Alastair Sawday's

Special Places to Stay

French
Bed & Breakfast

4 Contents

Before writing this introduction I trawled, heart in mouth as I do every year, through a collection of the latest Special Places to join us in France. Would we still be ploughing an unusual furrow of our own? Would the range of tastes and styles still startle me? Would there be the customary mix of ancient and modern, rural and urban, mad and trad, wild and tame? Would there be sumptuous comfort in castle turrets, Spartan design genius in old cottages? Above all, would we still be celebrating a random collection of fascinating, unconventional and conventional people? Would there be genius, originality, pioneering agricultural work, wine-making, craft and art and humanity in all its glorious miscellany?

YES! A hundred times yes – we've done it again, and I salute all those who have pulled this glittering collection together. The only visible difference is that there are, inevitably, fewer of the places that once set me alight when I began: crumbling farmhouses with crumbling farmers who could barely totter around serving the breakfast coffee. Time, simply, has taken its toll on them and the culture they were part of. Their successors are as fascinating in their own way – if more comfortable and 'modern European'.

We have vineyards, a spa, luxurious town houses in the very heart of Paris – one a stroll from Montmartre. We have ample places to get healthy, to unwind and be sybaritic. There are polished floors, medieval flagstones, wildlife enthusiasts, eco-houses and manors in many acres. You can breakfast on home-laid eggs, homemade pâtisseries and jams, on terraces, in farmyards and behind battlements. Homemade champagne can be served, as can any number of homemade wines. You can be alone or in company, dine in exquisite solitude or conviviality – and enjoy a minor resurgence of table d'hôtes. I feared it would disappear with the arrival of health and safety, but travellers now like to eat where they stay. We've visited all these places and we love them, why shouldn't you?

Alastair Sawday

Photo left: Tom Germain
Photo right: Vendangeoir d'Orgeval, entry 36

It's simple. There are no rules, no boxes to tick. We choose places that we like and are fiercely subjective in our choices. We also recognise that one person's idea of special is not necessarily someone else's so there is a huge variety of places, and prices, in the book. Those who are familiar with our Special Places series know that we look for comfort, originality, authenticity, and reject the insincere, the anonymous and the banal. The way guests are treated comes as high on our list as the setting, the architecture, the atmosphere and the food.

Inspections

We visit every place in the guide to get a feel for how both house and owner tick. We don't take a clipboard and we don't have a list of what is acceptable and what is not. Instead, we chat for an hour or so with the owner and look round – closely (it involves bouncing on beds, looking at linen, testing taps). It's all very informal but it gives us an excellent idea of who would enjoy staying there and our aim is to match places and guests. If the visit happens to be the last of the day, we may stay the night. Once in the book, properties are re-inspected every three to four years so that we can keep things fresh and accurate.

Feedback

In between inspections we rely on feedback from our army of readers, as well as from staff members who are encouraged to visit properties across the series. This feedback is invaluable to us and we always follow up on comments.

So do tell us whether your stay has been a joy or not, if the atmosphere was great or stuffy, the owners and staff cheery or bored. The accuracy of the book depends on what you, and our inspectors, tell us. A lot of the new entries in each edition are recommended by our readers, so keep telling us about new places you've discovered too. Please use the forms on our website at www.sawdays.co.uk.

However, please do not tell us if the bedside light was broken, or the shower head was scummy. Tell the owner, immediately, and get them to do something about it. Most owners are more than happy to correct problems and will bend over backwards to help. Far better than bottling it up and then writing to us a week later!

Subscriptions

Owners pay to appear on our pages. Their fee goes towards the high costs of inspecting and writing, of developing our website and producing an all-colour book. We only include places that we like and find special for one reason or another, so it is never possible for anyone to buy their way onto these pages. Nor is it possible for an owner to write their own description. We will say if the bedrooms are small, or if a main road is near. We do our best to avoid misleading people and keep up our reputation for reliability.

Disclaimer

We make no claims to pure objectivity in choosing these places. They are here simply because we like them. Our opinions and tastes are ours alone and this book is a statement of them; we hope you will share them. We have done our utmost to get our facts right but apologise unreservedly for any mistakes that may have crept in.

You should know that we don't check such things as fire regulations, swimming pool security or any other laws with which owners of properties receiving paying guests should comply. This is the responsibility of the owners.

Do remember that the information in this book is a snapshot in time and may have changed since we published it; do call ahead to avoid being disappointed.

For many more photos, as well as special offers and our latest collections, visit www.sawdays.co.uk

Photo: Bagatelle, entry 330

Finding the right place for you

All these places are special in one way or another. All have been visited and then written about honestly so that you can decide for yourselves which will suit you. Those of you who swear by Sawday's books trust our write-ups precisely because we don't have a blanket standard; we include places simply because we like them. But we all have different priorities, so do read the descriptions carefully and pick out the places where you will be comfortable. If something is particularly important to you then check when you book: a simple question or two can avoid misunderstandings.

Maps

Each property is flagged with its entry number on the maps at the front. These maps are a great starting point for planning your trip, but please don't use them as anything other than a general guide — use a decent road map for real navigation. Most places will send you detailed instructions once you have booked your stay.

Symbols

Below each entry you will see some symbols; they are explained at the very back of the book. They are based on the information given to us by the owners. However, things do change: bikes may be under repair or a new pool may have been put in. Please use the symbols as a guide rather than an absolute statement of fact and double-check anything that is important to you — owners occasionally bend their own rules, so it's worth asking if you may take your child or dog even if they don't have the symbol.

Children – The 🛈 symbol shows places which are happy to accept children of all ages. This does not mean that they will necessarily have cots, high chairs, etc. If an owner welcomes children but only those above a certain age, we have put in these details, too. These houses do not have the child symbol, but even these folk may accept your younger child if you are the only guests. Many who say no to children do so not because they don't like them but because they may have a steep stair, an unfenced pond or they find balancing the needs of mixed age groups too challenging.

Pets – Our 🐕 symbol shows places which are happy to accept pets. Do let the owners know that you'd like to bring your pet – particularly if it is not the usual dog! Be realistic about your pet – if it is nervous or excitable or doesn't like the company of other dogs, people, chickens, or children, then say so.

Owners' pets – The 🐈 symbol is given when the owners have their own pet on the premises. It may not be a cat! But it is there to warn you that you may be greeted by a dog, serenaded by a parrot, or indeed sat upon by a cat.

Communicating with owners

As we say below, owners are living their own lives in their own homes and, ideally, receiving guests as friends – who happen to pay them something when they leave. This is why travellers choose to stay at B&Bs rather than anonymous hotels. It is also why the owners have every right to expect to be treated like friends not machines. Yet, in the 'century of information', they are reporting more and more cases of enquirers who never reply to emails, guests who book and simply don't turn up: no email, no telephone call, no explanation, let alone an apology. It isn't for lack of the means to do it, it's because they just don't think. Let's stem the tide of thoughtlessness and keep our owners in business.

Our owners are proud of the regions in which they live and are invaluable sources of knowledge about their local areas, which they love to share. Many of our owners comment that guests who only stayed one night, en route to elsewhere, wished that they had stayed longer to explore. Guests too, having arrived and stayed for one night, have also said that they wished they had booked for longer. So do consider stopping for more than one night where you might otherwise be 'travelling through'.

Types of places

Some places have rooms in annexes or stables, barns or garden 'wings', some of which feel part of the house, some of which don't. If you have a strong preference for being in the throng or for

Photo: Les Chambres Saint Martin, entry 344

being apart, check those details. Consider your surroundings, too: rambling châteaux may be cooler than you are used to; city places and working farms may be noisy at times; and that peacock or cockerel we mention may disturb you. Some owners give you a front door key so you may come and go as you please; others like to have the house empty between, say, 10am and 4pm. Remember that B&Bs are people's homes, not hotels.

Do expect:
• a genuine personal welcome
• a willingness to go the extra mile
• a degree of informality, even family-life chaos, i.e. a fascinating glimpse of a French way of life

Don't necessarily expect:
• a lock on your bedroom door
• gin and tonic at 2am
• your room cleaned, bed made and towels changed every day
• a private table at breakfast
• access to house and garden during the day

• an immediate response to your booking enquiry

Rooms

Bedrooms — We tell you if a room is a single, double, twin/double (i.e. with zip and link beds), suite (a room with space for seating or two rooms sharing a bathroom), family room (a double bed + single beds), or triple (three single beds). If 'antique beds' sound seductively authentic, remember they are liable to be antique sizes too (190cm long, doubles 140cm wide); if in doubt, ask, or book a twin room (usually larger). Owners can often juggle beds or bedrooms, so talk to them about what you need before you book. It is rare to be given your own room key in a B&B and your room won't necessarily have a television.

Bathrooms — Most bedrooms in this book have an en suite bath or shower room; we only mention bathroom details when they do not. So, you may have a 'separate' bathroom (yours alone but not in your room) or a shared bathroom. Under certain entries we mention that two rooms share a bathroom and are 'let to same party only'. Please do not assume this means you must be a group of friends to apply; it simply means that if you book one of these rooms you will not be sharing a bath with strangers. For simplicity we may refer to 'bath'. This doesn't necessarily mean it has no shower; it could mean a shower only. If these things are important, please check.

Sitting rooms — Most B&B owners offer guests the family sitting room to share, or they provide a sitting room especially for guests.

Meals

Unless we say otherwise, breakfast is included. This will usually be a good continental breakfast — traditionally fresh baguette or pain de campagne with apricot jam and a bowl of coffee, but brioche, crêpes, croissants, and homemade cake may all be on offer too. Some owners are fairly unbending about breakfast times, others are happy just to wait until you want it, or even bring it to you in bed.

Apart from breakfast, no meals should be expected unless you have arranged them in advance. Many places offer their guests a table d'hôtes dinner — the same food for all and absolutely must be booked ahead — but it will not be available every night. (We have indicated the distance to the nearest restaurant when dinner isn't offered; but be aware that rural restaurants stop taking orders at 9pm and often close at least one day a week.) Often, the meal is shared with other guests at a communal table. These dinners are sometimes hosted by Monsieur or Madame or both and are usually a wonderful opportunity to get to know your hosts and to make new friends among the other guests. Meal prices are quoted per person, though children will usually eat for less. Ask your hosts about reduced meal rates if you're travelling with little ones.

When wine is included this can mean a range of things, from a standard quarter-litre carafe per person to a barrel of table

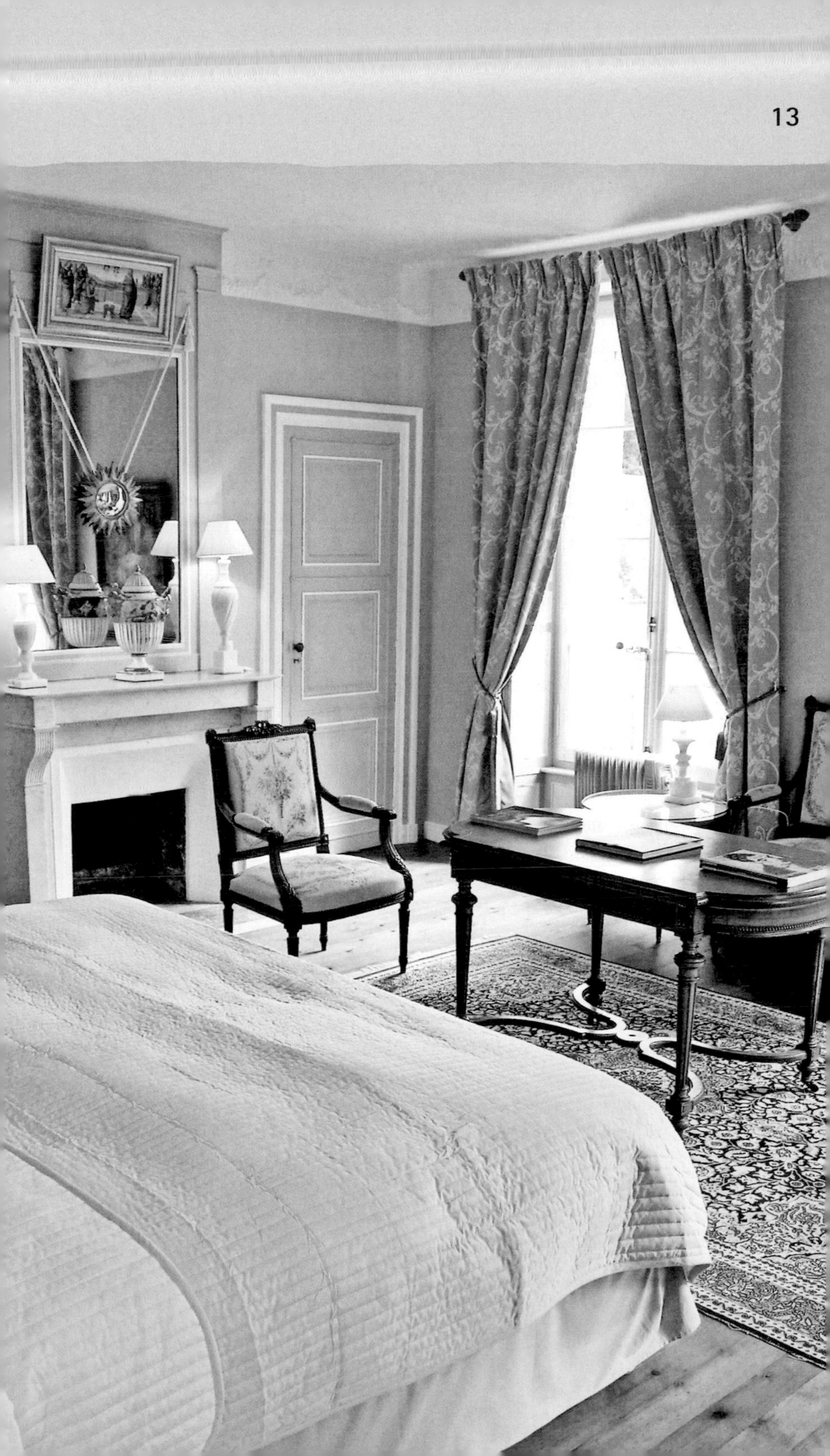

wine; from a decent bottle of local wine to an excellent estate wine.

Summer kitchens

Well before the ubiquitous barbecue came upon us, the French had come up with a daring idea for their places of summer residence: a minimal kitchen outside, half in the garden, and not doing 'proper' cooking. A summer kitchen is at ground level and partially open to the elements; generally under an overhang or in an adapted outbuilding, it typically contains a couple of bottled-gas burners or hotplates, a mini-refrigerator and a source of water; also crockery and cutlery. These facilities are for family and/or hosted garden meals and some owners who don't do table d'hôtes will allow guests to use the summer kitchen and picnic in their garden.

Prices and minimum stays

Most entries give a price PER ROOM with breakfast for two people. If this is not the case, we generally say so. The price range covers a one-night stay in the cheapest room in low season to the most expensive in high season. Some owners charge more at certain times (during festivals, for example) and some charge less for stays of more than one or two nights. Some owners ask for a two-night minimum stay and we mention this where possible.

Prices quoted are those given to us for 2017 onwards but are not guaranteed, so do double-check when booking.

Taxe de séjour is a small tax that local councils can levy on all paying visitors; it is rarely included in the quoted price and you may find your bill increased by €0.50–€2 per person per day to cover this.

Public holidays

As well as the usual public holidays which we take in the UK, the French also celebrate on various other dates. It is likely that B&Bs will be booked up well in advance around these days, so do plan ahead if you are going to be travelling then.

8 May – Victory 1945 Day
Ascension Thursday and Whit Monday
14 July – Bastille Day
15 August – Assumption of the Blessed Virgin Mary
1 November – All Saints' Day
11 November – Armistice 1918 Day

Booking and cancellation

Do be clear about the room booked and the price for B&B and for meals. It is essential to book well ahead for July and August, and wise for other months. If you practise the last-minuting habit which seems to be spreading, you deprive yourself of choice and make life harder for your hosts. Owners may send you a booking form or contrat de location (tenancy contract) which must be filled in and returned, and commits both sides. Requests for deposits vary; some are non-refundable, some owners may charge you for the whole of the booked stay in advance.

Some cancellation policies are more stringent than others. It is also worth noting that some owners will take this deposit directly from your credit/debit card without contacting you to discuss it. So ask them to explain their cancellation policy clearly before booking so you understand exactly where you stand; it may well avoid a nasty surprise.

Remember that the UK is one hour behind France and people can be upset by telephone enquiries coming through late in their evening.

Payment

Cash is usually the easiest way to pay. Virtually all ATMs in France take Visa and MasterCard. Some owners take credit cards but not all. If they do, we have given them the appropriate symbol. (Check that your particular card is acceptable.) Euro travellers' cheques will usually be accepted; other currency cheques are unpopular because of commission charges.

Tipping

Owners do not expect tips. If you have been treated with extraordinary kindness, write to them, or leave a small gift. Please tell us, too – we love to hear, and we do record, all feedback.

Arrivals and departures

Say roughly what time you will arrive (normally after 4pm), as most hosts like to welcome you personally. Be on time if you have booked dinner; if, despite best efforts, you are delayed, phone to give warning.

Closed

When given in months this means the whole of the month(s) stated. So, 'Closed: November–March' means from 1 November to 31 March.

Photo: Villa du Roc Fleuri, entry 683

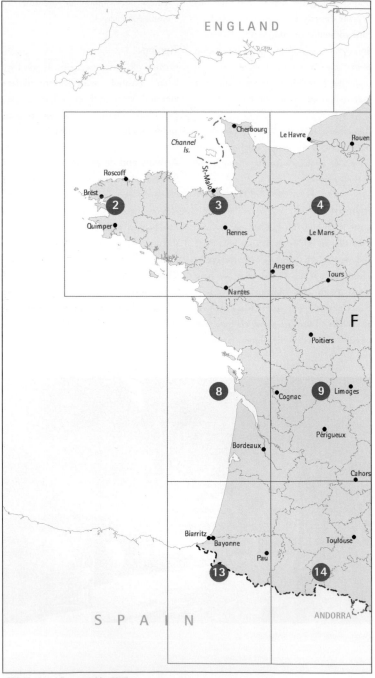

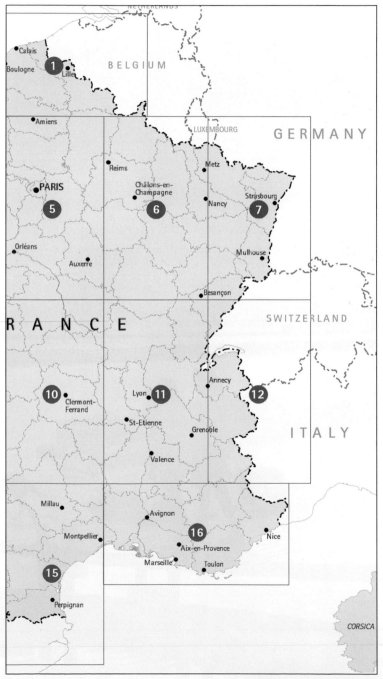

Photo: La Souqueto, entry 557

Map 1   19

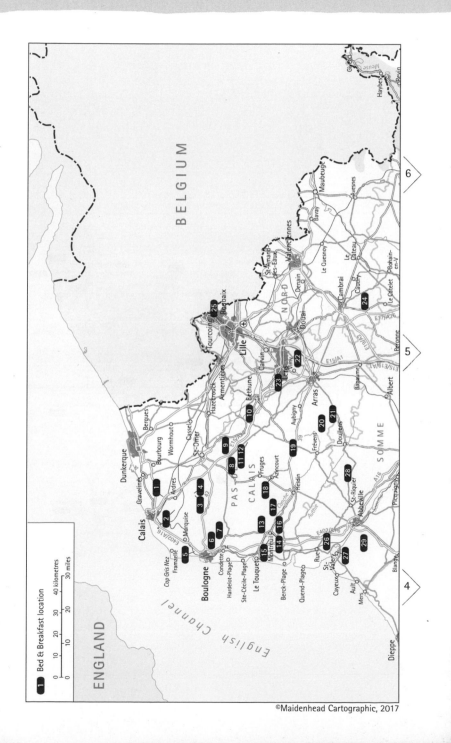

©Maidenhead Cartographic, 2017

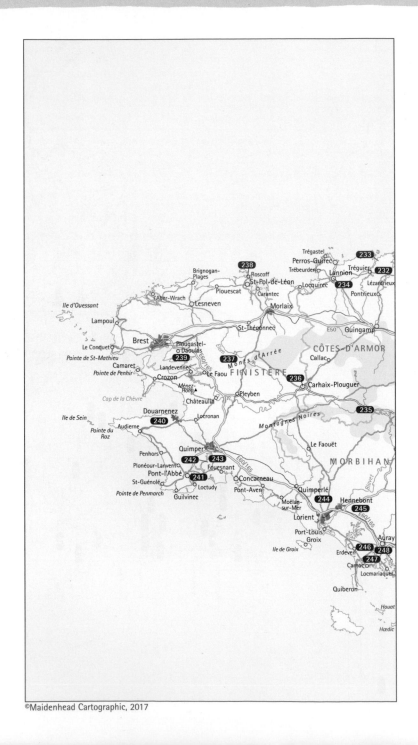

©Maidenhead Cartographic, 2017

Map 3 21

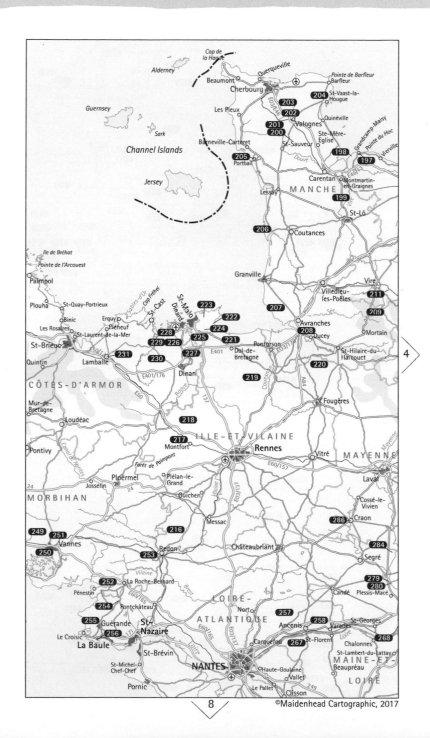

©Maidenhead Cartographic, 2017

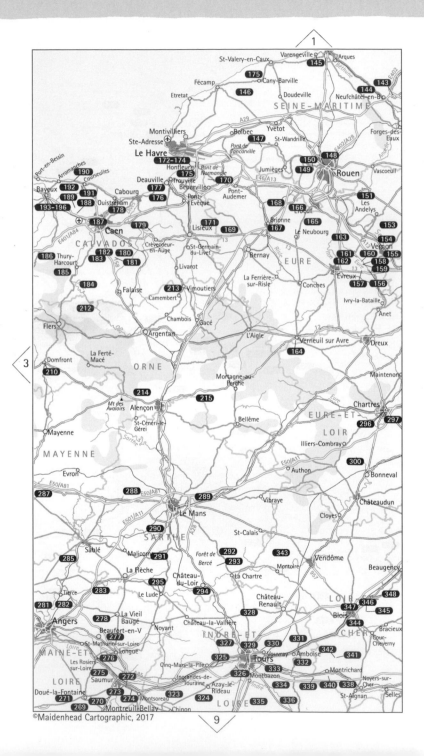

©Maidenhead Cartographic, 2017

Map 5

23

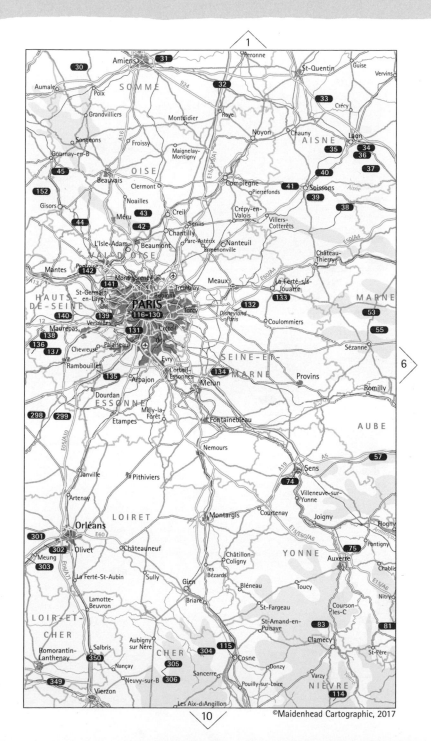

©Maidenhead Cartographic, 2017

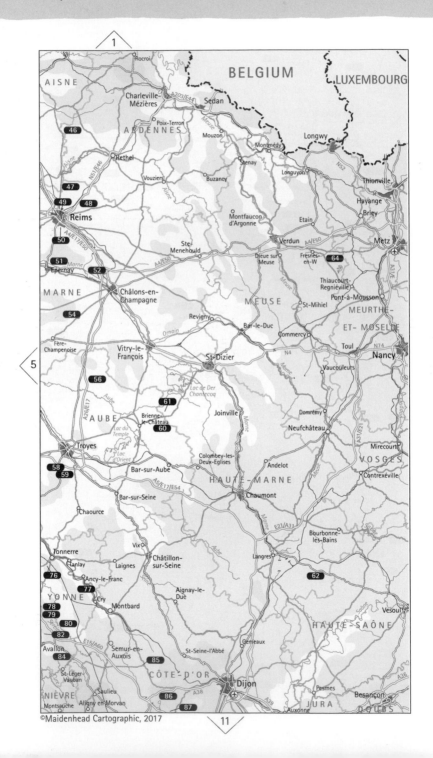

Map 7   25

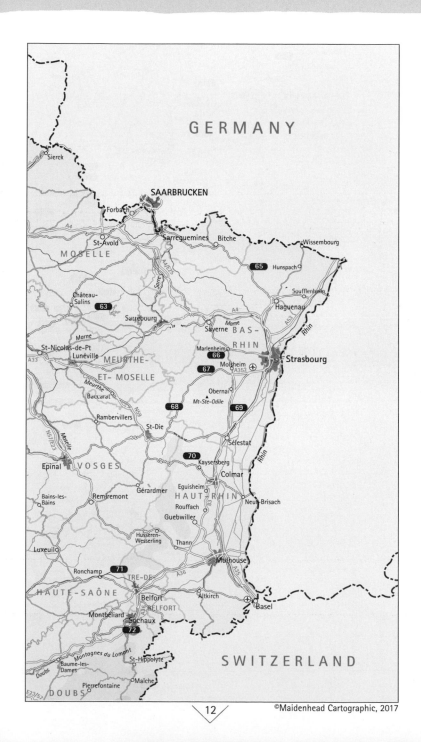

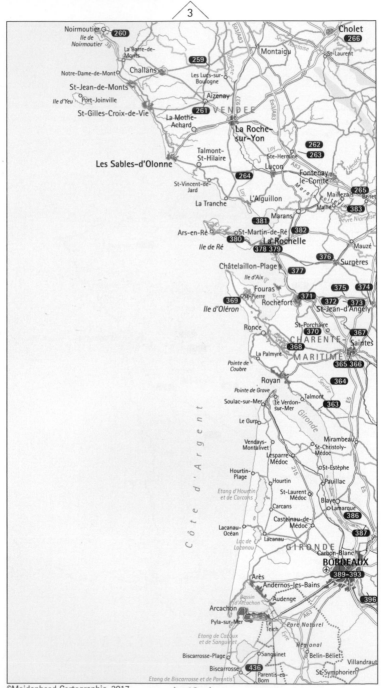

Map 9

27

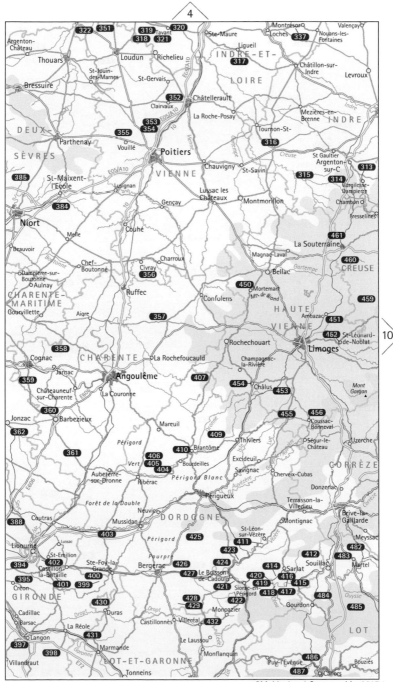

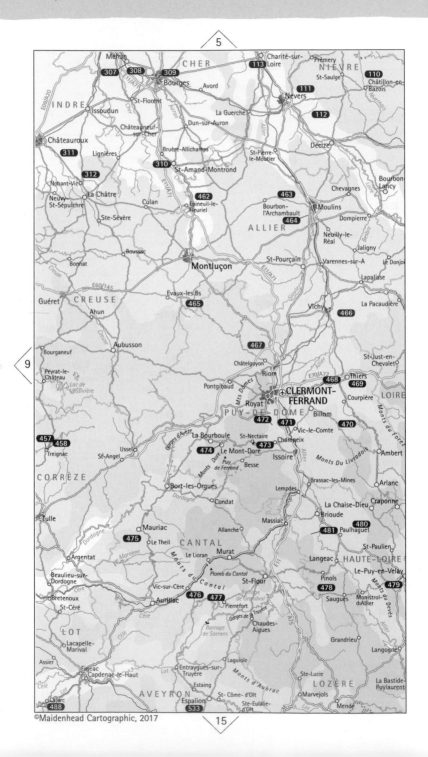

Map 11 29

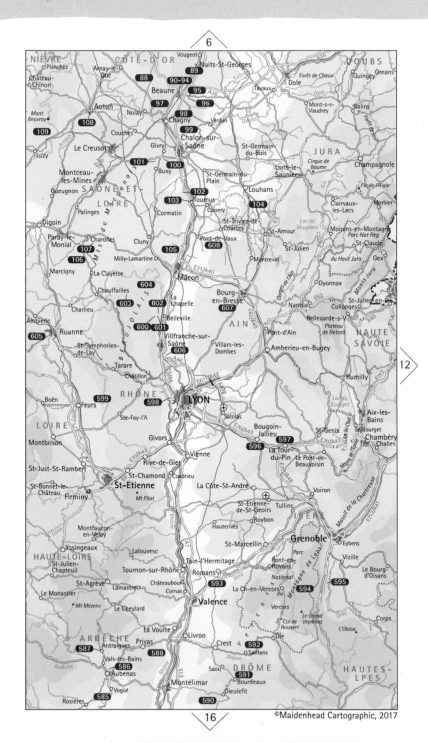

6

NIÈVRE · CÔTE-D'OR
○Planchez
○Château-
Chinon

Vougeot○
Arnay-le-
Duc
88
89
Nuits-St-Georges
Forêt de Chaux
Quingey○ Ornans○
DOUBS
Dole

Beaune **90-94** **95** A36
Tavaux○
Mont-s-s-
Vaudrey
Salins○
JURA

Autun
Nolay○
97 **96**
Verdun○
Mont-s-s-
Vaudrey

Mont
Beuvray▲
109 **108**
Couches○
98
Chagny
99
Chalon-sur-
Saône
St-Germain-
du-Bois
Cirque de
Baume
Champagnole○

Luzy○
Le Creusot○
Givry○
101 **100**
Buxy○
St-Germain-
du-Plain
Lons-le-
Saunier
Pic de l'Aigle

Montceau-
les-Mines
SAÔNE-ET
LOIRE
102
St-Germain-
Plain
Louhans○
Clairvaux-
les-Lacs
Morbier○

Gueugnon○
Palinges○
103
Tournus
Cuisery○
104

Digoin○
Cormatin○
St-Trivier-de-
Courtes
St-Amour○
Moirans-en-Montagne
Parc Nat Reg
St-Claude○

Paray-le-
Monial
○Charolles
107
Cluny○
105
Pont-de-Vaux○
St-Julien○
du Haut Jura
Gex○

106
Milly-Lamartine○
608
Montreval○

Marcigny○
○La Clayette
Mâcon
Oyonnax○
Monts Jura

Chauffailles○
604
La
Chapelle
Bourg-
en-Bresse
607
Nantua○
St-Julien-en-G

Charlieu○
603 **602**
Belleville○
Collonges○

Ambierle○
605
Roanne○
600 **601**
Villefranche-sur-
Saône
606
AIN
Pont-d'Ain○
Bellegarde-s-V
Plateau
de Retord
HAUTE
SAVOIE

St-Symphorien-
de-Lay
Villars-les-
Dombes○
Amberieu-en-Bugey○

Tarare○
Châtillon○
Rumilly○

Boën○
599
RHÔNE
598
LYON
Lac du
Bourget

Feurs○
Ste-Foy-l'A○
Satolas○
St-Genix○
Aix-les-
Bains

LOIRE
Givors○
Bougoin-
Jallieu
597
Le Bourget○
Chambéry○
Challes○

Montbrison○
Vienne○
596
La Tour-
du-Pin
Le Pont-de-
Beauvoisin

St-Just-St-Rambert○
Rive-de-Gier○

St-Bonnet-le-
Château○
St-Chamond○
Condrieu○
La Côte-St-André○
Voiron○
Massif de la Chartreuse

Firminy○
St-Etienne
Mt Pilat▲
St-Etienne-
de-St-Geoirs
Tullins○
ISÈRE

Montfaucon-
en-Velay○
Hauterives○
Roybon○

Yssingeaux○
Lalouvesc○
St-Marcellin○
Grenoble
○Eybens

HAUTE-LOIRE
St-Julien-
Chapteuil○
Parc
Pont-en-
Royans
Vizille○

St-Agrève○
Tournon-sur-Rhône○
Tain-l'Hermitage○
National
Le Bourg-
d'Oisans○

Le Monastier○
Lamastre○
Châteaubourg○
Romans○
593
du
594 **595**

▲Mt Mézenc
Le Cheylard○
Cornas○
La Ch-en-Vercors○
Vercors
Le Grand
Veymont▲
Corps○

Valence
Col de
Rousset
L'Obiou▲

ARDÈCHE
La Voulte○
Livron○
Crest○
592
Die○

Privas○
587
Antraigues○
588
Saillans○
HAUTES-
LPES

Vals-
les-Bains○
586
Saou○
DRÔME
591

Aubenas○
Montélimar○
Bourdeaux○
Dieulefit○

Vogüé○
585
590

Rosières○

16

©Maidenhead Cartographic, 2017

Map 13   31

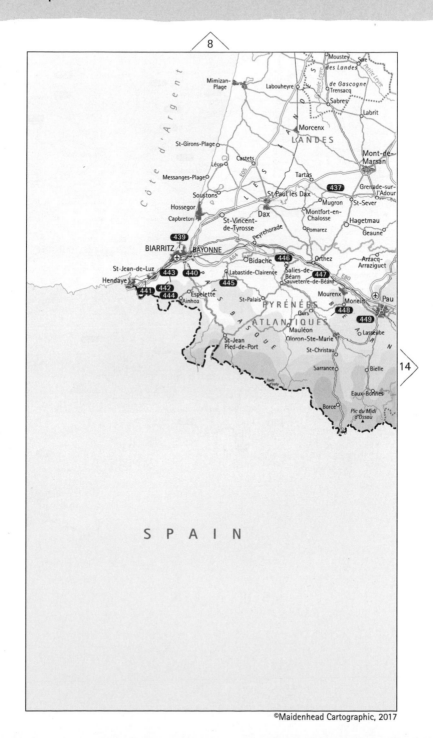

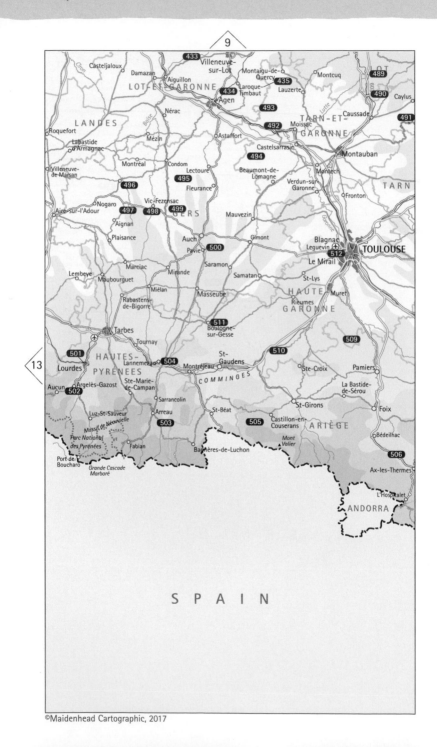

Map 15   33

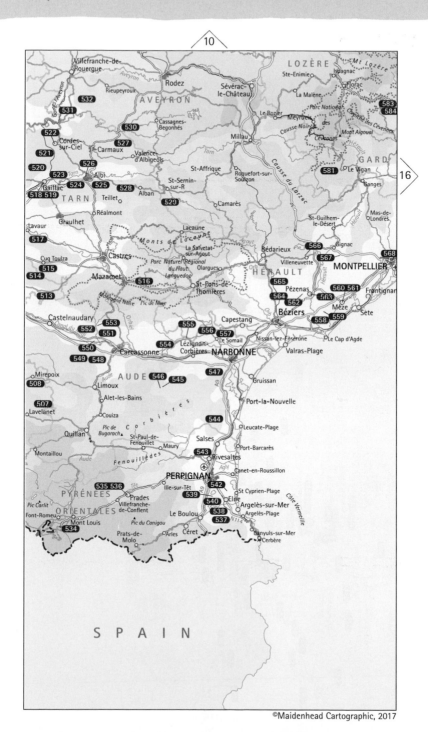

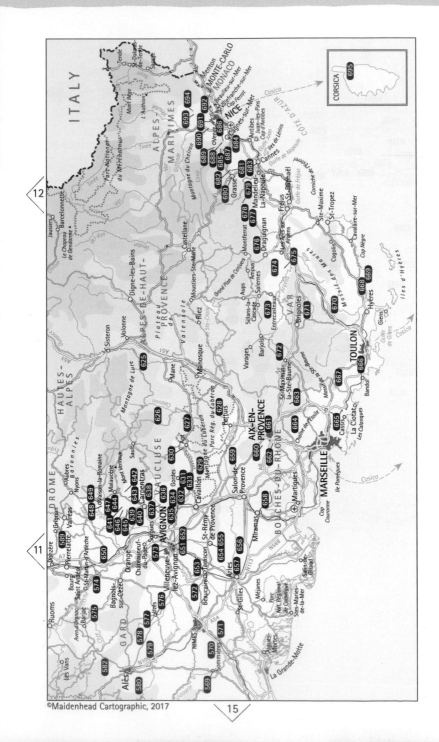

©Maidenhead Cartographic, 2017

The North • Picardy

Ardres Bridge Cottage

A canal-side setting among rolling agricultural plains, usefully close to Calais. The gardens are peaceful and the owners offer friendly table d'hôtes. The ground-floor bedroom gives onto the flowery borders, the other has its own little balcony overlooking the pond, where farmyard fowl frolic; the shower room is downstairs. Both are country cosy and comfortable with floral bed linen and wooden furniture; bathrooms are among the best. You share the young and charming owners' sitting room: long and spacious with a big fire and plenty of squishy sofas; and you breakfast round a farmhouse table. Utterly touching and authentic.

Rooms	1 double: €60–€75. 1 triple with separate shower: €60–€75. Extra bed/sofabed available €15 per person per night.
Meals	Dinner with wine, €25.
Closed	Rarely.

Laurent Blanquart
Ardres Bridge Cottage,
678 rue du Fort Bâtard,
62610 Pont d'Ardres,
Pas-de-Calais

Tel	+33 (0)3 21 96 63 92
Mobile	+33 (0)6 82 02 13 47
Email	blanquart.laurent@gmail.com
Web	www.ardres-bridge-cottage.com

Entry 1   Map 1

Villa Héloïse

An endearing place with an owner to match. Chatty hard-working Marie-Christine does everything herself in her pretty red-brick home; she's even built a treehouse in the garden. Stay in the family suite in the main house, a wonderland of plants and collected items old and new, or the independent wooden-decked apartment. It comes without a sitting room but Madame has buckets of personality to make up for this, and you can dine outside on that high decked terrace. Evergreens and shrubs provide the backdrop, fields surround you, Calais and Belgium are less than 30 minutes away. Wander the dunes, cycle, fish.

Rooms	1 family room for 4: €55–€90. 1 apartment for 2: €60.
Meals	Dinner with wine, €25.
Closed	Rarely.

Marie-Christine Debriel
Villa Héloïse,
683 rue de l'Église,
62340 Andres,
Pas-de-Calais

Tel	+33 (0)3 21 35 15 01
Mobile	+33 (0)6 87 12 51 02
Email	marie-christine.debriel@wanadoo.fr
Web	www.villaheloise.net

Entry 2   Map 1

La Ferme de Beaupré

Lut, a music teacher from Belgium (who speaks English) is one of those lovely gentle people who takes you happily into her home. It's a gorgeous old house at the end of a pretty tree-lined drive with perfect, peaceful bedrooms (one in taupes, off-whites, toile de Jouy and a tiny room off with a bed for a child, the other modern red, white, rattan and wood). Breakfast is a treat: homemade yogurt and jams, bread and pastries from the local boulangerie; dinner too is available sometimes so do ask. You have sole use of the living room; the garden bursts with peonies, lupins, roses and cherries. An adorable, very special place.

Le Manoir

The trompe l'œil and frescoed friezes are lavish, from the dining panelling to the staircase 'marble'. In spite of being known in the village as Le Château it's not really big but, with the original details intact, it is a historian's delight. All four guest rooms (one a two-bedroom family suite, another an elegant tribute to Africa) have been remodelled and beautifully refurbished, combining spectacular antiques with modern fabrics. The bathrooms are luxurious and the garden views, to box parterre and trees, are soothing. Welcoming Sylvie and Pierre offer you a delicious dinner, and a living room just for guests.

Rooms	1 double: €68-€75.
	1 family room for 2: €68-€125.
	Dinner, B&B €60-€64 per person.
	Extra bed/sofabed available €20 per person per night.
Meals	Dinner with wine, €25.
Closed	Christmas.

Rooms	3 doubles: €75.
	1 suite for 4: €110.
Meals	Dinner with wine, €28-€40.
Closed	Rarely.

Lut & Jean-Michel Louf-Degrauwe
La Ferme de Beaupré,
129 rue de Licques,
62890 Bonningues lès Ardres,
Pas-de-Calais
Tel +33 (0)3 21 35 14 44
Email lut.degrauwe@nordnet.fr
Web www.lafermedebeaupre.com

Sylvie & Pierre Bréemersch
Le Manoir,
40 route de Licques,
62890 Bonningues lès Ardres,
Pas-de-Calais
Tel +33 (0)3 21 82 69 05
Email pierre.breemersch@wanadoo.fr
Web www.lemanoirdebonningues.com

Entry 3 Map 1

Entry 4 Map 1

La Villa Sainte Claire

Friendly Catherine lends you bikes — so pedal off to Wimereux, a sweet seaside town a mile down the road. Then return to a 18th-century house in the lee of a village church, its long elegant façade distinguished by tall white windows perfectly beshuttered. The bedrooms are fresh, spacious and uncluttered, with views to a beautiful front garden, and it's a treat to stroll the rambling grounds, dotted with statues, punctuated by topiary. Wake to fresh local croissants and homemade jams; set off for the markets and shops of Boulogne… and a lovely lunch in the historic old town. The coastline is wild and wonderful.

Rooms	2 doubles: €95. Extra bed/sofabed available €15 per person per night. Additional room available for 2 children. Cot available.
Meals	Restaurant 50m.
Closed	16 October to 7 November & 14 December to 8 January.

Catherine Debatte
La Villa Sainte Claire,
11 rue du Presbytère,
62126 Wimille,
Pas-de-Calais

Tel	+33 (0)3 21 91 99 58
Mobile	+33 (0)6 16 70 84 26
Email	contact@villa-sainte-claire.fr
Web	www.villa-sainte-claire.fr

Entry 5   Map 1

Le Clos d'Esch

The golden stone of the oldest farmhouse in the village is now fronted by a large glass sunroom, and flowers flourish in the lower garden where two new houses stand. Discreetly friendly, relaxed and obliging, owners Olivier and Véronique (this was her pioneering parents' B&B) serve delicious breakfasts and for dinner there are a couple of good places in the village, which is small and charming. Bedrooms are simple, traditional, pristine, one in an outbuilding overlooking the courtyard and wooded hills, another (the triple) with its own patio overlooking the lawns. There's a neat and tidy sitting room, too. Good value.

Rooms	1 double, 2 twins: €54–€63. 1 triple: €79.
Meals	Auberges in village, 200m.
Closed	Rarely.

Véronique Boussemaere & Olivier Chartaux
Le Clos d'Esch,
62360 Echinghen,
Pas-de-Calais

Tel	+33 (0)3 21 91 14 34
Mobile	+33 (0)6 89 04 72 78
Email	veronique.boussemaere@wanadoo.fr
Web	www.leclosdesch.fr

Entry 6   Map 1

Le Clos de Tournes

Tranquil meadows, pastoral bliss: a metaphor for your calm, smiling fishmonger hosts. Caroline grew up with B&B: her parents were pioneers, she loves it. The fine old farmhouse, with pale façade and garden dotted by shady fruit trees, is an immaculate B&B retreat, while the outbuildings house two busy gîtes. The adventurous bedrooms are a surprise after the classic French dining room (long table, high upholstered chairs). Urban-chic in deep red and mustard, one is swathed in rich oriental toile de Jouy, the other in intensely patterned wallpaper and billowing taffeta. Caroline is graceful and sociable.

Les Dornes

Table d'hôtes round the convivial table is the inspiration behind this B&B – which, being perfectionists, this couple do so well. Dinner, locally sourced, sounds delicious, while vegetables come from an immaculate potager. The interiors of their new but traditional village house are equally manicured: the L-shaped living room; the bedrooms, colour-themed and French-cosy, two on the ground floor, their tiles topped by rugs, two under the eaves with honey-coloured boards; all large and super-comfortable. Historic St Omer is a must – for music and markets, bric-a-brac and breweries. Tremendous value.

Rooms	1 double, 1 twin: €65. Extra bed €20. Tourist tax €1 per person per night.
Meals	Seafood platter with wine, €35; not Fridays or Sundays. Restaurant 2km.
Closed	Rarely.

Rooms	3 doubles, 1 twin: €65.
Meals	Dinner with wine, €25; not Sundays.
Closed	Rarely.

Caroline Boussemaere
Le Clos de Tournes,
1810 route de Tournes,
62360 Echinghen,
Pas-de-Calais
Tel   +33 (0)3 91 90 48 78
Mobile   +33 (0)6 07 09 21 14
Email   reservation@leclosdetournes.com
Web   www.leclosdetournes.com

Jaqueline & Gilles Blondel
Les Dornes,
520 rue des Deux Upen,
Upen d'Aval, 62129 Delettes,
Pas-de-Calais
Tel   +33 (0)3 21 95 87 09
Mobile   +33 (0)6 88 82 55 96
Email   lesdornes@lesdornes.com
Web   www.lesdornes.com

Entry 7   Map 1

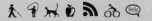

Entry 8   Map 1

Château de Moulin le Comte

A beautiful wooden floor in the 'green' bedroom and the black and white tiled hall are original touches still on show in this small château, renovated recently and completely by the Van der Elsts. Your Belgian hosts — father, mother, son — are serious about succeeding in their new venture and you will excuse the wonderfully kitsch china chihuahuas when you are relaxing in one of their spacious rooms; expect textured wallpapers and smart showers. Dinner in the elegant green and gold dining room might feature local watercress, colourful St Omer cauliflowers or veal with mustard, cooked by multilingual Francis.

Le Château de Philiomel

Unwind on a 15-acre estate — the owners live next door — in immaculate solitude. Overlooking parkland and lake, this commanding Italianate mansion has the right ingredients (pillars, portico, marble fireplaces) to give you grand ideas, yet is run with a light, friendly touch. Large lofty bedrooms, uncarpeted, uncluttered, are hotel-spotless in muted colours and the suite has its own balcony. You wake to delicious breakfasts at private tables in a light-flooded dining room with white walls and polished parquet, and you can stroll into town for dinner. With the A26 close by, this is a really nice stopover en route to Calais.

Rooms	4 twin/doubles: €104–€124. 1 family room for 4: €124–€184. Singles €84–€124. Extra bed/sofabed available €30 per person per night.
Meals	Dinner, 5 courses, €29.99. Restaurant 1.5km.
Closed	Rarely.

Rooms	3 doubles: €90–€100. 1 suite for 2-4: €130. Singles €75–€95. Extra bed/sofabed available €25 per person per night.
Meals	Restaurants 2km.
Closed	Rarely.

Francis Van der Elst
Château de Moulin le Comte,
44 rue Principale, Moulin le Comte,
62120 Aire sur la Lys,
Pas-de-Calais

Tel	+33 (0)3 21 88 48 38
Mobile	+33 (0)6 24 21 08 91
Email	info@chateaudemoulinlecomte.com
Web	www.chateaudemoulinlecomte.com

Frédéric Devys
Le Château de Philiomel,
Rue Philiomel,
62190 Lillers,
Pas-de-Calais

Tel	+33 (0)3 21 61 76 76
Mobile	+33 (0)6 09 10 81 95
Email	contact@philiomel.com
Web	www.lechateaudephiliomel.com

Les Cohettes

Fanny cares deeply that everyone be happy, and does brilliant table d'hôtes. A full house makes quite a crowd and when B&B and gîte guests come together there can be a dozen at table. But the big garden opens its arms to all and has some comforting mature trees under which guests may link up for summer pétanque. Dark beams have been painted pale, furniture has been sanded and smudge-finished. Pretty and cosy bedrooms — in the long low farmhouse attic — are colour-coded, while the studio is snug with its own little patio. The garden is peaceful and readers love it all.

Ferme de la Vallée

This is a real farm, so don't expect pretty-pretty — but Madame is a character and her welcome is top class. Guests return, for the authentic atmosphere and the delicious food. Amazing how much space lies behind the simple frontage of this street-side farmhouse; every little corner is crammed with 40 years' worth of collecting: porcelain, plates, jugs, crystal decanter stoppers, baskets, collectable plastics... the list is long. Come for comfy beds, spacious dayroom areas, billiards, table football (a vintage table) and games. It's intrinsically French despite the eccentricities, and Madame is a delight.

Rooms	3 doubles, 1 twin: €60-€70. 1 family room for 4-5: €65-€119. 1 studio for 2: €65. Singles €55.
Meals	Dinner, with wine, €27. Guest kitchen.
Closed	Rarely.

Rooms	1 double: €56. 1 suite for 4: €85. 1 triple: €66. Singles €40.
Meals	Dinner with wine, €23.
Closed	Rarely.

Fanny Bulot
Les Cohettes,
28 rue de Pernes,
62190 Auchy au Bois,
Pas-de-Calais

Tel	+33 (0)3 21 02 09 47
Mobile	+33 (0)6 07 06 65 42
Email	ginabulot@gmail.com
Web	www.lescohettes.fr

Brigitte de Saint Laurent
Ferme de la Vallée,
13 rue Neuve,
62190 Auchy au Bois,
Pas-de-Calais

Tel	+33 (0)3 21 25 80 09
Email	brigitte.de-saint-laurent@wanadoo.fr
Web	www.lafermedelavallee.com

Le Vert Bois

Ancient peace, delightful people, fields as far as the eye can see. And it's majestic for a farm — handsome house, outbuildings and courtyard are immaculately preserved. Étienne, Véronique and their family grow cereals, keep cows and look after guests — charmingly — in a converted farm building. Upstairs are a fresh cosy double and a pretty twin; ceilings slope, walls are spotless, bedcovers quilted, shower rooms small and newly fitted. Breakfasts, we're told, are lovely. The fine old town of Montreuil is just three kilometres away for restaurants and "astonishing points of view". Near Calais but feels like the heart of France.

Maison 76

Within the walls of Montreuil, a house of surprises. Affable English host and long term resident Tim balances fine antiques and modern touches within original features: parquet floors, panelled walls, high ceilings. Stylish bedrooms have stripped floorboards, accent wallpapers, soft grey tones and period pieces. Bathrooms are designer-sharp. Rent the whole house to include the loft suite with copper bathtub. Breakfast on homemade produce, raid the pantry at tea time for freshly baked cake (you have your own sitting room), then explore the city, Le Touquet and lovely villages. Return to sunset drinks in the walled garden. Sublime.

Minimum stay: 2 nights on weekends.

Rooms	1 double, 1 twin: €65-€85.
Meals	Restaurants 3km.
Closed	Rarely.

Rooms	3 doubles: €185-€225. 1 suite for 2: €250-€300. Whole house available as self-catering.
Meals	Dinner, 2-3 courses, €20-€25. Wine €12-€60. Restaurants within walking distance. Picnic sets & picnics available (book in advance).
Closed	Rarely.

	Étienne & Véronique Bernard Le Vert Bois, 62170 Neuville sous Montreuil, Pas-de-Calais
Tel	+33 (0)3 21 06 09 41
Mobile	+33 (0)6 08 74 79 43
Email	etienne.bernard6@wanadoo.fr
Web	www.gite-montreuilsurmer.com

	Tim Matthews Maison 76, 76 rue Pierre Ledent, 62170 Montreuil-sur-Mer, Pas-de-Calais
Tel	+33 (0)3 60 85 08 49
Email	info@maison76.com
Web	www.maison76.com

Le Pré Rainette

Relax with beautiful colours around you – turquoise, striking purples, soft Egyptian reds – and admire the abundance of old wood found in brocantes and used throughout to soften the interiors. 'Violette' is a perfect family room or spacious for a couple; 'Hortense' and 'Lilas' share a super modern shower room; 'La Petite Maison' has huge windows overlooking a small lake. Anne-Marie and Christophe, intelligent, helpful hosts, built the long red-roofed house in 2003, and named it 'tree frog prairie' after the quietly croaking wildlife. Have a go at rowing, use the pool, borrow bikes, or use the beach hut at Le Touquet – bliss.

Ferme du Saule

Guests have called Le Saule "a little treasure". And we know that the Trunnets' smiles are genuine, their converted outbuilding handsome and perfectly finished (down to mosquito nets on windows), the ground-floor rooms solidly traditional, the beds excellent, the dayroom proud of its beautiful armoire, and you get your own little table for breakfast. Monsieur and his son are only too happy to show you the flax production process (it's fascinating); young Madame looks after her three little ones and cares beautifully for guests. Proclaimed "the best cowshed I've ever stayed in" by one happy visitor.

Rooms	2 suites for 2-4: €120-€210. 1 apartment for 2-4: €150-€250.
Meals	Restaurants 3km.
Closed	11 November to 15 March. Open Christmas & New Year.

Rooms	2 doubles: €60. 1 suite for 4: €85-€100. 2 family rooms for 3: €70. Singles €50. Extra bed/sofabed available €15 per person per night.
Meals	Restaurants 6km.
Closed	Rarely.

	Anne-Marie de Gastines Le Pré Rainette, 1515 Grande Rue, 62170 Sorrus, Pas-de-Calais
Mobile	+33 (0)6 48 18 90 83
Email	prerainette@hotmail.fr
Web	www.prerainette.com

	Trunnet Family Ferme du Saule, 20 rue de l'Église, 62170 Brimeux, Pas-de-Calais
Tel	+33 (0)3 21 06 01 28
Email	fotrunnet@wanadoo.fr
Web	www.ferme-du-saule.com

Entry 15   Map 1

Entry 16   Map 1

Un Matin dans les Bois

He bakes delicious brioche, she adores birds and will take you to the marches, there are cats, dogs, ducks and plans for horses, and four-year-old Archie to make friends with you. The house, concealed in woods with rolling hill views, dates from the 15th century. Bedrooms, scattered between barn, stables and pigeonnier, are inspired, one with a wall of glass, another with a bedhead of silver birch trunks; beds are big, deep, sumptuous. There's a restaurant to walk to and a guest kitchen in a rustic-chic extension. Swing in the tree chairs, swim a lap in the pool, wander the woods with a lantern from your room. Magical!

Minimum stay: 2 nights in high season.

La Gacogne

Enter a 1750 arched orangery (the tower) filled with a very long table, an open fire and 101 curiosities. Alongside teddies are chain-mail bodices, longbows, crossbows and similar armoured reminders of nearby Agincourt (Azincourt). It is a treat to be received in this most colourful and eccentric of parlours for hearty continental breakfasts (the seed cake is delicious!), hosted by motherly Marie-José and knightly Patrick who've lived here for years. Small bedrooms in the outbuilding are farmhouse simple with heavy-draped medieval touches, a lush garden melts into a conifer copse and your hosts are utterly charming.

Rooms	3 doubles: €130–€140. 1 suite for 4: €160–€230.		Rooms	2 doubles: €70–€80. 1 family room for 3: €80.
Meals	Restaurants 3km. Guest kitchen.		Meals	Restaurant 1km.
Closed	Rarely.		Closed	1 November to 31 March.

M & Madame Dubrulle
Un Matin dans les Bois,
100 Impasse le Fresnoy,
62990 Loison sur Créquoise,
Pas-de-Calais
Mobile +33 (0)6 52 89 55 56
Email   info@unmatindanslesbois.com
Web   www.unmatindanslesbois.com

Patrick & Marie-José Fenet
La Gacogne,
62310 Azincourt,
Pas-de-Calais
Tel   +33 (0)3 21 04 45 61
Email fenetgeoffroy@aol.com
Web   www.gacogne.com

Le Loubarré

The period of each piece shows on its face, so you expect the elegantly coffered ceilings, the deeply carved woodwork, the vast Louis XIII dresser... but nothing prepares you for the neo-gothic stone fireplace! The rooms in the stables, some up, some down, are pretty and spotless, each with good fabrics, some antiques, a neat shower room, and you can use the comfortable family sitting room. Madame loves telling tales of the house and its contents, and has two dogs, a few goats and four donkeys (a weekend car-racing track in the valley, though). Both your hosts work constantly on their beloved house.

Château de Grand Rullecourt

A remarkable mix of place and people. This dynamic family – once eight of them! – have rebuilt their monumental château and brightened their escutcheon while being publishers in Paris and brilliant socialites: fascinating people, still energetic, and with a natural hospitality that makes up for any winter chill. Built in 1745, the château has many rooms and striking grandeur; come play lord and lady in chandeliered, ancestored salons, discover an aristocratic bedroom with big windows, walk the rolling green parkland as if it were your own. Breakfast is basic but it's another world.

Rooms	1 double, 2 twins: €60.
Meals	Guest kitchen. Restaurants within walking distance.
Closed	Rarely.

Rooms	4 doubles: €120.
	1 suite for 5: €250.
Meals	Restaurants within 4km.
Closed	Rarely.

	Marie-Christine & Philippe Vion
	Le Loubarré,
	550 rue des Montifaux,
	62130 Gauchin Verloingt,
	Pas-de-Calais
Tel	+33 (0)3 21 03 05 05
Email	mcvion.loubarre@wanadoo.fr
Web	www.loubarre.com

	Patrice & Chantal de Saulieu
	Château de Grand Rullecourt,
	3 place du château,
	62810 Grand Rullecourt,
	Pas-de-Calais
Tel	+33 (0)3 21 58 06 37
Mobile	+33 (0)6 07 12 89 08
Email	psaulieu@routiers.com
Web	www.chateaux-chambres-hotes.com

Château de Saulty

The re-lifted stately face looks finer than ever in its great park and apple orchards (15 varieties); it is a truly lovely setting. Inside, a warm, embracing country house with a panelled breakfast room, an amazing, museum-worthy, multi-tiled gents cloakroom and, up the wide old stairs, quietly luxurious bedrooms, some huge, furnished with printed fabrics and period pieces. Be charmed by wooden floors and plain walls in sunny tones, perhaps an old fireplace or a mirrored armoire. Quiet and intelligent, Sylvie is a natural at making guests feel at home.

Le Château

In a private park, in a small village, lies this peaceful 'Manoir.' It was built in 1928 to replace a chateau destroyed in WWI; the Vimy War Memorial is close by. Light pours in through numerous Art Deco windows and interiors have been enhanced by Madame's modern good taste. Sofas face a cosy log-burner in the monumental hall, bedrooms are immaculate (satin sheets, electric shutters, smart antiques), and you wake to wonderful breakfasts at a table set with porcelain. Charming hosts offer bikes, umbrellas, a sauna, a gym, and simple-but-elegant dinners in each first-floor bedroom.

Parking on-site.

Rooms	1 double: €75.
	1 family room for 4: €100.
	2 triples: €85. Singles €65.
Meals	Restaurants 16km.
Closed	January.

Rooms	2 doubles: €125-€149.
	1 suite for 2-3: €139-€159.
	Children under 2, €30. Child's bed €60.
	Sport & sauna, €12/hour per person.
Meals	Light dinner €28.
	Restaurants 10km.
Closed	15-28 August.

	Emmanuel & Sylvie Dalle
	Château de Saulty,
	82 rue de la Gare,
	62158 Saulty,
	Pas-de-Calais
Tel	+33 (0)3 21 48 24 76
Email	chateaudesaulty@nordnet.fr
Web	www.chateaudesaulty.com

	Jannick Blavier
	Le Château,
	9 rue du Puits,
	62580 Fresnoy en Gohelle,
	Pas-de-Calais
Mobile	+33 (0)6 22 19 87 25
Email	contact@lechateau-fresnoy-en-gohelle.com
Web	www.lechateau-fresnoy-en-gohelle.com

Ferme du Moulin

Terraced houses in front, a perfect little farmyard behind, the kindest of hosts within – it's a privilege to meet such a splendid person. A farmer's widow of old-fashioned simple good manners, she is comfortably maternal, delighting in her short travels and guests' conversation. Her modest, authentically timeworn French farmers' house is stuffed with collections of bric-a-brac and her genuine chambres d'hôtes – a threatened species – are family-furnished, floral-papered, draped with all sorts and conditions of crochet; the loo is across the landing. Breakfasts are good and you are perfectly placed for those battlefields.

Ferme de Bonavis

The Delcambre family home, originally one of the Abbaye de Vaucelles farms, rebuilt after WWI, is a friendly, unpretentious place to stay. Bedrooms are traditionally furnished, with tall windows and polished floorboards: 'Alize', in pretty toile de Jouy wallpaper, overlooks the garden; the 'Mozart' two-roomed suite is on the road side (not busy at night). Shower rooms are simple too. Breakfast – fresh bread, homemade brioche – is at one long table under ornate plasterwork in the dining room and Carole loves to share the history of her home and region. It's a pleasant walk to the Abbey, and there's a restaurant over the way.

Rooms	1 double with separate bath or shower, sharing wc with triple: €48. 1 triple with separate bath or shower, sharing wc with double: €48–€58.
Meals	Restaurants 500m.
Closed	Rarely.

Rooms	1 suite for 6: €82–€150. 1 family room for 4: €75–€120. Singles €58–€60.
Meals	Restaurants 2-minute walk.
Closed	Rarely.

	Madame Agnès Dupont Ferme du Moulin, 58 rue du Quatre Septembre, 62800 Liévin, Pas-de-Calais
Tel	+33 (0)3 21 44 65 91
Mobile	+33 (0)6 81 04 46 96

	Carole Delcambre Ferme de Bonavis, 59266 Banteux, Nord
Tel	+33 (0)3 27 78 55 08
Email	contact@bonavis.fr
Web	www.bonavis.fr

Entry 23   Map 1

Entry 24   Map 1

The North

Le Jardin d'Alix

A quiet, elegant residential quarter – but hop on the tram and in 20 minutes you're in the historic centre of Lille. Alexandra's light, airy house, tucked away from the road, was built a mere half century ago by a well-known local church architect. Use your host's sitting room during the day; the passage leading to the bedrooms has internet, and books galore, for the evening. Bedrooms, small and attractive, give onto the gorgeous garden – Alexandra's passion – and are hung with her paintings. Breakfast on homemade bread and jams served on fine porcelain in a spotless high-tech kitchen.

Rooms	1 double: €70.
	1 suite for 2: €85–€100.
Meals	Restaurants 3 minutes by tram.
Closed	Rarely.

Alexandra Hudson
Le Jardin d'Alix,
45 bis av de la Marne,
59200 Tourcoing,
Nord

Tel	+33 (0)3 20 36 72 08
Email	alexandra.hudson@ymail.com
Web	www.lejardindalix.com

Entry 25   Map 1

Picardy

La Tour Blanche

In grand French style, stable your steeds in fine boxes beneath the immensely tall sheltering trees, swirl up the staircase to superb rooms, each a symphony in fabric and colour – red or blue, green or white – with good beds on polished floors and a gentle view of the little church: all is handsome, sober and serene. And bathrooms are brand new. Your active, intelligent young hosts happily share their generous family house and big garden with guests, two children and half a dozen horses. There are games to play, bikes to hire, Amiens to visit and the shimmering Somme estuary to walk you into bird heaven.

Rooms	2 doubles: €88–€120.
	1 suite for 5: €152–€235.
	1 family room for 3: €104–€145.
	Singles €95–€100.
	Extra bed/sofabed available €20–€25 per person per night. Discounts available on stays over 2 nights.
Meals	Dinner with wine, €40.
	Guest kitchen.
Closed	Rarely.

Hélène & Benoît Legru-Plancq
La Tour Blanche,
10 rue de la Ville,
80120 Forest Montiers,
Somme

Tel	+33 (0)3 22 23 69 13
Mobile	+33 (0)6 88 61 31 62
Email	helene.legru-plancq@wanadoo.fr
Web	www.latourblanche.net

Entry 26   Map 1

Château du Romerel

Set in parkland in the middle of the town with views over the bay, this classic 19th-century villa exudes quiet privilege. Graciously furnished rooms include two chandeliered salons – lavish with curtains and deep sofas – and a polished dining room for elegant breakfasts with fruits from the orchard. Dinners, too. Light-flooded bedrooms are country-house-luxurious with soft colours, thick carpets and fine antiques. Most have bay views. Go seal-spotting or cycling; visit Abbeville and Amiens. Sit by the pool or drift amongst the garden's ancient trees and discover its secret bowers. Amélie takes delicious care of you.

Les Mazures

An architect-designed eco house, whose beauty lies in its simplicity. And the garden is glorious, a blaze of colour and form – rock, Japanese and wild flower, carefully gauged scent and colour combos to attract bees, butterflies and other such beasties. Bright white bedrooms have their own entrance and are immaculate, paired with sparkling bathrooms. At the heart, an airy open-plan living room that guests share with owners Peter and Vincent whose nationalities (English and French) are reflected in their cooking – tasty regional and British. Birdwatching, markets and WWI cemeteries are nearby. Fresh, peaceful, convivial.

Rooms	3 doubles: £183–£223. 1 triple: £243–£263.	Rooms	2 doubles, 1 twin: €62. Singles €59.
Meals	Dinner €35. Restaurant within walking distance.	Meals	Dinner with wine, €20. Restaurant 4km.
Closed	Rarely.	Closed	Rarely.

Odile Mulon & Eva Guitteau
Château du Romerel,
15 quai du Romerel,
80230 Saint-Valery sur Somme,
Somme
Tel   +33 (0)3 22 26 54 10
Email   info@chateaudenoyelles.com
Web   www.chateauduromerel.com

Peter Clark & Vincent Caplier
Les Mazures,
2b rue de la Prairie,
80370 Beaumetz,
Somme
Tel   +33 (0)3 22 32 80 52
Email   info@lesmazures.com
Web   www.lesmazures.com

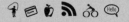

Entry 27   Map 1

Entry 28   Map 1

Château de Béhen

Surrounded by wooded parkland, the handsome château started life as a holiday house. In the 1950s the Cuveliers moved in, adding paddocks, a pond for swans and a deeply traditional décor. Big bedrooms come with solid oak floors and rugs, and French flourishes. Two-tone panelling graces the first-floor rooms, those above have sloping ceilings and a beam or two; bathrooms are hotel-perfect with double basins of mottled marble. Delicious dinner is at one lively table (or a single one if preferred). Saddle up and enjoy a guided trek – for a day or even two. Fun, friendly people, donkeys to stroke and 15 horses to ride.

Les Chambres d'Aumont

In the grounds of a stately 18th-century château, a cleverly converted outbuilding with four peaceful rooms overlooking the garden and stables. Where grain and wood were once stored, guests now find light, smartly furnished bedrooms with coir floors and luxurious en suites. Breakfast in the vast, bright communal room is a pleasure… Feast on homemade Mirabelle plum jam, local cake, cheese and charcuteries. Wonderfully calm and rural, you could happily pass the day dozing under an apple tree, but there's plenty to see in this lovely part of Picardy – Amiens Cathedral is a half hour drive and the Somme battlefields are close too.

Parking available.

Rooms	2 doubles, 1 twin: €125–€213. 1 suite for 2: €180–€202. 2 family rooms for 4: €185–€244.	Rooms	3 doubles: €92. 1 family room for 4: €110–€130.
Meals	Dinner with wine, from €43; book 2 days ahead.	Meals	Restaurant 10km.
Closed	Rarely.	Closed	Rarely.

Cuvelier Family
Château de Béhen,
8 rue du Château,
80870 Béhen,
Somme
Tel   +33 (0)3 22 31 58 30
Email norbert-andre@cuvelier.com
Web   www.chateau-de-behen.com

Stephanie Danzel d'Aumont
Les Chambres d'Aumont,
Le Château, 2 rue d'Hornoy,
80640 Aumont,
Somme
Tel   +33 (0)3 22 90 67 16
Email stephanie@chambresdaumont.fr
Web   www.chambresdaumont.fr

Entry 29   Map 1

Entry 30   Map 5

Le Macassar

This gem of a 19th-century house was restyled in the Twenties and Thirties to please a pretty young wife – but it's more 'femme fatale' than blushing belle. Suave bathrooms, extra fine bed linen, feather duvets – only the best. The master suite has turquoise velvet walls, a carved stone fireplace and fine contemporary art, and another an exotic bathroom accessed through an ornate Moorish door. Downstairs are corners in which to lounge and admire the art, the books and glassware. Outside: a flowering Italianate courtyard with a fountain. Splendid breakfasts are included in the price, the hosts are charming and Amiens is close.

Over 12s welcome. Parking on-site.

Château d'Omiécourt

On a working estate, Omiécourt is a proudly grand 19th-century château and elegant family house (the Thézys have four teenage children), with tall slender windows and some really old trees. Friendly if formal, communicative and smiling, your hosts have worked hugely to restore their inheritance and create gracious French château guest rooms, each with an ornate fireplace, each named for a different period. In an outbuilding near the two pools is a neat apartment for self-caterers; there's a 'boutique', too, of pretty things. A house of goodwill where you will be very comfortable.

Self-catering available.

Rooms	1 double, 1 twin: €180.
	4 suites for 2: €200-€260.
Meals	Hosted dinner with wine, €55;
	Sunday only. Groups on request.
	Restaurants 5-minute walk.
Closed	January/February.

Rooms	3 doubles: €145-€165.
	1 suite for 3: €165-€195.
	1 family room for 4: €195.
	Extra bed €30.
Meals	Gourmet room service dinner, €35.
	Restaurants 12km.
Closed	Rarely.

Miguel de Lemos
Le Macassar,
8 place de la République,
80800 Corbie,
Somme
Tel   +33 (0)3 22 48 40 04
Email   bookings@lemacassar.com
Web   www.lemacassar.com

Dominique & Véronique de Thézy
Château d'Omiécourt,
80320 Omiécourt,
Somme
Tel   +33 (0)3 22 83 01 75
Email   contact@chateau-omiecourt.com
Web   www.chateau-omiecourt.com

La Commanderie

Up here on the hill, not easy to find, is a Templar hamlet and a millennium of history: an enclosed farmyard, a ruined medieval chapel framing the sunrise, a tithe barn with high oak timbers – and this modern house. José-Marie, an unhurried grandmother of generous spirit, loves the history, harvests her orchards and vegetables, and welcomes genuinely. Bedrooms and bathrooms are in plain, dated farm style but open the window and you fall into the view that soars away on all sides of the hill, even to Laon cathedral. Homely, authentic, simple and great value – but not for you if you need all the mod cons and aren't keen on dogs.

Rooms	1 double: €50–€55.
	2 family rooms for 4: €60–€70.
Meals	Restaurants 10km.
Closed	Last week October to February, except by arrangement.

José-Marie Carette
La Commanderie,
Catillon du Temple,
02270 Nouvion & Catillon,
Aisne
Tel   +33 (0)3 23 56 51 28
Mobile +33 (0)6 82 33 22 64
Email carette.jm@wanadoo.fr
Web   www.gite-templier-laon.fr

Entry 33   Map 5

Le Clos

Genuine country hospitality and warmth are yours in the big old house. Madame is kindly and direct; Monsieur is the communicator (mainly in French), knows his local history and loves the hunting horn. His 300-year-old family house is cosily unposh: floral curtains, French-papered walls, original wainscotting, funny old prints in bedrooms, comforting clutter in the vast living room, posters in the corridors. The master bedroom is superb, others are simple and fine; one has a ship's shower room, all look onto green pastures. And there's a pretty lake for picnics across the narrow road.

Rooms	2 doubles, 1 twin: €50–€60.
	1 suite for 5: €70–€120.
	Extra bed €20.
Meals	Occasional dinner with wine, €22.50.
	Restaurant in village.
Closed	Mid-October to mid-March, except by arrangement.

Michel & Monique Simonnot
Le Clos,
02860 Chérêt,
Aisne
Tel   +33 (0)3 23 24 80 64
Email leclos.cheret@club-internet.fr
Web   www.lecloscheret.com

Entry 34   Map 5

Domaine de l'Étang

The village on one side, the expansive estate on the other, the 18th-century wine-grower's house in between. There's a civilised mood: Monsieur so well-mannered and breakfast served with silver and fine china in the comfortably elegant guest dining room. Wake to church-spire and rooftop views in rooms with soft comfort where, under sloping ceilings, French toile de Jouy is as inviting as English chintz (your hosts spent two years in England). Bathrooms are frilled and pretty. Shrubs hug the hem of the house, a pool is sunk into the lawn behind and Laon trumpets one of France's first gothic cathedrals.

Vendangeoir d'Orgeval

Passionate brocante buff, welcoming Nathalie has an interior deco shop in Laon and a sure eye for the soft grey-green-taupe tones. Her quiet, country-chic B&B spaces in the old stables are warmly comforting without being cluttered. The big raftered room for three, up a steep iron stair off the living room, has an antique claw-foot bath. The double room on the ground floor next door is just as softly cosy; you go down a wee spiral stair to a little vaulted cellar with a pebble-decorated floor: the bathroom. They share the communal room where breakfast and dinner are served and you can picnic if you like.

Minimum stay: 2 nights.

Rooms	2 doubles, 1 twin: €60–€75.
	Tourist taxes €0.75 p.p. per night.
Meals	Restaurants 6km.
Closed	Rarely.

Rooms	1 double: €85.
	1 family room for 3: €75–€100.
Meals	Dinner €30; min. 3, Saturdays only.
	Restaurants 3km.
Closed	Rarely.

	Patrick Woillez
	Domaine de l'Étang,
	2 rue St Martin,
	02000 Mons en Laonnois,
	Aisne
Tel	+33 (0)3 23 24 44 52
Mobile	+33 (0)6 26 62 36 41
Email	gitemons@sfr.fr
Web	www.domainedeletang.fr

	Nathalie & Bernard Vinçon
	Vendangeoir d'Orgeval,
	13 Grande Rue,
	02860 Orgeval,
	Aisne
Mobile	+33 (0)6 82 56 16 95
Email	vendangeoir.orgeval@netcourrier.com
Web	www.vendangeoirs-orgeval-picardie.com

La Grange

Hidden down lanes, behind an undulating wall, glimpsed through wrought-iron gates, is this big converted barn; Tony and Thierry have been looking after guests, with great pleasure, for years. Rambling gardens and a bountiful vegetable plot run down to wide open pasture. Under the high glass atrium of the breakfast room lies the heart of the house with wood-burner, piano and windows opening to undulating views, while peaceful and immaculate bedrooms hop from fabric-swathed opulence to a more simple country elegance. Hosted dinners are convivial and delicious; Reims, rich in history and gastronomy, is under an hour.

Ferme de Ressons

Ressons is home to a warm, dynamic, intelligent couple who, after a hard day's work running this big farm (Jean-Paul) or being an architect (Valérie) and tending three children, will ply you in apparently leisurely fashion with champagne, excellent dinner and conversation; they also hunt. The deeply carved Henri III furniture is an admirable family heirloom; bedrooms (two en suite) are colour-coordinated, views roll for miles and sharing facilities seems easy. A house of comfort and relaxed good manners (smoking is in the study only), whose decoration and accessories reflect the owners' travels.

Rooms	2 doubles: €79.
	1 apartment for 4: €149.
	Singles €69. Extra bed/sofabed
	available €20 per person per night.
Meals	Dinner, 4 courses with wine, €29.
	Restaurant 10km.
Closed	Rarely.

Rooms	2 doubles, sharing bath & 2 wcs;
	1 double, with bath, sharing wc;
	1 twin, sharing bath & 2 wcs;
	1 twin, with bath, sharing wc:
	€55–€80.
Meals	Dinner €19. Wine €14;
	champagne €18.
Closed	Rarely.

	Tony Bridier & Thierry Charbit
	La Grange,
	6 impasse des Prés,
	02160 Cuiry les Chaudardes,
	Aisne
Tel	+33 (0)3 23 25 82 42
Email	lagrangecuiry@orange.fr
Web	www.lagrangecuiry.fr

	Valérie & Jean-Paul Ferry
	Ferme de Ressons,
	02220 Mont St Martin,
	Aisne
Tel	+33 (0)3 23 74 71 00
Mobile	+33 (0)6 80 74 17 01
Email	ferryressons@orange.fr

Entry 37 Map 5

Entry 38 Map 5

La Cressonnière

Come and be pampered in gothic cathedral land. Audrey, Philippe and their children are loving their new venture into hospitality with B&B rooms, a gîte, a gypsy caravan and a little house in the woods. In this group of intelligently converted farm buildings they have installed all worldly comforts, including a state-of-the-art spa, and a calm country atmosphere. The two big airy B&B rooms marry the best new bedding with antique carved doors and some great designer touches. You share a pretty breakfast room, where home-cooked dinner can be served, too. Your young enterprising hosts want you to have the best holiday possible.

La Quincy

An old family home, faded and weary yet timeless and romantic. All is peaceful, and Marie-Catherine is natural and quietly elegant. Find a mellow, laid back atmosphere; corridors cluttered with books, magazines and traces of family life lead to an octagonal tower, its great double room and child's room across the landing imaginatively set in the space. A handsome antique bed on a polished floor, charming chintz, erratic plumbing and two parkland views will enchant you. Shrubs hug the feet of the 'troubadour' château, the garden slips into meadow, and summer breakfast and dinner (good wine, book ahead) are in the lived in orangery.

Rooms	2 doubles: €198.
Meals	Dinner €30. Restaurants 2km.
Closed	Rarely.

Rooms	1 family room for 3: €70-€110. Pets €8.
Meals	Occasional dinner with wine, €25.
Closed	Rarely.

	Audrey & Philippe Bertholus Deram
	La Cressonnière,
	4 rue d'en Bas,
	02200 Noyant et Aconin,
	Aisne
Tel	+33 (0)3 23 54 64 01
Mobile	+33 (0)6 50 91 07 60
Email	la-cressonniere@orange.fr
Web	www.gite-chambres-hotes-soissons.com

	Jacques & Marie-Catherine Cornu-Langy
	La Quincy,
	02880 Nanteuil la Fosse,
	Aisne
Tel	+33 (0)3 23 54 67 76
Mobile	+33 (0)7 86 99 37 95
Email	la.quincy@yahoo.fr

Entry 39   Map 5

Entry 40   Map 5

Domaine de Montaigu

Languid and pleasant gardens – pillows of lavender, dripping wisteria – hem in the large fountain'd courtyard, and neat pathways lead to stone terraces embracing the hill: welcome to this 18th-century wine domain. Gardening is one of the enthusiasms of new owner Claire (along with horses and champagne). She and Philippe love their B&B life and offer you cosy comfortable bedrooms decorated in traditional French style, three pretty with toile de Jouy. There are two sitting rooms, one large, one snug, a swimming pool for summer and a big convivial table for breakfasts of pastries and homemade jams.

Rooms	2 doubles: €80–€95.
	1 family room for 3, 1 family room for 5: €80–€130. Extra bed/sofabed available €25 per person per night.
Meals	Restaurant 5km.
Closed	Rarely.

Philippe de Coster
Domaine de Montaigu,
16 rue de Montaigu,
02290 Ambleny,
Aisne

Tel	+33 (0)3 23 74 06 62
Email	info@domainedemontaigu.com
Web	www.domainedemontaigu.com

Entry 41   Map 5

La Maison & L'Atelier

In the lush countryside outside of Chantilly – famed for its château, horse racing, lace and cream – lies a typical village house in unusual style. Clare's creative energy swirls around in the bold cubes and stripes, trompe l'oeil tiles, designer chairs and leafy plants. Carlos crafted the solid wood kitchen table at which you breakfast on home baked goodies, fresh fruits and juices from the village bakery or dine on a light charcuterie platter and a glass of good wine. Cats snooze by the fireplace in a light-filled sitting room bright with paintings by artist friends. And you will snooze well in one of two exquisite bedrooms overlooking a beautiful garden.

Rooms	2 doubles: €100–€120.
Meals	Dinner with wine, €20.
	Restaurants 15-minute drive.
Closed	Rarely.

Clare Howarth
La Maison & L'Atelier,
26 rue des Croix,
63530 Crouy-en-Thelle,
Oise

Mobile	+33 (0)6 80 04 38 04
Email	hello@lamaisonetlatelier.com
Web	www.lamaisonetlatelier.com

Entry 42   Map 5

L'Echappée Belle

Nadine looks after you impeccably in her family home filled with antiques and modern art. Breakfast is a bonanza of homemade pastries and jam, fresh croissants, local cheeses, served in the dining room at separate tables; traditional evening meals using local ingredients can be organised in advance and eaten on the terrace in summer. Sleep well in spacious, beamed bedrooms with good furniture, modern lighting, old prints and stencils, comfortable beds; bathrooms are bang up to date with posh smellies. You have your own sitting room, and there's seating galore in the beautiful garden, but you could borrow a bike, or go fishing.

Le Clos

The sprucest of farmhouses, whitewashed and Normandy-beamed, sits in its lush secret garden, reached via a door in the wall. Indoors, you find a remarkably fresh, open-plan and modernised interior, with a comfortable sitting room to share. The bedroom above the garage is spacious, neat, uncluttered and warm; bedding is the best, bathrooms spotless and modern with coloured towels. Dine with your informative hosts by the old farm fireplace on *tarte aux pommes du jardin*. Philippe, the chef, receives much praise. Chantal, a retired teacher, keeps you gentle company. A peaceful spot, close to Paris.

Rooms	4 doubles: €95–€150. Extra bed €25.
Meals	Dinner €27; children €17. Restaurants 6km.
Closed	One week around Christmas & occasionally.

Rooms	2 family rooms for 2-3: €60–€72.
Meals	Dinner with wine, €27.
Closed	3 weeks in winter.

	Nadine Guirriec
	L'Echappée Belle,
	1 rue Émile Delaere, Château Rouge,
	60730 Cauvigny,
	Oise
Tel	+33 (0)3 44 08 78 23
Email	naguirriec@gmail.com
Web	www.maison-hote-oise.com/

	Philippe & Chantal Vermeire
	Le Clos,
	3 rue du Chêne Noir,
	60240 Fay les Étangs,
	Oise
Tel	+33 (0)3 44 49 92 38
Email	philippe.vermeire@wanadoo.fr
Web	www.leclosdefay.com

Entry 43   Map 5

Entry 44   Map 5

Les Chambres de l'Abbaye

Chloé and her artist husband have the most unusual, delightful house in a village with a fine Cistercian abbey. You are free to roam a series of beautiful rooms downstairs, read a book in the pale blue formal salon, admire Jean-François' striking, exciting pictures (though sadly illness is making it harder for him). The family room is on the first floor, the two others higher up; all are fresh, and immaculate. You should eat well: much is homemade, including walnut wine and liqueur from their own trees. Walk it off round the partly unmanicured garden with its summerhouse and pond. It's a fascinating house and a pleasure to stay in.

Rooms	2 doubles: €95-€100.
	1 family room for 3: €100-€125.
	Extra bed/sofabed available €25 per
	person per night.
Meals	Dinner with wine & coffee, €30.
Closed	24-26 December.

Chloé Comte
Les Chambres de l'Abbaye,
2 rue Michel Greuet,
60850 St Germer de Fly,
Oise

Tel	+33 (0)3 44 81 98 38
Mobile	+33 (0)6 09 27 75 41
Email	comte.resa@free.fr
Web	www.chambres-abbaye.com

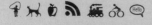

Entry 45   Map 5

Champagne – Ardenne

Champagne – Ardenne

Le Presbytère de Sévigny

You'll love your hosts: Jatin, attentive and hands-on; Laurence, easy, serene and a good cook (try her nougat ice cream!). The wing of their 19th-century presbytery, once used for christenings and confirmations, has become a plush and pretty gîte, with bedrooms that can be rented individually. Extremely cosy and comfortable, they come in fashionable muted colours or in Asian style; mattresses are deep and firm, and garnished with square French pillows. Downstairs are the sitting and dining rooms, elegant and cool. The village is remote with a 13th-century church; beyond are the vineyards of Champagne.

Rooms	3 doubles: €80-€95.
	1 triple: €95-€130.
	Discounts on stays of 3+ nights.
	Children under 6 stay free.
	Cot available free of charge.
Meals	Dinner, 3 courses, €28.
	Restaurants 11km.
Closed	Rarely.

Laurence & Jatin Janray
Le Presbytère de Sévigny,
7 rue du Cabas,
08220 Sevigny-Waleppe,
Ardennes

Tel	+33 (0)3 24 72 26 31
Email	info@lepresbyteredesevigny.com
Web	www.lepresbyteredesevigny.com

Champagne – Ardenne

La Grange Champenoise

Twenty minutes from Reims, this giant limestone barn has been rebuilt to create five flawless bedrooms (new kingsize mattresses, top toiletries) and a handsome breakfast room and sitting room besides. Oak floors are impeccable, colours are ivory and cream, and bedrooms open onto a huge sunny courtyard with a low hedging trim. Enjoy an excellent French breakfast served at a convivial table with white dining chairs. Gently spoken Florent farms the estate, friendly unassuming Emmanuelle makes the pastries, and if you order champagne it arrives on a silver platter.

Rooms	4 doubles: €90-€95.
	1 family room for 4: €120-€190.
	Extra bed €35 per night.
	Cot available €15 on request.
	Singles €80-€85 (except weekends
	& bank holidays).
Meals	Restaurant 7km.
Closed	Late December to early March.

Florent & Emmanuelle Guillaume
La Grange Champenoise,
Rue du 151 R.I.,
51110 Auménancourt,
Marne

Tel	+33 (0)3 26 97 54 21
Mobile	+33 (0)6 21 61 62 52
Email	contact@lagrangechampenoise.com
Web	www.lagrangechampenoise.com

La Closerie des Sacres

An easy drive from Reims, these former stables have changed radically. Large, cool, downstairs areas – the mangers and tethering rings remain – are pale-tiled with dark leather sofas, games and books, an open fire, a glass-topped dining table, wrought-iron chairs. And you can do your own cooking in the fully fitted kitchen. Bedrooms are solid oak-floored, draped and prettily coloured with well-dressed beds, cushions, teddy bears, electric blinds and jacuzzi baths. The Jactats have farmed here for generations and tell of the rebuilding of their village in 1925. Take time to talk, and play boules in the sheltered garden.

La Demeure des Sacres

A privileged spot for a privileged mansion. Reims Cathedral is 150 yards away: you can see it from the balcony of the Suite Royale. All the rooms are 'royale' here: suave, spacious, voluptuous, and the quietest facing the garden. Courteous Céline cares for house, family and guests and offers an elegant breakfast buffet of homemade cookies, crêpes and jams in the classical dining room (at one table, or several – you choose), or on the terrace on summer days, overlooking lawn, roses, shrubs and swings. You get minibars, safes, superb bathrooms, snow-white linen... and a sweeping Art Deco day room.

Parking 50m.

Rooms	1 double: €94. 1 suite for 5: €120-€180. 1 triple: €94-€115. Singles €78-€100.
Meals	Guest kitchen available. Restaurants 2km.
Closed	Rarely.

Rooms	2 twin/doubles with separate shower & wc: €153. 1 suite for 2-4, 1 suite for 2-5: €228-€253. Extra bed/sofabed available €35 per person per night.
Meals	Restaurants within walking distance.
Closed	Rarely.

Sandrine & Laurent Jactat
La Closerie des Sacres,
7 rue Chefossez,
51110 Lavannes,
Marne
Tel   +33 (0)3 26 02 05 05
Email   contact@closerie-des-sacres.com
Web   www.closerie-des-sacres.com

Céline Songy
La Demeure des Sacres,
29 rue Libergier,
51100 Reims,
Marne
Mobile   +33 (0)6 79 06 80 68
Email   contact@la-demeure-des-sacres.com
Web   www.la-demeure-des-sacres.com

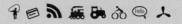

Entry 48   Map 6

Entry 49   Map 6

Champagne – Ardenne

Domaine Ployez-Jacquemart

The grand old mansion sits in green, serene gardens near the outskirts of a small champagne village; Ployez-Jacquemart is an exceptional domain whose fizz ranges from buttery-rich to fruity-fresh. Courteous staff (who live off site) serve breakfast at one big table, and show you to rooms decorated in impeccable French style. Ask for one that faces the vineyards ('Nature', distinguished by its gentle colours and polished boards, is on the first floor, 'Savane' and 'Provence' are on the second). The communal spaces are chic, the gardens are elegant, the breakfasts are delicious and you can wander at will.

Minimum stay: 2 nights at weekends.

Domaine Sacret

A dynamic, humorous and creative couple, these two. James was born into a small champagne dynasty and started the B&B with Stéphanie as a natural extension of his wine-tasting sessions. Their large newly-done rooms go from coolly sober to dramatically red, all with character and great bathrooms. The bar-restaurant-salon is as big and welcoming as James himself. He runs champagne tastings every evening, Stéphanie serves delicious platters of local specialities at the long convivial table, happy wine buffs relax in leather chesterfields or at the bright red pool table, and Mr Supercat lords it over all. A happy place to be.

Parking on-site.

Rooms	3 doubles, 1 twin: €135-€145. 1 family room for 4: €200-€210.
Meals	Gourmet dinner €135; minimum 6 guests. Restaurants 10km.
Closed	Rarely.

Rooms	3 doubles, 1 twin/double: €160-€190.
Meals	Dinner €25. Restaurants 5-minute walk.
Closed	March.

Laurence Ployez
Domaine Ployez-Jacquemart,
8 rue Astoin,
51500 Ludes,
Marne
Tel   +33 (0)3 26 61 11 87
Email   contact@ployez-jacquemart.fr
Web   www.ployez-jacquemart.fr

Stephanie Chevillet
Domaine Sacret,
3 rue Billecart,
51160 Ay,
Marne
Tel   +33 (0)3 26 56 99 20
Mobile +33 (0)6 60 69 58 86
Email   james-chevillet@orange.fr

Château de Juvigny

Oozing old-world charm, this handsome 1705 château wraps you in its warmth. The family have occupied one wing for 200 years and, thanks to Brigitte, it has a wonderfully easy-going elegance. There are chandeliers, polished floorboards, wainscotting and antiques, old-fashioned bathrooms, cracked floor tiles, rustic outbuildings. Bedrooms, in the old servants' quarters, are informally stylish with marble fireplaces, pretty bedcovers and views over the park, the formal gardens and the lake. You breakfast, colourfully, beneath a vast (and deteriorated!) portrait of an ancestor. Charming, unfussy country comfort.

Ferme de Bannay

The deep-country house in the pretty village brims with new chintz and old beams. Bedrooms dressed in ivory and white have quilted bedcovers and scatter cushions; sprays of artificial flowers brighten nooks and crannies; and there's a bathroom behind a curtain. Little English is spoken but the welcome is so endearing, the generosity so genuine, the food so delicious, that communication is easy. Just a few cows on the farm now, and the odd tractor passing, but the vegetable garden is handsome and much of the produce ends up on your (delightfully antique) plate.

Rooms	3 doubles, 1 twin: €95–€150. 1 suite for 4: €150–€200. Extra bed €25.
Meals	Restaurant 10km.
Closed	Mid-October to 1 April, except by arrangement.

Rooms	1 suite for 2-3 with kitchen: €84–€148. 1 triple: €70–€88. 1 quadruple: €70–€106.
Meals	Dinner with wine, €42; with champagne €61. Restaurant 3km (weekdays), 12km (weekends).
Closed	Rarely.

Brigitte Caubère d'Alinval
Château de Juvigny,
8 av du Château,
51150 Juvigny,
Marne
Mobile +33 (0)6 78 99 69 40
Email information@chateaudejuvigny.com
Web www.chateaudejuvigny.com

Muguette & Jean-Pierre Curfs
Ferme de Bannay,
1 rue du Petit Moulin,
51270 Bannay,
Marne
Tel +33 (0)3 26 52 80 49
Email leschambresdemuguette@orange.fr

Entry 52   Map 6

Entry 53   Map 5

Au Pré du Moulin

The big 1789 farmhouse deep in the country has been in the Coulmier family for two generations. Luckily, one half of the main house has been given over to guests; an interconnecting suite (poppy-print wallpaper, wooden floors) provides family-sized space to match a child-friendly garden. Elsewhere, rooms are French 'rustic chic' to a tee; white lacquered bedsteads and cornflower-blue floral details in one, stylish dark wood and Burgundian limestone with tiny black cabochons in another. Valérie and Didier are lovely, friendly and knowledgeable hosts and will share delicious organic home-grown fare with you.

Auprès de l'Église

New Zealanders Michael and Glenis do excellent table d'hôtes and love sharing their restored 19th-century house full of surprises: some walls are unadorned but for the mason's scribbles. The upstairs suite is separated by a fabulous wall of bookcases and an attic stair, the ground floor has a French country feel. Another big, cleverly designed room leads off the courtyard where you sit in the shade of birch trees and dine (and enjoy a champagne aperitif). Oyes church has no chiming clocks: you'll sleep deeply here. Plenty of fun and funky brocante yet the comforts are modern. Charming Sézanne is a 20-minute drive.

Rooms	1 double: €55–€70.
	1 suite for 4: €90–€100.
	1 triple: €55–€85.
	Extra bed/sofabed available €15 per person per night.
Meals	Dinner with wine, €30.
Closed	Christmas & New Year.

Rooms	2 suites for 2-4: €120–€160.
	Singles €80. Extra bed/sofabed available €20 per person per night.
Meals	Dinner with wine, €40.
	Children's dinner, 2 courses, €10.
Closed	Rarely.

Valérie & Didier Coulmier
Au Pré du Moulin,
4 rue du Moulin,
51130 Clamanges,
Marne
Tel   +33 (0)3 26 64 50 16
Email   reservation@aupredumoulin.fr
Web   www.aupredumoulin.fr

Glenis Foster
Auprès de l'Église,
2 rue de l'Église,
51120 Oyes,
Marne
Tel   +33 (0)3 26 80 62 39
Mobile   +44 (0)7808 905233
Email   titusprod@me.com
Web   www.champagnevilla.com

Entry 54   Map 6

Entry 55   Map 5

La Parenthèse

Lovely! A half-timbered longhouse in a drowsy village between Épernay and Troyes. Elegant Madame Debelle managed the renovation to show off timber, tile and stonework and create rustic chic bedrooms — a harmonious balance of traditional with contemporary touches. A grand fireplace takes centre stage downstairs where you breakfast at the long, benched kitchen table (homemade jams a speciality) and bedrooms have kitchenettes; the biggest has its own roof terrace. Madame can provide supper and advice on itineraries: all things Champagne, medieval Troyes. The superb Reims cathedral and the lesser-known St Rémy are an hour away.

Domaine du Moulin d'Eguebaude

A delightful mill — and trout farm. The secluded old buildings in the lush riverside setting are home to a fish restaurant, several guest rooms and 50 tons of live fish. Delicious breakfast and dinner are shared with your enthusiastic hosts, who started the business 40 years ago; groups come for speciality lunches, anglers come to fish. Bedrooms under the eaves are compact, small-windowed, simply furnished, decorated in rustic or granny style, the larger annexe rooms are more motel-ish. Lots of space for children, and good English spoken. More guest house than B&B.

Rooms	1 double: €75. Extra bed €20.
Meals	Dinner with wine, €30; children €10. Restaurant 10km.
Closed	Rarely.

Rooms	2 doubles, 1 twin: €77–€82. 2 family rooms for 4: €112–€128. 1 triple: €87.
Meals	Dinner with wine, €28. Guest kitchen.
Closed	Rarely.

Mathilde & Éric Debelle
La Parenthèse,
38 rue de La Lhuitrelle,
10700 Dosnon,
Aube
Tel   +33 (0)3 25 37 37 26
Email   contact@gites-laparenthese.com
Web   www.gites-laparenthese.com

Alexandre & Sandrine Mesley
Domaine du Moulin d'Eguebaude,
36 rue Pierre Brossolette,
10190 Estissac,
Aube
Tel   +33 (0)3 25 40 42 18
Email   moulineguebaude10@gmail.com
Web   www.moulineguebaude.jimdo.com

Entry 56   Map 6

Entry 57   Map 5

Domaine de la Creuse

You're well away from the main road but a short walk from the village in this stone farmhouse dated 1742. B&B rooms are in various outbuildings set around a pretty courtyard with trees, shrubs and flowers: each is different but all have exposed oak beams, half-timbered walls, comfortable seats with views and fresh white embroidered cotton sheets on good thick mattresses. All have a seating area too. Breakfast is in the airy dining room, or the rambling garden – smiley Madame makes her own jams and yogurts and buys the best croissants and bread from the local artisan baker. Golf, walks, cycling and watery fun are all near.

Parking on-site.

Rooms	2 doubles: €110–€135.
	2 suites for 2-4: €110–€170.
	1 family room for 4: €135–€195.
	Extra bed/sofabed available €15–€30 per person per night.
Meals	Buffet on arrival available €35 for 2 (no drinks included), by arrangement. Restaurants 5km.
Closed	22 December to 5 January.

Marie-Christine Deroin-Thevenin
Domaine de la Creuse,
D444,
10800 Moussey,
Aube

Mobile +33 (0)6 07 89 99 49
Email deroin.thevenin.ph@wanadoo.fr
Web www.domainedelacreuse.fr

Entry 58   Map 6

À l'Aube Bleue

Madame is a collector of intriguing finds (including the Peugeot 203). Her two family-friendly garden-facing bedrooms make good use of compact space: one has the double bed on the mezzanine floor and children sleep below; the other, pretty in pale colours, sleeps three. The disabled access room is larger, also simply furnished, with a baldequin bed. You breakfast at one big table next to the kitchen. Do arrange a meal in the sheltered outdoor dining area, too; it's fun and hung with agricultural bits and bobs, and the food will be good. All in a quiet village, in open country 18km south of medieval Troyes.

Rooms	1 double: €68.
	1 family room for 4: €100.
	1 triple: €85. Singles €58.
	Extra bed/sofabed available €20 per person per night.
	Dinner, B&B extra €25 per person.
Meals	Dinner with wine & coffee, €29; children over 5, €9; under 5, €6.
Closed	Rarely.

Christine Degois
À l'Aube Bleue,
6 rue du Viard,
10320 Assenay,
Aube

Tel +33 (0)3 25 40 29 58
Mobile +33 (0)6 85 10 43 50
Email contact@chambres-hotes-aube-bleue.fr
Web www.chambres-hotes-aube-bleue.fr

Entry 59   Map 6

Champagne – Ardenne

Champagne Ardenne

La Pierre Écrite

The Nachbroun, kindly people, simply love mills. This one began life in the 13th century – property then of the Earl of Champagne – and its history entwines with village folklore. The bedrooms – modern retro style with painted panelling, brocante prints and big monochrome shower rooms – overlook the mill pond: a treat for all seasons whether dizzying with dragonflies or mist-rising on a frosty morning. Breakfast is a grand spread of sweet and savoury; there's a corner kitchen downstairs, a garden barbecue, and a decent restaurant you can easily walk to in attractive, historic and watery Soulaine-Dhuys.

Domaine de Boulancourt

This large and splendid farmhouse is irresistible. For fishermen there's a river, for birdwatchers a fine park full of wildlife (come for the cranes in spring or autumn); for architecture buffs, the half-timbered churches are among the "100 most beautiful attractions in France". Bedrooms are comfortable and handsome; afternoon tea is served by the piano in the elegant panelled salon; dinner, including fresh fruits and vegetables from the B&B, local meats, cheeses and wine from the Haute-Marne (south of the department), is eaten around one table with your delightful hosts. You will feel like a member of the family.

Rooms	2 doubles: €80.
Meals	Restaurant within walking distance.
Closed	Rarely.

Rooms	2 doubles, 1 twin: €85–€95. 1 suite for 2: €85. 1 single: €65. 20% discount for 2nd night; 30% discount for 3rd night. Extra bed €20.
Meals	Dinner with wine, €35.
Closed	21 November to 2 May.

Jean-Claude Nachbroun
La Pierre Écrite,
Le Moulin,
4 rue des Tanneries,
10200 Soulaine Dhuys,
Aube
Tel   +33 (0)3 25 27 07 37
Mobile   +33 (0)6 80 91 61 31
Email   lapierreecrite@orange.fr

Philippe & Christine Viel-Cazal
Domaine de Boulancourt,
Le Désert,
52220 Longeville sur la Laines,
Haute-Marne
Tel   +33 (0)3 25 04 60 18
Mobile   +33 (0)6 33 18 84 92
Email   dom.boulancourt@wanadoo.fr
Web   www.domaine-de-boulancourt.com

Entry 60   Map 6

Entry 61   Map 6

Le Relais du Puits

Regular guests of Michel and Évelyne in their tiny medieval village in Champagne will find this charming couple in a 'new' 200-year-old home. Just three rooms now, all reflecting Évelyne's quirky humour: snow-white "Romantic", chic "Belle-Époque", extravagant "Medieval" with a gothic, dark orange décor, daggers and tapestries. Bathrooms are gorgeous, the garden large, and dinners – Évelyne's cider chicken, Michel's chocolate mousse – fabulous value. After 18 years your hosts know just what guests want, whether it's free internet, a roaring fire in the sitting room, or bicycles for the surrounding forests and country lanes.

Rooms	1 double, 1 twin with separate bath: €74. 1 quadruple: €84–€125. Extra bed €20. Cot €12.
Meals	Dinner with wine, €18; children under 10, €10; under 3, free. Restaurant 8km.
Closed	Rarely.

Évelyne & Michel Poope
Le Relais du Puits,
15 rue Augustin Massin,
52500 Pressigny,
Haute-Marne

Tel	+33 (0)3 25 88 80 50
Email	e.m.poope@orange.fr
Web	www.le-relais-du-puits.com

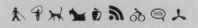

Entry 62   Map 6

Lorraine • Alsace • Franche Comté

Lorraine

Château d'Alteville

A genuine eco-friendly family château (several generations run the estate) in a privileged setting: wake to a chorus of birds. Bedrooms are deliciously *vieille France*; bathrooms are functional and adequate. The real style lies in the utterly French salon and the dining room – reached through halls, past library and billiards – where dinners are enjoyed by candlelight in the company of your charming hosts. David, a committed environmentalist, cooks local produce with skill, Agnieszka joyfully deals with two lovely children and fills the place with flowers. The lake on the doorstep is a marvel of peace and birdlife.

Rooms	4 doubles, 1 twin: €91.
Meals	Dinner €31–€38.50.
	Wine €5–€15.
Closed	Rarely.

David Barthélémy
Château d'Alteville,
Tarquimpol,
57260 Dieuze,
Moselle

Tel	+33 (0)3 87 05 46 63
Mobile	+33 (0)6 72 07 56 05
Email	chateau.alteville@free.fr
Web	www.chateaudalteville.com

Entry 63   Map 7

Lorraine

Les 3 Officiers

The prosperous looking manor by the church (once a modest farmhouse) has become a splendid B&B. Tea in the salon with Frederick – Anglophile restorer with a great sense of humour – is civilised and fun, while dinner at the big table (homemade orange wine, local organic produce) with both hosts, and perhaps other guests, is a gorgeous feast. As for the bedrooms, they have been designed in the spirit of the house, one à la Napoleon III, the other Louis Philippe. Towels are snowy, bed linen crisp and all is generous and bright. Wake to fruit compotes served on antique china, come home to a beautiful box-hedged garden.

Parking available.

Rooms	2 doubles: €90. Singles €80.
	Extra bed €30 per night.
Meals	Dinner, 3 courses with wine, €29;
	children under 7, €15.
	Restaurant 5km.
Closed	Rarely.

Frederick Metz
Les 3 Officiers,
Rue de Verdun,
55210 Woël,
Meuse

Email	les3officiers.resa@orange.fr
Web	www.chambres-3officiers-lorraine.com

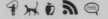

Entry 64   Map 6

Le Moulin

The thermal waters of Niederbronn have drawn visitors since Roman times, and the town, in a half moon of hills in the Northern Vosges, retains an authentic Alsatian atmosphere. Madame and Monsieur welcome you in the same spirit to their peaceful estate, where a stream driven mill, now gîtes, sits amid ancient trees, a pool and rose walk. The elegant manor has two history-filled guest rooms, pretty in pastel and catching the morning sun, and a fire in the salon. Quietly green, your hosts run an electric car and serve home-pressed apple juice at breakfast. Roam UNESCO forests to medieval villages and ruined châteaux.

86 rue du Général de Gaulle

A real old Alsatian farmhouse in the wine-growing area, where you can be in a beautiful, bustling village street one minute and your own peaceful little world the next. It is on a main road but the bedrooms are in the guest wing at the back, protected by the courtyard. Their simplicity is reflected in the price. Your friendly hosts retired from milk and wine production in order to have more time for guests; breakfast is served in the garden or in the dining room, and Paul makes a wicked eau de vie. A useful place to know at the start of the Route des Vins, and close to gorgeous, glamorous Strasbourg.

Rooms	1 twin/double: €90.
	1 suite for 4-5: €130-€140.
Meals	Restaurant 1km.
Closed	1 January to 31 March.

Rooms	3 doubles: €40-€44.
	Extra bed €8.
Meals	Restaurants within walking distance.
Closed	Rarely.

Henri & Marianne Mellon
Le Moulin,
44 route de Reichshoffen,
67110 Niederbronn les Bains,
Bas-Rhin
Email   marianne.mellon@gmail.com
Web   gite.moulin.free.fr

Paul & Marie-Claire Goetz
86 rue du Général de Gaulle,
67520 Marlenheim,
Bas-Rhin
Tel   +33 (0)3 88 87 52 94
Email   goetz.paul@wanadoo.fr

Ermitage du Rebberg

Beams, baby grands and a botanical guide, library, sauna, gym… tradition and luxury meet. Thirty acres of mature gardens and woodlands surround the villa and Madame's welcome is genuine. Aromatic pastries and charcuterie appear for breakfast, taken socially or in privacy according to guests' whims. Dinner is framed by the tropical conservatory or sunny patio, with menus fit for a gourmand and wines to match. Spacious rooms (four in a former barn) compete for the top spot – Citrine is a favourite – and jacuzzi baths abound. The pool is a refreshing island in a sea of cool green. Visit Strasbourg, follow the Route des Vins.

Bluets et Brimbelles

The mountain house by the village church has been exquisitely revived, and you feel welcome the moment you enter. Fresh oak, spruce and larch abound, many features have been preserved and all is cosy and draft-free. Catherine and Thierry love to speak English and do bountiful table d'hôtes at the long table, or on the terrace in summer (the gardens are sheer delight). She is a chef and pâtissier, produces for local shops in her shining new bakery and gives courses in the large spotless kitchen, he is proud possessor of a fleet of 2CVs. Tour the mountains with the roof down… return to log fires, delicious beds, drenching showers. Bliss.

Rooms	9 doubles: €140-€210.
	1 family room for 5: €150-€195.
	Singles €130-€200.
	Sofabeds available in some rooms.
Meals	Dinner with apéritif, €55;
	children over 12, €33;
	children 5-12 years, €22.
	Restaurants 1km.
Closed	Rarely.

Rooms	2 doubles: €70-€90.
	1 suite for 4: €80-€150.
	1 family room for 4: €70-€120.
	Extra bed/sofabed available €20 per
	person per night.
Meals	Dinner with wine, €25.
	Restaurants 2-minute walk.
Closed	3-18 October & Christmas.

Elisabeth Goetzmann
Ermitage du Rebberg,
49 rue de la Hoube,
67280 Urmatt,
Bas-Rhin
Tel   +33 (0)3 88 47 33 31
Email   info@ermitagedurebberg.com
Web   www.ermitagedurebberg.com

Catherine Habersetzer
Bluets et Brimbelles,
4 rue de l'Eglise,
67420 Saulxures,
Bas-Rhin
Mobile   +33 (0)6 32 09 99 78
Email   bluetsetbrimbelles@laposte.net
Web   www.bluetsetbrimbelles.fr

Ambiance Jardin

In a small Alsatian village is an 18th-century house surrounded by an exquisite garden. Gravel paths wander past bird-filled trees and charming benches, clipped shrubs and secret corners. Pierrette and Jean-Luc, warm, friendly and fluent in several languages, have set aside a barn with four first-floor bedrooms – immaculate, spacious and overlooking the garden. Wake to homemade pâtisseries and jams, served all morning at rustic tables. Cycle your way through Alsace's vineyards, hop on a ferry and cross the Rhine, or come as a group and take the barn over; there's a cosy sitting room and kitchen downstairs.

Parking on-site.

La Haute Grange

On the side of a hill, looking down the valley, this 19th-century farmhouse is surrounded by forests and wildflower meadows. Rural and indulging all at once, it is a place for de-stressing... deeply comforting bedrooms, subtle and spicy colours, the whole house filled with the smell of baking in the morning. The large sitting room has an open fireplace, an honesty bar and hundreds of books; step onto the patio and enjoy the heart-lifting views. A warm, German-speaking couple, Margaret and Philippe will help you plan days of discovery. There are a great selection of restaurants less than fifteen minutes away by car.

Rooms	4 doubles: €88–€98. 10% discount for stays of 7 nights or more. Extra bed €20 per person per night.
Meals	Restaurants 2-minute walk.
Closed	Rarely.

Rooms	3 doubles, 1 twin/double: €110–€150. Singles €95–€135.
Meals	Restaurants 6km.
Closed	Rarely.

Pierrette Kieny
Ambiance Jardin,
12 rue de l'Abbé Wendling,
67230 Diebolsheim,
Bas-Rhin
Tel +33 (0)3 88 74 84 85
Email contact@ambiance-jardin.com
Web www.ambiance-jardin.com

Margaret & Philippe Kalk
La Haute Grange,
La Chaude Côte,
68240 Fréland,
Haut-Rhin
Tel +33 (0)3 89 71 90 06
Mobile +33 (0)6 15 72 15 15
Email lahautegrange@aol.com
Web www.lahautegrange.fr

Entry 69 Map 7

Entry 70 Map 7

Maison d'Hôtes du Parc

Appreciate the finer things in life in Emmanuel and Mark's 1860s riverside home: gourmet cuisine, gorgeous gardens, inspired design. Polished, harmonious interiors waft with shades of mushroom, raspberry and moss, with period antiques, exquisite objets, a harp in the vast salon, a grand piano in the library. Fine china appears at four-course dinners as you chat over tender lamb cutlets with garden thyme. Rooms are cosily sumptuous, views spilling over well-tended gardens of scampering roses, manicured hedges, a summer house and potager. Beyond centennial trees is a gem: Le Corbusier's sensually spiritual chapel.

Rooms	2 doubles, 1 twin: €110-€130.
	1 suite for 2: €130.
	1 single: €79.
Meals	Dinner, 4 courses, €25.
	Restaurants nearby.
Closed	Rarely.

Emmanuel Georges
Maison d'Hôtes du Parc,
12-14 rue du Tram, 70250
Ronchamp,
Haute-Saône
Tel +33 (0)3 84 63 93 43
Email leparc-egeorges@wanadoo.fr
Web www.hotesduparc.com

Entry 71   Map 7

La Maison de Juliette

There are bikes to borrow and the countryside is a 500m ride away. The moment you enter the gardens of this charming edge-of-town house, built for a wealthy family in 1904, all feels peaceful. Your hosts – she with perfect English – are among the warmest we know, their generosity extending from homemade brioche at breakfast to billowing whiter-than-white muslin and tip-top mattresses. Bathrooms are minimalist with an antique touch; the two double rooms have a shared kitchen and doors opening onto a terrace. Breakfast can be served outside or in the conservatory – gluten and dairy-free if preferred. Guests love it here.

Rooms	2 doubles: €75-€85.
	1 family room for 4: €90-€150.
Meals	Restaurants 1km. Guest kitchen.
Closed	Rarely.

Françoise Gauthé
La Maison de Juliette,
8 rue des Combes St Germain,
25700 Valentigney,
Doubs
Tel +33 (0)3 81 91 88 19
Email maisondejuliette@orange.fr
Web www.maisondejuliette.fr

Entry 72   Map 7

La Maison d'à Côté

Arlette does shabby-chic as only a Frenchwoman can. Stone stairs spiral to an apartment of lofty 19th-century rooms, a gorgeous mix of vintage and contemporary. Retro cinema seats, pretty mirrors and old hat-boxes sit amongst metal-topped tables and industrial lights. Polished floors, wooden shutters and panelled walls ensure a gracious tone. Choose between a quirkily elegant or cool contemporary bedroom — both have organic soaps and shampoos. Charming and fun, Arlette cooks brilliantly (her restaurant is nearby) serving delicious organic breakfasts. In the centre of mountain-town Pontarlier, this will suit outdoors-lovers.

Rooms	1 double, 1 twin/double: €105–€110.
Meals	Owner's restaurant, 50m.
Closed	Rarely.

Arlette Laude
La Maison d'à Côté,
11 rue Jules Mathez,
25300 Pontarlier,
Doubs

Tel	+33 (0)3 81 38 47 18
Email	arlette.laude@orange.fr
Web	www.lamaison-da-cote.fr

Entry 73   Map 12

Photo: La Maison Chaudenay,
entry 98

Burgundy

La Maison d'Aviler

On each floor, eight tall windows look down on the resplendent garden that shelters Aviler from noise. At the back is the Yonne where barges peacefully ply: what a setting. The house was originally a workhouse – destitution in 18th-century France had its compensations. Your hosts were interior decorators by trade and are collectors by instinct, so expect subtle but sumptuous detail in elegantly French bedrooms. Sens has a memorable cathedral, a tempting market, and the shops and restaurants of this lovely town simply yell 'quality'.

Château de la Resle

This handsome house sits on an impeccable estate of landscaped gardens with neat lavender-lined paths. Johan and Pieter, your smiley hosts, came from Holland several years ago and have made everything elegant, modern and stylish. A fine stone staircase leads to spacious, view-filled rooms painted in muted hues; fabulous modern art hangs on the walls. There's a further suite in a cottage outside. Bathrooms are spotless with state-of-the-art showers. Tuck into a fine breakfast then set off for vineyards and wine tastings, pretty villages with ancient half-timbered houses, walks and cycle rides. Fabulous in every way.

Minimum stay: 2 nights at weekends & in high season. Children over 10 welcome.

Rooms	3 suites for 3: €90. Extra person €30
Meals	Restaurants in Sens.
Closed	Mid-January to mid-February.

Rooms	1 double, 1 twin/double: €195-€295. 3 suites for 2, 1 suite for 4: €250-€475. Extra bed/sofabed available €25 per person per night.
Meals	Dinner available on request, depending on occupancy. Restaurant 2km.
Closed	Mid-November to mid-February.

	Christiane & Bernard Barré
	La Maison d'Aviler,
	43 quai du Petit Hameau,
	89100 Sens,
	Yonne
Tel	+33 (0)3 86 95 49 25
Email	daviler@online.fr
Web	www.daviler.online.fr

	Johan Bouman & Pieter Franssens
	Château de la Resle,
	89230 Montigny la Resle,
	Yonne
Mobile	+33 (0)6 86 11 29 22
Email	info@chateaudelaresle.com
Web	www.chateaudelaresle.com

Entry 74   Map 5

Entry 75   Map 5

Burgundy

Château de Béru

Château life as you'd dream it, and windows that survey vineyards for miles. Home to the Comtes de Béru since 1627, the estate includes a working vineyard. Harvested by hand, the grapes are grown naturally, mostly organically – a delectable extra as you tour the cellars. It's a place that transports you to another era, yet the choice antiques and tasselled tie-backs harmonise with contemporary backdrops: raw brickwork and pretty fabrics, fresh linens, chic bathrooms; we loved 'Havane'. Have breakfast in the sitting-dining room, by the pool, or in bed. Lunch and dinner are available in the wine bar at the stables.

Rooms	3 doubles: €150-€180. 1 suite for 5: €250-€270.
Meals	Lunch & dinner €30. Platter from €5. Wine €18-€40. Restaurant 7km.
Closed	Rarely.

Laurence & Athénaïs de Béru
Château de Béru,
32 Grande Rue,
89700 Béru,
Yonne

Tel +33 (0)3 86 75 90 43
Email laurencedeberu@gmail.com
Web www.chateaudeberu.com

Entry 76   Map 6

Burgundy

Le Petit Village

You are on the outskirts of a medieval village close to the Armançon river and this is perfect for families. Choose between the cottage or coach house – each has attractively decorated rooms with oak beams, flagstone floors, great mattresses and good fabrics. Bathrooms are clean and modern and there's a play barn full of toys. Breakfast is served at one convivial table – freshly baked bread and pastries or the Full Monty from Annabella's trusty Aga. She will cook you a delicious dinner too if you ask. Warm, friendly hosts, a heated pool, private gardens, a tearoom and gift shop on site make this is a jewel. Enchanting.

Minimum stay: 7 nights in high season.

Rooms	1 double, 1 double with separate bathroom: €70-€80. 1 cottage for 4, 1 cottage for 6: €125-€150. Dinner, B&B €65-€100 per person per night.
Meals	Breakfast €6-€8. Dinner, 4 courses, €25. Restaurant 3km.
Closed	Rarely; self-catering only in August.

Annabella Ware
Le Petit Village,
33 route de Genève,
89160 Fulvy,
Yonne

Tel +33 (0)3 86 75 19 08
Email le-petit-village@orange.fr
Web www.le-petit-village.com

Entry 77   Map 6

Carpe Diem

In a tranquil Burgundy village lies this handsome old farmhouse. Peek through the gate: all is verdant with vines and the garden is picnic perfect. Eat convivially on a pretty terrace or in a grand dining room with luxurious décor and a fireplace. With home-grown veg and local produce (the Charolais beef is as sweet as a nut), dinner is well worth booking. Immaculate bedrooms are romantic in toile de Jouy with pepperings of fine paintings and antiques. Ask for Chambre Diane in the main house with its big bath, or choose the beautiful stables — children will love the secret mezzanine rooms.

Over 12s welcome. Minimum stay: 2 nights in July/August.

Le Verger

You're in the middle of a proper Burgundian village by the church. Rooms are filled with character and beautiful things — a dining room with a wonderful beamed ceiling, a sitting room with Persian rugs, vast fireplace, pink tiled floor. Charming Alan and Rosemary give you breakfasts with homemade jams at one big table, outdoors in fine weather. Bedrooms — one in one house, two in the other — are fresh as a daisy and warm as toast with fine antiques and good art — one packed with books from floor to ceiling. Explore culture, taste wine, nip to Époisses for some remarkably smelly cheese. A super place to stay.

Rooms	4 doubles, 1 twin/double: €72–€105. Singles €64–€87. Extra bed €25.
Meals	Dinner with wine, €37; not Thursdays. Restaurants 4km.
Closed	Rarely.

Rooms	1 double sharing bathroom with family room: €80–€90. 1 family room for 3; 1 family room for 3 sharing bathroom with double: €80–€90.
Meals	Restaurants 3km.
Closed	Rarely.

	Patrick Cabon
	Carpe Diem,
	53 Grande Rue,
	89440 Massangis,
	Yonne
Tel	+33 (0)3 86 33 89 32
Email	carpediem.ser@gmail.com
Web	www.b-and-b-burgundy.com

	Alan Ravenscroft & Rosemary Stones
	Le Verger,
	9-11 rue du Gravelain,
	89440 Coutarnoux,
	Yonne
Mobile	+44 (0)7768 840313
Email	piazza@btinternet.com
Web	www.burgundyhols.com

Burgundy

Maison Crème Anglaise

From a Tintin collection to Custard the dog, this gracious old house is full of surprises. Swallows nest in a medieval archway, a staircase winds up a tower and the garden falls steeply away giving unforgettable views. Sumptuous rooms are bright with flowers, bedrooms are pretty, cosy, comfy, appealing and the charming bathroom is shared. Graham and Christine, open, enthusiastic, entertaining, hands-on, go the extra mile for their guests and hold evening recitals and exhibitions for local artists in the courtyard. The garden pool is delicious, the hilltop village is historic, the peace is a balm.

Rooms	2 doubles, 1 twin sharing bathroom: €80–€90.
Meals	Buffet supper available on request. Special events catered for. Restaurants 6km.
Closed	Rarely.

Graham & Christine Battye
Maison Crème Anglaise,
22 Grande Rue,
89420 Montréal,
Yonne
Tel +33 (0)3 86 32 07 73
Email grahambattye@maisoncremeanglaise.com
Web www.maisoncremeanglaise.com

Burgundy

Girolles les Forges

Beyond the hamlet's church, in gardens where birds sing and hens roam, is a blue-shuttered 'maison de maître.' Corinne and Christian love nothing more than to share their life and their home, its regal sitting room, its elegant dining room, its long table laden with seasonal fruits, organic breads and homemade jams at breakfast. Discover historic Avallon and the fine wines of Chablis; return to polished boards, lush linen, a soothing massage. One bedroom is at the top of the steep dovecot stair, three are in the house, and the cellar suite, off the garden, is stunning. As for dinner, don't miss it: Christian is a fabulous chef.

Rooms	2 doubles: €75–€95. 3 suites for 4: €87–€180. Extra bed €10 per child per night.
Meals	Dinner with wine, €40; children €11. Restaurants 7km.
Closed	Rarely.

Christian & Corinne Sauer
Girolles les Forges,
8 rue Bouchardat,
89200 Girolles,
Yonne
Tel +33 (0)3 86 33 59 61
Email girolleslesforges@orange.fr
Web www.girolleslesforges.com

La Cimentelle

After an astoundingly beautiful drive you reach this handsome family house built by titans of the cement industry at the turn of the last century: now a pool sits on top of the old factory. Come for extraordinary food (both hosts are gourmet cooks), thoughtfulness, friendly chat and the loveliest rooms. Three are works of art with a touch of fun: a Murano mirror, an antique desk, pink faux-baroque wallpaper and stunning white linen curtains. Swish bathrooms shine with monogrammed towels and showers of Italian mosaic. Family rooms at the top of the house are huge. Don't miss it, you'll need at least two nights.

Auberge de la Tuilerie

Surrounded by acres of woodland and pasture, a blissfully remote Burgundy farmhouse with charming rooms. Retired journalists Lee and Philippe have transformed their historic home into a mellow countryside retreat. Parquet floors and oak beams endure in light, spacious bedrooms filled with antiques; each has a sparkling modern bathroom. Lee's bountiful vegetable garden provides much of the produce for superb regional meals eaten communally. Only birdsong disturbs the deep peace, so go slow and laze by the inviting pool, explore the wild gardens, take a siesta… or head out to Vézelay hilltop village or medieval Clamecy. Wonderful.

Minimum stay: 2 nights in high season. Pets by arrangement.

Rooms	3 doubles: €90–€125.
	2 family rooms for 6: €170–€370.
Meals	Dinner with wine, €46.
Closed	Rarely.

Rooms	3 doubles, 2 twin/doubles: €95.
	Singles €75. Extra bed/sofabed
	available €20 per person per night.
Meals	Dinner €35. Restaurant 4km.
Closed	Rarely.

	Nathalie & Stéphane Oudot
	La Cimentelle,
	4 rue de la Cimentelle,
	89200 Vassy lès Avallon,
	Yonne
Tel	+33 (0)3 86 31 04 85
Email	lacimentelle@orange.fr
Web	www.lacimentelle.com

	Philippe Chamaillard
	Auberge de la Tuilerie,
	La Tuilerie,
	89480 Andryes,
	Yonne
Mobile	+33 (0)6 76 79 26 77
Email	auberge.tuilerie@gmail.com
Web	www.auberge-tuilerie.com

Burgundy

Les Champs Cordois

Welcome to deepest Burgundy: pastures as far as the eye can see, sheep and Charolais cattle. The building is rambled by roses, and the garden, Dominique's pride and joy, climbs the hill. The hub of this handsome old house is its huge, slopey ceiling'd living room with friendly tables and leather sofas and chairs, and a wonderful terrace just off it. Enjoy jams from their own fruits at breakfast, and hearty dishes at dinner: genuine table d'hôtes. The big private family room is on the ground floor, the first-floor rooms interlink, and the style is cottage cosy. Great for groups.

Rooms	2 doubles, 2 twins: €72–€123. 1 family room for 4: €82–€150. Children under 3, €5. Twins & doubles can interconnect to form 2 family suites for 4.
Meals	Lunch picnic €12. Dinner 4-courses €27. Restaurant 4km.
Closed	Rarely.

Martine Goichon
Les Champs Cordois,
46 route de Rouvray,
89630 Bussieres,
Yonne
Tel   +33 (0)3 86 33 01 31
Email   les.champs.cordois@wanadoo.fr
Web   www.les-champs-cordois.com

Burgundy

L'Étoile Argentée

In a courtyard where coaching horses once rested, now there are colourful gardens where children can play. Breakfast out here on croissants and homemade jams, or sit out with a glass of wine and a book from the library. In winter, cuddle up by the wood-burner amid Monsieur's choice of antiques and paintings. South-facing bedrooms, up wide oak stairs, are elegantly decorated by Madame, an interior designer. Two have modern en suite showers but loos are shared. There are good restaurants in the village, plus a pool and tennis for summer. You can spend happy days fishing, golfing and walking in pristine countryside.

Minimum stay: 2 nights on weekends. Male dogs welcome. Smoking permitted outside.

Rooms	1 twin/double, sharing wc with twin; 1 twin/double with separate bath/shower room & wc; 1 twin, sharing wc with twin/double: €65–€95. Extra twin room available to let with twin/double only, €50 p.n.
Meals	Dinner €25. Wine €12–€20. Restaurants within walking distance.
Closed	Rarely.

Isabelle van Delft
L'Étoile Argentée,
2 av Carnot,
21350 Vitteaux,
Côte-d'Or
Tel   +33 (0)3 80 30 70 52
Email   letoileargentee@gmail.com
Web   www.letoileargentee.com

Clos de Fougères

Idyllic country roads bring you to the village of Montoillot, then climb to the hamlet above and this dapper stone farmhouse, with barns, stables, delicious gardens and pool. Bedrooms are spacious, harmonious, delightful (beams, books, sofas, antiques) and unusually private, from the sprawling suite in its old-stone 'annexe' to the country-chic treehouse beyond... our idea of heaven. The owners – humorous, generous and kind – deliver breakfasts to one big table indoors or out (or privately should you prefer): a tempting spread of cheeses, hams, pain d'épices, fruit tarts, home eggs and homemade jams.

Pets by arrangement.

Domaine de Serrigny

Just yards from a pretty stretch of the Burgundy Canal, a fine 18th-century house with high walls and magnificent views to perfect little Châteauneuf en Auxois. Charles and Marie-Pascale are stylish, informal and huge fun; so is their house. Fabulous antiques, interesting art and textiles, space outside for children to cavort. Bedrooms are a beautiful mix of styles with something for everyone, from grand salon to zen attic; all are delightful, bathrooms are bliss. Relax in the garden with its big lawn, colourful pots, decked pool and tennis court; have breakfast here or in the large open-plan sitting/dining room. Heaps of charm.

Rooms	1 double, 2 twin/doubles: €100–€115. 1 suite for 2: €115–€125. Treehouse – 1 double: €115–€130. Extra bed €30.
Meals	Restaurants 10km.
Closed	Rarely.

Rooms	1 double: €98–€108. 1 suite for 2, 1 family room for 4: €122–€139. Children under 8 free.
Meals	Auberge opposite (closed Mondays).
Closed	Rarely.

	Catherine Beaufremez Clos de Fougères, Rue de L'Église, 21540 Montoillot, Côte-d'Or
Tel	+33 (0)3 80 49 24 64
Mobile	+33 (0)6 64 15 66 31
Email	closdefougeres@wanadoo.fr
Web	www.closdefougeres.com

	Marie-Pascale Chaillot Domaine de Serrigny, Lieu dit "le Village", Route Départementale, 21320 Vandenesse en Auxois, Côte-d'Or
Tel	+33 (0)3 80 49 28 13
Mobile	+33 (0)6 86 89 90 07
Email	chaillot.mp@wanadoo.fr
Web	www.manoir-de-serrigny.com

Burgundy

La Saura

For those wishing to escape to a sweet Côte d'Or village near Beaune – and some of the world's greatest wines – come here. The house and stables are charming and peaceful, the renovation is recent, the décor is delicious, the pool is a boon. Irresistible Madame smiles easily and loves her guests, gives you generous breakfasts before the log fire and big airy bedrooms with classic colours and lavish touches – and views; she also plans an enchanting guests' hideaway off the garden (for WiFi, books and games). Bed linen is antique and embroidered, towels carry the La Saura logo, paths lead into the hills. Bliss.

Children over 10 welcome. Pets by arrangement.

Rooms	2 doubles: €110–€125.
	1 suite for 3: €130–€145.
	Extra bed/sofabed available €35 per
	person per night.
Meals	Restaurant 100m.
Closed	20 December to 5 January.

Jocelyne-Marie Lehallé
La Saura,
Route de Beaune,
21360 Lusigny sur Ouche,
Côte-d'Or
Tel   +33 (0)3 80 20 17 46
Mobile   +33 (0)6 81 29 57 42
Email   la-saura@wanadoo.fr
Web   www.la-saura.com

Entry 88   Map 11

Burgundy

Les Hêtres Rouges

A pretty old Burgundian hunting lodge, 'Copper Beeches' stands in a walled garden full of ancient trees; and its village setting is a delight. There's an unexpected air of Provence inside: beautifully judged colour schemes (Madame paints), fine furniture, numerous *objets*, a tomcat or two. Your hosts extend a warm, genuine yet ungushing welcome to the weary traveller, and can organise wine tours that are perfect for you. Up a steep stair are low rooms with dark character and fine linen. Breakfast has the savour of yesteryear: yogurt, fresh bread, homemade jam, delicious coffee.

Rooms	1 twin/double, 1 twin: €90–€104.
	Extra bed €32.
Meals	Restaurants 8km.
Closed	Rarely.

Jean-François & Christiane Bugnet
Les Hêtres Rouges,10 route de
Nuits, Antilly, 21700 Argilly,
Côte-d'Or
Tel   +33 (0)3 80 62 53 98
Mobile   +33 (0)6 78 47 22 29/
         +33 (0)6 75 07 65 01
Email   leshetresrouges@free.fr
Web   www.leshetresrouges.com

Entry 89   Map 11

Les Planchottes

If you find yourself in the Mecca of Wine, in the very heart of old Beaune, then surely you should stay with a family of winegrowers like the Bouchards? They are charming people, passionate about food, wine and matters 'green'; Cécile's breakfasts linger long in the memory. Once three cottages, the conversion of this old townhouse is immaculate: the craftsmanship of new oak and stone, the quiet good taste of the colours, the space in the comfortable bedrooms, the ultra modern bathrooms. Chill out in the walled, lush, flowered garden (replete with pet rabbit), glimpse the vineyards on the horizon. Outstanding.

Rooms	1 double, 1 twin: €110. Extra bed/sofabed available €25 per person per night.
Meals	Restaurants within walking distance.
Closed	Mid-December to mid-February.

Christophe & Cécile Bouchard
Les Planchottes,
6 rue Sylvestre Chauvelot,
21200 Beaune,
Côte-d'Or

Tel	+33 (0)3 80 22 83 67
Email	lesplanchottes@gmail.com
Web	www.lesplanchottes.fr

Entry 90 Map 11

Chez Les Fatien

A lovely surprise through an unassuming oak door... This 300-year-old vine workers' house is set round a tranquil courtyard and has been beautifully revived. The beamed colonial style breakfast room/lounge has ancient flagstones, leather sofas and a custom-made zinc bar. Bedrooms (one on the ground floor) come with snow white linen, art, gorgeous showers, antique basins. Madame gives you good breakfasts of local cheeses, charcuterie, eggs, hot chocolate and croissants. Underneath the chambres d'hôtes lie the family's 14th-century Cistercian cellars, where winemaker Charly Fatien can guide you through a tasting of Maison Fatien wines.

Garage available €15 per night.

Rooms	2 doubles: €255-€305. 1 suite for 2; 1 suite for 2-4 with separate shower room: €299-€335. Extra sofabed available €55 per night.
Meals	Restaurants 5-minute walk.
Closed	December/January.

Madame Fatien
Chez Les Fatien,
17 rue Ste Marguerite,
21200 Beaune,
Côte-d'Or

Tel	+33 (0)3 80 22 82 84
Email	reservation@chezlesfatien.com
Web	www.maisonfatien.com

Entry 91 Map 11

Burgundy

La Maison Blanche

Nadine speaks excellent English and lives two minutes away. Upon arrival she escorts you to her amazing wine cellar/ breakfast room/ salon, where coffee and tea is on tap and you help yourself to wine (pay later). Each minimalist bedroom (one with three double beds) is reached via a white-painted stair; floors are slate, colours grey and white, art is erotic and chic bathrooms lie behind partitioned walls. Breakfast is flexible and there's a designer guest kitchen should you wish to prepare a meal. As for fascinating Beaune, beneath its cobbled streets lies a maze of corridors filled with a million bottles of wine.

Minimum stay: 2 nights in high season. Ask about parking.

Rooms	2 doubles: €162.
	1 triple: €162-€366. Whole house available, €1,000 for 2 nights.
Meals	Brunch on request. Guest kitchen available. Restaurants nearby.
Closed	Rarely.

Nadine Belissant-Reydet
La Maison Blanche,
3 rue Jules Marey,
21200 Beaune,
Côte-d'Or

Mobile	+33 (0)6 60 93 51 84
Email	contact@lamaison-blanche.fr
Web	lamaison-blanche.fr

Entry 92   Map 11

Burgundy

Sous le Baldaquin

Once Yves — the perfect host — swings open the huge doors of his townhouse in the heart of Beaune, the 21st-century disappears, the serene garden tugs at your soul and peace descends. Play the count, countess or courtesan as you mount the stone stair to your small perfect cocoon, past walls and ceiling painted in pale trompe-l'œil allegory. Gracious and elegant are the aubergine and willow-green taffeta drapes and beribboned baldaquin, charming the bathroom with its ancient double-basin, beautiful the view to the rambling roses. To call this romantic is an understatement — and Yves is the nicest host.

Rooms	1 double: €100-€110.
	Extra bed €25.
Meals	Restaurants 5-minute walk.
Closed	Rarely.

Yves Cantenot
Sous le Baldaquin,
39 rue Maufoux, 21200 Beaune,
Côte-d'Or

Tel	+33 (0)3 80 24 79 30
Mobile	+33 (0)6 80 17 72 51
Email	yves.cantenot@laposte.net
Web	www.souslebaldaquin.fr

Entry 93   Map 11

Les Jardins de Loïs

The owners are wine buffs and their pride and joy is their cellar. Inside this 200-year-old house every detail delights, while bedrooms, reached by a splendid exterior stair, are lavish and beautiful. Antique armoires flatter oriental rugs, Italian bathrooms are immaculate with monsoon showers, and the garden suite is housed in a private outbuilding with its own sitting room and huge bath. Breakfast and homemade jams are enjoyed in the elegant, airy dining room. Stroll Beaune's ancient cobbles, sample the fruits of the region's wine capital. Then retire with a bottle of their own fine burgundy to a gem of a half-hectare garden.

La Terre d'Or

The Martin family — Jean-Louis and Christine now joined by son Vincent — run three wonderful houses, each surrounded by mature trees and a terraced garden. The modern, multi-levelled main house has five large and lovely bedrooms while the stone cottage, for B&B or self-catering, is traditional, the third house being more independent. The noble old beams and rosy tomette floors frame a fine contemporary look warmed with stylish lighting, crisp linen and polished country pieces. The honeymoon suite has a private piece of garden. It's bliss to relax on the main terrace and gaze across vineyards to the ramparts of old Beaune.

Rooms	3 doubles: €160.
	2 suites for 2: €185–€195.
Meals	Restaurant 150m.
Closed	Christmas & New Year.

Rooms	1 twin: €220.
	4 suites for 2: €150–€270.
	1 cottage for 4, 1 cottage for 6: €395–€510.
Meals	Breakfast €13. Picnic available. Restaurant 400m.
Closed	Rarely.

	Anne-Marie & Philippe Dufouleur
	Les Jardins de Loïs,
	21200 Beaune,
	Côte-d'Or
Tel	+33 (0)3 80 22 41 97
Mobile	+33 (0)6 73 85 11 47
Email	contact@jardinsdelois.com
Web	www.jardinsdelois.com

	Vincent, Christine & Jean-Louis Martin
	La Terre d'Or,
	Rue Izembart La Montagne,
	21200 Beaune,
	Côte-d'Or
Tel	+33 (0)3 80 25 90 90
Email	jlmartin@laterredor.com
Web	www.laterredor.com

Le Clos Champagne Saint Nicolas

Le Clos is nicely set back from the main road and Beaune is a ten-minute stroll. Built to take guests, the new wing has spanking new bedrooms, modern bits in the bathrooms and a salon overlooking the garden. Fabrics, bedding and antiques reveal Anne as a woman of taste who thinks of everything, even a guest kitchen for your morning spread of homemade jams, cake, croissants, bread, yogurt and fresh fruit. Bruno has a passion for vintage cars, especially if they're English. Knowledgeable natives and hospitable hosts, they fill you in on the sights, restaurants and vineyards over a welcoming glass of wine.

Rooms	1 double, 2 twin/doubles: €110.
Meals	Guest kitchen. Restaurants within walking distance.
Closed	Rarely.

Bruno & Anne Durand de Gevigney
Le Clos Champagne Saint Nicolas,
114 ter route de Dijon,
21200 Beaune,
Côte-d'Or

Tel	+33 (0)3 80 61 24 92
Mobile	+33 (0)6 61 82 39 63
Email	closchamp.stnicolas@free.fr
Web	closchamp.stnicolas.free.fr

Entry 96　Map 11

Clos Saint Jacques

Wine-lovers' heaven! In a magnificent, ancient village this 18th-century winery looks its handsome 300-year old self, but has all the right mod cons. Your engaging, enthusiastic and knowledgeable hosts are keen to share their local contacts; Monsieur is in the wine trade, Madame takes huge care of guests with memorable breakfasts and big, deeply comfortable beds. Lovely rooms, in the old worker's house and *cuverie*, are either rustic and beamed or more brightly modern; everyone's welcome to relax in sofas by the fire. Pilgrims bound for Santiago gathered in Meursault and the tradition of hospitality continues.

Rooms	3 apartments for 2, 1 apartment for 4: €98–€198. Extra bed €20 only for Sous les Etoiles.
Meals	Restaurants 3-minute walk.
Closed	Rarely.

Anne & Denis Duveau
Clos Saint Jacques,
1 rue Pierre Mouchoux,
21190 Meursault,
Côte-d'Or

Mobile	+33 (0)6 08 93 25 82/ +33 (0)6 80 99 10 91
Email	contact@clossaintjacques.fr
Web	www.clossaintjacques.fr

Entry 97　Map 11

La Maison Chaudenay

Stéphane's family have been making wine for eight generations; Florence's background is in the restaurant trade – who better to look after you? This is a gracious house with grand gates, a superb garden (with 200-year old sequoia) and habitable outbuildings, where the owners live – giving you free run of the house. Bedrooms, pale and rich, have taste, antiques and modern bathrooms, generous breakfasts are served in the main dining room, or on the verandah in the sunshine. There's a weekly market in the courtyard, astronomy evenings and good restaurants in Chagny – but ask about eating in, the owners plan to offer dinner soon.

Minimum stay: 2 nights.

Domaine de l'Oiseau

Peeping out from under low slanting eaves and climbing plants, the lovely 18th-century buildings frame a courtyard. The village-end setting is secluded riverside woodland; feast by the pool on valley views *and* food. Bedrooms sing with serenity and good taste: the suite, graceful and feminine, in the old bakery, the rest peacefully in the Pavilion. Each has a dressing room, a small perfect bathroom and enchanting old *tomette* floor. Relax in the glorious beamed barn, now the guest library; sample the local fine wines in the cellar below under the guidance of your friendly, extrovert hosts. An exceptional place.

Rooms	3 doubles: €70-€110.
	2 family rooms for 4: €85-€130.
	Extra bed €20.
Meals	Summer kitchen. Restaurants 3km.
Closed	Rarely.

Rooms	2 twin/doubles with separate wc: €130.
	1 suite for 2-4 with separate wc: €130-€160.
	1 triple with separate wc: €140-€160.
Meals	Dinner with wine, from €50.
Closed	December – March.

Stéphane & Florence Balu
La Maison Chaudenay,
26 rue de Tigny,
71150 Chaudenay,
Saône-et-Loire

Tel   +33 (0)3 85 87 35 98
Email   info@maisonchaudenay.com
Web   www.beaunebedandbreakfast.com

Dominique & Philippe Monnier-Pictet
Domaine de l'Oiseau,
17 rue Chariot, 71590 Gergy,
Saône-et-Loire

Tel   +33 (0)3 85 91 61 26
Mobile   +33 (0)6 23 46 59 07
Email   info@domoiseau.com
Web   www.domoiseau.com

Entry 98   Map 11

Entry 99   Map 11

Domaine de Nesvres

There are Michelin stars in Chagny, châteaux all around and the Route des Vins beyond the door; this is a great spot for a civilised holiday. In the small village of St Désert, at the end of the private driveway, you stay on a fortified farm steeped in history and owned by a lovely French couple. Outside is vast and full of rustic charm; inside is cosy and comfy. Find billiards, books, beams, a sitting room for guests (games, music, WiFi, TV), five airy bedrooms (the family room with good antiques) and Adeline's delicious food, perhaps homemade 'pain d'épices' at breakfast, and poulet de Bresse at dinner.

L'Orangerie

Enter gardens that are secluded, charming, full of colour. Light spills into the sitting room through arched vine-clad windows while cream walls and Indian rugs add to the simple elegance of this *maison de maître*. Antiques and travel are the owners' passion: a grand staircase, interesting paintings and oriental fabrics add up to a mix of styles that work beautifully. Bedrooms vary in size and have lovely seersucker linen and antique prints; bathrooms are classically tasteful. Terraced lawns lead down to the heated pool, lavish breakfasts include unusual homemade jams, and the wonderful Voie Verte cycle route runs nearby.

Minimum stay: 2 nights. Over 12s welcome.

Rooms	1 double, 1 twin: €75–€85. 1 family room for 3, 1 family room for 4: €85–€140. 1 triple: €85–€115. Pets welcome, €5 p.n.
Meals	Dinner with apéritif and wine, €35. Restaurants 5km.
Closed	Rarely.

Rooms	3 twin/doubles: €80–€110.
Meals	Hosted dinner with wine, €25–€40. Restaurants 4km.
Closed	3 November to 17 March.

Adeline & Michel Courcenet
Domaine de Nesvres,
Route de Buxy,
71390 Saint Désert,
Saône-et-Loire
Mobile +33 (0)6 16 13 30 50
Email micourcenet@aol.com
Web domainedenesvres.jimdo.com

David Eades & Niels Lierow
L'Orangerie,
20 rue des Lavoirs, Vingelles,
71390 Moroges,
Saône-et-Loire
Tel +33 (0)3 85 47 91 94
Email info@orangerie-moroges.com
Web www.orangerie-moroges.com

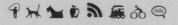

Entry 100   Map 11

Entry 101   Map 11

Le Crot Foulot

Gutsy Jan and Annie sold their prize-winning restaurant in Brussels and filled their cellar while putting the finishing touches to this handsome wine-grower's house. Golden stones outside, a clean minimalism inside: Belgians always pull this off with flair. An elegant glass and wood staircase leads to muted bedrooms with delicate pale timbers revealed and glorified. In the open kitchen you can watch Jan whip up his mussel mousse while a farmyard chicken sizzles with citrus fruits in the oven. Annie will have brought up the perfect nectar for the menu. All is well in Burgundy tonight!

La Tour du Trésorier

Hoping for ancient? Find a 15th-century town gate in a 10th-century wall; a 17th-century tower, added by the abbey treasurer, now an intriguing mix of old beams, embossed tiles, spiral stairs and wooden doors. Original paintings, some by Thierry, grace the walls of the grand dining room. Light-filled bedrooms are just as artistic, with sculpted furniture and unusual objets. Outside, a jacuzzi bubbles in the orchard; century-old trees stand in the park; loungers and terraces gaze on lush countryside. Sophie and Thierry love sharing their passion for south Burgundy and fine wine: Thierry is a sommelier, the wine list is superb.

Rooms	3 twin/doubles, 1 twin: €110–€140. 1 family room for 3: €168–€198.
Meals	Dinner €39. Wine from €15.
Closed	November – February.

Rooms	1 double, 3 twin/doubles: €150–€170. 1 suite for 4 with jacuzzi: €190–€250.
Meals	Restaurants 1-4 km.
Closed	Rarely.

Annie Coeckelberghs & Jan Hostens
Le Crot Foulot,
71240 Jugy,
Saône-et-Loire
Tel   +33 (0)3 85 94 81 07
Email   info@crotfoulot.com
Web   www.crotfoulot.com

Sophie & Thierry Lindbergh
La Tour du Trésorier,
9 place de l'Abbaye, 71700 Tournus,
Saône-et-Loire
Tel   +33 (0)3 85 27 00 47
Email   info@tour-du-tresorier.com
Web   www.tour-du-tresorier.com

Burgundy

La Ferme de Marie-Eugénie

La Ferme belonged to Marie-Eugénie's grandmother and the deft renovating flair of this ex-Parisian couple (formerly in advertising) is on show everywhere, from whitewashed beams to shabby-chic leather sofas. The pretty half-timbered barn (owners live in the cottage) overlooking a big lawned garden is now a fashionable maison d'hôtes. Be charmed by light-flooded rooms, pale tiled floors and exposed limestone walls. Bedrooms are comfortable, delightful – soft colours, modern art; there's an inviting, books-and-magazines salon and a slick dining-kitchen for delicious meals. Glossy-mag perfection meets deep rural sleepiness.

Rooms	3 doubles, 1 twin: €135. Extra bed/sofabed available €3 per person per night.
Meals	Dinner €35. Wine €25-€70. Restaurants in Louhans, 9km.
Closed	Christmas.

Marie-Eugénie Dupuy
La Ferme de Marie-Eugénie,
225 allée de Chardenoux,
71500 Bruailles,
Saône-et-Loire
Tel   +33 (0)3 85 74 81 84
Email   info@lafermedemarieeugenie.fr
Web   www.lafermedemarieeugenie.fr

Entry 104   Map 11

Burgundy

Le Clos de Clessé

Set in superb gardens (mature olive trees, clipped box hedges, gravel paths, stone-edged beds, delicious roses) the old manor by the church is the life's dream of delightful Tessy and André, Cordon Bleu cooks both – don't miss dinner! Two gorgeous cottages with split-level bedrooms overlook the garden and there's a pretty, bare-beamed guest room in the main house. Natural stone, old fireplaces, terracotta tiles and flagstones worn satin-smooth offset modern fittings and antique pieces perfectly. Vineyards and châteaux galore… though the tempting and secluded pool may be as far as you'll get.

Minimum stay: 2 nights in high season. Pets by arrangement.

Rooms	2 doubles: €105-€145. 1 suite for 4: €120-€205. Singles €100-€115. Extra bed/sofabed available €30 per person per night.
Meals	Dinner, 4 courses, €40; with wine €45; children under 12, €20; available twice a week. Restaurant 3km.
Closed	Rarely.

Tessy & André Gladinez
Le Clos de Clessé,
11 place de l'église,
71260 Clessé,
Saône-et-Loire
Tel   +33 (0)3 85 23 03 56
Email   info@closdeclesse.com
Web   www.closdeclesse.com

Entry 105   Map 11

Château de Vaulx

Vaulx was described in 1886 as "well-proportioned and elegant in its simplicity". It is as lovely now and in the most beautiful position, high on a hill with views that stretch to distant mountains. Delightful Marty will escort you to the west wing then create a delicious dinner. Expect big bedrooms full of character, a panelled drawing room with chandeliers, a huge dining room with fresh flowers, and manicured lawns and box balls tightly topiaried – stroll down the romantic avenues in dappled sunlight. In the village, a 13th-century bell tower; nearby, one of the best chocolate makers in France (monthly tastings and lessons).

La Tour

The terraced garden is brimful of stepping stones and flowers, ginger tabbies wend through the irises, bucolic views stretch across undulating pastures: this is a deeply rural ensemble. June, widely travelled, kind, attentive, a great reader and lover of art in all its forms, lives in a long stone farmhouse in a cluster of outbuildings that go back to 1740. The airy two-bedroom suite in its own wing has a fine stone fireplace on its ground floor; floorboards are honey-coloured, the bathroom is a treat, and scrumptious breakfasts are served on charming country china. Lovely.

Rooms	2 doubles: €110-€130.
	2 family rooms for 4: €149.
	1 apartment for 5: €195.
	Price per night: €36-€100 per person.
Meals	Dinner €33. Wine €20.
	Restaurant 3km.
Closed	Rarely.

Rooms	1 suite for 3: €85-€95.
	Extra bed €15.
Meals	Dinner with wine, €24.
	Vegetarian meals available.
	Restaurants 7km.
Closed	Rarely.

Marty Freriksen
Château de Vaulx,
71800 St Julien de Civry,
Saône-et-Loire
Tel   +33 (0)3 85 70 64 03
Email   marty@chateaudevaulx.com
Web   www.chateaudevaulx.com

June Bibby
La Tour,
71120 Marcilly La Guerce,
Saône-et-Loire
Tel   +33 (0)3 85 25 11 67
Mobile   +33 (0)6 87 59 78 29
Email   bibbyjune@gmail.com
Web   www.latourbandb.com

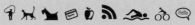

Moulin Renaudiots

Bordering the ancient Forest of Planoise and overlooking idyllic Burgundy countryside, this former water mill is a tranquil retreat. A stream babbles quietly in the background and, as the sun sets, a chorus of crickets provide accompaniment. Classic mid-century Danish furniture features throughout the five beautifully renovated rooms, while wooden floors and exposed beams give contemporary interiors a natural feel. Breakfast on home-made jam, pastries and fruit from the gorgeous gardens... Twice a week your lovely hosts offer convivial dinners too. By day, cool off in the sparkling pool, work out in the gym, taste wine in the new cellar or visit fascinating Autun.

Minimum stay: 2 nights in high season. Pets by arrangement.

Château de Villette

Coen and Catherine – he Dutch, she Belgian – fell in love with this little château, then had their wedding here: they love their adopted country. They've opened just five rooms to guests (the suites are twin-roomed) and one very private cottage so they can spoil you properly. And get to know you over dinner. (Though, should you prefer a romantic dinner for two, they'll understand.) Bedrooms, large, light and airy, with warm colours and polished floors, are dressed in château-style finery. Views sail out of great windows to meadows and woodland and families will love it. Beaune and the vineyards lie temptingly close.

Rooms	3 doubles: €130–€165. 1 suite for 2-4; 1 family room for 2-3: €145–€155. Extra beds available €30.		Rooms	3 doubles: €195–€265. 3 suites for 5: €340–€410. 1 cottage for 2: €285.
Meals	Dinner with wine, coffee & apéritif, €52, Sat & Mon. Cold plates available Weds & Fri. Restaurants 4km.		Meals	Dinner €55. Wine €18–€100.
Closed	November – March.		Closed	12 September to 15 January.

	Trevor Morgan Moulin Renaudiots, Chemin du Vieux Moulin, 71400 Autun, Saône-et-Loire			**Catherine & Coen Stork** Château de Villette, 58170 Poil, Nièvre
Tel	+33 (0)3 85 86 97 10		Tel	+33 (0)3 86 30 09 13
Email	contact@moulinrenaudiots.com		Email	catherinestork@chateaudevillette.eu
Web	www.moulinrenaudiots.com		Web	www.chateaudevillette.eu

Entry 108   Map 11

Entry 109   Map 11

Manoir du Chagnot

At this historic estate deep in Burgundy countryside, Belgian owner Gisèle encourages guests to forget everyday stresses and soak up the peaceful surroundings. The original house, all high ceilings and imposing presence, is thought to have been designed by Louis XIV's military engineer Vauban. A wide staircase leads to rooms modernised with bold, colourful murals; more paintings hang in the dining room and home grown produce is on the menu. A serene sitting room is perfect for morning meditation – you can book massage or mindfulness too. For outdoor action, swim in the pool, walk, cycle or explore Morvan National Park.

Minimum stay: 2 nights.

Château de Nyon

A pretty little château in a secluded valley in the heart of utterly unspoilt countryside. The remarkable Catherine inherited the house and has been doing B&B for 20 years. Her bedrooms, all on the first floor, echo the 18th-century character of the house. Toile de Jouy is charmingly splashed across pink paper and fabrics, bathrooms have big tubs or walk-in showers, glorious views to the garden reveal an avenue of lime trees and a hornbeam maze. Friendly Madame serves a beautiful breakfast of fresh pastries and home honey. It's hard to leave this blessed setting; the nearest restaurant is ten kilometres away.

Pets by arrangement.

Rooms	1 double, 2 twin/doubles: €105–€125. 1 family room for 3: €150–€175.
Meals	Dinner with coffee, €25–€28. Restaurants 3km.
Closed	Rarely.

Rooms	2 doubles: €65–€85. 1 family room for 4: €150.
Meals	Restaurant 10km.
Closed	Rarely.

	Gisèle Lievens Manoir du Chagnot, Le Renaudin, 58110 Mont et Marre, Nièvre
Tel	+33 (0)3 86 78 14 51
Mobile	+33 (0)6 78 22 86 24
Email	salonderlevenskunst@gmail.com
Web	www.salonderlevenskunst.com

	Catherine Henry Château de Nyon, 58130 Ourouër, Nièvre
Tel	+33 (0)3 86 58 61 12
Email	chateaudenyon@gmail.com
Web	www.chateaudenyon.com

Entry 110   Map 10

Entry 111   Map 10

Burgundy

Château de Prye

The rooms are vast, the marble stables are palatial and the corridors heave with antlers and stag heads from previous ancestors; the history is intriguing. The young Marquis and Marquise have joyfully taken up the challenge of running both château and estate (they breed Charolais cattle) and host their guests with grace. Each cavernous bedroom is furnished with splendid antiques; bathrooms are en suite. Take a peek at the château kitchen... from here breakfast is dispatched to an oak-panelled dining room with sumptuous views. This rambling château, its woodlands, gentle river and trees are dreamy... relish the fairy tale.

Rooms	3 doubles: €115-€190.
	2 suites for 2-4: €115-€190.
Meals	Dinner €35. Wine €8-€105.
Closed	Mid-October to mid-April.

Magdalena & Antoine-Emmanuel
du Bourg de Bozas
Château de Prye,
58160 La Fermeté,
Nièvre

Tel	+33 (0)3 86 58 42 64
Email	info@chateaudeprye.com
Web	www.chateaudeprye.com

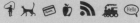

Entry 112   Map 10

Burgundy

Château de la Marche

Marie-Paule and Yves – elegant, enthusiastic, engaging – live in a house of Palladian grandeur built on the banks of the river Loire. Surrounded by great trees and expertly planted borders (their business is garden design), the only sound is birdsong and the lovely church bell. Inside is... Italy, all bathed in light. Find a hall with frescoes, a cushy salon, mirrors, chandeliers and tall windows for views. Bedrooms have pastel panelling and glossy parquet; bathrooms are shiny and bright. On your doorstep is La Charité sur Loire, a World Heritage treasure. Return to billiards, table tennis and a leisurely pool-side bask.

Rooms	3 doubles: €95-€132.
	Extra bed/sofabed available €30 per
	person per night.
Meals	Restaurants 5km.
Closed	15 November to 13 April.

Yves Wallaert
Château de la Marche,
Grande Rue,
58400 La Marche,
Nièvre

Mobile	+33 (0)7 85 12 54 91
Email	yves.wallaert@orange.fr
Web	www.chateaudelamarche.fr

Entry 113   Map 10

La Villa des Prés

Deep in real peace-wrapped country, this place of secluded old-style comfort and breathtaking views of the Morvan has new and rightly enthusiastic Dutch owners: it's gorgeous. Inside are open fires, antique beds, sympathetic period decorations, antique linen and super modern showers. Rooms are vast and there are two salons, one gloriously golden green, for lazing about. A baronial double stair leads down to the fine garden and the ha-ha where, rather endearingly, chickens may be roaming. A base for church, château and vineyard visits — a peaceful paradise.

Minimum stay: 3 nights.

Le Prieuré Saint Agnan

Beneath the bell tower of Cosne sur Loire's historic church, five characterful B&B rooms in an old Benedictine priory. Surrounded by tranquil gardens, the handsome stone building stands on the banks of the Loire, within walking distance of the town's restaurants, and a cycle ride from Sancerre and Pouilly Fumé vineyards. Bedrooms are spacious and colourful, with river or courtyard views, and immaculate en-suite shower rooms. A continental breakfast, including local goat's cheese and ham, is served at a large wooden table in the light-filled dining room or in the garden. Take a dip in the heated pool or explore local châteaux.

Parking on-site.

Rooms	5 twin/doubles: €80–€105.
Meals	Complimentary dinner with wine for 7-night stays (Sun only). Guest kitchen. Restaurant 3km.
Closed	October – March.

Rooms	5 doubles: €110–€140. Extra bed/sofabed available €30 per person per night.
Meals	Restaurants within walking distance.
Closed	Rarely.

	Kees & Inge Stapel
	La Villa des Prés,
	Route de Corbigny,
	58420 St Révérien,
	Nièvre
Tel	+33 (0)3 86 29 03 81
Mobile	+31 (0)6 51 18 89 67
Email	villa-des-pres@orange.fr
Web	www.villa-des-pres.com

	Gilles Cégretin
	Le Prieuré Saint Agnan,
	1 Rue des Forges, Impasse du Prieuré, Place St Agnan,
	58200 Cosne sur Loire,
	Nièvre
Email	leprieuresaintagnan@gmail.com
Web	www.prieuresaintagnan.com

Région Parisienne

Martinn – Key2Paris

A gem of a pied-à-terre for two, right there in the middle of old Paris. Step through the secluded cobbled courtyard to this ground-floor flat; the door opens into the small, uncluttered bedroom with a book-filled living room beyond. Find a purple taffeta bedcover, pretty paintings, snazzy bathroom, and a corner kitchen for rustling up your own meals after Martinn's welcoming dinner (breakfast too if you want); all is beautifully decorated. The neighbourhood teems with busy brasseries, pavement cafés, fashionable shops; easy stroll to Pompidou centre, Louvre, Marais district. Martinn is charming, and eager to share Paris with you.

Minimum stay: 3 nights.

Bonne Nuit Paris

Absolute Paris, 300-year-old timbers, crazy wonky stairs and modern comforts, independent rooms and a warm welcome, little streets, friendly markets: it's real privilege. Charming, intelligent Jean-Luc serves his honey, Denise's jams and fresh bread in their generous, rambling living room upstairs. To each room, be it ground or first floor, a colourful shower, a lot of quirk (the last word in creative basins), an appealing mix of antique woodwork and modern prints, and a sense of seclusion. Simplicity, panache and personality, attention and service: these are the hallmarks. No communal space, but a lovely peaceful courtyard.

Rooms	1 apartment for 2–3: €90–€150. Dinner, B&B extra €35–€45 per person. Extra bed/sofabed available €40 for 3-7 nights.
Meals	Dinner available by arrangement. Restaurants within walking distance.
Closed	Rarely.

Rooms	3 doubles: €175–€225. 2 triples: €275–€300. Extra bed €75.
Meals	Restaurants within walking distance.
Closed	Rarely.

	Martinn Jablonski-Cahours
	Martinn – Key2Paris,
	Rue d'Argout,
	75002 Paris
Mobile	+33 (0)6 03 48 29 29
Email	info@key2paris.com
Web	www.key2paris.com

	Denise & Jean-Luc Marchand
	Bonne Nuit Paris,
	63 rue Charlot, Le Marais,
	75003 Paris
Tel	+33 (0)1 42 71 83 56
Email	jean.luc@bonne-nuit-paris.com
Web	www.bonne-nuit-paris.com

Entry 116   Map 5

Entry 117   Map 5

Parc Royal Marais

Tourists, hipsters, fashionistas: everyone loves the new Le Marais – also known as 'Old Paris'. Strolling distance from Place des Vosges is an elegant 18th-century mansion, formerly a factory, now a condominium. Here lives sweet Assia in her second-floor flat, overlooking elegant gardens. A well-travelled Parisian who worked for the UN, she offers you two sophisticated, top-of-the-range rooms, peaceful and awash with light. Comforts include electric blinds, sleek floors, wool mattresses, mini bars, safes and TV. Breakfast, at the long stylish dining/sitting room table, includes fresh orange juice and the best *viennoiseries*.

Minimum stay: 2 nights. Secure parking available, €20 per day.

Rooms	1 double: €160. 1 studio for 2: €190. Singles €150–€180.
Meals	Restaurants 2-minute walk.
Closed	Rarely.

Assia Bedjaoui
Parc Royal Marais,
16 rue du Parc Royal,
75003 Paris

Mobile	+33 (0)6 19 61 09 69
Email	contact@parcroyalmarais.com
Web	www.parcroyalmarais.com

Notre Dame district

At the end of the street are the Seine and the glory of Notre Dame. In a grand old building (with a new lift by the 17th-century stairs), the two unaffected rooms, one above the other, look down to a little garden. The mezzanined family room has its bathroom off the landing; a simple breakfast of shop-packed items is laid here. Upstairs is the smaller room: bed in the corner, timeworn shower room and your own entrance. Madame is polyglot, active and eager to help when she is available; she leaves breakfast ready if she has to go out. She and her daughter appreciate the variety of contact guests bring. A gem in the heart of Paris.

Minimum stay: 2 nights.

Rooms	1 double: €95. 1 family room for 4 with separate bath & breakfast area: €115–€140.
Meals	Continental breakfast left ready if owner has to go out (for the family room only). No breakfast offered for the double.
Closed	Rarely.

Brigitte Chatignoux
Notre Dame district,
75005 Paris

Tel	+33 (0)1 43 25 27 20
Email	brichati@hotmail.com

My Open Paris

In the heart of the city, set away from the road, this 19th-century townhouse is peaceful. Determined to make your stay special, hosts Eanjo and her husband greet you warmly and deliver a generous breakfast of fresh pastries, baguette, eggs and cheese to your door. Bright, compact bedrooms (one on the ground floor, some up a spiral staircase) are decorated in fresh colours with wooden floors and tasteful furniture; all have spotless bathrooms and a dinky kitchenette. Just a short walk from public transport, markets, restaurants and tourist spots, you couldn't pick a better launchpad for exploring France's delightful capital.

Minimum stay: 2 nights; 3 nights in high season.

Les3chambres

Colour and soft comfort, family antiques and atmosphere are here in buckets thanks to Laurent's flair for interiors (he's a lighting designer) and his love of meeting people. Easy and relaxed, he is a walking encyclopaedia on Paris and serves a succulent breakfast. Storm blue fades into bright turquoise, khaki is married to terracotta, old floorboards meet thick new carpet, gilt-framed oils hang beside good contemporary works, purple plush lifts modern sofas and brocades flatter old fauteuils. Bedrooms have splendid beds, high-tech gadgets and neat little designer shower rooms. Place and person are a delight, old Paris is at your door.

Minimum stay: 2 nights.

Rooms	2 doubles, 3 twin/doubles: €170-€190. 1 suite for 4: €285. Extra bed/sofabed available €30-€50 per person per night.		Rooms	3 doubles: €184-€204.
Meals	Restaurants 1-minute walk.		Meals	Restaurants within walking distance.
Closed	Rarely.		Closed	August.

	Eanjo Dudragne My Open Paris, 35 rue de Lyon, 75012 Paris			**Laurent Rougier** Les3chambres, 14 rue Bleue, 75009 Paris
Mobile	+33 (0)6 13 79 83 28		Tel	+33 (0)1 42 47 07 42
Email	contact@myopenparis.com		Email	contact@les3chambres-paris.com
Web	www.myopenparis.com		Web	www.les3chambres-paris.com

Entry 120   Map 5

Entry 121   Map 5

ELIEL

Live like a hip Parisian. From the Belle Époque elevator and carved cornices to the glass dining table and original art, Madame's second-floor apartment makes you feel like a true native. Parquet-floor, white-on-white panelled bedrooms are luxuriously minimal – marble, mirrors, leather – with elegant splashes of colour – perhaps an Hermès scarf or Chinese cloisonné jar. Bathrooms are elegantly stunning. Madame is glamorous, adorable and has her finger on the pulse of the city's fashion, art and eating scenes, and will advise. Breakfast on top-quality teas, preserves and pastries then explore nearby Montmartre and boho Marais.

Rooms	2 doubles, 1 twin: €180–€240. Singles €150–€190. Extra child's bed available.
Meals	Restaurants within walking distance.
Closed	Rarely.

Sabine Wu
ELIEL,
91 rue La Fayette,
75009 Paris

Mobile	+33 (0)6 70 80 51 72
Email	sabine@eliel.fr
Web	www.eliel.fr/en/

Entry 122   Map 5

Côté Montmartre

Walk in and touch an 1890s heart: floral inlay on the stairs, stained-glass windows behind the lift. On the top landing, a curly bench greets you. Young and quietly smiling, Isabelle leads you to her personality-filled living room, a harmony of family antiques and 20th-century design, and a gift of a view: old Paris crookedly climbing to the Sacré Cœur. Breakfast may be on the flowering balcony, perhaps with fat cat Jules. Your big white (no-smoking) bedroom off the landing with independent entrance is modern and new-bedded in peaceful rooftop seclusion; the shower room a contemporary jewel. Interesting, cultured, delightful people, too.

Rooms	1 double: €135–€155. Extra bed €30.
Meals	Restaurants nearby.
Closed	Rarely.

Isabelle & Jacques Bravo
Côté Montmartre,
11 bis rue Jean Baptiste Pigalle,
75009 Paris

Tel	+33 (0)1 43 54 33 09
Mobile	+33 (0)6 14 56 62 62
Email	isabelle.c.b@free.fr
Web	www.cotemontmartre.com

Entry 123   Map 5

52 Clichy

If you want conviviality for two, choose to share your host's stylish and peaceful top-floor flat, its immaculate blue bedroom and en suite bathroom with a private loo just over the passage. Rosemary will chat about her many-facetted traveller's life, serve breakfast on the pretty balcony or at the walnut table in her relaxing chiaroscuro living room. If you prefer privacy for two to four, choose the modern third-floor apartment in chocolate and fire-red and breakfast at your own table. Rosemary knows a million Parisian things and will point you to the Paris that suits you. You will be well cared for.

Studio Amélie

In Montmartre village, in a quiet street between bustling boulevard and pure-white Sacré Cœur, Valérie and her architect husband offer a super-chic and ideally autonomous studio off their charming, pot-planted and cobbled courtyard with your bistro table and chairs. A bed dressed in delicate red against white walls, an antique oval dining table, a pine-and-steel gem of a corner kitchen, a generous shower, a mirror framed in red. Valérie's discreet decorative flourishes speak for her calm, positive personality and her interest in other lands. A delicious Paris hideaway you can call your own.

Minimum stay: 3 nights.

Rooms	1 twin/double with separate wc: €115–€135.
	1 apartment for 4: €160–€200.
Meals	Restaurants 100m.
Closed	Rarely.

Rooms	1 twin/double with kitchenette: €98; €680 per week.
	Extra bed available.
Meals	Breakfast at the boulangerie next door. Guest kitchen. Restaurants nearby.
Closed	Rarely.

	Rosemary Allan
	52 Clichy,
	75009 Paris
Tel	+33 (0)1 44 53 93 65
Mobile	+33 (0)6 66 01 75 44
Email	rosemarylouise@52clichy.com
Web	www.52Clichy.com

	Valérie Zuber
	Studio Amélie,
	Montmartre,
	75018 Paris
Mobile	+33 (0)6 30 93 81 35
Email	studiodamelie@wanadoo.fr

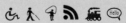

Entry 124   Map 5

Entry 125   Map 5

Région Parisienne

Villa Montabord

If ever there was a hidden treasure in Paris, La Cité des Fleurs is it! Imagine opening a gate onto a peaceful, private lane of grand houses and sumptuous gardens – the busy city melts away. All that's missing from this utterly untouched view of La Belle Époque is a penny-farthing and children playing marbles... The Sciards are kind hosts with an eye for elegant detail. Red doors open to a hall of chequered tiles and stained glass; airy bedrooms have marble fireplaces and white linen. Breakfasts of homemade cakes, gourmet teas and viennoiseries are taken en famille in the dining room or internal courtyard. Visit nearby museums, wander Montmartre.

Underground parking 3-minute walk, €30 per day.

Région Parisienne

Copernic

Feel Parisian here with Sylvie and her husband. Enter the large limestone building and up the spiral staircase (or the tiny lift) to the third floor. Relax and chat in the modern-feeling large kitchen/living area, eat breakfast at a time to suit you, order dinner too – Sylvie is a grand cook. Bedrooms are all off the guest corridor: expect marble fireplaces, shelves filled with books, large mirrors, new mattresses and floor to ceiling windows with views to the quiet street. You're within walking distance of the tourist traps, super restaurants and shops, museums, galleries and the wide open spaces of the Bois de Boulogne.

Rooms	2 doubles, 2 doubles with Italian shower: €160–€199.
Meals	Restaurants 5-minute walk.
Closed	Rarely.

Rooms	1 double, 1 twin: €100–€150. 1 single: €90–€120.
Meals	Restaurants 2-minute walk.
Closed	Rarely.

	Isabelle Sciard
	Villa Montabord,
	3 Cité des Fleurs,
	75017 Paris
Email	villamontabordparis@gmail.com
Web	www.villamontabordparis.com

	Sylvie Petit
	Copernic,
	39 rue Copernic,
	75116 Paris
Mobile	+33 (0)6 95 09 14 27
Email	sylvie.petitnivard@gmail.com

Villa du Square

Return from museum or shopping pleasures to a gorgeous Parisian guesthouse and its quiet garden that rubs shoulders with Le Corbusier's Villa Jeanneret. Revel in fine art and antiques, ancient and modern all beautifully put together by your warm, friendly and super-chic hosts; they live on the top floor with three well-behaved teenagers and a small dog. Bedrooms are sumptuous in their fine objets and lovely fabrics (the largest has its own garden door), wonderful walk-in mosaic showers and fabulous washbasins. Beds are superb, towels deluxe, breakfast fresh and delicious and there's a grand piano among the family portraits.

Minimum stay: 3 nights in high season. Children over 10 welcome.

Rooms	5 doubles: €175–€305.
Meals	Restaurant 2-minute walk.
Closed	Rarely.

	Marie-Victoire Gicqueau
	Villa du Square,
	26 rue Raffet,
	75016 Paris
Tel	+33 (0)1 71 72 91 33
Mobile	+33 (0)6 10 11 83 42
Email	contact@villadusquare.com
Web	villadusquare.com

Entry 127   Map 5

Relais 12 Bis

In the rich and rarefied core of the capital, this beautiful first-floor apartment has the trappings of a top end hotel with the welcoming air of a B&B. Rooms are understated and sophisticated: white walls, parquet floors, huge beds, stylish modern furniture. Each has its own spotless chrome, glass and marble bathroom, replete with soft white towels and heavenly lotions and potions. Sound-proofing and triple glazing means nothing disturbs your tranquillity – the only time you'll be aware of your neighbours is in the elegant dining/sitting room, where you breakfast on homemade cake, bread, pastries, cheese and delicious jams.

Minimum stay: 2 nights.

Rooms	4 doubles: €220–€300.
	1 suite for 4: €320–€440.
	Extra bed/sofabed available €40 per person per night.
Meals	Restaurants 5-minute walk.
Closed	Rarely.

	Philippe Schwarz
	Relais 12 Bis,
	12 bis rue Desaix,
	75015 Paris
Mobile	+33 (0)6 80 92 65 68
Email	reservation@relais12bis.com
Web	www.relais12bis.com

Entry 128   Map 5

Les Toits de Paris

The light-filled rooms, generous breakfasts and most courteous young owners are all of a lovely piece: quiet, clothed in gentle earthy colours, natural materials and discreet manners. You will feel instantly at ease in this cultured atmosphere. The attic room has a super-comfy bed, a convertible sofa and a darling little writing desk beneath the sloping beams; the beautiful bathroom has everything. The family rooms and studio have kitchenettes and sparkling shower rooms. Walk round 'the village', discover its quirky shops, its restaurants for all tastes and budgets – then head for the riches of central Paris.

Pension Les Marronniers

It's an honest-to-goodness pension de famille and as personal and cluttered as anything in Balzac. Find pictures, portraits and photographs, statues and plants galore, a grass-green armoire topped with candlesticks – plus a motley crew of friendly dogs. Marie coddles her guests and loves cooking for them: she clearly enjoys food herself, especially vegetarian, and makes sure others do too. The bedrooms for short-stayers have less personality, rather as if they have been furnished with what was left over. But what counts is the wonderful welcome, from Marie, the tradition and the food.

Rooms	1 double: €130. 2 family rooms for 4: €150–€180. 1 studio for 3: €130–€150. Extra bed €20.		Rooms	3 twin/doubles: €85–€105. 6 twin/doubles each with shower & separate wc: €78–€99. Singles €23.
Meals	Restaurants nearby.		Meals	Full board, except Saturdays & Sundays; breakfast on Saturdays included.
Closed	Rarely.		Closed	Rarely.

	Matthieu & Sophie de Montenay Les Toits de Paris, 25 rue de l'Abbé Groult, 75015 Paris		**Marie Poirier** Pension Les Marronniers, 78 rue d'Assas, 75006 Paris
Mobile	+33 (0)6 60 57 92 05	Tel	+33 (0)1 43 26 37 71
Email	resa@chambrehotesparis.fr	Email	o_marro@club-internet.fr
Web	www.chambrehotesparis.fr	Web	www.pension-marronniers.com

Entry 129   Map 5

Entry 130   Map 5

Le Clos des Princes

Paris is 20 minutes by train, Versailles 15 by motorway. Here, behind wrought-iron gates in an elegant suburb, the French mansion sits in an exuberant town garden of pergolas, box bushes and mature trees. Your kind, attentive hosts – she an ex-English teacher, he with a passion for Sully Prudhomme – may give you the poet/philosopher's two-room first-floor suite; he lived here in 1902. Polished floorboards, pretty prints, choice antiques, decorative perfume bottles by a claw-footed tub, all dance to the 19th-century theme. Breakfast unveils gorgeous porcelain and delicious homemade muffins and jams. Outstanding.

Le Moulin de St Martin

Agnès is gentle, with artistic flair, Bernard is gregarious, charming, convivial: together they have created a delectable B&B. The old mill is on an island encircled by Corot's Grand Morin river; lovely old willows lap the water, the pretty villages of Voulangis and Crécy lie beyond. A warm sober elegance prevails: there are 17th-century floorboards topped by oriental rugs; Asian antiques and art in gilt frames; cherry-red toile and snowy bed linen; terraces for summer views; log fires for nights in. Disneyland Paris, a world away, maybe a short drive but, above all, fine châteaux beckon.

Minimum stay: 2 nights.

Rooms	1 suite for 2: €105–€120.
	1 family room for 4: €95–€110.
	Sofabed available for children.
Meals	Restaurant 400m.
Closed	Rarely.

Rooms	1 double, 1 twin/double: €85–€95.
Meals	Dinner €28. Wine €18.
Closed	Rarely.

Christine & Éric Duprez
Le Clos des Princes,
60 av Jean Jaurès,
92290 Châtenay Malabry,
Hauts-de-Seine
Tel +33 (0)1 46 61 94 49
Email ce.duprez@yahoo.com
Web www.leclosdesprinces.com

Bernard & Agnès Gourbaud
Le Moulin de St Martin,
7 rue de St Martin,
Voulangis,
77580 Crécy la Chapelle,
Seine-et-Marne
Tel +33 (0)1 64 63 69 90
Email moulindesaintmartin@orange.fr

Entry 131   Map 5

Entry 132   Map 5

Le Clos de la Rose

For seekers of garden peace, for champagne and architecture buffs (vineyards and historic Provins nearby), this gorgeous green retreat from crazed Paris – cool, quiet, stylishly homely – has been restored with fine respect for 200-year-old origins: limewash, timbers, country antiques, a gathering of books. Charming Brendan (he's Irish) and gentle, organised Véronique have a lovely family and, amazingly, time to chat over aperitifs. Bedrooms have pretty colours, antique linen and patchwork charm, the adorable cottage (with kitchen) is ideal for a longer stay. Don't miss dinner, hot or cold: you choose.

Pets by arrangement.

Ferme de Vert Saint Père

Cereals and beets grow in wide fields and show-jumpers add elegance to the landscape. A generous farm courtyard surrounded by lovely warm stone buildings encloses peace and a genuine welcome from hosts and labradors alike, here where Monsieur's family has come hunting for 200 years. Find family furniture (the 1900s ensemble is most intriguing) and planked floors in beautiful bedrooms, immaculate mod cons and a handsome guest living room where breakfast is served at a convivial table surrounded by honey, polished floors and oriental-style rugs. Utter peace, a remote setting, and a Michelin-rated auberge in the village.

Rooms	2 doubles: €94–€146.
	1 cottage for 3: €99–€181.
	Extra bed/sofabed available €25 per person per night. Self-catering options available in cottage.
Meals	Breakfast €11. Dinner €29. Wine €20–€34. Champagne €32. Restaurant 10-minute drive.
Closed	Rarely.

Rooms	1 family room for 3: €76–€86.
	2 apartments for 4: €120–€125.
Meals	Restaurant in village, 1.5km.
Closed	Christmas.

Véronique & Brendan Culligan
Le Clos de la Rose,
11 rue de la Source, L'Hermitière,
77750 St Cyr sur Morin,
Seine-et-Marne

Tel	+33 (0)1 60 44 81 04
Mobile	+33 (0)6 82 56 10 54
Email	resa@clos-de-la-rose.com
Web	www.clos-de-la-rose.com

Philippe & Jeanne Mauban
Ferme de Vert Saint Père,
77390 Crisenoy,
Seine-et-Marne

Tel	+33 (0)1 64 38 83 51
Mobile	+33 (0)6 71 63 31 36
Email	mauban.vert@wanadoo.fr
Web	vertsaintpere.com

Nid de Rochefort

Wander among fruit trees in Stephane's tranquil walled garden; hard to believe that Paris is just 30 minutes by train. Wake to birdsong, and fabulous views of ancient Rochefort and the forest beyond. Breakfast is a convivial delight – feast on pancakes, pastries and honey (fresh from their own hives) in the elegant sitting room. Stylish, brightly painted doubles and a spacious family suite are split between the 18th-century house and a blue-shuttered cottage, or seek privacy in an extra room in the garden with its own kitchen: DIY breakfast, or sneak some from the house. Stroll to the unspoilt village for divine pastries.

À l'Ombre Bleue

Let the willows weep over the village pond; you go through the high gate into a sheltered paradise. The prettiest rooms have masses of old pieces, dolls, books, pictures to intrigue you, a chirruping garden with two rescue dogs to play with and the most caring hostess to provide an exceptional brunch. Have dinner too if you can (Catherine teaches cookery and sources locally: it's delicious). The miniature garden house is a lovers' dream: tiny salon downstairs, bedroom sporting superb bath up. Fulsome towels, extras of all sorts: charming, chatty Catherine thinks of everything.

Rooms	3 doubles: €82-€90.
	1 suite for 5: €115-€195.
	1 studio for 2 with kitchenette:
	€120-€150. Singles €78-€105.
	Extra bed/sofabed available €15 per
	person per night.
Meals	Restaurants in village
Closed	Rarely.

Rooms	1 double: £80-£100.
	2 family rooms for 2-4: €80-€160.
	Singles €65-€85.
	Extra sofabeds available.
Meals	Dinner with wine, €25.
	Light supper €15.
Closed	Rarely.

Stephane Jacquerez
Nid de Rochefort,
34 rue Guy le Rouge,
78730 Rochefort-en-Yvelines,
Yvelines

Tel	+33 (0)1 78 97 02 82
Mobile	+33 (0)6 13 24 50 99
Email	stephane.jacquerez@gmail.com
Web	www.lenidderochefort.fr

Catherine Forget-Pépin
À l'Ombre Bleue,
22 rue de la Mare, Les Pâtis,
78125 Mittainville,
Yvelines

Tel	+33 (0)1 34 85 04 73
Email	catherine@alombrebleue.fr
Web	www.alombrebleue.fr

Domaine des Basses Masures

The serene and beautiful Rambouillet forest encircles this hamlet and the house is a former stables; horses still graze in the field behind. Long, low and stone-fronted, cosily draped in Virginia creeper and wisteria, it was built in 1725. Madame, hospitable and easy-going, does B&B at one end; the gîte is at the other. The B&B bedrooms are friendly and charming, with pretty paintings and mirrors on the walls, antiques, books and places to sit. Breakfast is served in the sitting room or garden. Come to walk or ride, or visit the cities and sights: Versailles is 20 minutes, Paris not much further.

Cosi à la Moutière

In an 18th-century building that once housed a legendary auberge (frequented by Orson Welles, Ava Gardner, statesmen and royals) is an elegant chambres d'hôtes in a peaceful old town. Imagine white orchids and muslin, board games and books, spaciousness and light, and stylish taupe sofas before a grand fire. Dine at one table or on the wide terrace, wake to Micaela's lemon jams, muffins and clafoutis; all is delicate and delicious. Pedal off to explore Montfort-l'Amaury's cobbled streets, return to big boutique bedrooms with monsoon showers and myriad cushions – dazzling symphonies in grey, butterscotch and white.

Rooms	2 doubles: €90-€95. Both rooms rented together: €170. Extra bed/sofabed available €30 per person per night.
Meals	Restaurant 2km.
Closed	Rarely.

Rooms	1 twin/double: €115. 1 family room for 4: €125-€160. Singles €85-€95.
Meals	Restaurants within walking distance.
Closed	Rarely.

	Mme Walburg de Vernisy
	Domaine des Basses Masures,
	13 rue des Basses Masures,
	78125 Poigny la Forêt,
	Yvelines
Tel	+33 (0)1 34 84 73 44
Mobile	+33 (0)6 95 41 78 46
Email	domainebassesmasures@gmail.com
Web	www.domaine-des-basses-masures.com

	Micaela Tomasino
	Cosi à la Moutière,
	12 rue de la Moutière,
	78490 Montfort l'Amaury,
	Yvelines
Mobile	+33 (0)6 29 37 56 23
Email	maisondecosi@yahoo.fr
Web	www.chambresdhotes-cosi.com

Entry 137   Map 5

Entry 138   Map 5

Villa de la Pièce d'Eau des Suisses

Ah, Versailles! The gilded grandeur of the château, the tiny backstreets of the old town, the great lake of the Swiss Guards and, in between, a discreet door opening to a rambling house warmed by cultured parents, well-mannered teenagers, friendly pets and the smell of beeswax. Bathe in books, colour and art (Laure is an accomplished artist and dress designer); a garden too. Climb two gentle floors (pictures to absorb at every step) to large light rooms with views over the Royal Gardens. Add unusual family furniture and a superb new biscuity shower room: this genuine family B&B is a rare privilege.

Les chambres de Beynes

With Paris and Versailles a short hop away, these charming, modern rooms suit explorers and business types. Owner Alexandra is kind and thoughtful and cooks for you by arrangement. There's a bedroom in the large 18th century house and two more in the cottage across the pretty garden, one designed for wheelchair users. All are spotless and comfortable, with their own bathrooms and terraces. Choose a continental breakfast of delicious breads and pastries or a full English outside or in the shared dining room. You're a short stroll from shops and restaurants, and a twice-weekly table d'hôte showcases Alexandra's splendid cooking.

Parking on-site.

Rooms	1 double, sharing bathroom with twin/double, 1 twin/double, sharing bathroom with double: €140–€160. Extra bed/sofabed available €60 per person per night.
Meals	Restaurants within walking distance.
Closed	Rarely.

Rooms	3 doubles: €95–€105. Singles €85–€95. Cot available.
Meals	Dinner, 3 courses with wine, €25; Monday & Thurs only. Restaurants 5-minute walk.
Closed	1 week in July.

Laure de St Chaffray
Villa de la Pièce d'Eau des Suisses,
6 rue de la Quintinie,
78000 Versailles,
Yvelines

Tel	+33 (0)1 39 53 65 40
Mobile	+33 (0)6 22 60 05 84
Email	bedinversailles@gmail.com
Web	www.bedinversailles.com

Alexandra Joseph
Les chambres de Beynes,
1 place de l'Estandart,
78650 Beynes,
Yvelines

Mobile	+33 (0)6 66 30 42 24
Email	alexandra@leschambresdebeynes.com
Web	www.leschambresdebeynes.com

Entry 139   Map 5   Entry 140   Map 5

Région Parisienne

Les Colombes

On the doorstep of Paris, in the grounds of a royal château, surrounded by quiet tree-lined residential avenues, it's a trot from an atmospheric racecourse, almost on the banks of the Seine, with forest walks, good restaurants, efficient trains to and from Paris, impeccable, harmonious rooms, table d'hôtes and a deeply pretty garden to relax in. What Les Colombes lacks in old stones it makes up for in a welcome steeped in traditional hospitality – and that includes generous breakfasts, home-grown fruit and veg at dinner – and glowing antiques. Courteous, caring French hosts and great value.

Rooms	2 doubles, 1 twin: €82–€100. Extra bed/sofabed available €40 per person per night.
Meals	Dinner with wine, €48.
Closed	Rarely.

Irène & Jacques James
Les Colombes,
21 av Béranger,
78600 Maisons Laffitte,
Yvelines

Tel	+33 (0)1 39 62 82 48
Mobile	+33 (0)6 71 13 51 05
Email	jacques.james@orange.fr
Web	www.chambresdhotes-lescolombes.fr

Entry 141   Map 5

Région Parisienne

Les Tourelles de Thun

The neo-gothic brick pile rearing above its suburban street to peer across the Seine valley astonishes. Built by an ancestor in the 1850s as a summer residence, decorated with Corentin's father's varied and talented art, it has tall windows, big rooms – the modern salon is vast – and huge personality. Breakfast and dinner are in the 'medieval' dining room, the library is alive with books, scrolls and prints, there are armchairs and thick carpets in each big bedroom, from 'Hector' you can spy the Eiffel Tower. Charming, informative and eager, Nathalie uses simple colour schemes and good fabrics to create warm comfort – and she loves cooking.

Rooms	3 doubles: €82–€98. 1 suite for 3: €112–€162. Dinner, B&B €109 per person; €129 for two.
Meals	Dinner with wine, €32; children under 15, free.
Closed	Rarely.

Nathalie & Corentin Delhumeau
Les Tourelles de Thun,
25 rue des Annonciades,
78250 Meulan en Yvelines,
Yvelines

Tel	+33 (0)1 30 22 06 72
Email	contact@tourellesdethun.com
Web	www.chambredhotetourellesdethun.com

Entry 142   Map 5

Normandy

Château de Bouelles

Chandeliers on every ceiling, oil paintings on the walls and views in every direction make this a place of memorable luxury. This 19th-century manor, approached by a tree-lined drive, commands 88 acres of grazing land and sits in beautiful gardens (with tennis court and pool). Light-filled reception rooms feed off a white entrance hall, and big, light bedrooms are reached via a carved wood staircase. Here you'll find tip-top mattresses, oriental rugs and stylish bathrooms. Breakfast is at the large dining room table, a feast of bread, pastries, fresh fruit and local ham and cheese. Smiling reception presides over arrivals.

23 Grand Rue

Peter loves his wines (he was in the trade), Madeleine is energetic and vivacious, both welcome you generously at their 'maison bourgeoise' on the edge of a château village. Set back from the road behind fence and clipped hedge are three cosy classically furnished bedrooms: books and fresh flowers, immaculate duvets, smart French furniture, a calvados nightcap on the landing. Shower rooms are small and beautifully tiled. There's a conservatory for breakfast, a front room for relaxing and, at a table dressed with silver, French dinners are served. Dieppe, Rouen, Honfleur: all are wonderfully close.

Rooms	4 doubles: €150–€180.
	1 suite for 5: €250. Extra bed €35
	per night. Cot available, €25.
Meals	Restaurants 5km.
Closed	Rarely.

Rooms	2 doubles, 1 twin: €70.
	Singles €60.
Meals	Dinner with wine, €27.
Closed	Rarely.

	Colas Guyonnaud
	Château de Bouelles,
	76230 Bouelles,
	Seine-Maritime
Mobile	+33 (0)6 58 91 06 35/
	+33 (0)6 58 66 50 47
Email	contact@chateauexperiences.com
Web	www.chateaudebouelles.com

	Peter & Madeleine Mitchell
	23 Grand Rue,
	76270 Mesnières en Bray,
	Seine-Maritime
Tel	+33 (0)2 32 97 06 31
Email	info@23grandrue.com
Web	www.23grandrue.com

Saint Mare

A fresh modern house under a steep slate roof in a lush green sanctuary; it could not be more tranquil. The garden really is lovely and worth a wander – a tailored lawn, a mass of colour, huge banks of rhododendrons for which the village is renowned (three of its gardens are open to the public). Claudine runs home and B&B with effortless efficiency and gives you homemade brioches for breakfast; smiling Remi leads you to guest quarters in a freshly wood-clad house reached via stepping stones through the laurels. Bedrooms are comfortable, sunny, spotless, shining and utterly peaceful – two are big enough to lounge in.

Le Clos du Vivier

The lush garden shelters bees, bantams, sleek cats and a phenomenal variety of shrubs and flowering plants. Monsieur is retired and he looks after all this while Madame tends to their guests, with respect for everyone's privacy; Madame also offers guidance on hiking, and there's tennis and fishing nearby. She is an intelligent, active and graceful person, her bedrooms, some under sloping ceilings, are cosily colourful, her bathrooms big and luxurious, her breakfast richly varied. After a jaunt, you can read their books, relax among their lovely antiques or make tea in their breakfast room. The cliffs at Étretat are 20 minutes away.

Rooms	1 suite for 4, 1 suite for 4 with kitchenette, 1 suite for 5: €85–€135. Extra beds available €20 per person per night.
Meals	Restaurants 20-minute walk.
Closed	Rarely.

Rooms	1 twin/double: €120. 1 suite for 5: €150–€170. 1 triple: €120–€140.
Meals	Restaurants in Valmont, 1km.
Closed	Rarely.

	Claudine Goubet Saint Mare, Route de Petites Bruyères, 1 chemin des Sablonnières, 76119 Varengeville sur Mer, Seine-Maritime
Tel	+33 (0)2 35 85 99 28
Mobile	+33 (0)6 18 92 28 20
Email	claudine.goubet@chsaintmare.com
Web	www.chsaintmare.com

	Dominique Cachera-Gréverie Le Clos du Vivier, 4 chemin du Vivier, 76540 Valmont, Seine-Maritime
Tel	+33 (0)2 35 29 90 95
Email	le.clos.du.vivier@wanadoo.fr
Web	www.leclosduvivier.com

Entry 145   Map 4

Entry 146   Map 4

Mille Roses

Poised on a hillside gazing south over the Seine, this proud red-brick mansion was once home to opera tenor Placide Poultier. Now Patsy will welcome you in; a teacher and guide, she is well versed in local history and happy to share the local secrets over a light breakfast. At the top of the house are two modern, simple twin bedrooms and a sitting room where you can browse a guide book over a cup of tea; bathrooms are separate but private and everything is spotless. Outside, a huge copper beech and blue cedar sprinkle shade into a lush, sloping garden where a barbecue and hammock promise lazy summer afternoons.

Chambres avec Vue

The elegant black door hides a little house of treasures, curios, art and character, an easy walk (25 minutes) from the centre of Rouen. Dominique, full of energy and enthusiasm, has a flair for decoration – as her paintings, coverings and light, bright furniture declares. Oriental rugs on parquet floors, French windows to balcony and garden, bedrooms brimful of interest. Nothing standard, nothing too studied, a very personal home and leisurely breakfasts promising heavenly surprises. The house's hillside position in this residential area is equally special. Great value, great views.

Rooms	2 twins, each with separate bathroom & shared living area,: €80–€90.
Meals	Dinner, 4 courses, €25 (on first evening only). Restaurant nearby.
Closed	March – May & October/November.

Rooms	3 doubles: €65. Singles €45.
Meals	Restaurant 1km.
Closed	October/November.

	Patsy Musto
	Mille Roses, 9 rue Jean Le Gaffric,
	76490 Villequier, Seine-Maritime
Tel	+33 (0)2 32 70 44 32,
	+44 (0)1527 873645
Mobile	+33 (0)6 48 85 92 19,
	+44 (0)7768 886407
Email	patsy.musto8@orange.fr
Web	www.frenchencounters.com

	Dominique Gogny
	Chambres avec Vue,
	22 rue Hénault,
	76130 Mont St Aignan,
	Seine-Maritime
Tel	+33 (0)2 35 70 26 95
Mobile	+33 (0)6 62 42 26 95
Email	chambreavecvue@free.fr
Web	chambreavecvue.online.fr

Entry 147   Map 4

Entry 148   Map 4

Le Brécy

Jérôme has happy childhood holiday memories of this elegant 17th-century manor house; he and delightful Patricia moved to join grand-mère who had been living here alone for years. A long path flanked by willows leads down to the Seine: perfect for an evening stroll. One suite is on the ground floor, in classically French coral and cream, its windows opening to a walled garden; the second, equally refined, is in the attic. Breakfast is when you fancy: brioches, walnuts, fresh fruit in a pretty green-panelled room. Ask about the Abbey and walks to its gardens. A charming rural paradise just 15 minutes from Rouen Cathedral.

Manoir de Captot

The drive curves through paddocks and pillared gates to this serene 18th-century mansion. The forest behind may ring with the stag's call, the heads and hooves of his kin line the grand staircase. The fine classic French interior is peacefully formal: a gorgeous primrose-yellow dining room with an oval mahogany table for breakfast feasts, a collection-filled drawing room, a beautiful first-floor bedroom with the right curly antiques and pink Jouy draperies. Michelle cherishes her mansion and resembles it: gentle, attentive, courteous. Giverny is near, Rouen and its heaps of lovely restaurants are ten minutes away.

Children over 10 welcome.

Rooms	1 suite for 2, 1 suite for 3: €99–€109.
Meals	Restaurant in village.
Closed	Rarely.

Rooms	1 double: €95–€110.
	1 suite for 2-3: €95–€110.
	Extra double occasionally available.
Meals	Restaurant 900m.
Closed	Rarely.

Jérôme & Patricia Lanquest
Le Brécy,
72 route du Brécy,
76840 St Martin de Boscherville,
Seine-Maritime

Tel   +33 (0)2 35 32 00 30
Mobile   +33 (0)6 62 37 24 22
Email   lebrecy@gmail.com
Web   www.lebrecy.com

Michelle Desrez
Manoir de Captot,
42 route de Sahurs,
76380 Canteleu,
Seine-Maritime

Tel   +33 (0)2 35 36 00 04
Email   captot76@yahoo.fr
Web   www.captot.com

Entry 149   Map 4

Entry 150   Map 4

Normandy

Château de Bonnemare

A Renaissance gatehouse leads to a remarkable 16th-century brique de St Jean façade as you enter the grounds of this enticing 'monument historique'. Alain and Sylvie, generous and charming, have restored two elegant ground-floor rooms in the north wing, and two with listed decoration on the first floor. Find French classical elegance, chandeliers, mouldings, deep mattresses and pleasing modern bathrooms. Breakfast in the vaulted Great Kitchen with embroidered napkins, fresh fruits and flowers, pâtisseries and homemade jams. The estate walls enclose chapel, farm, cider press, bakery, barns and 44 acres of park and woodland. Grand.

Rooms	1 double: €112–€145.
	3 suites for 2-3: €202–€235.
	Singles €112.
Meals	Shared guest kitchen.
	Restaurant 6km.
Closed	1 December to 15 February.

Sylvie Vandecandelaere
Château de Bonnemare,
990 route de Bacqueville,
27380 Radepont,
Eure

Tel	+33 (0)2 32 49 03 73
Mobile	+33 (0)6 03 96 36 53
Email	sarlbonnemare@nordnet.fr
Web	www.bonnemare.com

Entry 151   Map 4

Normandy

La Lévrière

The garden laps at the river bank where moorhens nest; trout swim, birds chirrup, deer pop by – it's the dreamiest village setting. Madame is charming and takes everything (including escapee horses) in her stride and her young family love it when guests come to stay. Breakfast is at a grey-painted table with crimson plexiglass chairs; garden loungers are a temptation to stay. Bedrooms are across the way, two in the granary, one up, one down, the third in the immaculate coach house attic with a fine garden view. Creamy walls, sweeping floors, rafters, toile de Jouy, fresh flowers... stay a long while.

Rooms	1 double: €85. 1 suite: €85–€105.
	1 triple: €85–€115.
Meals	Restaurant 5km.
Closed	Rarely.

Sandrine & Pascal Gravier
La Lévrière,
24 rue Guérard,
27140 St Denis le Ferment,
Eure

Tel	+33 (0)2 32 27 04 78
Mobile	+33 (0)6 79 43 92 77
Email	contact@normandyrooms.com
Web	www.normandyrooms.com

Entry 152   Map 5

Chambres d'hôtes de la Bucaille

In a small hamlet surrounded by 600 acres of land is a farmhouse where Sophie and her children live, and a four-square brick mansion for the guests. You'll find a breakfast room, sitting room and TV room downstairs, and five bedrooms up, with choice fabrics, period furniture and fine new bathrooms. Breakfast is served on antique tablecloths and white china, and elegant wallpapers and north African rugs are scattered throughout. All feels polished, pleasing, and hospitable. Say hello to the horses, borrow the bikes, visit Richard the Lionheart's Château Gaillard; it's one of many historic sites.

Château de la Madeleine

Originally a priory, the château sits back from the road, surrounded by 22 unmanicured acres and sheltered by venerable trees. Here live a gentle young family, running a most hospitable B&B. Interiors are resolutely period with upholstered French chairs and marquetry flooring, woodland falls into the surrounding valley and the views are green and astounding. Your bedrooms, ranging from large to huge, are linked by a (part-open) marble stair, and spread across the top floors; two have private roof terraces. Paul and Marie serve breakfast at clothed tables and you feast on freshly squeezed orange juice, delicious pastries and Italian mountain ham.

Rooms	1 double, 3 twin/doubles: €80–€110.
	1 apartment for 5: €90–€150.
Meals	Restaurant 8km.
Closed	Rarely.

Rooms	2 suites for 3: €160.
	2 family rooms for 5: €200.
	Extra bed €20.
Meals	Restaurants 4km.
Closed	November – March.

Sophie Hamot
Chambres d'hôtes de la Bucaille,
2 rue Jean Lucas,
27700 Guiseniers,
Eure
Tel   +33 (0)2 32 54 58 45
Email   hamot.jerome@orange.fr
Web   www.chambres-hotes-labucaille.com

Marie Mathe
Château de la Madeleine,
27510 Pressagny l'Orgueilleux,
Eure
Mobile +33 (0)6 26 60 27 80
Email   lamadeleine-27@orange.fr
Web   www.chateau-madeleine.com

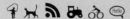

Normandy

La Réserve

You will like Valérie, lively mother of four, and her quietly refined house. And after breakfast at the big guest table you will want to stay forever. Over home-grown eggs and homemade jams, cake of the day, cheeses, charcuterie and fruit kebabs, conversations flourish, friendships bud. Outside, limewash walls stand among lavender-edged lawns and orchards, kindly Flaubert the Leonberger ambles, cows graze; inside are grey woodwork and gorgeous rooms, superb beds, handsome rugs on parquet floors, fine antiques and touches of brocante. Monet's ineffable gardens are just down the hill.

Rooms	2 doubles, 4 twin/doubles: €135–€165. Extra bed €40. Whole house available.
Meals	Restaurants 1km.
Closed	November – March, except by arrangement.

Valérie & François Jouyet
La Réserve,
27620 Giverny,
Eure

Tel	+33 (0)2 32 21 99 09
Email	mlreserve@gmail.com
Web	www.giverny-lareserve.com

Entry 155   Map 4

Normandy

Les Hautes Sources

Three golden farmhouses around a central lawned terrace, with views that sail over the valley to a distant church spire: an incomparable setting. Enthusiastic Amaury and Audrey arrived with their family in 2012 and give you three bedrooms in the second house and a family cottage in the third: uncluttered, gorgeous, luxurious. Imagine decorative floors, white-painted beams, muted colours and snowy linen. Wake to five homemade jams that include apple caramel, set off for Monet's beautiful Giverny, wander the lovely gardens, splash in the pool, sink into sofas by the great stone fire. You will unwind here.

Rooms	1 twin/double, 1 twin: €120–€140. 1 suite for 2: €160–€170. 1 cottage for 5: €170–€200.
Meals	Restaurants 3km.
Closed	Rarely.

Amaury de Tilly
Les Hautes Sources,
32 rue Roederer,
27120 Ménilles,
Eure

Mobile	+33 (0)6 72 84 91 89
Email	amaury.detilly@hotmail.fr
Web	www.les-hautes-sources.fr

Entry 156   Map 4

Les Granges Ménillonnes

An active farm until 1950, it sits beside a pretty garden in the prettiest countryside in the Eure valley, 20 minutes from Monet's gardens at Giverny, midway between Rouen and Paris. In converted outbuildings, big comfortable bedrooms, one with a balcony, furnished with warm colours, honeyed floorboards and country quilts beneath a riot of beams overlook a lily pond and loungers that beckon you to doze over a book – though excellent walking abounds. Chantal and Michel, energetic hosts, offer speciality breads and up to 15 different jams for breakfast, and run a farm shop in the village.

Clos de Mondétour

Tiny church to one side, lazy river behind, views to weeping willows and majestic limes – the house oozes grace and tranquillity. Grégoire and Aude have created a calm, charming atmosphere inside: this is a family home. Lofty, light-drenched bedrooms with polished floorboards, antiques and monogrammed bed linen are beautifully refined; bathrooms are light and luxurious. The living area, with a striking tiled floor and bold colours, is a restful space in which to settle in front of a log fire – or enjoy a special breakfast among fresh flowers and family silver. Aude's horses graze in the meadow behind.

Rooms	2 doubles, 1 twin: €73.
	1 suite for 4, 1 suite for 7: €120-€145.
Meals	Restaurant 3km.
Closed	Rarely.

Rooms	1 double, 1 twin/double: €130.
	1 family room for 4: €100-€150.
	1 triple: €140.
Meals	Restaurants 2km.
Closed	Rarely.

Michel & Chantal Marchand
Les Granges Ménillonnes,
2 rue Grand'Cour,
27120 Ménilles,
Eure

Mobile	+33 (0)6 70 46 87 57
Email	chant.mich.marchand@gmail.com
Web	www.lesgranges27.com

Aude Jeanson
Clos de Mondétour,
17 rue de la Poste,
27120 Fontaine sous Jouy,
Eure

Tel	+33 (0)2 32 36 68 79
Mobile	+33 (0)6 71 13 11 57
Email	aude.jeanson@closdemondetour.com
Web	www.closdemondetour.com

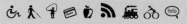

Entry 157   Map 4

Entry 158   Map 4

Les Logis du Moulin

Welcome to a serene green paradise – a converted water mill and burgeoning B&B. Across deckchair'd lawns linked by meandering paths (clogs and umbrellas provided!) are two separate cottages, sober, simple, fresh and warm; total tranquillity. In the first, the main bedroom is downstairs and the single is up, leading through to a rustic-stylish shower. In the converted bread oven, bucolically on the river bank, is a double with an extra bed for child. Find floors of rosy terracotta, arched windows hung with muslin, pretty beds topped with quilts. In the handsome dining room, gentle Elisabeth serves a breakfast worth lingering over; and you can, until 11am.

Pets by arrangement.

L'Aulnaie

Michel and Éliane have invested natural good taste in their restoration of this lovely 19th-century farmhouse in a particularly pretty village. Guests share a self-contained part of the house with its own dayroom and breakfast area – there's lots of space to settle in – with books, music and open fire. Bedrooms are gentle, beautiful, fresh, with Jouy-print fabrics, plain walls and honey-coloured floors. Enthusiastic, charming Éliane is an amateur painter and inspired gardener, pointing out the rich and the rare; lawns sweep down to a stream that meanders beneath high wooded cliffs. Such value!

Rooms	1 double: €85. 1 suite for 3: €105. Singles €65-€70. Extra bed/sofabed available €15 per person per night.
Meals	Assiette gourmande, with cider, €16. Restaurant 3km.
Closed	Rarely.

Rooms	1 double, 1 twin: €100.
Meals	Restaurants 2km.
Closed	Rarely.

	Elisabeth Lamblardy
	Les Logis du Moulin,
	4 rue du Moulin,
	27120 Fontaine sous Jouy,
	Eure
Tel	+33 (0)2 32 26 06 07
Email	elisabeth.lamblardy@orange.fr
Web	www.leslogisdumoulin.fr

	Éliane & Michel Philippe
	L'Aulnaie,
	29 rue de l'Aulnaie,
	27120 Fontaine sous Jouy,
	Eure
Tel	+33 (0)2 32 36 89 05
Mobile	+33 (0)6 03 30 55 99
Email	contact@aulnaie.com
Web	aulnaie.co.uk

La Ferme des Isles

Approach this sprawling 19th-century farm through a watercolour of mills, meadows and bridges… friendly French hosts await with a menagerie of four-legged friends. With vintage chairs, suspended lamps, billiards and book-filled mangers, it's perfect for fun social soirées and François's four-star dinners. Beams break up modern bedrooms – a triangular bath and a sunburst bed will astound you. Breakfast in the cavernous barn (on goat's cheese, grainy breads, garden fruits); end the day amongst fireplaces, convivial tables and chesterfields in stone-walled sitting and dining rooms. For nature lovers, couples and families – huge fun.

Clair Matin

Handsomely carved Colombian furniture, strong colours, interesting prints – not what you expect to find at a long, low, 18th-century village homestead with a turret at each end. Your kind and very lovely Franco-Spanish hosts raised five children in South America before renovating their French home. Bedrooms, not huge, are solidly comfortable, bathrooms are immaculate and there's a new games room in an outbuilding. At the huge Andean breakfast table you will enjoy fresh breads, homemade jams and good conversation. Jean-Pierre is a passionate gardener and his plantations burst with every kind of shrub and flower!

Rooms	5 doubles: €95–€165.		Rooms	1 double: €70–€85.
Meals	Dinner, 4 courses with wine, €47.50.			1 suite for 2: €85–€120.
	Restaurants 300m.			1 family room for 4: €70–€100.
Closed	Rarely.		Meals	Auberges 6km.
			Closed	Rarely.

	François & Sophie Breban		**Jean-Pierre & Amaia Trevisani**
	La Ferme des Isles,		Clair Matin,
	7 chemin des Isles,		19 rue de l'Église,
	27490 Autheuil Authouillet,		27930 Reuilly,
	Eure		Eure
Tel	+33 (0)2 32 36 66 14	Tel	+33 (0)2 32 34 71 47
Mobile	+33 (0)6 63 46 00 45	Email	bienvenue@clair-matin.com
Email	lafermedesisles@gmail.com	Web	www.clair-matin.com
Web	www.lafermedesisles.com		

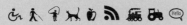

La Londe

The big beautiful garden flows down to the river Eure – what a setting – and the old farmhouse and yesteryear buildings are as neat as new pins. Delightful Madeleine devotes herself to home and guests and bedrooms are neat, clean, pretty, sober and relaxing; the double's French windows open to the garden, the perfect small suite sits under the eaves. Expect antique lace, silver snuff boxes, a kitchen/salon for guests and very delicious breakfasts with garden views. A form of perfection in a privileged and peaceful spot: woods and water for walking, canoeing, fishing; Giverny – or Rouen – a half-hour drive.

Rooms	1 double: €65–€70.
	1 suite for 3: €67–€95.
	Extra bed/sofabed available €20 per person per night.
Meals	Guest kitchen. Restaurants 5km.
Closed	Rarely.

Madeleine & Bernard Gossent
La Londe,
4 sente de l'Abreuvoir,
27400 Heudreville sur Eure,
Eure
Tel   +33 (0)2 32 40 36 89
Mobile   +33 (0)6 89 38 36 59
Email   madeleine.gossent@online.fr
Web   www.lalonde.online.fr

Entry 163   Map 4

Château de la Puisaye

A fine château which oozes 19th-century elegance (pale façade, shuttered windows) in 27 acres of rural bliss. Find large airy bedrooms with antiques, huge mantelpiece mirrors, glass-panelled doors that flood spaces with light; ivory paintwork and snowy linen create an ordered calm. Diana, a stylish cook, will prepare a light supper or dinner on request, perhaps foie gras then truffle-stuffed guinea fowl; fruit and veg come from the potager, the 19th-century greenhouse and local markets. Lounge in the book-filled library, borrow a bike and pedal the grounds; relax in the infra-red sauna among delicious aromatherapy oils.

Rooms	3 doubles, 1 twin: €98–€128.
	1 suite for 4: €185.
Meals	Dinner with wine, €35.
	Menu gourmand €55.
	Normandy platter with cider, €17.
Closed	Rarely.

Bruno & Diana Costes
Château de la Puisaye,
Lieu-dit La Puisaye,
27130 Verneuil sur Avre,
Eure
Tel   +33 (0)2 32 58 65 35
Email   info@chateaudelapuisaye.com
Web   www.chateaudelapuisaye.com

Entry 164   Map 4

Au Vieux Logis

They are full of character and terribly French, this artist owner and her crooked house marked by the slings and arrows of 500 years: wonky floorboards, bathrooms among the beams, old-fashioned floral bedrooms and a sensuous garden full of old favourites: lilac and honeysuckle, luscious shrubs and fruit trees. Set in the middle of the village, the quiet old house has an atmosphere that inspires ease and rest. (Saint-Exupéry, author of the *Le Petit Prince* and a friend of Madame's father, stayed here.) Madame, a good, generous soul, was once an antique dealer so breakfast is served on old silver.

Le Vertbois

Step into the pages of a fairy-tale. Three tiny, half-timbered cottages, all soft grey and white, sit beside a creeper-covered chalet (a former shooting lodge), surrounded by deep woodland that begs to be explored. Each cottage is a self-contained, very pretty, suite. One is stylishly rustic with terracotta tiles and dark antiques; another has an Asian theme (and extra loft bedroom); the third glows with pale-painted furniture and soft drapes. All have terraces and shiny bathrooms. Breakfast at leisure in the owners' cosy living room. Explore Rouen or the coast, play tennis, borrow a bike. Relaxed hosts, pretty surrounds.

Rooms	2 doubles: €50. 1 triple: €80. 1 quadruple: €100.
Meals	Dinner €17. Wine €15.
Closed	Rarely.

Rooms	1 double, 1 twin/double: €105. 1 family room for 4: €130–€150.
Meals	Restaurants 7km.
Closed	Rarely.

Annick Auzoux
Au Vieux Logis,
27370 St Didier des Bois,
Eure
Tel +33 (0)2 32 50 60 93
Email levieuxlogis5@orange.fr
Web www.levieuxlogis.fr

Catherine Collemare & François Vadot
Le Vertbois,
19 Route de Bourgtheroulde,
27370 La Haye du Theil,
Eure
Tel +33 (0)2 32 36 66 85
Email le.vertbois@orange.fr
Web www.vertbois.fr

Entry 165   Map 4

Entry 166   Map 4

Manoir d'Hermos

The sedately old-French bedrooms with good antiques and satin touches in the 16th-century house (in Madame's family for 100 years) are large, light and lovely. All sit in peace by pastoral meadows, a birdy orchard and spreading lake. Béatrice is full of spontaneous smiles, puts flowers everywhere, organises big parties on a theme (not when B&B guests are here), serves good breakfasts and brunches at one table and keeps four gentle donkeys. The orchards produce cider and trees are being carefully and meticulously planted to Napoleonic plans discovered in the archives. A super place to stay, filled with interesting history.

Le Logis des Monts

The house, picturesquely timbered and behind wrought-iron gates, lies on the edge of a hamlet. The setting is rural; the large garden is delightful. Françoise and her Spanish greyhound are the friendliest hosts. The sitting room is shared (log fireplace, overhead beams) and the colourful, immaculate bedrooms are in the guest wing, the cosiest under the eaves. After a fine continental breakfast – brioche, homemade jams, fruit salad – served in the conservatory at flexible times, set off for Rouen, Honfleur and glamorous Deauville. Table d'hôtes is offered everyday on request – don't miss it: Françoise is an excellent cook.

Rooms	1 suite for 3 (with kitchen): €108.
	1 quadruple: €94-€138.
Meals	Restaurants 2km.
Closed	Rarely.

Rooms	2 doubles: €58. Singles €48.
Meals	Dinner with drinks, coffee &
	apéritif €18.
	Restaurants 7km
Closed	Rarely.

	Béatrice & Patrice Noël-Windsor
	Manoir d'Hermos,
	27800 St Éloi de Fourques,
	Eure
Tel	+33 (0)2 32 35 51 32
Mobile	+33 (0)6 11 75 51 63
Email	contact@hermos.fr
Web	www.hermos.fr

	Françoise Hannedouche
	Le Logis des Monts,
	26 impasse des monts nord,
	27520 Theillement,
	Eure
Tel	+33 (0)2 32 57 25 88
Mobile	+33 (0)6 85 42 38 07
Email	lelogisdesmonts@orange.fr
Web	www.lelogisdesmonts.fr

Entry 167   Map 4

Entry 168   Map 4

Les Clématites

An enchanting maison de maître, one of several that housed the nimble-fingered ribbon weavers, with the bonus of fine table d'hôtes. Hidden amid the fields of the Normandy plains, it stands in a dream of a garden, overgrown here, brought to heel there, flanked by a majestic walnut and age-old pears, filled with shrub roses; the odd forgotten bench adds to the Flaubertian charm. Inside, Marie-Hélène, bright-eyed and eager, has used Jouy cloth and elegant colours to dress the country-French bedrooms that fill the first floor. These ex-Parisian hosts are courteous, considerate, truly endearing.

Ailleurs sous les Etoiles

In an idyllic setting of orchards and pastures is a 19th-century farmhouse with two half-timbered cottages – a bucolic spot for Normandy B&B. The grounds are landscaped and large, there's a heated pool for all to share, and the only sound you'll hear is the braying of the donkey, the odd tractor, and the birds. Denis (ex-hospitality) and Isabelle (fashion) have created two immaculate light-filled bedrooms, one in the eaves, both with tip-top bathrooms and pretty green views. Exemplary breakfast includes homemade brioche and orchard fruits. For dinner you can pop into neighbouring Beuzeville or bustling Honfleur.

Rooms	1 double, 1 twin: €72.
	1 triple: €87.
Meals	Supper, 3 courses with wine, €21.
Closed	Rarely.

Rooms	2 doubles: €95-€130.
Meals	Restaurants 3.5km.
Closed	Rarely.

Marie-Hélène François & Hughes de Morchoven
Les Clématites,
Hameau de la Charterie,
27230 St Aubin de Scellon, Eure
Tel   +33 (0)2 32 45 46 52
Mobile   +33 (0)6 20 39 08 63
Email   la.charterie@orange.fr
Web   monsite.orange.fr/la.charterie

Isabelle & Denis Block
Ailleurs sous les Etoiles,
616 route de l'Ermitage,
La petite campagne,
27210 Manneville la Raoult,
Eure
Tel   +33 (0)2 77 18 53 80
Email   contact@ailleurssouslesetoiles.com
Web   www.ailleurssouslesetoiles.com

Bergerie de la Moutonnière

Sheep graze behind this charming old bergerie, in the grounds of your hospitable Dutch hosts' manor house. Great independence here: a rustic, open kitchen on the covered terrace, and a spacious suite with a super-comfortable bed and big bathroom below. Find warm gentle colours, lofty rafters, traditional colombage walls and wooden floors; there are armchairs and a sofa by the wood-burning stove and you can order a breakfast hamper to be delivered. After walking, golf, visiting old churches, farmers' markets and Trouville, return to the beautiful, peaceful gardens. A magical place – guests love it, and children and dogs are welcome too.

Au Grey d'Honfleur

There's a fairytale feel to this pair of tall narrow houses in a quiet cobbled backstreet. You don't quite know what to expect but you know you're somewhere rare and special. Inside, stairs and steps in all directions link little rooms; age-old beams and sloping ceilings contrast with imaginative décor and modern luxury. Josette, a globe-trotting lawyer, knows a thing or two about what's required of a guest bedroom… Looking down over the haphazard roofs of medieval Honfleur, the miniature terraced garden and fountain, delightfully formal, add to the pleasure. Breakfasts are divine.

Minimum stay: 2 nights.

Rooms	1 suite for 2: €95–€110. Space for cot or child's bed.
Meals	Breakfast €10. Evening meals on request. Restaurants 4km.
Closed	Rarely.

Rooms	2 doubles: €125–€160.
Meals	Restaurants within walking distance.
Closed	Rarely.

	Rudolf Walthaus Bergerie de la Moutonnière, 295 chemin du Mesnil, 14590 Le Pin, Calvados
Tel	+33 (0)2 31 62 56 86
Email	walthaus@mac.com
Web	www.bergerienormandy.com

	Josette Roudaut Au Grey d'Honfleur, 11 rue de la Bavole, 14600 Honfleur, Calvados
Mobile	+33 (0)6 85 07 50 45
Email	info@augrey-honfleur.com
Web	www.augrey-honfleur.com

Beehome

Down a country lane minutes' from Honfleur, this modern, arty, brick and timber-clad house is full of light, surrounded by an immense lawned garden with a discreet swimming pool. You sleep in great comfort in fresh, inviting rooms with huge beds and a fascinating array of artwork: ink drawings, watercolours, pastels, photographs. Bathrooms are modern and immaculate. You breakfast continental-style, and generously, with homemade jams and organic honey from the owners' own hives. Dinner is a treat, too. The big guest sitting room is wonderfully quirky, with a mix of furniture old and new, and the Merciers themselves are delightful.

Minimum stay: 2 nights in high season. Pets by arrangement.

Le Clos Bourdet

Welcome to chic, charming B&B, off a residential street, in a big hilly garden high above town. Françoise ran a tea room for 25 years, Jean-Claude is a photographer whose black-and-white prints beautify elegant rooms. Tall windows pull in the light in a sitting room heaving with books, crowned by a chandelier. Wend your way up the corkscrew staircase (past a collection of vintage bird cages that catch the eye) to bedrooms with antique wicker chairs on seagrass floors and soft-raspberry walls showing off turquoise taffeta. There are monsoon showers and a big terrace view... such fun to be in historic Honfleur!

Minimum stay: 2 nights at weekends.

Rooms	3 doubles: €135.
	1 family room for 3: €160.
Meals	Dinner €27. Restaurants 1.5km.
Closed	Rarely.

Rooms	4 doubles: €125–€180.
	1 suite for 2: €150–€195.
	Extra bed €35.
Meals	Restaurants within walking distance.
Closed	Rarely.

	Brigitte Mercier
	Beehome,
	47 chemin des Charmilles, Vasouy,
	14600 Honfleur,
	Calvados
Tel	+33 (0)2 31 88 51 87
Mobile	+33 (0)6 07 10 59 17
Email	contact@beehome.fr
Web	www.beehome.fr

	Françoise Osmont
	Le Clos Bourdet,
	50 rue Bourdet,
	14600 Honfleur,
	Calvados
Mobile	+33 (0)6 07 48 99 67
Email	info@leclosbourdet.com
Web	www.leclosbourdet.com

Entry 173   Map 4

Entry 174   Map 4

La Petite Folie

Just steps from the old harbour, these three townhouses are havens from the artistic bustle. The main house (B&B), built for a sea captain in the 1830s, has heavy shutters over grand mansard windows. Its more modest neighbour contains three apartments over three floors. Up the street are two more apartments with views onto a beautiful garden. Penny and Thierry give you handsome bedrooms with plump duvets, lacquered armchairs, mahogany chests of drawers. Breakfast is a daily treat. The ground-floor sitting room is as wide as the house and the garden has a summerhouse with sea views. All this, and delightful hosts.

Minimum stay: 2 nights. Over 12s welcome; children under 12 welcome in 1 apartment.

Le Clos aux Masques

Ceramic masks on the façade of this charming Norman B&B greet you with a smile. Delightful Anne and convivial Andrea have transformed this half-timbered longère into a peaceful rural retreat. Ancient beams remain in some cosy bedrooms, offset by white walls and colourful bed linen, but creatively tiled en-suites are supremely modern and views soar over the big, lawned, garden. Huddle around the open fire in a sitting room furnished with antiques and comfy sofas. Feast on hearty breakfasts of fresh bread, local cheese and Sicilian pastries. Sandy beaches are close – you can borrow the family's beach hut at Blonville!

Self-catering also available; enquire with owners.

Rooms	4 doubles, 1 twin: €145-€175. 3 apartments for 2, 2 apartments for 4: €195-€295.	Rooms	2 doubles: €85-€99. 2 family rooms for 3: €95-€145. 1 family room for 4: €130-€169.
Meals	Breakfast to apartments on request. Restaurants nearby.	Meals	Restaurants 4km.
Closed	Early January to mid-February.	Closed	Rarely.

	Penny & Thierry Vincent La Petite Folie, 44 rue Haute, 14600 Honfleur, Calvados		**Anne & Andrea Acquanegra** Le Clos aux Masques, Le Bourg, 14950 Saint Pierre Azif, Calvados
Mobile	+33 (0)6 74 39 46 46	Mobile	+33 (0)6 46 82 71 53
Email	lapetitefoliehonfleur@gmail.com	Email	contact@clos-aux-masques.com
Web	www.lapetitefolie-honfleur.com	Web	www.clos-aux-masques.com/

Entry 175   Map 4

Entry 176   Map 4

La Mascotte

In the animated seaside town of Villers sur Mer — next to legendary Trouville — is a 19th-century villa built by a librettist. An airy hall leads to a stylish sitting room with French windows to a terrace, and a table at which stupendous breakfasts are served: breads, pastries, fruits, yogurts, homemade waffles and jams. Your gentle, discreet hostess, a passionate golfer, can direct you to one of numerous courses. Then it's back to boudoir armchairs, comfy beds and polished parquet: the bedrooms (one with a balcony, one a roof terrace) are a joy — all overlook the garden and rooftops, all have distant views of the sea.

Parking on-site.

Château de Bénéauville

Down the plane-flanked drive to an immaculate Renaissance château in harmonious grounds. Find painted 17th-century beams in perfect condition, heads of antelope and oryx surprising the walls, a panelled library, a powder-blue dining room, and fireplaces imposing and theatrical. Here live the Augais family, with horse, hens and handsome gundogs. In big peaceful bedrooms with tall windows are chestnut floors and grey-washed beams, oriental carpets, quilted bedspreads, boudoir armchairs, deep baths (with shower attachments) and exquisite curtain tassels. Take a dip in the discreet pool; set off for culture in Caen. Marvellous.

Rooms	1 double, 1 twin/double: €100–€140.
	1 family room for 4: €100–€180.
Meals	Restaurants 3-minute walk.
Closed	January or February.

Rooms	3 doubles: €190–€250.
	1 suite for 5: €270–€420.
	2 of the doubles can form a suite: €250–€310.
Meals	Restaurants 5km.
Closed	1 October to 1 June.

Ségolène de la Serre
La Mascotte,
11 rue de la Comtesse de Béarn,
14640 Villers-sur-Mer,
Calvados
Mobile   +33 (0)6 76 98 20 34
Email   contact@guesthouse-lamascotte.com
Web   www.guesthouse-lamascotte.com

Philippe Augais
Château de Bénéauville,
Bénéauville,
14860 Bavent,
Calvados
Tel   +33 (0)2 31 72 56 49
Email   reservation@chateaudebeneauville.fr
Web   www.chateaudebeneauville.fr

Entry 177   Map 4

Entry 178   Map 4

Le Fresnay

Playfully guarded by a flock of sculpted sheep, this beautiful half-timbered manor house stands proudly in acres of pastures, orchard, woodland and garden. Courteous Italian owner Mr Fabra has created a chic, peaceful sanctuary in the Normandy countryside. Breakfast on pastries and home-produced honey; sleep in stylish terracotta-floored rooms with stone fireplaces and contemporary bathrooms. Gently wake to birdsong and the prospect of a day exploring the Cider Trail local markets. In the evenings, read by the open fire in one of the sumptuous sitting rooms or drive to a nearby village for dinner. Bliss.

Château du Mesnil d'O

The approach to this 18th-century château lifts the spirit. Stone pillars and tall iron gates mark the entrance: the setting is lovely. Bedrooms scented by fresh flowers are on the first floor up a staircase of white Caen stone with a wrought-iron handrail and balustrade. A landing with a view over the park is the perfect place to spread your newspaper on a lovely old table; bookshelves bursting with books line the length of one wall, family portraits line the corridors. Breakfast is taken in the dining room with painted scenes above the doors and a Louis XVI buffet displaying its collection of beautiful china plates.

Rooms	3 doubles, 2 twin/doubles: €90–€110.
Meals	Restaurants 2.5km.
Closed	Rarely.

Rooms	3 doubles: €110.
	1 suite for 4: €170.
Meals	Restaurants within 5km.
Closed	Rarely.

	Matteo Fabra
	Le Fresnay,
	2630 chemin d'Englesqueville,
	14340 Cambremer,
	Calvados
Mobile	+33 (0)6 89 82 95 40
Email	lefresnay@gmail.com

	Guy de Chabaneix
	Château du Mesnil d'O,
	14270 Vieux Fumé,
	Calvados
Tel	+33 (0)2 31 20 01 47
Email	lemesnildo@wanadoo.fr
Web	www.lemesnildo.com

Entry 179   Map 4

Entry 180   Map 4

Ferme de la Ruette

The gates glide open to a gravelled sweep and a tree'd lawn, with an old stone cider press to the side. Elegant, compassionate Isabelle looks after house, garden, guests — and rescue cats and horses — with warmth and charm; Philippe, a friendly GP, fills the game larder. The barn houses two bedrooms plus a delightful family suite under the rafters (up a steep private stair) and a cosy guest sitting room with a bar. Rooms have pretty striped wallpapers, seagrass floors and elegant Louis XV-style chairs, quirky objets on shelves and in crannies, beds dressed with white heirloom spreads. Vivacious, bustling Caen is an easy drive.

Château des Riffets

Period ceilings and parkland views make Riffets a gracious château experience. Admire yourself in myriad mirrors, luxuriate in a jacuzzi, bare your chest to a supersonic shower and lie, at last, in an antique bed. The walls of the huge hall and the galleried landing are an elegant foil for tapestries, plants and austere antique pieces. Wry Monsieur was a psychologist, gentle Madame an English teacher, and a fine breakfast is served at one big table. Take a stroll in the park, hire a nearby horse or a canoe, enjoy a lap in the pool. Caen's historic treasures are a ten-minute drive, Bayeux and Mont St Michel are an hour away.

Rooms	2 doubles: €60–€80.
	1 suite for 4 with kitchenette:
	€60–€80.
	Extra bed €10.
Meals	Restaurant 5km.
Closed	Rarely.

Rooms	2 doubles: €125–€175.
	2 suites for 2: €125–€175.
Meals	Restaurant 1km.
Closed	Rarely.

Isabelle & Philippe Cayé
Ferme de la Ruette,
5 chemin Haussé, 14190 Cauvicourt,
Calvados

Tel	+33 (0)2 31 78 11 82
Mobile	+33 (0)6 28 26 22 61
Email	laruette@gmail.com
Web	www.fermedelaruette.fr

Anne-Marie & Alain Cantel
Château des Riffets,
14680 Bretteville sur Laize,
Calvados

Tel	+33 (0)2 31 23 53 21
Mobile	+33 (0)6 14 09 74 93
Email	chateau.riffets@wanadoo.fr
Web	www.chateau-des-riffets.com

Entry 181   Map 4

Entry 182   Map 4

La Vieille Abbaye

In rural Calvados: a place for families to come and live the dream. Stephan and Kate are doing what they love best… running a modern dairy farm, caring for a menagerie of animals (miniature goats, horses, ponies) and opening their immaculate doors to guests. Roses climb the walls of the farmhouse, there's a play barn next door, swings and slides outside, and a dining room that's the heart of the house, a perfect place for breakfasts of free-range eggs laid by the family's hens, farm milk, local pastries and homemade butter and jams. Two opulent rooms wait upstairs, one with a super little kitchen and a romantic four-poster, and the other tailormade for families.

Minimum stay: 2 nights in high season.

Château de la Pommeraye

A big shuttered mansion (1646 with later additions) surrounded by meadows and woodland, this part-moated house is flanked by 12th-century towers and outbuildings. Your ex-Parisian hosts, a young family, give you perfect bedrooms – find handsome carpets on polished boards, vast beds heaped with pillows, a selection of pictures (oils, icons, engravings) and classic porcelain hand basins. Downstairs: pale painted wainscoting and moss-green velvet chairs, log fires and stone flooring. Spa, golf and riding breaks can be arranged, there's 'Suisse Normande' for rock climbing and canoeing, Caen for culture and shopping.

Rooms	1 four-poster: €100–€150. 1 family room for 4: €100–€150. Extra bed €10–€15. Cot available.
Meals	Dinner €20–€40; children €10. Restaurants 4km.
Closed	Rarely.

Rooms	4 twin/doubles: €175–€225. 2 suites for 2: €245–€295. Extra bed €40.
Meals	Breakfast €15. Restaurant 2-minute walk.
Closed	Rarely.

Kate Le Moigne
La Vieille Abbaye,
Rue de la Fromagerie,
14220 Barbery,
Calvados
Tel   +33 (0)2 31 78 31 48
Mobile   +33 (0)6 78 24 67 84
Email   katelemoigne@googlemail.com
Web   www.frenchfarmhouse.fr

Alexandre Boudnikoff
Château de la Pommeraye,
14690 La Pommeraye,
Calvados
Tel   +33 (0)2 31 69 87 86
Email   alexandre.boudnikoff@orange.fr
Web   www.chateaudelapommeraye.com

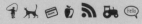

Entry 183   Map 4

Entry 184   Map 4

Château La Cour

Welcome to a 13th-century castle, once owned by the Ducs d'Harcourt, full of comfort and joy. There are Lloyd Loom chairs and marble fireplaces, one bedroom has a curved stair to a lavish bathroom, all are beautifully decorated and face the garden. Breakfast includes home-grown fruits, homemade yogurt and eggs from the château's hens, while English china, damask and candelabra grace the dinner table. David's potager is a wonder; Lesley's cooking is delicious. The Cravens are conservationists, too; barn owls nest in the end wall and the birdwatching is fabulous. Don't miss the Normandy beaches, or Bayeux.

Children over 12 welcome.

Le Gaudin

Shooting through the centre of this 18th-century farmhouse is a chimney of 4,500 bricks. Clive knows: he built it! Every feature conveys space, age and the care and creativity of your British hosts. Exposed stone walls; an old manger, now a wine rack; Denise's upholstered coffee table; a doll's house in the sunny breakfast room, and the long table at which guests gather for Clive's superb dinners. Deeply comfortable bedrooms have hand-sewn fabrics and fine French antiques. Fish the lake in the wooded grounds; join the ancient pilgrims' walk to Mont St Michel; go canoeing in nearby Thury-Harcourt. No wonder people return.

Rooms	3 doubles, 1 twin: €160.
Meals	Hosted dinner with wine, €35–€50.
Closed	November – February.

Rooms	3 doubles, 1 twin: €70–€90.
Meals	Dinner with wine, €38.
Closed	January – March.

David & Lesley Craven
Château La Cour,
14220 Culey le Patry,
Calvados
Tel   +33 (0)2 31 79 19 37
Email   info@chateaulacour.com
Web   www.chateaulacour.com

Clive & Denise Canvin
Le Gaudin,
Route d'Aunay,
14260 Campandré Valcongrain,
Calvados
Tel   +33 (0)2 31 73 88 70
Email   legaudin14@yahoo.co.uk
Web   www.legaudin.co.uk

Entry 185   Map 4

Entry 186   Map 4

Chez Laurence du Tilly

Laurence has a passion for cool, contemporary style – and good food. Her central 18th-century townhouse has an elegantly hip salon – honesty bar, open fire, Danish chairs, music – then, up ancient spiral stairs to a choice of three apartments. The first floor is classic in white offset by modern pieces; the second has stripped boards and funky designer pieces; the cosy under the eaves one has animal skin rugs, black parquet and a roof top terrace. Beds are well dressed, bathrooms snazzy, kitchens state-of-the-art. Fab food can be delivered to your table. The ferry port is close, and Caen is a great little city to explore on foot.

Parking on-site.

Château les Cèdres

This elegant 18th-century château on the edge of the pretty town of Bretteville l'Orgueilleuse has a friendly, family feel – owners Aude and Franck are raising four children here as well as welcoming guests. The three bedrooms on the first floor are airy and light, kilims and floorboards underfoot, beams overhead, white walls and minimal fuss, each with a stylish modern bathroom. Tall windows overlook the beautiful lawned gardens with space to roam or relax, perhaps with an apéritif from the honesty bar. Breakfast at the family table in the dining room is an ample array of French fare, ideal for fuelling forays into Normandy.

Rooms	1 apartment for 2, 2 apartments for 4: €150–€200. Extra bed €25. Cot & sofabed available.
Meals	Full breakfast €20. Dinner €25–€30. Restaurants 1-minute walk.
Closed	January/February.

Rooms	3 twin/doubles: €140–€180. Singles €125–€165.
Meals	Restaurants 2-minute walk.
Closed	Rarely.

	Laurence du Tilly Chez Laurence du Tilly, 9b rue pémagnie, 14000 Caen, Calvados
Mobile	+33 (0)7 86 23 28 28
Email	chez-laurence@dutilly.fr
Web	www.chez-laurence.dutilly.fr

	Franck de Saint Roman Château les Cèdres, 9 rue de Bayeux, 14740 Bretteville l'Orgueilleuse, Calvados
Mobile	+33 (0)6 13 14 91 23
Email	franckdeserre@aol.com
Web	www.chateau-les-cedres.fr

Entry 187   Map 4

Entry 188   Map 4

Ferme Manoir de Cacharat

Step through the magnificent arched porch to find a beautifully restored 17th-century manoir of majestic proportions. Here lives gentle Valerie. All is close by: D-Day beaches, 20 minutes; Caen and Bayeux, 15 minutes; and, in the restored stables, books, board games, sofas and a fire await your return. Bedrooms lie above, in an immaculate hayloft at the top of a spiral stair. Both have new beds, pale pine floors, restful colours, and overlook the garden or the quadrangle. There's an orchard at the back, outbuildings to the side, and a vast salon in the house, for bountiful breakfasts and delicious "assiettes gourmandes". Perfect peace prevails.

Parking on-site.

Rooms	1 double, 1 twin/double: €95. Extra beds available €20.
Meals	Dinner, with cider, €15. Restaurants 6km.
Closed	1 November to 1 April.

Valerie Gallouin
Ferme Manoir de Cacharat,
Rue de Cacharat,
14740 Secqueville en Bessin,
Calvados

Tel	+33 (0)2 31 08 17 83
Mobile	+33 (0)6 30 08 59 24
Email	valeriegallouin@gmail.com
Web	www.manoirdecacharat.fr

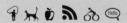

Entry 189   Map 4

La Malposte

It's just plain lovely, this little group of stone buildings with a wooden footbridge over the rushing river, ancient steps, moss, trees, a fine garden with flowers and hens. The age-old converted mill is for the family, the hunting lodge (and an enchanting annexe for four) is for guests. Patricia's talented decoration weaves nostalgia with designer tones; the spiral stair winds to an enchanting dayroom with guest kitchen and homemade preserves (superb fig jam); sun pours into the bedroom at the top. Woods for nut-gathering, beaches nearby, table tennis and that playful stream. Your hosts are sweet and love having families.

Rooms	2 doubles: €98. 1 family room for 3, 1 family room for 4: €118–€154. 1 annexe for 4: €154.
Meals	Guest kitchen. Restaurants 2km.
Closed	Rarely.

Patricia & Jean-Michel Blanlot
La Malposte,
15 rue des Moulins,
14470 Reviers,
Calvados

Tel	+33 (0)2 31 37 51 29
Email	jean-michel.blanlot@wanadoo.fr
Web	www.lamalposte.com

Entry 190   Map 4

Ferme Le Petit Val

Close to landing beaches, village markets, the Bayeux Tapestry and jolly Caen is this perfectly maintained and very French farmstead. Outside, shrubs, conifers and a profusion of flowers; inside, country comfort and handsome furniture. It's been in the family for six generations, all is immaculate and the Lesages look after you with an easy charm. Off a Frenchly wallpapered landing, with views of garden and pretty gravelled courtyard, are the two biggest and most characterful bedrooms. Expect good china and jams at breakfast's long tables, tourist brochures on the sideboard, mountain bikes to borrow.

Le Mas Normand

A fun place, warm and colourful, run with great charm by Mylène and Christian. They've done a fine job on their 18th-century house: old stonework and beams, super showers, a modern-rustic style, and Provençal fabrics and soaps from Mylène's native Drôme. Bedrooms are sheer delight: the sunny much-furnished double on the ground floor, the charming suite across the yard, filled with good pieces including an 'armoire de mariage'. The new family rooms? Two delightful fisherman's cabins in the garden, with great showers. Ducks, geese and hens roam; the beach is 300 yards. Generous and special.

Rooms	1 double: €63–€73.
	1 family room for 3: €63–€99.
	Barn – 1 double, 1 twin: €63–€73;
	1 family room for 3: €63–€99.
	Singles €59. Extra bed/sofabed
	available €26 per person per night.
Meals	Restaurants 3km.
Closed	December – March.

Rooms	1 double: €80–€90.
	2 family rooms for 4: €100–€160.
	Extra charge for pets.
Meals	Restaurants 5km.
Closed	Rarely.

Gérard & Anne Lesage
Ferme Le Petit Val,
24 rue du Camp Romain,
14480 Banville,
Calvados

Tel	+33 (0)2 31 37 92 18
Mobile	+33 (0)6 87 03 85 52
Email	fermelepetitval@wanadoo.fr
Web	www.ferme-le-petitval.com

Christian Mériel & Mylène Gilles
Le Mas Normand,
8 impasse de la Rivière,
14114 Ver sur Mer,
Calvados

Tel	+33 (0)2 31 21 97 75
Email	lemasnormand@wanadoo.fr
Web	www.lemasnormand.com

Entry 191   Map 5

Entry 192   Map 4

Les Glycines

This lovely couple are kindness itself, she softly spoken and twinkling, he jovial, talkative, utterly French. Having retired from farming, they moved into the heart of Bayeux. You can glimpse the cathedral spires from their house, once part of the old bishop's palace. Beyond the gates and the wisteria, the door opens to a lofty beamed living room rejoicing in good antiques and a monumental fireplace; through another is the kitchen. Up the ancient stone stairs are pretty bedrooms – immaculate bedding, pastel-tiled showers – that look quietly over a pocket-handkerchief garden. Delicious breakfasts, history all around, and no need for a car.

Clos de Bellefontaine

Come to be pampered and effortlessly spoiled at this elegant townhouse, a ten-minute stroll from the famous Tapestry. Bedrooms are chic and gracious with choice antiques, colours are mocha and white, floors polished parquet or seagrass. Choose the top floor for snugness and charm, the first floor for grandeur and space. With a walled garden and two handsome ground-floor salons – antiques, family photographs, help-yourself refreshments – to lounge around in, you'll not miss home. Carole's breakfasts, with homemade tarts, fruit compotes and cheeses, are the highlight of the stay.

Rooms	2 doubles: €69.
	1 family room for 3: €95.
	Singles €59.
Meals	Restaurant 50m.
Closed	Rarely.

Rooms	1 double, 1 twin: €135–€175.
	Extra bed/sofabed available €20 per
	person per night.
Meals	Restaurants nearby.
Closed	Rarely.

Louis & Annick Fauvel
Les Glycines,
13 rue aux Coqs,
14400 Bayeux,
Calvados

Tel +33 (0)2 31 22 52 32
Mobile +33 (0)6 89 39 84 79
Email louisfauvel@orange.fr

Carole & Jérôme Mallet
Clos de Bellefontaine,
6 rue de Bellefontaine,
14400 Bayeux,
Calvados

Mobile +33 (0)6 81 42 24 81
Email clos.bellefontaine@wanadoo.fr
Web www.clos-bellefontaine.fr

Le Petit Matin

You're on a residential street overlooking the Place Charles de Gaulle, a short walk from the astonishing 11th-century cathedral at the heart of this ancient town. Helpful Pascal has transformed his antique-filled handsome town house into a lovely place to stay with beautiful lawned gardens (for lazing in the shade or playing boules). Bedrooms are comfortable and elegant, full of space and light, each with their own smart modern bathroom – one on the ground floor has its own entrance and terrace. Breakfasts are a paean to the baker's art, with fruit, yoghurt, homemade jam and much more. Explore historic Bayeux.

Parking on-site.

La Tour Louise

Your hosts' warmth and enthusiasm for their new venture make this rather funky little place bang in the centre of town special. You can walk to everything, the cathedral tower peeps into the courtyard and Sandrine makes you delicious cakes. The elegant 1800s house with 1950s furniture has a garden for fine-weather breakfasts or aperitifs (possibly accompanied by tabby cat Gustave) and plenty of space in the living room. Up the lovely stone staircase, on the first and second floors, find four virtually identical bedrooms with a turquoise wall, soft grey wool retro chair and crisp white linen. Make sure you see the Bayeux tapestry.

Minimum stay: 2 nights in high season. Children over 6 welcome.

Rooms	4 doubles, 1 twin/double: €75-€140. Extra bed €50. Cot available.
Meals	Picnics available. Restaurants 5-minute walk.
Closed	Rarely.

Rooms	2 doubles: €95-€125. 2 family rooms for 3: €125-€155.
Meals	Restaurants 5-minute walk.
Closed	2 weeks in February & occasionally.

	Pascal Lebret
	Le Petit Matin, 9 Rue des Terres,
	Place Charles de Gaulle,
	14400 Bayeux, Calvados
Tel	+33 (0)2 31 10 09 27
Mobile	+33 (0)6 08 28 65 59
Email	lepetitmatin@hotmail.fr
Web	www.chambres-hotes-bayeux-lepetitmatin.com

	Sandrine Camus
	La Tour Louise,
	4 rue Tardif,
	14400 Bayeux,
	Calvados
Mobile	+33 (0)6 32 83 74 22
Email	contact@latourlouise.com
Web	www.latourlouise.com

Le Château

The château dates proudly from 1580; once, Emile Zola stayed here. In the yard, restored to tremendous shape and character as a garden area for guests, an arched barn houses three beamy bedrooms (admire astounding roof timbers through a trap window). Just beyond the flowering stone steps: a fourth room in a tiny cottage. They are country rooms, simple, elegant, traditional with toile fabrics and sweet antiques. Madame is a vibrantly warm, well-read and discreet person, who loves having guests and can discourse at fascinating length about the history. Dinner? It is fresh, delicious and washed down by pommeau, wine and calvados.

Ferme-Manoir de la Rivière

Breakfast by the massive fireplace may be oil lamp-lit on winter mornings in this 13th-century fortress of a former dairy farm, with its ancient tithe barn and little watchtower. Isabelle is proud of her family home, its flagstones worn smooth with age, its high vaulted stone living-room ceiling, its second-floor rooms, one narrow with a shower in a tower, another with exposed beams and *ciel de lit* drapes. Her energy boundless, she is ever improving her rooms, gives you homemade brioche and jam for breakfast and really good organic dinners – much supported by Gérard.

Rooms	2 doubles, 1 twin: €70-€85. 1 suite for 5: €70-€85.
Meals	Dinner with wine or cider, €35; children €20. Restaurants nearby.
Closed	December to mid-January.

Rooms	1 double: €70-€80. 2 triples: €95-€115.
Meals	Dinner with cider or wine, €27-€30.
Closed	Rarely.

Dominique Bernières
Le Château,
14450 Grandcamp Maisy,
Calvados
Tel   +33 (0)2 31 22 66 22
Email   dominiquebernieres@orange.fr
Web   perso.wanadoo.fr/
          alain.marion/gbindex.html

Gérard & Isabelle Leharivel
Ferme-Manoir de la Rivière,
14230 Géfosse Fontenay,
Calvados
Tel   +33 (0)2 31 22 64 45
Mobile +33 (0)6 81 58 25 21
Email   leharivel@wanadoo.fr
Web   www.lemanoirdelariviere.net

La Vimonderie

Sigrid's big country kitchen and crackling fire are the heart of this fine 18th-century granite house and you know instantly you are sharing her home: the built-in dresser carries pretty china, her pictures and ornaments bring interest to the salon and its Normandy fireplace, and she proudly tells how she rescued the superb elm staircase. A fascinating person, for years a potter in England, she has retired to France and vegetarian happiness; she loves to cook for guests. Bedrooms have colour, unusual antiques and original beams. Five acres of garden mean plenty of space for children and grown-ups alike. Great value.

Minimum stay: 2 nights.

Le Petit Ruisseau

In the hamlet of Le Douit is a 350-year-old house, rather grand with its own little turret, a delicious piece of Norman history. Linda's welcome is generous and warm, and her knowledge of World War Two second to none; her father-in-law was a renowned photo journalist and his black and white photos are captivating. There are books, antiques, squishy sofas too, and a kitchen with a big old Aga. Linda loves real food so her suppers and dinners reflect the seasons and you can eat under the old walnut tree in summer. All this, feather quilts, fresh flowers and deep mattresses, and a young garden backed by pastures – enchanting!

Rooms	2 doubles: €50–€60.
Meals	Dinner with wine, from €18.
	Light supper from €10.
	Picnics from €5. Guest kitchen.
Closed	January/February.

Rooms	1 twin/double: €70–€80.
Meals	Dinner with wine & coffee, €35.
	Light supper €17.50.
	Restaurants 4km.
Closed	Rarely.

Sigrid Hamilton
La Vimonderie,
50620 Cavigny,
Manche
Tel   +33 (0)2 33 56 01 13
Mobile   +33 (0)6 59 21 48 07
Email   sigrid.hamilton@googlemail.com
Web   www.lavimonderie.com

Linda Malindine
Le Petit Ruisseau,
9 chemin de L'Église,
50390 Biniville,
Manche
Tel   +33 (0)2 33 41 47 05
Email   lande.la@orange.fr
Web   www.normandybandb.co.uk

Ferme de Banoville

Sarah, Andy, and their two young children moved here four years ago. The aim is to be self-sufficient so they've planted a willow coppice and fitted solar panels. Down a bumpy track from the village, ringed by countryside, the rustic farmhouse and outbuildings huddle round an ancient oak and duck pond. At one end of the family home find three simple bedrooms (one en suite) and a guest salon/dining room where you breakfast: eggs from the hens, home-pressed apple juice, the usual pastries. Part of the fun of staying is joining your hosts for supper; perhaps lamb or duck raised on the farm. You can explore both coasts from here.

Manoir de Bellauney

Even the smallest bathroom oozes atmosphere through its *œil de bœuf*. The youngest piece of this fascinating and venerably ancient house is over 400 years old; its predecessor stood on the site of a monastery, the fireplace in the lovely Medieval bedroom carries the coat of arms of the original owners. To furnish the rooms, your ex-farmer hosts hunted out carved *armoires de mariage*, lace canopies, footstools – and hung tapestry curtains at the windows. They share their energy enthusiastically between this wonderful house, its small dense garden, and their guests. Sheer comfort among warm old stones.

Rooms	1 double, 2 doubles with separate bathroom: €59.
Meals	Dinner with wine & coffee, €19. Restaurants 5km.
Closed	Rarely.

Rooms	1 double: €70–€100. 3 suites for 3: €70–€120.
Meals	Restaurants 4km.
Closed	November – April.

	Sarah Beale Ferme de Banoville, 50260 Négreville, Manche
Tel	+33 (0)2 33 08 05 36
Email	banoville@gmail.com
Web	www.banoville.com

	Christiane & Jacques Allix-Desfauteaux Manoir de Bellauney, 50700 Tamerville, Manche
Tel	+33 (0)2 33 40 10 62
Email	manoirdebellauney@gmail.com
Web	www.bellauney.com

Bruce Castle

Live graciously — even if it's only for a stopover (Cherbourg is 15km away). The Fontanets are a charming and amusing couple and their 1914 neo-classical mansion is full of pretty antiques. From the restrained elegance of the hall a handsome white staircase sweeps up to big, serene bedrooms with garden and woodland views; oriental rugs and crystal chandeliers add another dash of luxury. Breakfast off white porcelain with antique silver cutlery in a charming dining room then retire to the elegant 'library' overlooking the gardens. In the 20-acre grounds are the ruins of an 11th-century castle… to stay here is a massive treat.

Manoir de la Fèvrerie

Your blithe, beautiful, energetic hostess is a delight, forever indulging her passion for interior decoration. Her exquisite rooms are a festival of colours, textures, antiques and embroidered linen. It's a heart-warming experience to stay in this wonderful old Normandy farmhouse where the great granite hearth is always lit and a breakfast of superb local specialities is served on elegant china; there is a richly carved 'throne' at the head of the long table. Find a deep courtyard at the entrance, a pretty garden behind; soft countryside surrounds you and Barfleur and the coast is a short drive.

Rooms	3 doubles: €110–€130.
Meals	Restaurant 8km. Simple bistro 3km.
Closed	Rarely.

Rooms	3 twin/doubles: €72–€80.
	Fifth night free (not July/August).
	Children's room available.
Meals	Restaurants 3km.
Closed	Rarely.

Anne-Rose & Hugues Fontanet
Bruce Castle,
13 rue du Castel, 50700 Brix,
Manche

Tel	+33 (0)2 33 41 99 62
Mobile	+33 (0)6 72 95 74 23
Email	bruce-castle@orange.fr
Web	www.bruce-castle.com

Marie-France Caillet
Manoir de la Fèvrerie,
4 route d'Arville,
50760 Ste Geneviève,
Manche

Tel	+33 (0)2 33 54 33 53
Mobile	+33 (0)6 80 85 89 01
Email	lafevrerie@orange.fr
Web	www.lafevrerie.fr

La Roque de Gouey

A fishing and sailing port and a bridge with 13 arches: a pretty place to stay. The enchanting *longère* is the home of two of our favourite owners: Madame, the same honest open character as ever and Monsieur, retired, who has time to spread his modest farmer's joviality. Your side of the house has its own entrance, dayroom and vast old fireplace where old beams and *tomettes* flourish. The bedrooms up the steepish outside stairs are small, with pretty bedcovers and antiques that are cherished, the ground-floor room is larger, and the breakfast tables sport flowery cloths. Brilliant value.

Manoir de Coutainville

Secluded rooms with views over rooftops and sparkling seas are a traveller's joy. Add a cultured hostess, delectable dining and a 15th-century manoir and you have a dash of French magic. Through pale stone arches serenity awaits, genteel apéritifs ushering in five-course dinners that showcase fish and seafood. Sophie Véron provides spare wellies and captivating conversation, her fashion career informs her calm interiors — a rare mix of charm and luxury — and history resonates through every sea-view room. Downstairs in the annexe find library armchairs and a scullery kitchen. Stroll to Coutainville, watch the sailing boats.

Rooms	2 doubles: €57. 1 family room for 3, 1 family room for 5: €75–€110.
Meals	Guest kitchen. Restaurants 500m.
Closed	Rarely.

Rooms	2 doubles, 1 twin with separate shower: €180–€270. 2 suites for 4: €240–€380. Extra bed/sofabed available €40 per person per night.
Meals	Dinner with wine, €58.
Closed	Rarely.

	Bernadette Vasselin La Roque de Gouey, Rue Gilles Poërier, 50580 Portbail, Manche
Tel	+33 (0)2 33 04 80 27
Email	vasselin.portbail@orange.fr

	Sophie Véron Manoir de Coutainville, 2 rue de la Maugerie, 50230 Agon Coutainville, Manche
Tel	+33 (0)2 33 47 05 90
Mobile	+33 (0)6 07 55 29 77
Email	sophie-veron@manoir-de-coutainville.com
Web	www.manoir-de-coutainville.com

Château de Chantore

Set in peaceful countryside and just 5km from the sea, this striking 18th-century château has been restored with great care by Bernard and Inaki. It is filled with startlingly bold colours, striking fabrics, fine paintings and antique pieces. Bedrooms have big canopied beds, marble fireplaces and spotless bathrooms with individual flourishes. You breakfast on fresh bread and apple cake from the local baker, honey from the estate hives and eggs from the chickens. Take the bikes for a spin, visit nearby seaside towns and discover bracing coastline before returning to supper on the terrace and a stroll through the grounds.

Parking on-site.

2 Le Bois de Crépi

Madame's welcome is as cheerful and bright as her bedrooms – and she loves to cook. The Gavards' immaculate 1980s house, resting in one pretty acre (lawns, roses, little footbridge over the pond) is the perfect stopover: near the autoroute yet truly tranquil. Borrow bikes and cycle the 'voie verte' to Mont St Michel or spend the day in St Malo. Then come home to friendly table d'hôtes and a great-value menu that reflects the seasons. There's a guest sitting room to retire to, with guide books, games, TV; and bedrooms are under the eaves, warm, simple, characterful, with brand new beds and flowers. Bathrooms gleam.

Rooms	2 doubles, 1 twin: €150–€205. 2 suites for 4: €225–€340. Extra bed/sofabed available £36 per person per night.
Meals	Restaurants 5km.
Closed	Rarely.

Rooms	2 family rooms for 4: €53–€58. Singles €48. Extra bed/sofabed available €12 per person per night. Under 3's free.
Meals	Dinner, 3 courses with wine, €20; children €10. Restaurants 1 km.
Closed	Rarely.

Bernard Legal
Château de Chantore,
50530 Bacilly,
Manche
Tel +33 (0)9 60 52 82 73
Email contact@chateaudechantore.com
Web www.chateaudechantore.com

Jean-Paul & Brigitte Gavard
2 Le Bois de Crépi,
Poilley, 50220 Ducey,
Manche
Tel +33 (0)2 33 48 34 68
Mobile +33 (0)6 65 31 99 99
Email jpgavard@club-internet.fr

La Maison Launay

It's the Barbieux who make this place special – they really are exceptionally warm people. Their pretty house is 18th century, faces south and has a large garden you're free to explore. This is simple B&B, with wellies, cagoules and maps on tap, homemade jams and brioche for breakfast and lots of books to read. There's a sitting room with a clic-clac sofa, a dining room with one big table, and three guest rooms upstairs. The twin with its doll's house is for children and the nicest is under the roof, light and airy with a balcony. Monsieur is a very keen cook, a big fan of Raymond Blanc and a whizz at pâtisserie: eat in.

Belle Vallée

Built in 1800, the tall house stands in acres of woods, pastures and landscaped gardens, with outbuildings (the owners' quarters) and cottage. Footpaths meander to a lovely walled orchard, the kitchen garden provides for table d'hôtes, the hens donate the eggs. Inside are corridors alive with books, five delightful bedrooms – vintage beds, polished floors, boudoir chairs, divine duvets – and an inviting sitting room with a log fire. In the panelled dining room, hospitable Richard and Victoria, both from the catering industry, serve continental breakfast at crisp tables. Domfront on its hill is wonderfully close.

Rooms	3 doubles: €62-€72.
Meals	Dinner, 4 courses with wine, €25-€30. Restaurants 10-minute walk.
Closed	Rarely.

Rooms	3 doubles: €70-€90. 2 quadruples: €100-€120. Extra bed €15.
Meals	Dinner, 4 courses with wine, €23. Restaurants 5-minute drive.
Closed	Rarely.

Joëlle Barbieux
La Maison Launay, Launay,
50140 St Clément Rancoudray,
Manche
Tel   +33 (0)2 33 50 92 99
Mobile   +33 (0)7 88 64 60 90
Email   lamaisonlaunay@gmail.com
Web   lamaisonlaunay.wix.com/
         lamaisondubocage

Victoria & Richard Hobson-Cossey
Belle Vallée,
61700 Domfront,
Orne
Tel   +33 (0)2 33 37 05 71
Email info@belle-vallee.net
Web   www.belle-vallee.net

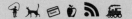

Orchard Gites

At Alison's rose-covered farmhouse, wrapped in bucolic views, you feel you're staying with family – and Fudge, the friendly terrier. Breakfasts, with homemade jams, are in the kitchen; the cosy sitting-room and garden are yours to share. The small simple bedroom under the eaves is colourful and homely, with a window at floor level through which the late afternoon sun pours, and you have a view of an apricot tree. Gardener-turned-artist Alison loves sharing her local knowledge and, on request, cooks delicious suppers from her 'potager'. Simple, unshowy, with a garden of quiet places in which to dream.

Pets by arrangement.

Manoir de Bénédicte

A really wonderful house, bursting with history and beautiful architecture. Bénédicte is warm, engaging and a delight to stay with, opening her home and also the impressive grounds in an informal, relaxed way. Light floods in to a rich red dining room with oak parquet floor and picture windows overlooking lawns and river; the salon is calming and has equally fine views; upstairs are lofty-ceilinged bedrooms with Persian rugs and family antiques. Breakfast is round the large table: freshly-squeezed orange juice, local cheeses, bread from the local bakery, homemade cakes and jams. Energetic walks abound – or just stroll the parkland.

Parking on-site.

Rooms	1 double with separate bathroom: €45–€50. Singles €40–€45.		Rooms	3 doubles: €125–€155. Extra bed €25.
Meals	Dinner €15.		Meals	Restaurants 3km.
Closed	Rarely.		Closed	End October to April.

Alison Smith
Orchard Gites,
La Foucaudiere,
61800 St Quentin les Chardonnets,
Orne
Tel   +33 (0)2 33 65 32 09
Email   alisonsmith@orange.fr
Web   www.orchardgites.lowernormandy.com

Bénédicte de Saint Pol
Manoir de Bénédicte,
Les Planches, 61430 Cahan,
Orne
Tel   +33 (0)6 74 13 17 49
Mobile   +33 (0)6 74 13 17 49
Email   xb.desaintpol@club-internet.fr
Web   www.lemanoirdebenedicte.fr/en/

Entry 211   Map 3

Entry 212   Map 4

Le Prieuré Saint-Michel

An atmospheric time warp for the night on the St Michel pilgrim route: traditional décor in the timbered 14th-century monks' storeroom with tapestry wall covering and antiques, or the old dairy, or a converted stable; a huge 15th-century cider press for breakfast in the company of the Ulrichs' interesting choice of art; a chapel for yet more art, a tithe barn in magnificent condition for fabulous receptions, perfectly stupendous gardens, a sort of medieval revival. Your hosts are totally devoted to their fabulous domain and its listed buildings and happy to share it with guests who appreciate its historical value.

La Louvière

Charming hostess Isabelle says the 18th-century manor house has "une ambiance de soie": a chandelier sparkles above lace tablecloths in the dining room, pale chintz dresses elegant windows in the sunny salon. Take an aperitif on the terrace, get sporty on the tennis court, and dream in the gardens, fragrant with roses, buzzing with bees, and fecund with potager crammed with vegetables and herbs. Inside, an oak staircase curves up to the bedrooms, daintily, exquisitely romantic, decorated with fine fabrics and antiques. Everything you could want is here: a heated pool, tennis court, small fishing lake, happiness and peace.

Rooms	2 doubles, 1 twin/double: €100-€115. 2 suites for 3: €120-€130. Singles €95-€105. Extra bed/sofabed available €15 per person per night.
Meals	Restaurant 4km.
Closed	Rarely.

Rooms	3 doubles; 1 double with separate private bathroom: €95-€160. 1 suite for 4: €190.
Meals	Dinner with wine & coffee, €39.
Closed	Rarely.

Jean-Pierre & Viviane Ulrich
Le Prieuré Saint-Michel,
61120 Crouttes,
Orne
Tel +33 (0)2 33 39 15 15
Email leprieuresaintmichel@wanadoo.fr
Web www.prieure-saint-michel.com

Isabelle & Alain Groult
La Louvière,
Le Fault,
61420 Saint Denis sur Sarthon,
Orne
Tel +33 (0)2 33 29 25 61
Email isabelle@louviere.fr
Web www.louviere.fr

Entry 213   Map 4

Entry 214   Map 4

Normandy

Les Larry

Just beyond the village of St Quentin de Blavou, this 19th-century farmhouse has long sweeping views across the valley and Norman countryside. Isobel is a bubbly Englishwoman who settled here in 2004; her Shetland and Connemara ponies keep her busy – she teaches, too – but she's still a hands-on hostess. The cosy double has a sloping roof and beams; use the second room, where the bed doubles as a divan, as your sitting room – or sit and chat with Isobel in hers. In fine weather you can breakfast on the terrace and drink in the view. Head out to the countryside for biking and hiking – the peace is divine!

Rooms	1 double, sharing bathroom with single: €55. 1 single, sharing bathroom with double: €45.
Meals	Restaurants 7km.
Closed	Rarely.

Isobel Jagger
Les Larry,
61360 St Quentin de Blavou,
Orne

Mobile	+33 (0)6 03 09 25 06
Email	chambresdhotesleslarry61360@gmail.com
Web	www.chambresdhotesleslarry61360.com

Brittany

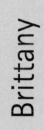

Château de Bézyl

At the end of a long drive on a 230-acre estate, a late 19th-century country manor restored with a flair for all things art deco, from light fittings to bespoke wallpapers. Owner Aly and her three dogs are often on hand to greet you. Revel in your huge room with bold colours, fine furnishings, views of the surrounding grounds, and modern, luxurious bathroom. Meals are taken together in either the dining room or at the kitchen table. Tuck in to fulsome breakfasts then head out to explore the grounds, visit the cathedral at Rennes or have a day on the beach. Return to the peace of your estate and a four-course dinner.

Parking on-site. Well-behaved dogs welcome.

Château du Pin

The small château with its pretty faded shutters is now inhabited by the Josses. Modern furniture rubs shoulders with brocante finds, bookshelves burst with books and art, bold red walls brighten up the salon where breakfast is served. Up to soft-hued bedrooms, their swathes of ruched silk clasped by tassels, their beds delicious with hand-painted headboards and luxurious covers. Outside: masses of park and woodland for children to roam. A light supper is available at separate tables: a platter of smoked salmon, a hot gratin – ideal for the first night. You're within easy reach of the Emerald coast, the gulf of Morbihan, Dinard and St Malo.

Helipad available.

Rooms	3 doubles: €140-€190. Extra bed €30.
Meals	Dinner €33; children €18. Bar snacks. Restaurants 7km.
Closed	November – March

Rooms	1 double, 2 twin/doubles: €88-€163. 2 family rooms for 4: €88-€163. 1 cottage for 4: €140. Extra person €29.
Meals	Breakfast €14. Dinner €29, on request. Wine €10-€30. Restaurant 5km.
Closed	Rarely.

Aly Roos
Château de Bézyl,
35550 Sixt Sur Aff,
Ille-et-Vilaine
Tel   +33 (0)2 99 70 10 31
Mobile   +33 (0)6 32 48 11 07
Email   info@chateaudebezyl35.com
Web   www.chateaudebezyl35.com

Marie France & Jean-Luc Josse
Château du Pin,
Route départementale 125,
La Veronnière, 35750 Iffendic,
Ille-et-Vilaine
Tel   +33 (0)2 99 09 34 05
Email   josse.jeanluc@free.fr
Web   www.chateau-pin.fr

Château du Quengo

Anne, descendant of an ancient Breton family, and Alfred, who is Swiss, are passionate about animals, gardens, music, life! They welcome you open-armed to their inimitable house: a private chapel, a bio garden, rare trees, 1800s wallpapers, a carved staircase, a mosaic'd floor. She runs willow-weaving classes and plies you with homemade delights; he builds organs; both love the slow life. Bedrooms have antique radiators and are properly old-fashioned, our favourite being the family room. No plastic anything, few mod cons, just intelligent, humorous hosts and a house steeped in atmosphere, beauty and peace.

Château de la Ballue

The formal gardens are listed and open to the public, a French reverie of paths and groves sprinkled with modern sculptures gazing over Mont St Michel. Baroque recitals may ring in the courtyard and Purcell odes float over marble fireplaces, antique paintings, gilded mirrors and orchids. This is no museum, however, but a family home enlivened by children. Sleep deeply in dreamy canopied beds, wake to silver cutlery and a fine continental spread in a blue-panelled breakfast room. Some bedrooms have tented *cabinets de toilette,* birds sing in the *bosquet de musique.* Baroque, family-friendly, enchanting.

Rooms	1 double: €82.
	1 suite for 5: €87.
Meals	Guest kitchen. Restaurants 1.5km.
Closed	Rarely.

Rooms	3 doubles: €210-€250.
	1 suite for 4: €260-€385.
	1 triple: €270-€290. Extra bed €40.
Meals	Breakfast €20. Restaurants 15km.
Closed	Rarely.

Anne & Alfred du Crest
de Lorgerie
Château du Quengo,
35850 Irodouër,
Ille-et-Vilaine
Tel   +33 (0)2 99 39 81 47
Email   lequengo@laposte.net
Web   chateauduquengo.free.fr

Marie-Françoise Mathiot-Mathon
Château de la Ballue,
35560 Bazouges la Pérouse,
Ille-et-Vilaine
Tel   +33 (0)2 99 97 47 86
Email   chateau@la-ballue.com
Web   www.la-ballue.com

Entry 218   Map 3

Entry 219   Map 3

Les Touches

In rolling countryside at the end of the track is an immaculately restored 350-year-old farmhouse. The setting? Three acres of beautifully tended gardens that fall to a babbling brook. In the stone barn are three pretty bedrooms — two cosily under dark beams, the third, for families, with a secluded courtyard aglow with roses and birdsong. Owners Sue and Jerry, full of beans, love hosting four-course table d'hôtes at their big rustic table. Swings, trampoline and smooth rocks for playing on, an above-ground pool for splashing in, and sofas, books and small log-burner for cosy nights in. Perfect.

Château de Mont Dol

An elegant, quietly sophisticated destination which will suit those who adore good food. The overall feel is one of unassuming good taste: find a large salon with chalky or exposed stone walls, an open fire, ecru and grey soft furniture and vases of hydrangeas — some gorgeous antiques too. Bedrooms are exquisite in a country style and with spick and span bathrooms. But you're here for the food — breakfasts of homemade yogurt, jams from the garden, croissants from the local bakery, and through the beautiful garden (low clipped box hedges, a fountain, gravel paths) you'll find the restaurant: a fixed menu, three courses, delicious.

Minimum stay: 2 nights at weekends & in high season.

Rooms	2 doubles: €75-€85. 1 family room for 4: €85-€121. Extra bed €18. Cot €10.
Meals	Dinner, 4 courses with wine, €35. Auberge 3km.
Closed	Rarely.

Rooms	4 doubles: €105-€119. 1 family room for 4: €149-€155. Singles €105-€115. Extra bed/sofabed available €25 per person per night. Dinner, B&B €96-€101 per person.
Meals	Dinner with wine, coffee & apéritif, €43. Restaurants 5-minute walk.
Closed	15 November to 2 February.

Sue & Jerry Thomas
Les Touches,
35420 St Georges de Reintembault,
Ille-et-Vilaine
Tel   +33 (0)2 99 17 09 91
Email   sue@lestouches.info
Web   www.lestouches.info

Yannick Goulvestre
Château de Mont Dol,
1 rue de la Mairie,
35120 Mont Dol,
Ille-et-Vilaine
Mobile +33 (0)6 24 31 87 49
Email   yannick.goulvestre@wanadoo.fr
Web   www.chateaumontdol.com

La Seigneurie

In a seaside town of wide sands and blue sea hides an 18th-century house in a church-side garden: Phillipe's B&B. Across the courtyard, in stable and barn, is the gorgeous sitting room: a minstrels' gallery, books, magazines, tapestries, an ornate chandelier... and smouldering embers scenting the air. Big bedroom suites are just as enchanting, one on the ground floor, another up private stairs. Fresh flowers and macaroons welcome you, antiques and silver coffee pots delight you, walls are in soft blues and greys, and breakfast arrives in wicker baskets stuffed with local and homemade treats. Seduction by the sea!

La Petite Ville Mallet

You can spot the sea before you arrive — at this traditional-but-new white-shuttered house on the edge of St Malo. Pet sheep and goats mow the grass and Monsieur's fruit garden spilleth over! Inside all is comforting and inviting and your retired hosts — proud descendants of the swashbuckling corsairs — are a joy to meet. Sun spills through French windows at breakfast, and elegant carpeted bedrooms have armchairs for relaxing cups of tea. Circle the ramparts of seafaring St Malo or 15th-century Dinan (small, exquisite), catch the ferry to Jersey or a boat to the isles off the Emerald Coast.

Rooms	1 double: €90.
	3 suites for 2-5: €95-€130.
Meals	Shared seafood platter with wine,
	€29-€58. Restaurants 300m & 7km.
Closed	Rarely.

Rooms	1 double: €85-€90.
	1 suite for 4: €140-€150.
	1 triple with separate bathroom:
	€100-€110.
Meals	Restaurants 3km.
Closed	Rarely.

	Françoise Busson
	La Seigneurie,
	35114 St Benoit des Ondes,
	Ille-et-Vilaine
Tel	+33 (0)2 99 58 62 96
Mobile	+33 (0)6 72 43 06 97
Email	contact@la-seigneurie-des-ondes.net
Web	www.la-seigneurie-des-ondes.net

	Joëlle & Henri-Pierre Coquil
	La Petite Ville Mallet,
	Le Gué,
	35400 St Malo,
	Ille-et-Vilaine
Tel	+33 (0)2 99 81 75 62
Email	lapetitevillemallet@orange.fr
Web	www.lapetitevillemallet.com

Entry 222   Map 3

Entry 223   Map 3

Brittany

Malouinière des Trauchandières

This handsome manoir in big peaceful gardens has been lovingly restored by Claude, who speaks six languages, and equally well-travelled Agnès; both are charming and friendly – to you and your dog. Theirs is a fascinating house dating from 1510, with French windows opening to a south-facing terrace and a salon lined with oak panelling; relax by the blazing fire. Bedrooms, comfortable, traditional and upstairs, are dominated by dark ships' timbers; the port of St Malo is close, so are golden sand beaches – perfect for woofy walks. Breakfast is served beneath the chandelier and there's an annual garden party in the grounds. Marvellous.

Dogs welcome free of charge.

Rooms	4 twin/doubles: €80–€100.
	1 suite for 4: €120–€130.
Meals	Hosted dinner with wine, €35.
	Restaurants in St Méloir,
	5-minute drive.
Closed	Rarely.

	Agnès François
	Malouinière des Trauchandières,
	Albiville, St Jouan des Guérets,
	35430 St Malo,
	Ille-et-Vilaine
Tel	+33 (0)2 99 81 38 30
Mobile	+33 (0)6 22 80 47 97
Email	agnesfrancois@hotmail.com
Web	www.les-trauchandieres.com

Entry 224   Map 3

Brittany

Les Mouettes

House and owner are imbued with the calm of a balmy summer's morning, whatever the weather. Isabelle's talent seems to touch the very air that fills her old family house (and smokers are not spurned!). Timeless simplicity reigns; there is nothing superfluous: simple carved pine furniture, an antique wrought-iron cot, dhurries on scrubbed plank floors, palest grey walls to reflect the ocean-borne light, harmonious gingham curtains. Starfish and pebbles keep house and little garden sea-connected, whimsical mobiles add a creative touch. The unspoilt seaside village, popular in season, is worth the trip alone.

Rooms	4 doubles, 1 twin: €55–€65.
Meals	Restaurants in village.
Closed	Rarely.

	Isabelle Rouvrais
	Les Mouettes,
	17 Grande Rue,
	35430 St Suliac,
	Ille-et-Vilaine
Tel	+33 (0)2 99 58 30 41
Email	contact@les-mouettes-saint-suliac.com
Web	www.les-mouettes-saint-suliac.com

Entry 225   Map 3

Manoir du Clos Clin

Monsieur found this ancient, grand farmhouse derelict and has lavished huge attention on it. He's done it immaculately, from re-roofing and installing geothermal underfloor heating, to creating smart, comfortable and historically themed bedrooms and bathrooms; the Louis XIII-style four-poster is exemplary. Formal family portraits hang in the huge living room – gen up on things local and play the piano. Fresh breakfasts come from the open-plan kitchen. Pedal the cycle path to Dinan; you're on the outskirts of Pleurtuit, a couple of miles from Dinard and can lounge peacefully in the lawned garden, or immerse yourself in the hedge maze.

La Vallée de la Rance

All is funky, bright and contemporary at smiling Hervé and Anne's apartments converted from a 19th-century longère and perfectly positioned on the shores of the estuary. Plenty of fun touches: a teacup light, amusing caricatures on the walls – just mind your head in the mezzanine double. Delicious breakfast served in a cheery dining room overlooking the Rance is a leisurely affair before everyone tumbles out for a swim in the pool. After crêpes with Anne's famous caramel beurre salé, St Malo yogurts, Breton cakes and butter, you might need a bit of exercise! A wonderful, friendly spot to stay en famille.

Rooms	3 doubles: €64-€150. 1 family room for 4: €112-€200. 10% discount for 2 nights; 20% for 3+ nights. Please see owners reservation page of their website to book and pay online.	Rooms	1 double: €80-€90. 2 suites for 4, 2 suites for 6: €80-€165. Extra person €20.
Meals	Restaurants 500m.	Meals	Dinner from €20.
Closed	Rarely.	Closed	Rarely.

	Guy Macquart de Terline Manoir du Clos Clin, Le Clos Clin, 35730 Pleurtuit, Ille-et-Vilaine		**Anne & Hervé Desert** La Vallée de la Rance, La Vallée, 22490 Plouer sur Rance, Côtes-d'Armor
Mobile	+33 (0)6 88 17 93 91	Tel	+33 (0)2 96 89 11 53
Email	gmacquart@orange.fr	Email	valleedelarance@gmail.com
Web	www.manoirclosclin.fr/ bedandbreakfast-stmalo/	Web	www.valleedelarance.com

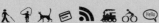

Entry 226 Map 3

Entry 227 Map 3

Le Clos Saint Cadreuc

Peace in a hamlet a pebble's throw from the coast, driving distance from ten golf courses (bring your clubs!) and a good stopover for St Malo. There's a welcoming atmosphere in this stone farmhouse, and colour and space in the living/dining room. The guest quarters are in the converted stables, comfortable, very French, with great walk-in showers and hotel-like extras; the bright airy family room is super and spacious. Your warm hosts put Breton dishes on your plate and pour organic wines; between house and stables is a pretty sheltered garden, for DIY barbecues and picnics.

La Belle Noë

Chantal is a dynamo of energy and artistic endeavour, loves animals (dog, cats, goats, donkeys), loves brocante, was a florist (flowers flow from the potager) and is full of smiles. Her charming 'longère' is immaculate inside and surrounded by pasture and gardens. After a day spent exploring chic Dinard, medieval Dinan or checking out the area's Michelin stars, what a pleasure to retreat to bedrooms with comfy mattresses, well-lit showers and little containers of biscuits and bonbons. As for breakfast, it's a marvel of homemade yogurts, pancakes, madeleines, compotes, cheeses and exquisite jams, served at gleaming tables.

Minimum stay: 2 nights on weekdays.

Rooms	2 doubles: €75.
	1 family room for 4: €80–€135.
	1 triple: €80–€100.
	1 quadruple: €75.
Meals	Dinner with wine, €28.
Closed	Rarely.

Rooms	5 doubles: €85–€115.
Meals	Restaurants 1.5km.
Closed	Rarely.

Brigitte & Patrick Noël
Le Clos Saint Cadreuc,
22650 Ploubalay,
Côtes-d'Armor

Tel	+33 (0)2 96 27 32 43
Mobile	+33 (0)6 82 14 94 66
Email	clos-saint-cadreuc@wanadoo.fr
Web	www.clos-saint-cadreuc.com

Chantal Bigot
La Belle Noë,
22130 Crehen,
Côtes-d'Armor

Tel	+33 (0)2 96 84 08 47
Email	belle.noe@wanadoo.fr
Web	www.crehen.com

Entry 228   Map 3

Entry 229   Map 4

Brittany

Manoir du Plessix-Madeuc

Glide through a tall wrought iron gate to find a quiet atmosphere at this ancient manor house. The Dupuys have created three apartments which are let to artists during the winter; here they host artistic soirées and exhibitions. Enter your apartment through the bottom of the tower; up steps find two large, lofty bedrooms: soaring beams, polished antiques; the connecting bathroom is old-fashioned but pristine; views are over the manicured garden. Breakfast is left for you outside your room – perfect independence. The small town nearby has remarkable remains of a Roman villa, and you're not far from miles of stunning coastline.

Parking on-site.

Rooms	1 apartment for 4: €95–€115.
Meals	Restaurants 3km.
Closed	Rarely.

Bérénice Dupuy
Manoir du Plessix-Madeuc,
Le Plessix-Madeuc, 22130 Corseul,
Côtes-d'Armor
Tel   +33 (0)2 96 27 99 57
Email berenicedupuy@gmail.com
Web   manoirduplessixmadeuc.com/
       le-plessix

Brittany

Le Manoir de la Villeneuve

Embraced by rolling lawns, wooded parkland and sweeping drive, this manor house seems untouched by the 21st century. Light airy pools of calm – high ceilings, tall windows, polished boards – are furnished with a contemporary elegance while plain walls, beams and tomette floors have been allowed to glow. Beautiful bedrooms have soothing colours, pretty antiques, delicious soaps, beams in some and sloping ceilings; the suite has a vast bathroom and its own salon. Breakfast handsomely at the convivial table, then explore Dinan, St Brieuc, the coast. Return for a dip in the new summer pool. Charming Nathalie oversees all.

Rooms	3 doubles, 1 twin/double: €70–€150.
	1 suite for 3: €130–€150.
Meals	Restaurant 2km.
Closed	Rarely.

Nathalie Peres
Le Manoir de la Villeneuve,
22400 Lamballe,
Côtes-d'Armor
Tel   +33 (0)2 96 50 86 32
Email manoirdelavilleneuve@wanadoo.fr
Web   www.chambresaumanoir.com

Manoir de Coat Gueno

The 15th-century, country-cocooned manor house, close to fishing ports, headlands and long sandy beaches, is a treasure. Beautifully restored over decades, every detail has been considered yet Christian is not so precious that he stops the blue tits nesting in a nook in the stone work! The salon's 'lit clos' is a treat, as is the vast stone fireplace, crackling with logs in winter. Gaze from a florally furnished suite onto the lawns below, enjoy the splashing of the pool or the crack of the billiards. The games room and the charming cottage (with its own fire) are in the grounds, and your host is the perfect French gentleman.

Children over 7 welcome if they can swim.

Manoir d'Hôtes de Troëzel Bian

A finely restored, peaceful old farmhouse, the manor is warm and comfortable. Your hosts, a chatty Franco-British couple of former scientists are loving their new life as B&B owners; founts of local knowledge they will point you expertly to what to do and see — even starting you off on the coastal path or giving you a guided tour of Tréguier cathedral. Their gourmet dinners feature organic and home-grown produce with some twists on traditional French cuisine. With its suite-like bedrooms upstairs, two sitting rooms, original stone fireplace, a wood stove and lots of garden, this is a place to relax after your days exploring a beautiful part of the Breton coast.

Rooms	2 suites for 2-4: €110–€170. 1 cottage for 2: €100–€170. 10% discount on stays of 6+ nights; 20% discount on stays in May/June.	Rooms	4 twin/doubles: €85–€95. Singles €75–€85. Extra bed/sofabed available €20–€30 per person per night.
Meals	Restaurants 4km.	Meals	Dinner, 3 courses with wine, €30. Restaurants 10-minute walk.
Closed	September – April.	Closed	Rarely.

	Christian de Rouffignac		Armelle & Tony Sébilleau
	Manoir de Coat Gueno,		Manoir d'Hôtes de Troëzel Bian,
	Coat Gueno,		Troëzel Bian,
	22740 Pleudaniel,		22610 Kerbors,
	Côtes-d'Armor		Côtes-d'Armor
Tel	+33 (0)2 96 20 10 98	Tel	+33 (0)9 52 61 47 36
Email	coatguen@aol.com	Email	ctrobian@gmail.com
Web	mapage.noos.fr/coatgueno	Web	www.troezelbian.com

Entry 232   Map 2

Entry 233   Map 2

Manoir de Kerguéréon

Such gracious hosts with a wonderful sense of humour: you feel you are at a house party; such age and history in the gloriously asymmetrical château: tower, turrets, vast fireplaces, low doors, ancestral portraits, fine furniture; such a lovely garden, Madame's own work. Up the spiral stone staircase are bedrooms with space, taste, arched doors, a lovely window seat to do your tapestry in, good bathrooms; and the great Breton breakfast can be brought up if you wish. Apéritifs among the roses, breakfast before the crackling fire; their son breeds racehorses on the estate and their daughter-in-law runs the B&B. Sheer delight.

Toul Bleïz

There may be badgers and wild boar on the moors but civilisation is a five-minute drive – and you breakfast when you want to in a courtyard trilled by birds. Julie offers 'painting with picnics' and Jez concocts delicious vegetarian dishes for your supper (take these 'en famille' or in private by the summerhouse). This is an enchanting Breton cottage with French windows pouring light into a snug ground-floor bedroom with a patchwork quilt and lace pillows, armchairs, barbecue and summerhouse kitchenette, and an outdoor deck with lavender and sweeping views – what better place for an apéritif! The village is delightful, the Abbey de Bon Repos is near. Flexible, and great value.

Rooms	1 double, 2 twins: €120. Singles €80. Extra bed €30.
Meals	Restaurants 7km.
Closed	Rarely.

Rooms	1 double: €75.
Meals	Vegetarian dinner with wine, 2 courses, €22. Picnic available. Summerhouse with kitchenette & BBQ.
Closed	Rarely.

Arnauld de Bellefon
Manoir de Kerguéréon,
Ploubezre, 22300 Lannion,
Côtes-d'Armor

Tel +33 (0)2 96 38 80 59
Mobile +33 (0)6 03 45 68 55
Email arnaud.debellefon@nordnet.fr
Web www.de-bellefon-arnaud.e-
monsite.com

Julie & Jez Rooke
Toul Bleïz,
22570 Laniscat,
Côtes-d'Armor

Tel +33 (0)2 96 36 98 34
Mobile +33 (0)6 88 57 75 31
Email jezrooke@hotmail.com
Web www.phoneinsick.co.uk

Manoir de Kerledan

Everyone loves Kerledan, its gargoyles, its sophisticated theatrical décor, its owners' enthusiasm. Peter and Penny have made it stunningly original. Sisal and unstained oak, limed walls, the odd splash of antique mirror or gilded bergère with fake leopard skin create a mood of luxury and calm; stone-floored bathrooms are delicious, candlelit, cut-glass dinners are legendary. Sit by the great dining room fire, stroll in the lovely gardens (baroque courtyard, palisade hornbeam allée, potager), lounge in antique linen in a perfect bedroom and let yourself be pampered by your hosts: arrive as strangers, leave as friends.

Kergudon Chambres d'Hôtes

On the outskirts of tiny Saint Cadou is a 17th-century presbytery flanked by two houses, a place of serenity and charm. Ben and David, generous to a fault, have created four immaculate gîtes at the end of the lane... and if you're a couple, you can do B&B. Choose between 'Hayloft' (kitchen, log-burner, sweet sunny garden) and 'Stable', an adorable studio with sliding doors to its own patio. Eggs Breton, porridge, fresh continental, full English — whichever breakfast you go for it'll be delicious, and delivered to your door. Fly-fish at lovely Lake Drennec (a 10-minute stroll) or hop on the bikes and cycle the *Voie Vert*.

Minimum stay: 3 nights in high season. Pets by arrangement.

Rooms	2 doubles, 1 twin/double: €90–€115. 1 family room for 4: €110–€155
Meals	Dinner, 2-3 courses, €23–€28. Wine from €5.
Closed	Mid-November to March.

Rooms	2 apartments: €80–€90. Cot available.
Meals	Dinner, 3 courses, €70. Restaurants 3km.
Closed	Rarely.

Peter & Penny Dinwiddie
Manoir de Kerledan,
Route de Kerledan,
29270 Carhaix Plouguer,
Finistère
Tel +33 (0)2 98 99 44 63
Email kerledan@gmail.com
Web www.kerledan.com

Ben Dickins
Kergudon Chambres d'Hôtes,
Hent Gorreker,
29450 Saint Cadou,
Finistère
Tel +33 (0)2 98 24 16 98
Email ben@kergudon.com
Web www.kergudon.com

Entry 236 Map 2

Entry 237 Map 2

Un Balcon sur la Mer

Pop over to Roscoff to this historic 16th-century merchant's house with its cosy salons, exquisite Art Nouveau staircase, nautically-themed rooms and light, bright bathrooms. Charming Parisians Françoise and Jean-Michel have created an elegant and enchanting home, where the waves crash against the back wall and a deluge of fresh coastal light washes in through the windows. Continental breakfast with sea views sets you up for a day wandering cobbled streets, browsing shops or simply hunkering down with a book in front of the fire. Parking's tricky so come on foot: walk, cycle, take a trip to car-free Île de Batz.

Domaine de Moulin Mer

Bordeaux shutters against white-washed walls, graceful steps rising to the front door, attendant palm trees… Stéphane has restored this manor house to its full glory. The luxurious rooms are a masterly combination of period elegance and tasteful minimalism, the gardens a riot of shady trees – olives, palms, eucalyptus and mimosas. Across the road you can glimpse the waters of the estuary and a fine old mill. Stéphane, who used to work in Dublin, is an amusing, genial host and a collector of furniture and art. He will cook you (according to availability and his whim) an inventive dinner using fresh local produce.

Rooms	1 double: €100–€180.
	1 suite for 3: €100–€180.
	Extra bed €30.
Meals	Restaurants 2-minute walk.
Closed	November to mid-March.
	Open Christmas & New Year.

Rooms	2 doubles: €80–€110.
	2 suites for 2: €120–€150.
Meals	Dinner €35. Wine from €10.
Closed	Rarely.

Françoise & Jean-Michel Brochet
Un Balcon sur la Mer,
23B Place Lacasse Duthiers,
29680 Roscoff,
Finistère

Mobile   +33 (0)6 87 72 96 36/
           +33 (0)6 07 10 86 61
Email   contact@unbalconsurlamer.fr
Web   www.unbalconsurlamer.fr

Stéphane Pécot
Domaine de Moulin Mer,
34 route de Moulin Mer,
29460 Logonna Daoulas,
Finistère

Tel   +33 (0)2 98 07 24 45
Email   info@domaine-moulin-mer.com
Web   www.domaine-moulin-mer.com

Entry 238   Map 2

Entry 239   Map 2

Manoir de Kerdanet

Irresistible cakes, savouries, fruits and teas are served in a salon with a vast granite fireplace and logs that flicker at the first sign of cold weather. Off a country road, down an alley of trees, and there it is, a beautiful manor house 600 years old, lived in and loved by urbane hosts with a talent for making you feel instantly at home. A spiral stone staircase leads to authentic and timeless bedrooms, comfortable with crisp sheets and woollen blankets, coordinated furnishings and dark Breton antiques. Walkers and sailors will love the coast… watch out for the regattas at Douarnenez!

Cottage for 2 also available.

La Ferme de Kerscuntec

In the bucolic heart of the country, yet close to white sand beaches, the 17th-century cider farm has become a heavenly B&B. Elegant bedrooms are fresh and calming, one with its own decked terrace; the garden is prolific, Anne is creative and humorous, breakfasts are exceptional: wake to muffins and hedgerow jams. Tempting confections are displayed in glass jars for guests to enjoy, zinc pots are stuffed with flowers, bathrooms are for lingering in, sparkling windows frame the fields. Visit the fishing boats in Sainte Marine harbour and the grand shops of Quimper, set off for the islands. Seafood restaurants abound.

Minimum stay: 2 nights.

Rooms	2 doubles: €114.
	1 suite for 4: €134-€194.
Meals	Restaurants 5km.
Closed	Mid-October to mid-May.

Rooms	5 doubles: €85-€140.
	Singles €90-€150.
Meals	Restaurant 2km.
Closed	Rarely.

Sid & Monique Nedjar
Manoir de Kerdanet,
29100 Poullan sur Mer,
Finistère
Tel   +33 (0)2 98 74 59 03
Email manoir.kerdanet@wanadoo.fr
Web   www.manoirkerdanet.com

Anne & Bruno Porhiel
La Ferme de Kerscuntec,
Kerscuntec, 29120 Combrit,
Finistère
Tel   +33 (0)2 98 51 90 90
Mobile +33 (0)6 86 99 78 28
Email   contact@lafermedekerscuntec.fr
Web   www.lafermedekerscuntec.fr

Entry 240   Map 2

Entry 241   Map 2

Brittany

Château de Penfrat

You can ride or hike freely around 100 hectares of forested parkland, and watch birds on the banks of the Odet. As for the château – it's a tall handsome hunting lodge built by eccentric nobles, now owned by Patrick and Barbora. Enjoy life's simple pleasures: a good book, an easy chair, light jazz, crêpes at breakfast with chèvre frais, and an apéro before dinner (come winter) with your hosts. There's a retro feel to the salons, and a sunny feel to the bedrooms: tall windows, low beds, candlelit baths. Explore the fish markets of Quimper, the tall ships of Locronan, the artists' village of Pont-Aven. Then back for a delicious massage.

Rooms	1 double: €95–€115.
	1 suite for 3, 1 suite for 4:
	€130–€180.
Meals	Dinner €3; not in summer.
	Wine €8–€20. Restaurant 5km.
Closed	1 December to 15 January.

Barbora Kairyte & Patrick Viossat
Château de Penfrat,
25 chemin de Penfrat,
29950 Gouesnach,
Finistère
Mobile +33 (0)6 33 33 37 63
Email   info@penfrat.fr
Web   www.penfrat.fr

Entry 242   Map 2

Brittany

Tregont Mab

There's a faded elegance about this 16th-century stone manor with its lingering smell of woodsmoke and grand features that whisper its fine heritage. Up a spiral staircase find – 'Anne de Bretagne', a two-bedroomed suite for three with separate bathroom, and 'Les Cordeliers', for two, with en suite. Both are unfussy yet inviting. Breakfast is a treat in front of a crackling fire: fresh breads, pastries, local honey. Mme Voisard will gladly give you the grand tour, or you can wander free-range: find the little chapel in the grounds, cosy-up in the guest salon, explore the forest. Bustling Quimper and the coast are close.

Minimum stay: 2 nights.

Rooms	1 double: €85–€110.
	1 suite for 3 with separate bath:
	€85–€125.
Meals	Restaurants 1km.
Closed	Rarely.

Mai Voisard
Tregont Mab,
Chemin de Tregont Mab,
29000 Quimper,
Finistère
Mobile +33 (0)6 87 35 19 85
Email   contact@tregontmab.fr
Web   www.tregontmab.fr

Entry 243   Map 2

Brittany

Histoire de...

At the edge of a small village and surrounded by fields, this blue-shuttered longère is just the place to recharge your batteries. Charming Sophie is on hand to welcome you and – seeing as you're the only guests – can give you her full attention. Your ground floor bedroom is pleasant, spacious and thoughtfully furnished, with your shower room and loo just a few steps down the corridor. Start your day with a breakfast of organic produce at the kitchen table before heading out on a bike ride or a trip to historic Quimper. Once you're back, find a spot in the garden and sit with the cat at your feet and a book in your hand.

Rooms	1 double with separate bathroom: €85. Extra bed available €10.
Meals	Dinner, 3 courses, €25. Restaurants 5km.
Closed	Rarely.

Sophie Lucas-Robic
Histoire de...,
Kerunon, 56520 Guidel,
Morbihan

Tel	+33 (0)9 67 11 59 60
Mobile	+33 (0)6 71 96 34 42
Email	ssophss2@yahoo.com
Web	histoirede-chambresdhotes.fr

Brittany

Talvern

Steamer trunks and leather club chairs, deep-set windows and hefty beams, a family to greet you and Patrick's great food: welcome to an escape by the sea. Patrick was a chef in Paris (note the fine potager), Christine is the talent behind the quietly original bedroom décor (hemp, seagrass, organic colours) and the farmhouse once belonged to the château. There are walks in the woods and good cycling nearby, you are well placed for Vannes and the Gulf of Morbihan yet the coastal inlet is five minutes away. Separated from the road by a grassy courtyard, the wall encloses a sunny terrace on which children may play,

Pets by arrangement.

Rooms	2 doubles, 1 twin/double: €71-€84. 2 suites for 4: €123-€128. Extra bed/sofabed available €20 per person per night.
Meals	Dinner with wine, €27.
Closed	Rarely.

Patrick Gillot
Talvern,
56690 Landévant,
Morbihan

Tel	+33 (0)2 97 56 99 80
Mobile	+33 (0)6 16 18 08 75
Email	talvern@chambre-morbihan.com
Web	www.chambre-morbihan.com

Les Chaumières de Kerimel

The standing stones of Carnac are minutes away, beaches, coastal pathways and golf course close by. Kerimel is a handsome group of granite farm buildings in a perfect setting among the fields. Bedrooms are simple beauties: plain walls, some panelling, patchwork bedcovers and pale curtains, old stones and beams. The dining room is cottage perfection: dried flowers hanging from beams over a wooden table, a spring fire in the vast stone fireplace, breakfasts from grand-mère that promise an organic treat each day. A gentle, generous young family with excellent English, and passionately eco minded.

Minimum stay: 2 nights in high season. Pets by arrangement.

14 Kerpunce

Catherine and Régis' infectious joie de vivre – and boating in particular – is a real tonic. Widely travelled, they love to share their chosen region and cheerful, modern home. It's full of colour and maritime references; in a quiet hamlet four kilometres from the bustle of La Trinité-sur-Mer. The first-floor guest area a simple, spacious, jaunty retreat. Régis can skipper you aboard his two-masted ketch, to explore the lovely Golfe de Morbihan. Good French breakfasts have the added bonus of freshly baked bread and *galettes de blé noir*, home-laid eggs and a view of the south-facing garden; fields and woods beyond. Very easy and friendly.

Rooms	2 twin/doubles: €88–€98. 3 triples: €103–€113.
Meals	Crêpes supper with cider, €20. Restaurants 3km.
Closed	March – May & October/November.

Rooms	1 suite for 2: €80. 2 extra doubles, €70; let to same party only: sharing suite's bathroom. Whole house available on self-catering basis in summer; contact owner for details.
Meals	Restaurants 2.5km.
Closed	Rarely.

Nicolas Malherbe
Les Chaumières de Kerimel,
9 Kerimel,
56400 Ploemel,
Morbihan
Mobile +33 (0)6 83 40 68 56
Email chaumieres.kerimel@wanadoo.fr
Web www.chambres-kerimel.com

Catherine Ricquier & Régis Lobrichon
14 Kerpunce,
56950 Crach,
Morbihan
Mobile +33 (0)6 99 08 59 94 /
(0)6 43 62 36 32
Email cathricquier@yahoo.fr
Web www.monescaleenmorbihan.fr

Lueur des îles

A contemporary eco-build carved into a pine clad hillside smack in the middle of the Gulf of Morbihan and its National Park – only 300m from the sea. The friendly Jégous are thoroughly Breton and give you breakfasts of homemade pastries, breads, yogurts and jams (and organic eggs, ham and cheese if you wish). You'll find a high glazed living space with a huge modern fireplace, driftwood sculptures, decorative shells and pebbles. Nothing jars: colours are calm, paint is natural, white linen-clad beds are wide and deep, bath/shower rooms are well-designed and spacious. Come for all this and a heated pool, sauna and jacuzzi.

Parking on-site. Minimum stay: 2 nights.

Les Dames de Nage

Philippe has transformed this Breton farmhouse into an indulgent retreat; perfectly positioned between medieval Vannes, the Gulf of Morbihan and the wild Quiberon coast. A born host, you'll find him cultured and discreet. 'La Victoria' and 'La Vasa' (with a private terrace) are on a separate wing. Each has a big window, sparkling bathroom and seriously comfortable bed. A delicious, local breakfast is served in the glass atrium overlooking the vibrant flower gardens. There's a gym, indoor pool, and spacious guest lounge with games and TV. While away hot days lazing on the wooden deck with cooling dips in the outdoor pool.

Rooms	5 doubles: €98–€150.
	Sauna €10; jacuzzi €20.
Meals	Restaurants 10-minute walk.
Closed	Occasionally in winter.

Rooms	1 double: €98–€149.
	1 suite for 2-3: €98–€149.
	Extra beds available at no charge.
Meals	Restaurants 3km.
Closed	Rarely.

	Lionel Jégou
	Lueur des îles,
	39 rue du Lenn,
	56870 Baden,
	Morbihan
Email	lueur-des-iles@orange.fr
Web	www.lueur-des-iles.com

	Philippe Rabet
	Les Dames de Nage,
	Rescorles,
	56390 Grand-Champ,
	Morbihan
Mobile	+33 (0)6 40 88 23 60
Email	prabet@orange.fr
Web	www.lesdamesdenage.com

Maison de la Garenne

Ditch the car and dart down a side street to this impressively elegant townhouse – a secluded eyrie with luscious views of the public gardens and the old city ramparts. Sweep up the stairs (past Antoine and Christine's parents' quarters) to refined bedrooms each with a peaceful garden theme and views over the charming garden. Find the soft tones of the 19th century plus antiques, and the rich colours of the orient. Bathrooms are a treat – note the amusing portable bidet! Sip coffee from classy china in the breakfast salon, then stroll into Vannes to explore its historic harbour. Return home to evening sun in a cosy wee salon.

Pets by arrangement.

Domaine de Coët Bihan

Close to beautiful, medieval Vannes, Jantine and Jacques' house lies in undulating country where horses graze and clematis clambers. Light-filled bedrooms, the most luxurious on the first floor, are crisp and comfy with pukka linen and top-class showers. Feast on crêpes before setting off for walks and climbs and, from the top of wooded summits, views over the Gulf of Morbihan. Then a nap in the enclosed garden or an espresso in the tiny salon. If you're enjoying the indoor pool too much to be tempted by a local Michelin-starred restaurant (there are two), Jantine will make you a tasty platter.

Rooms	2 doubles, 1 twin: €95–€132. 1 family room for 4: €115–€178. Singles €83–€139. Extra bed/sofabed available €18 per person per night.
Meals	Restaurant 100m.
Closed	Rarely.

Rooms	4 doubles: €90–€105. Extra bed €15.
Meals	Cold platter €12–€20. Restaurants 4km. Kitchen & BBQ available.
Closed	Rarely.

Antoine & Christine Goursolas
Maison de la Garenne,
2 rue Sébastien de Rosmadec,
56000 Vannes,
Morbihan
Tel   +33 (0)2 97 67 00 31
Email   contact@maisondelagarenne.com
Web   www.maisondelagarenne.com

Jantine Guégan-Helder
Domaine de Coët Bihan,
Lieu-dit Coët Bihan, Monterblanc,
56250 Vannes,
Morbihan
Tel   +33 (0)2 97 44 97 22
Mobile   +33 (0)6 20 42 42 47
Email   domainedecoetbihan@gmail.com
Web   www.chambredhotes-vannes.fr

Entry 250   Map 3

Entry 251   Map 3

La Chaumine

This traditional 18th-century Breton farmhouse has stacks of character and sits in rolling countryside, just minutes from fine beaches. Friendly, enthusiastic hosts decamped from London to set up snug bedrooms under the eaves in nautical blue and white. A fresh, open living space downstairs with lofty beams, a huge granite fireplace, comfy sofas and a baby grand. Borrow bikes (excellent cycle routes) and kayaks and make for the glorious coastline; forage for oysters, take a ferry to tiny offshore islands. Nearby La Roche-Bernard has chic boutiques and eateries; there's a relaxing garden and small overground pool to come home to.

Parking on-site.

Préméhan

A place to unbend. Paul (ex-builder, blues musician) and Diana (florist with a good eye for furniture) are fuss-free hosts with a passion for their restored home and lots of local know-how. They feed you on stuff from their veg patch or nearby – do try the local cider – and can point you to local fêtes and markets. The south-facing house, spacious and light, has oak floors and beams and is filled with flowers, traditional French country furniture, old lamps, rugs, pictures and photos – all given a delightful edge thanks to son Joe's funky lighting. Nod off virtuously on a thick mattress with good linen – wake to birdsong.

Parking available.

Rooms	2 doubles: €60–€70.
	1 family room for 4: €70–€120.
Meals	Restaurants 5-minute drive.
Closed	Rarely.

Rooms	1 double; 1 double with separate disabled shower room; 1 double with separate shower room: €70–€75. 1 family room for 4: €85–€128. Extra bed €25.
Meals	Dinner with wine & coffee, €28. Restaurants 5 km.
Closed	Rarely.

Steve & Lisa Gosling
La Chaumine,
Kerbrochant, Cipry, Marzan,
56130 La Roche-Bernard,
Morbihan

Mobile +44 (0)7795 424979
Email chaumine56130@outlook.com
Web www.lachaumine-marzan.com

Paul & Diana Cowley
Préméhan,
56350 Allaire,
Morbihan

Tel +33 (0)2 99 72 69 99
Email paulcowleybluesman@gmail.com
Web www.premehan.com/index.html

Photo: Château de Chambiers,
entry 283

Western Loire

Château de Coët Caret

Come for a taste of life with the French country aristocracy – it's getting hard to find; the family have lived here for 13 generations. Gwénaël greets you on arrival and is on hand when needed. The château is tucked into the woods and 100 hectares of parkland with plenty of paths for wandering: serenity is guaranteed. Bedrooms are lived-in but comfortable; *Saumon*, under the eaves, comes with binoculars for the birds. Start the day with excellent bread, jams and coffee in the wonderful breakfast room. Gwénaël is full of tips and you are in the Brière Regional Park where water and land are inextricably mingled and wildlife abounds.

Le Manoir des Quatre Saisons

Welcome to a manoir with a fascinating history, and a delightful and attentive host. Jean-Philippe offers swimming robes and drinks by the pool on summer days, and leisurely breakfasts at the big table with eggs and cereals as well as local choices. Recently refreshed rooms (some in two-storey cottages in the grounds, some with kitchens, some with sea views) are colourfully co-ordinated with a traditional feel – stripes, patterns, French flourishes; little dishes of local fudge are a lovely extra. Beach, river and town are walkable but children (and dogs) will love romping in the garden with its many secret corners.

Minimum stay: 2 nights July / August & bank holiday weekends.

Rooms	3 doubles, 1 twin: €85–€120.
Meals	Restaurants 2-10km.
Closed	Rarely.

Rooms	3 doubles, 1 twin: €75–€95.
	1 quadruple: €95–€105.
	Extra bed €20.
Meals	Restaurants 1.5km.
Closed	Rarely.

Gwénaël de La Monneraye
Château de Coët Caret,
44410 Herbignac,
Loire-Atlantique

Tel	+33 (0)2 40 91 41 20
Email	coetcaret@gmail.com
Web	www.coetcaret.com

Jean-Philippe Meyran
744 bd de Lauvergnac,
44420 La Turballe,
Loire-Atlantique

Tel	+33 (0)2 40 11 76 16
Mobile	+33 (0)6 87 33 43 86
Email	manoirdes4saisons@gmail.com
Web	www.le-manoir-des-quatre-saisons.com

Entry 254   Map 3

Entry 255   Map 3

Villa La Ruche

Benoit's carefully restored 1903 villa is three minutes' walk from the famous beach of La Baule, at the peaceful end of the bay. Its swimming pool takes up most of the palm-fringed courtyard and its rooms – ground floor 'Les Pins', the biggest – are classy in an old-meets-new way: bold modern wallpaper, polished, original floorboards, local art. Bathrooms are generous, and striking – one's very New York 20s, another is lined with huge marble tiles. Breakfast jams and cakes are a homemade treat in the conservatory; the salon has an open fire, books, games, hot drinks. Your charming host, passionate about La Baule, will guide you.

Parking available: very quiet street.

Château de Cop-Choux

Where to start: the elegant house built just before the French Revolution (with later towers), the 18-hectare park, the pool, the rolling lawns? Or the 17 marble fireplaces and your friendly hosts? The house is full of light and bedrooms are lofty: fabric floating at tall windows, perhaps an exquisite carved bed. A river runs through the grounds, there are lakes and woods for ramblers, rare ferns for plant buffs, farm animals, even dromedaries in summer. Breakfast comes with a selection of teas in a pretty panelled room and dinner is served at separate tables. All feels calm and serene.

Rooms	3 doubles: €95-€135.
Meals	Restaurants 3-minute walk.
Closed	Rarely.

Rooms	4 twin/doubles: €95-€120.
	1 suite for 4: €160-€240.
	Extra bed/sofabed available €15-€20 per person per night.
Meals	Breakfast €9.
	Dinner with wine, €39.
	Restaurants 12km.
Closed	15 November to 28 November & Christmas.

	Benoit Colin
	Villa La Ruche,
	6 bis avenue du Général Berthelot,
	44500 La-Baule-Escoublac,
	Loire-Atlantique
Mobile	+33 (0)6 18 65 18 24
Email	contact@villa-laruche.com
Web	www.villa-laruche.com

	Patrick Moreau
	Château de Cop-Choux,
	44850 Mouzeil,
	Loire-Atlantique
Tel	+33 (0)2 40 97 28 52
Email	contact@copchoux.fr
Web	www.chateau-cop-choux.com

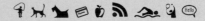

Entry 256   Map 3

Entry 257   Map 3

Loire-Séjours

An 18th-century townhouse run with love and pride by Breton Aline and London-Scot Andrew. Their home has a friendly feel; the sitting room has grand piano, parquet and books, elegant bedrooms have good beds. They know western Loire well – it's part of the old kingdom of Brittany and steeped in Celtic history. Breakfast is delicious: organic coffee, homemade jams and cakes, artisan bread and viennoiseries. The Loire à Vélo route is on the doorstep, Nantes is nearby; discover the vineyards of Muscadet and Coteaux d'Ancenis, and relax with a glass of wine in the pretty tiered garden on your return – Andrew might entertain you with his bagpipes!

On-street parking.

Rooms	3 doubles, 1 twin: €60–€75. 1 family room for 3: €68–€78.
Meals	Restaurants within walking distance.
Closed	Rarely.

Andrew Treppass
Loire-Séjours,
196 rue du Général Leclerc,
44150 Ancenis,
Loire-Atlantique

Tel	+33 (0)9 64 40 47 46
Email	info@loire-sejours.fr
Web	www.loire-sejours.com

Logis de Richebonne

Monsieur's parents bought this old *logis Vendéen* when he was six. Years later, researching the history of the house, he found his family had owned it in 1670! In the hall, Madame's family tree goes back to the 14th century. Both are warm, welcoming and not at all grand and the old house is full of personal touches: Madame painted the breakfast china and embroidered the beautiful tablecloths. Vast bedrooms have peaceful views and quantities of fresh and dried flowers. The suite is ideal for a family, the huge grounds hold two pretty ponds (unfenced) and a barbecue: you may picnic here. Wonderful all round.

Rooms	2 doubles: €75. 1 suite for 5: €75. Extra bed €20.
Meals	Picnic possible. Restaurant in village, 1.5km.
Closed	Rarely.

Alain & Françoise de Ternay
Logis de Richebonne,
7 impasse Richebonne,
44650 Legé,
Loire-Atlantique

Tel	+33 (0)2 40 04 90 41
Email	adeternay@wanadoo.fr
Web	www.logisderichebonne.com

Blanc Marine

A dreamy coastal light shimmers over the whole flat island, then comes the Atlantic breeze to blow happy birds, boaters and cyclists in all directions. Even in thronging summer, peace reigns inside the scented garden of this smart, comfortable modern house where each originally-furnished B&B room has its own entrance and wee hedged terrace. Delightful and enthusiastic, Jane makes guests feel very welcome; you will get to know her and the others over breakfast at one big table in the family living room. Binge on seafood and rare local potatoes, swim off wide sandy beaches, explore rock pools in this ideal holiday place.

Château de la Maronnière

Friendly Marie and François have excelled in restoring their luxurious, 18th-century château. Oak parquet is warm underfoot, copper leaf chandeliers light the circular hall and a stuffed fox surprises on the spiral staircase. Many rambling acres of green-fingered Eden await; take a wildlife walk or pluck cherries by the pool. Stylish shared spaces are immaculate with a baby grand in residence: 'Le Petit Bois' has carved antique furniture; 'La Rotonde' is marble grey with unusual panelling. Textiles and trimmings are sumptuous, bath robes fluffy; throw open the shutters and the views pour in. Stroll into Aizenay — or dine here.

Rooms	5 doubles, 2 doubles can interconnect: €85-€155. Extra bed available in 1 room, €25. Bikes available, €10 p.p. per day.
Meals	Brunch €10. Restaurants 10-minute walk.
Closed	Rarely.

Rooms	1 double, 2 twin/doubles: €125-€140. 1 suite for 4: €220. Extra child bed €25.
Meals	Dinner with wine, €35. Restaurants 500m.
Closed	Rarely.

Jean & Jane Dalric
Blanc Marine,
1 bis rue de l'Acquenette,
85330 Noirmoutier,
Vendée

Tel	+33 (0)2 51 39 99 11
Email	contact@blanc-marine.net
Web	www.blanc-marine.net

François-Xavier & Marie-Hélène
d'Halluin
Château de la Maronnière,
Route des Sables,
85190 Aizenay, Vendée

Mobile	+33 (0)6 25 02 00 55
Email	dhalluinmh@gmail.com
Web	www.chateauvendee.com

Entry 260 Map 8

Entry 261 Map 8

La Frelonnière

An elegant country house in a peaceful, pastoral setting – who would not love it? The 18th-century farmhouse, complete with musket holes and open rafters, is informal and delightful. Your English/Scottish hosts are fun, friendly and intimately acquainted with France – they brought their children up here. Now they generously open their living space to guests, their serene pool and their exquisite Monet-style garden. Quietly stylish bedrooms (coir carpets, white walls, fresh flowers, silk flourishes) are divided by a sofa'd library on the landing; dinners, served every night, may be romantic or convivial. A gem.

Rooms	4 doubles: €80.
Meals	Dinner with wine, €25.
Closed	Rarely.

Julie & Richard Deslandes
La Frelonnière,
85410 La Caillère–St Hilaire du Bois,
Vendée

Tel	+33 (0)2 51 51 56 49
Mobile	+33 (0)6 70 08 50 26
Email	julie@lafrelonniere.fr
Web	www.bandbvendee.com

Entry 262   Map 8

La Maison de Landerie

Annie used to have her own restaurant in Devon so whether you are outside on her little stone terrace overlooking open fields and forest or inside at her long antique table, it will be a Cordon Bleu breakfast. Multi-talented Annie could open an antique shop: her lovingly collected artefacts decorate this sweet little farmhouse like a dream from the past. The paint work is gorgeous, the vintage linens are sumptuous, the towels are thirsty, the mattresses are from heaven. You can walk to town, pick a trail in the forest or rent a canoe and follow the lazy river Lay. Annie's dinners are renowned, even the Mayor comes to dine.

Rooms	2 doubles: €70.
Meals	Dinner with wine, €30.
Closed	Christmas.

Annie Jory
La Maison de Landerie,
La Réorthe,
85210 Sainte Hermine,
Vendée

Tel	+33 (0)2 51 27 80 70
Email	richard.jory@wanadoo.fr
Web	www.lalanderie.com

Entry 263   Map 8

Le Clos du Marais

Spot egrets, herons and storks as you gaze across to the marshes beyond Jacqueline and Gil's whitewashed home. At the edge of a historic village close to the Vendée coastline, this beautifully renovated 1700s longère has two elegant rooms for guests. Cheery blue 'Hortensia' has an en suite with a roll top bath and scented stuff for pampering; romantic 'Les Dimes' has a walk-in shower and its own sitting room with a pair of stylish leather armchairs. Breakfast on pastries, homemade jam and local honey in the dining room or by the heated pool; book ahead for Gil's superb three-course dinners. Delightful stopover when travelling south.

Minimum stay: 2 nights in high season.

Le Rosier Sauvage

The pretty village is known for its exquisite abbey and some of that monastic serenity pervades these rooms. We love the family room under the rafters: massive oak door, cool tiled floor, a touch of toile, a simple mix of furniture. Through the family kitchen, breakfast is at a long polished table in the old stable: linger over cake and compote; the old laundry, its huge stone tub intact, is now a sitting room. Guests can picnic in the many-flowered walled garden, overlooked by the abbey and a glorious cedar tree. Energetic Christine is as charming as her house, which is also home to her husband and twin girls.

Rooms	2 doubles: €85–€105.
Meals	Dinner, 3-courses, €30.
Closed	Rarely.

Rooms	1 double, 1 twin: €49–€52. 1 family room for 3, 1 family room for 4: €59–€72.
Meals	Restaurants within walking distance.
Closed	October – April.

Jacqueline & Gil Darlavoix
Le Clos du Marais,
10 rue du Communal,
85540 Curzon,
Vendée

Tel	+33 (0)2 28 14 01 12
Mobile	+33 (0)6 21 74 75 01
Email	leclosdumarais@gmail.com
Web	www.leclosdumarais.com

Christine Chastain-Poupin
Le Rosier Sauvage,
1 rue de l'Abbaye,
85240 Nieul sur l'Autise,
Vendée

Tel	+33 (0)2 51 52 49 39
Email	lerosiersauvage@gmail.com
Web	www.lerosiersauvage.c.la

Entry 264   Map 8

Entry 265   Map 8

Château de la Frogerie

It's not often you can pretend to be medieval royalty but ascending the fabulous spiral staircase to your turret bedroom presents the ideal opportunity! Overlooking glorious Loire countryside, this petite château dates back to the fifteenth-century. Panelled-walls, a moat and parquet floors create historical atmosphere but charming owners, Jean-Christophe and Raymond-Pierre, have ensured that modern comfort co-exists. Antique beds are dressed in fine linen; cosy leather armchairs surround the fireplace and there's a pool shaded by ancient walls. Breakfast like a king on pastries, milk from the local Jersey herd and honey from the château's hives.

Parking on-site.

Rooms	3 doubles: €85–€152.
	1 family room for 4-5: €156–€260.
	Singles €69–€133.
Meals	Restaurant 6km.
Closed	Rarely.

Jean-Christophe Robert
Château de la Frogerie,
49360 Maulévrier,
Maine-et-Loire

Tel	+33 (0)2 41 30 60 67
Email	contact@chateau-frogerie.fr
Web	www.chateau-frogerie.fr

Le Mésangeau

The house is long-faced, and refined; the grounds (superb) come with a fishing pond and 'aperitif gazebo'. The Migons (hugely interesting and friendly) have expertly renovated this unusual house with its barn-enclosed courtyard, two towers and covered terrace. Big, north-facing bedrooms are elegant and comfortable behind their shutters, and keep the housekeepers busy. Expect leather sofas and a suit of armour, colourful beams above antique furniture, two billiard tables, and bikes, ping-pong and drums in the barn. You're within an easy drive of plenty of towns and villages where you can get a jolly good supper.

Rooms	3 doubles: €100–€120.
	1 suite for 4,
	1 suite for 5: €180–€240.
Meals	Restaurants 8km.
Closed	1 November to 31 March.

Brigitte & Gérard Migon
Le Mésangeau,
49530 Drain,
Maine-et-Loire

Tel	+33 (0)2 40 98 21 57
Email	le.mesangeau@orange.fr
Web	www.loire-mesangeau.com

La Rousselière

A hymn to peace, permanence and gentle living. The superb garden is Monsieur's pride and joy; château-like reception rooms open one into another – glass doors to glass doors, billiards to dining to sitting – like an indoor arcade; family portraits follow you everywhere; Mass is still said once a year in the chapel. But it's never over-grand. Bedrooms are highly individual with their antiques and hand-painted armoires (courtesy of an artistic sister), many bathrooms are new and Madame is the most delightful smiling hostess and a fine cook (veg, meat and eggs all home-grown). Your lovely hosts join you for an apéritif before dinner.

La Grande Maison d'Arthenay

Micaela was in the hotel trade, Sue worked at a Sussex winery, now they run an idyllic B&B on a former Saumur wine estate. The tours of their cellars and of the region are unmissable. The house dates from 1706, the potager is organic, and the outbuildings create a delicious hollyhock'd garden off which two rustic-chic bedrooms lie. The two in the house are equally lovely, one with an extra bed on the mezzanine: tuffeau walls, deep mattresses, soft beautiful colours. Start the day with a convivial breakfast (fresh figs, eggs from their hens), end it with a twice-weekly wine-tasting dinner at the big table.

Rooms	2 doubles, 2 twins: €70–€100.
	1 family room for 4: €150.
Meals	Dinner with wine, €30.
Closed	Rarely.

Rooms	3 twin/doubles: €105–€120.
	1 suite for 4: €125–€140.
	Singles €95.
Meals	Dinner with wine, coffee, tea &
	liqueur, €55
	(Sunday & Monday only).
Closed	November – March.

François & Jacqueline de Béru
La Rousselière,
49170 La Possonnière,
Maine-et-Loire
Tel   +33 (0)2 41 39 13 21
Mobile +33 (0)6 60 67 60 69
Email   larousseliere@unimedia.fr
Web   www.anjou-et-loire.com/rousseliere

Micaela Frow & Sue Hunt
La Grande Maison d'Arthenay,
Rue de la Cerisaie, Arthenay,
49700 Saumur,
Maine-et-Loire
Tel   +33 (0)2 41 40 35 06
Email   resv@lagrandemaison.net
Web   www.lagrandemaison.net

Entry 268   Map 3

Entry 269   Map 4

Manoir de Boisairault

Our inspector had an *Alice Through The Looking Glass* moment as she stepped off the street, through the unremarkable gate and into the wonderful gardens – a series of secret 'rooms' – that surround this elegant, 18th-century, cloistered manor. A labyrinth of caves, typical of the region, lies below and guests sometimes dine there with Jean-Pierre and Béatrice – your cultured, interesting hosts. Pray for the camembert sprinkled with pastis, cooked in the fire's embers – it's divine. Inside are an attractive dining room and three pretty bedrooms; the ground-floor one – all Louis XV – is particularly enchanting.

Le Clos de la Brète

Most of the houses in the village are owned by winemakers still, but this one is lived in by gentle Madame. With her adorable daughter, two cats and a handful of pretty hens, she does B&B that is perfect for families. There are troglodyte villages to visit and, just up the road, a bamboo-forested zoo, the famously animal-friendly Doue la Fontaine. Beds are beautiful and brand new, eiderdowns add colour to a neutral palette and everything feels sunny and warm. Wake to homemade yogurts, breads, cakes and jams, set off for the châteaux of the Loire, return to rambling lawns, toys to share, and a stylish grey sofa in front of the fire.

Rooms	2 doubles: €125–€140. 1 family room for 4: €180–€240.		Rooms	2 doubles: €65–€76. 1 suite for 5: €75–€155. Extra bed/sofabed available €16–€25 per person per night.
Meals	Hosted dinner with wine €35; children under 10, €15. Restaurants 10 km.		Meals	Restaurants 2km.
Closed	Rarely.		Closed	Rarely.

Jean-Pierre Delmas
Manoir de Boisairault,
8 rue de Pas d'Aubigné,
49260 Le Coudray Macouard,
Maine-et-Loire
Mobile   +33 (0)6 08 93 85 61
Email   contact@manoir-de-boisairault.com
Web   www.manoir-de-boisairault.com

Florence Lacroix
Le Clos de la Brète,
9 rue Jean de la Brète, Village d'Igné,
49700 Cizay la Madeleine,
Maine-et-Loire
Tel   +33 (0)2 41 50 46 26
Email   flodelabrete@orange.fr
Web   www.le-clos-de-la-brete.fr

Entry 270   Map 4   Entry 271   Map 4

Western Loire

Western Loire

Château de Beaulieu

Set back from the banks of the river Loire lies a château of character and charm, a perfect reflection of its delightful owners. The house was built in 1727 and the décor, traditional and authentic, captures the romance of that earlier age. Five bedrooms lead off an oak-beamed corridor and range from the dramatic to the cosy and intimate. Find antique armoires, ornate fireplaces, bold colours and dreamy views of the large, tree-brimmed garden – with a lovely pool and a small prospering vineyard. Snuggle down with a book from the library, try your hand at billiards, visit historic Saumur.

La Sterne de Loire

Véronique, who paints, is loving settling into the medieval village, gleaning crockery and furniture from brocantes and her own grandparents to bring a new life and soul to this delightfully eclectic 15th-century house. On a road beside the Loire, it has direct sightings of swooping "sternes" (terns), an authentically ancient atmosphere, small bedrooms with huge personality and pretty showers, a splendid fireplace with its original bread oven in the dark beamed dining room – and masses of steps. Your cosmopolitan, polyglot hostess knows all the fascinating things to do and see here.

Minimum stay: 2 nights in high season.

Rooms	4 doubles: €120. 1 suite for 4: €160-€200.
Meals	Restaurants 1km.
Closed	November to Easter.

Rooms	4 doubles: €95-€105. 1 triple: €120-€130.
Meals	Restaurants 5-minute walk.
Closed	Rarely.

Conor & Mary Coady-Maguire
Château de Beaulieu,
98 route de Montsoreau,
49400 Saumur,
Maine-et-Loire
Tel +33 (0)2 41 50 83 52
Email info@chateaudebeaulieu.fr
Web www.chateaudebeaulieu.fr

Véronique van Eetvelde
La Sterne de Loire,
26 rue des Ducs d'Anjou,
49400 Souzay-Champigny,
Maine-et-Loire
Mobile +33 (0)6 63 11 28 12
Email v_van_eetvelde@yahoo.fr
Web www.lasternedeloire.com

Entry 272 Map 4

Entry 273 Map 4

Domaine de Marconnay

Once a humble dwelling hewn into the cliff, this lovely old place took centuries to evolve. Now it is a deeply atmospheric, romantic B&B. Enter to find a private, wood-panelled, stone-floored salon with a 17th-century fireplace, a table that seats ten and a stone stair spiralling to the bedroom above. Warm, luminous and inviting, this exquisite uncluttered space combines pale blue panelling with hunks of bare stone, a fabulous shower and a view – of orangerie, farmhouse and countryside. Charming Madame lives across the courtyard, serves a fine breakfast and can pick you up from Saumur.

Parking on-site.

Rooms	1 double: €90.
Meals	Restaurants 1km.
Closed	Rarely.

Madame Huguette Goumain
Domaine de Marconnay,
49730 Parnay,
Maine-et-Loire
Tel +33 (0)2 41 38 13 38
Mobile +33 (0)6 83 17 07 59
Email jeangoumain@laposte.net

Entry 274   Map 4

Manoir de Montecler

Vivacious Madame Carpentier's small manor house lies on a hill above the village on the banks of the Loire. Neat bedrooms (including one in the tower) with period furniture and in calming hues enjoy views of the terraced gardens and across the river. Madame loves to cook and serves breakfast – with homemade cake – and seasonal dinners on the terrace or in the pretty kitchen dining area. Visit the châteaux of the Loire or, for horse lovers, the Cadre Noir riding school; return to the charming sitting room leading out to the peaceful gardens or, if staying in the double room, to your own private sauna.

Rooms	1 twin, 1 double with separate bathroom: €70-€120. 1 single with separate wc: €65-€75.
Meals	Dinner €29.
Closed	Rarely.

Brigitte Carpentier
Manoir de Montecler,
1 rue de la Barbacane,
49350 Chènehutte-les-Tuffeaux,
Maine-et-Loire
Tel +33 (0)2 41 38 43 49
Email brigittecarpentier49@orange.fr
Web www.lemanoirdemontecler.com

Entry 275   Map 4

Domaine de l'Oie Rouge

These new owners, warm-hearted epicureans, fell in love with a small riverside town between Saumur and Angers, and a handsome house in its own Belle Époque park. Settle in to a deep red sofa with an apéritif – and a mesmerising view of the flowing Loire. The décor is due for updating but the rooms are large and undoubtedly comfortable, one with a canopied bed, another with a splendid view. Set off on the bikes (six to hire) for the amphitheatre at Gennes or the Abbey of Fontevraud. And if Odile's madeleines are anything to go by, her dinners (tartelettes aux échalotes, blanquette de poule) are unmissable!

Le Logis du Pressoir

Birdsong and sunlight filter through eau de nil shutters into your cosy 18th-century cottage on this former wine pressing estate. A chestnut-panelled haven (pretty curtains, antique furniture, pale linens, a luxurious shower) it's all the work of friendly, knowledgeable Lisa and Mark. Lush parkland conceals four gîtes, whose guests share the heated pool with you. Breakfast amidst wisteria and lavender on your private terrace: summer fruits from the orchard, pâtisserie fresh from the village minutes away. A local restaurant delivers carefree dinners, and Lisa will pack a picnic for forays into historic wine country.

Minimum stay: 2 nights; 3 nights in high season.

Rooms	3 doubles: €83–€103. Singles €75–€103. Extra bed/sofabed available €19 per person per night.
Meals	Dinner with wine, €27. Restaurants 2-minute walk.
Closed	Rarely.

Rooms	1 double: €85–€95.
Meals	Restaurant 10-minute walk. Picnics available
Closed	1 November to 31 March.

Odile Bousselin
Domaine de l'Oie Rouge,
8 rue Nationale,
49350 Les Rosiers sur Loire,
Maine-et-Loire

Tel	+33 (0)2 41 53 65 65
Email	domainedeloierouge@gmail.com
Web	www.domaine-oie-rouge.com

Lisa & Mark Wright
Le Logis du Pressoir,
Les Bois d'Anjou, 49250 Brion,
Maine-et-Loire

Tel	+33 (0)2 41 57 27 33
Mobile	+33 (0)6 73 49 96 77
Email	info@logisdupressoir.com
Web	www.logisdupressoir.com

Les Bouchets

It's spotless now, with all mod cons, gleaming antiques, open fires and vases of fresh flowers. The house was a ruin when the Bignons found it but they managed to save all the old timbers and stones. The result is a seductively warm cheerful house with bedrooms cosy and soft, two upstairs, one with an entrance off a garden where swings invite children to play. Passionate about food, they used to run a restaurant where Michel was chef; note the coppers in the kitchen/entrance hall, and memorabilia in the family sitting room. Géraldine, bright, friendly and organised… and serving beautiful homegrown or local food and the wines of Anjou.

La Croix d'Étain

Frisky red squirrels decorate the stone balustrade, the wisteria is a glory in spring, and the wide swooshing river cascades over the weir. It feels like deep country yet this handsome manor has urban elegance in its very stones. Panelling, mouldings, subtly muted floor tiles bring grace; traditional French florals add softness. It looks fairly formal but sprightly Madame loves having guests and pampers them, in their own quarters, with luxury. Expect plush, lacy, flowery, carpeted bedrooms, three with river views, all with sunny bathrooms. The yacht-side setting is stunning – it could be the Riviera.

Rooms	1 double, 1 twin/double: €70-€75. 1 family room for 4: €120.
Meals	Dinner with wine, €29.
Closed	Rarely.

Rooms	1 double, 3 twin/doubles: €85-€100. Singles €75. Extra bed/sofabed available €25 per person per night.
Meals	Dinner with wine, €30. Crêperie 50m.
Closed	Rarely.

Michel & Géraldine Bignon
Les Bouchets,
lieu dit Les Bouchets,
49150 Le Vieil Baugé,
Maine-et-Loire

Tel	+33 (0)2 41 82 34 48
Mobile	+33 (0)6 71 60 66 05
Email	geraldinebignon@gmail.com
Web	www.lesbouchets.com

Jacqueline & Auguste Bahuaud
La Croix d'Étain,
2 rue de l'Écluse,
49220 Grez Neuville,
Maine-et-Loire

Tel	+33 (0)2 41 95 68 49
Email	croix.etain@loire-anjou-accommodation.com
Web	www.loire-anjou-accommodation.com

Manoir du Bois de Grez

An ancient peace lingers over the fan-shaped cobbled courtyard, the old well, the little chapel: the Manoir oozes history. Your doctor host, a talented gardener, and his charming wife, much-travelled antique-hunters with imagination and flair, offer guests warm generous bedrooms (including a superb family room) hung with well-chosen oriental pieces and paintings in good strong colours that reflect the garden light. Most wonderful of all are the specimen tree'd gardens, their great grassy carpets embracing a small lake. You share a big sitting room with your lovely hosts, lots of plants and a suit of armour.

Château de Montriou

The park will explode your senses – and once the visitors have gone home, what a treat to have it to yourselves: the lake, the famous sequoia, the waves of crocuses in spring, the centuries-old chapel with three statues of Marie. This 15th-century château has been lived in and tended by the same family for 300 years and Monsieur and Madame know exactly how to make you feel at home. A spiral stone staircase leads to properly formal bedrooms whose bold colours were design flavour of the period; wooden floors, thick rugs and antiques are only slightly younger. And the venerable library is now a guest sitting room. Special.

Rooms	2 doubles, 1 twin: €90–€110. 1 family room for 4: €110–€150.
Meals	Picnic on request. Guest kitchen. Restaurant 1.5km.
Closed	Rarely.

Rooms	2 doubles; 1 double with kitchen: €95–€130. 1 suite for 4 with kitchen: €175. Singles €85–€115.
Meals	Restaurant 6km.
Closed	1 November to 1 April.

Marie Laure & Jean Gaël Cesbron
Manoir du Bois de Grez,
Route de Sceaux d'Anjou,
49220 Grez Neuville,
Maine-et-Loire
Tel   +33 (0)2 41 18 00 09
Mobile   +33 (0)6 22 38 14 56
Email   cesbron.boisgrez@wanadoo.fr
Web   www.boisdegrez.com

Régis & Nicole de Loture
Château de Montriou,
49460 Feneu,
Maine-et-Loire
Tel   +33 (0)2 41 93 30 11
Email   chateau-de-montriou@wanadoo.fr
Web   www.chateau-de-montriou.com

Entry 280   Map 3

Entry 281   Map 4

Château de Montreuil sur Loir

An 1840s neo-gothic delight in a 16-hectare, deer-roamed park, a river for swimming and rowing, and a film set of an interior. The sitting room is splendidly 'medieval', the panelled drawing room pure 18th century, taken whole from a château, with superb hangings and immensely high doors. This was once a self-sufficient country estate with chapel, dovecote and mill (remains still visible). Large, lofty bedrooms have authentic wooden floors and carpets, antique cupboards, bucolic river views. Your hosts speak good English, are gracious, refined and humorous, and always there to receive guests.

Château de Chambiers

Another marvellous family château, this one surrounded by a deep forest. Smiling Madame (a good cook, and wonderful with children) speaks perfect English, is proud of her gardens and her big, beautiful rooms; she is a talented designer. Bedrooms have delicious antiques, one a French-Caribbean mahogany bed, floors are 18th-century oak with *terre cuite* borders – exquisite; some of the baths, washstands and fittings are period originals, so it's a huge treat to stay here if you appreciate history. There's a panelled *salon de thé*, a billiards room and books, and a playhouse and organic potager in the garden. Un coin de paradis!

Well-behaved pets welcome, €12.50 per night.

Rooms	2 family rooms for 3, 1 family room for 4: €100-€130.
Meals	Dinner with wine, €35.
Closed	1 November to 31 March.

Rooms	1 double: €167. 4 family rooms for 3: €137-€206. Extra bed/sofabed available €28 per person per night.
Meals	Dinner, 3-4 courses, €36.50-€49.50; children under 9, €14.50.
Closed	Rarely.

Marc & Alice Renard Bailliou
Château de Montreuil sur Loir,
49140 Montreuil sur Loir,
Maine-et-Loire

Tel	+33 (0)2 41 76 21 03
Mobile	+33 (0)6 67 33 27 05
Email	renardalice@hotmail.fr
Web	www.anjou-loir.com

Anne & Élie Crouan
Château de Chambiers,
49430 Durtal,
Maine-et-Loire

Tel	+33 (0)2 41 76 07 31
Email	info@chateauchambiers.com
Web	www.chateauchambiers.com

Château du Plessis Anjou

Sixteenth-century Le Plessis has been welcoming guests for years. Dinner, brought to a long table in a dining room grandly furnished with Roman Empire frescoes, might include duck with apricots, cheese, a crisp fruit tart. One bedroom is striking with oriental rugs and the bed in a deep alcove; others have lofty beamed ceilings. Children are welcome and the Renouls have two of their own, hence the playground and the trampoline, the rabbits and the goat. Madame invites children to gather breakfast's eggs, and the pool hides in the grounds; the trees are sublime. Terra Botanica is a 15-minute drive.

La Maison du Roi René

The famous old auberge has become a charming B&B. Scrunch up the drive serenaded by soft roses to a lovely welcome from Madame. Part medieval, part 18th century, like the village around it, it has corners, crannies and a stunning central stone fireplace. The Valicourts – they speak four languages! – are the happy new owners of these magnificent oak doors and rosy tomette floors; bedrooms are beamed and very pleasing – one opens to the garden, three to the tower. There's a pretty paved terrace for breakfast with viennoiseries and a room of auberge proportions for a light supper of cold meats and local specialities.

Rooms	3 doubles: €105-€180.
	2 suites for 2: €220-€250.
	Extra bed/sofabed available
	€25-€35 per person per night.
Meals	Hosted dinner €48.
	Wine €20-€240.
Closed	Rarely.

Rooms	2 doubles, 1 twin: €65-€85.
	1 suite for 2: €65-€85
	Extra sofabed available in twin.
Meals	Supper tray available, €15.
	Restaurant 100m.
Closed	Rarely.

	Valérie & Laurent Renoul
	Château du Plessis Anjou,
	49220 La Jaille Yvon,
	Maine-et-Loire
Tel	+33 (0)2 41 95 12 75
Email	plessis.anjou@wanadoo.fr
Web	www.chateau-du-plessis.com

	Dominique de Valicourt
	La Maison du Roi René,
	4 Grande Rue,
	53290 Saint Denis d'Anjou,
	Mayenne
Tel	+33 (0)2 43 70 52 30
Mobile	+33 (0)6 89 37 87 12
Email	roi-rene@orange.fr
Web	www.roi-rene.fr

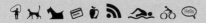

Entry 285   Map 4

Château de Craon

Such a close and welcoming family, whose kindness extends to include you. It's a magnificent place, with innumerable expressions of history, taste and personality, and gracious Loïk and Hélène, young grandparents, treat you like friends. A sitting room with sofas and a view of the park, an Italianate hall with sweeping stone stair, classic French bedrooms in lavender, blue, cream... an original washstand, a canopied bed, a velvet armchair. Everywhere a feast for the eyes; paintings, watercolours, antiques. Outside, 40 acres of river, meadows, lake, ice house, tennis court, pool, and a potager worth leaving home for.

Rooms	3 doubles, 1 twin: €100–€160. 1 suite for 4: €260. 1 single: €80. Extra bed/sofabed available €35 per person per night.
Meals	Dinner with wine, €45. Restaurants in village, within walking distance.
Closed	November – March.

Loïk & Hélène de Guébriant
Château de Craon,
53400 Craon,
Mayenne
Tel   +33 (0)2 43 06 11 02
Email   chateaudecraon@wanadoo.fr
Web   www.craoncastle.com

Entry 286   Map 3

Domaine de la Houzardiere

Marguerite welcomes with tea and cakes; within minutes, you're part of her family. Large bedrooms in the converted barn of her 19th-century farmhouse are furnished with antiques from her grandfather's château; elegant armoires, beds and tables. Colourful quilts cover the beds, bright rugs are laid on tiled or parquet floors, original paintings hang on the walls. Windows look to woods – beckoning for walks – or the walled garden. Breakfasts – dinners, too – are served in a beautiful, spacious barn on sunny days (with kitchen for rustling up lunches); in the farmhouse kitchen on cooler days. Wonderfully, traditionally French.

Rooms	3 doubles, 1 twin: €60. Extra bed €18 per night.
Meals	Dinner with apéritif, wine & coffee, €21. Children's dinner available. Restaurants 500m.
Closed	January/February.

Marguerite Moenner
Domaine de la Houzardiere,
Route de St Georges,
53170 Bazougers,
Mayenne
Tel   +33 (0)2 43 02 37 16
Email   marguerite@houzardiere.com
Web   www.houzardiere.com

Entry 287   Map 4

Château d'Éporcé

Grand and pure 17th century with a moat and magnificent avenue of trees leading to the door. Yet you discover a laid-back, lived-in atmosphere with three salons for guests and little change for 50 years. Find lofty ceilings, antiques, books, engravings and butterfly collections galore. Meals are easy-going, with drinks before and tea in the lounge afterwards. Bedrooms are charmingly faded; all face the sun and have lovely park views and rather eccentric, ancient bathrooms. First-floor rooms are the ones to go for – proper château stuff. Anglophile Rémy is a charming host; his gardens handsome, formal, wonderful. Pack a jumper in the winter...

La Maison du Pont Romain

Cross Montfort's exquisite stone bridge to this pretty house on the banks of the river. Enter the grounds and forget the world in heavenly peace among very old trees. Gentle Madame saved it all from ruin and gives you two comfortable rooms upstairs, privately off the courtyard, both with fine armoires. The suite in the old stables (salon below, bedrooms above) has a charming late 18th-century feel. There are delicious jams at the big table for breakfast and a family salon for guests. Visit Montfort's castle and the lovely, unsung villages and vineyards of the Sarthe. For children? Forest animals at Pescheray and an aquapark in the village.

Rooms	2 doubles, 1 twin/double: €90–€150.
Meals	Dinner with wine, €40.
Closed	Rarely.

Rooms	2 doubles: €65–€75.
	1 suite for 3-4: €65–€75.
Meals	Dinner with wine, €24.
Closed	Rarely.

Rémy de Scitivaux
Château d'Éporcé,
Éporcé,
72550 La Quinte,
Sarthe
Tel   +33 (0)2 43 27 70 22
Email   eporce@wanadoo.fr
Web   www.chateau-eporce.com

Chantal Paris
La Maison du Pont Romain,
26 rue de l'Église,
72450 Montfort le Gesnois,
Sarthe
Tel   +33 (0)2 43 76 13 46
Email   chantal-paris@wanadoo.fr
Web   www.le-pont-romain.fr

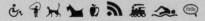

Entry 288   Map 4

Entry 289   Map 4

Château de Saint Frambault

You'll feel utterly spoilt on this elegant, traditional country château estate. Charming Madame's freshly baked cakes are memorable, so are beamed and beautiful rooms, reached by a handsome spiral stair and graced with family antiques, rich fabrics and beds of the greatest comfort. Reception rooms have fine 18th-century panelling and tapestry upholstered chairs; all is warm and very French. Wander the well-groomed grounds, admire the oaks, the lakes, the clipped yews; take an evening plunge in the lovely heated pool. All this in a gentle, wooded valley, five minutes from good restaurants and less than an hour by train from Paris.

Swimming pool available 6pm-9pm.

Rooms	5 doubles: €99-€180.
	Singles €99-€129.
	Extra bed/sofabed available
	€20-€30 per person per night.
Meals	Restaurants 5km.
Closed	11 June to 19 June, Christmas & New Year.

Emmanuel & Savina de Goulaine
Château de Saint Frambault,
Route de St Fraimbault,
72210 Roézé sur Sarthe,
Sarthe

Tel	+33 (0)2 43 77 21 40
Email	emmanueldegoulaine72@gmail.com
Web	www.manoir-saint-frambault.com

Entry 290   Map 4

Château de Montaupin

Outside, a Virginia creeper has the façade in its clutches — to pretty effect! Inside, wine and conversation flow. Mme David is friendly and welcoming and adores her house, family and guests. There's a laid-back feel, a cluttered elegance, a faded décor; the atmosphere is that of a happy household. A suspended spiral staircase leads to the upper floors and the best suite is right at the top, its roof timbers exposed. Families will feel at home. Breakfasts are robust and table d'hôtes is classic French, with much produce from the garden. Be sure you try the family wines!

Rooms	2 doubles: €75-€80.
	2 suites for 4, 1 triple: €75-€80.
	Extra person €20.
Meals	Dinner with wine, €22.50.
Closed	Occasionally.

Marie David
Château de Montaupin,
Montaupin,
72330 Oizé,
Sarthe

Tel	+33 (0)2 43 87 81 70
Mobile	+33 (0)6 83 56 60 40
Email	chateaudemontaupin@wanadoo.fr

Entry 291   Map 4

Le Chaton Rouge

The Le Mans race track is less than ten miles away, but life in St Pierre du Lorouer is lived at a slower pace. Opposite the church is a house that combines château grandeur with a cottagey feel – thanks to cheerful, generous, imaginative Sarah. Relax in the courtyard, climb the steps to the walled garden where the vegetable patch awaits. With luck its produce will end up on your plate: Sarah is a fabulous cook! There's a real fire for winter, an outdoor dining room for summer, and, up a sweeping stair, the bedrooms – fresh, white and uncluttered. One is cosily in the attic with kitchen, glass table and chandeliers.

Children over 5 welcome.

Le Moulin de St Blaise

A house of surprises: mill machinery in the dining room; vast bread oven in the kitchen; fruit and vegetable plot like a Garden of Eden. Come here for fantastic fresh food (dinners, too), the sounds of water, and freedom. Huge beamed dining and sitting rooms have books, games, billiards – and space for children to play. More space on the terrace and in the meadow and garden; keep an eye on children by the river. Airy, white bedrooms have garden and vineyard views; most have smart shower rooms. Friendly owners will point you to Le Mans, lakeside beach, châteaux. Catch fish for supper, or relax with a book and the rushing water.

Rooms	2 doubles; 1 double with separate shower: €90-€120. 1 family room for 4 with separate bathroom: €160-€200. Singles €70. Dinner, B&B €95 per person.
Meals	Lunch €10. Dinner €25. Restaurant 20m.
Closed	Rarely.

Rooms	1 double, 2 twins: €89-€149. 1 family room for 3: €89-€149. Extra bed/sofabed available €29-€49 per person per night. Cot available, but linen not provided.
Meals	Dinner with wine, €25. Restaurant 1km.
Closed	Rarely.

	Sarah Carlisle
	Le Chaton Rouge, 4 rue du Calvaire,
	72150 Saint Pierre du Lorouer,
	Sarthe
Tel	+33 (0)2 43 46 21 37
Mobile	+33 (0)6 44 17 23 74
Email	sarah@lechatonrouge.com
Web	www.lechatonrouge.com

	Elaine Love Miles
	Le Moulin de St Blaise,
	72340 Chahaignes,
	Sarthe
Tel	+33 (0)2 43 46 78 05
Email	philelaine2007@yahoo.co.uk
Web	www.moulinstblaise.com

Entry 292   Map 4

Entry 293   Map 4

La Châtaigneraie

Outside is a fairy tale: mellow old stone, white shutters, green ivy, a large leafy garden, a clematis-covered well, a little wood and glimpses of the 12th-century castle round the corner; La Châtaigneraie used to be the servants' quarters. Green-eyed Michèle, modern, intelligent and interested in people, shares the hosting with Michel. The suite is made up of three pastel-hued bedrooms that look onto garden or endless fields. Stay a while and connect – with the soft hills, the woods, the streams, the châteaux. Guests can be as independent as they like and can take one, two or three rooms. Dinner is great value.

Rooms	1 suite for 2-5: €65–€120.
Meals	Dinner with wine, €25; children €12. Restaurant 2km.
Closed	November – March.

Michèle Letanneux & Michel Guyon
La Châtaigneraie,
72500 Dissay sous Courcillon,
Sarthe
Tel   +33 (0)2 43 79 36 71
Mobile   +33 (0)6 16 44 45 97
Email   michelecretagne@yahoo.fr

Entry 294   Map 4

5 Grande Rue

On Le Lude's Grande Rue is a nobleman's house built around 1650, in its own walled garden, sunny and peaceful; from many of the windows you can glimpse the Château. Simon and Susan pay huge attention to detail, love having guests, offer tea, cakes or wine on arrival, and give you one of five big comfortable bedrooms upstairs. All have immaculate linen, sparkling bathrooms and original button cushions made by Susan. There's an illuminated dining terrace and a wonderful salon to come home to, and long, leisurely breakfasts to wake to. Wine caves and châteaux abound, including Bauge's with its 17th-century apothecary.

Rooms	4 doubles, 1 twin: €75–€99.
Meals	Dinner, 3 courses with wine, €25; with cheese €27. Restaurants 50m.
Closed	Rarely.

Simon & Susan Wachter
5 Grande Rue,
72800 Le Lude,
Sarthe
Tel   +33 (0)2 43 94 92 77
Email   info@5granderue.com
Web   www.5granderue.com

Entry 295   Map 4

Loire Valley

Maison Ailleurs

A short stroll from the glorious cathedral is the home of the former bishop. Valérie and her husband, after a life of international travel, fell for its beauty and brought it back to life. Now this young family live in the right wing and the suites are in the left, up a wide stone stair: one in the original chapel, with a modern four-poster and dramatic stripes, one overlooking the garden (idyllic, walled and full of roses), and one on the second floor, elegant in dove greys and soft yellows. Find iPod docks, Nespresso machines, flawless kitchenettes, lovely linen. Breakfasts are beautiful, the parking is a boon.

Maison JLN

Come to enjoy this gentle, charming family and the serene vibes of their old Chartrain house. Up two steep twisting spirals to the attic, through the family's little prayer room (a shell for each pilgrim who's stayed here), the sweet, peaceful bedroom feels like a chapel itself with its honey floorboards and small windows (no wardrobe). Lots of books: reminders of pilgrimage, just beneath the great cathedral. Madame artistic, friendly, offers artists a small studio to borrow; Monsieur speaks nine languages and is quietly amusing; both are interested in your travels. An unusual and special place, in a timeless town.

Rooms	2 doubles with kitchenettes: €135-€173. 1 suite for 2-3 with kitchenette: €179-€219. Extra bed/sofabed available €20 per person per night.
Meals	Restaurants within walking distance.
Closed	Rarely.

Rooms	1 twin with separate shower & wc on floor below: €57. Singles €46. Extra bed/sofabed available €14 per person per night.
Meals	Restaurants nearby.
Closed	Rarely.

	Valérie Genique Maison Ailleurs, 17 rue Muret, 28000 Chartres, Eure-et-Loir
Email	maisonailleurs@gmail.com
Web	www.maisonailleurs.com

	Jean-Loup & Nathalie Cuisiniez Maison JLN, 80 rue Muret, 28000 Chartres, Eure-et-Loir
Tel	+33 (0)2 37 21 98 36
Mobile	+33 (0)6 79 48 46 63
Email	chartres.maison.jln@gmail.com
Web	www.chambre-hotes-chartres.com

Le Moulin de Lonceux

A placid river sets ancient mill stones grinding and flour flows; ducks dip, swans preen, geese saunter; gardens are beset by roses, herbs, bantams, goats, a hammock. The mill has been ingeniously restored by this hard-working family into a home, museum, a ballroom for weddings and a B&B, wrapped around a courtyard. Sleep in stables complete with manger; a two-room loft suite; a smart Miller's Room with fireplace; a flint-walled cider press. Breakfast in the dayroom (sofa, games, candles, log fire) on fresh pastries from home-milled flour (of course). Chartres is close, Paris an easy train ride. A gem.

Château de Denonville

In deep rural plains, beneath skyscapes to die for, two millennia of history are stacked up here and you sleep on 14th-century foundations. In their east wing the delightful, welcoming owners serve a superior continental breakfast by the stone fireplace; in the vaulted, tapestry-hung salon there are prints, clocks and collections to explore, myriad books and two pianos. Bedrooms, properly draped and swagged, have good modern bathrooms. The main 19th-century stately home and its great gardens are open to the public while you're out visiting Chartres, the Loire châteaux, even Paris — before coming back to this superb place.

Parking on-site.

Rooms	3 doubles: €105–€120. 1 suite for 2-4: €170. Extra bed/sofabed available €20 per person per night.
Meals	Catered meals & cold tray on arrival, with wine, €15–€25 (on request). Restaurant 3km.
Closed	Rarely.

Rooms	2 doubles: €90. 1 suite for 2: €110–€140. 1 family room for 6: €110–€170. Extra bed €15.
Meals	Dinner, 4 courses with wine, €25; Sunday only. Restaurants 10-minute drive.
Closed	Rarely.

	Isabelle Heitz
	Le Moulin de Lonceux,
	Hameau de Lonceux,
	28700 Oinville sous Auneau,
	Eure-et-Loir
Mobile	+33 (0)6 70 00 60 45
Email	contact@moulin-de-lonceux.com
Web	www.moulin-de-lonceux.com

	Aurélie Capet-Pehuet
	Château de Denonville,
	28700 Denonville,
	Eure-et-Loir
Mobile	+33 (0)6 73 18 77 37
Email	chateau.denonville@gmail.com
Web	www.chateaudedenonville.fr

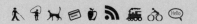

Entry 298   Map 5

Entry 299   Map 5

Moulin de la Ronce

A very fine mill, built in 1555, restored in 2008, beautifully and artfully transformed by Clément and bright smiling Laurence. Expect the best: homemade jams, tea from Paris, eggs from the hens, and, facing a central courtyard, eco-luxurious bedrooms in uncluttered style... an age-old flagged floor, a Philippe Starck bathtub, colourful towels, splashes of art. The waterside setting is timeless, the garden is thronged with weeping willows, there are books to plunder, grapes to pluck, a row boat for the hearty, a day room for summer, a log fire for winter, and, 15 miles away, the glorious cathedral of Chartres.

Château La Touanne

Lush trees and elaborate gates frame the graceful façade. Nicolas and Christine's courteous informality permeates their peaceful 17th-century château. Downstairs, ancestral portraits survey antiques, gilt mirrors and fine porcelain in sitting room and salon. Breakfast in the stately dining room, where locally sourced table d'hôtes dinners are also held. Bedrooms are sumptuous: marble fireplaces, high ceilings, fine oak parquet. The terrace leads into parkland, farm, and an orchard hiding the heated pool. Stroll through meadows to explore bosky riverside paths, borrow a boat. An authentic family château, just 90 minutes from Paris.

Rooms	1 double, 1 twin/double: €150–€170.
	1 suite for 2-4: €200.
	Singles €130–€140
Meals	Restaurants 6km.
Closed	Rarely.

Rooms	3 doubles, 1 twin/double: €130–€180.
	Singles €100–€150.
Meals	Dinner with wine, €35.
Closed	Rarely.

	Laurence & Clément Krief
	Moulin de la Ronce,
	28800 Alluyes,
	Eure-et-Loir
Mobile	+33 (0)6 31 17 48 80
Email	contact@moulin-de-la-ronce.com
Web	www.moulin-de-la-ronce.com

	Nicolas & Christine d'Aboville
	Château La Touanne,
	45130 Baccon,
	Loiret
Tel	+33 (0)2 38 46 51 39
Mobile	+33 (0)6 88 76 69 89
Email	nicolas.daboville@orange.fr
Web	www.chateau-latouanne.com

La Feuillaie

Monsieur's 'light and aromatic' dinners are paired with Loire Valley wines and served at Madame's beautifully dressed table. Risen gloriously from ruin, your hosts' 18th century home hides in rambling grounds amid a duck-filled lake and 40 species of trees. Eclectic objects catch the eye in soundproofed bedrooms: a sculpted elephant, grandma's lace, ornate wallpapers, claw-foot baths. After dinner, there's billiards or cards by the fire, a piano and literally hundreds of recipe and wine books. (Inspired? They run cooking courses.) Borrow a bike and follow the Loire from this charming village to châteaux, gardens and lakes.

Le Clos de la Vigneronne

You're just a few minutes from the A10, on the edge of a small village and surrounded by open fields on one side, tall bushy trees on the other. The house, built in 1850, is made of beautiful old white stone and has red shutters to add Gallic charm. Béatrice and Régis give you rather sleek modern bedrooms, a continental breakfast at separate tables and a kitchen with a wood-burner for rainy days. There's a small lending library too. Sleep peacefully in the quiet then discover châteaux, museums, gardens, sporty stuff in spades, regional wines and farmers' markets for foodies, all from this unfussy family home.

Parking on-site.

Rooms	4 doubles, 1 twin/double: €152–€170. Extra bed/sofabed available €35 per person per night. Children under 2, €15. Cot available on request.	Rooms	2 twin/doubles with separate wcs: €70–€85. 1 family room for 4: €95–€145. Extra child bed €25 per person per night, available in 1 double room, suitable for children aged 2-10; cot available.
Meals	Dinner, 3 courses with apéritif, wine & coffee, €52; children €15. Restaurants 2km.		
Closed	Rarely.	Meals	Restaurants 5-minute drive.
		Closed	New Year.

	Véronique & Philippe Frenette La Feuillaie, 4 rue Basse, 45130 Saint Ay, Loiret		**Béatrice Ecosse** Le Clos de la Vigneronne, 19 rue de Villeneuve, 45190 Messas, Loiret
Mobile	+33 (0)6 16 75 71 27	Mobile	+33 (0)6 87 04 65 46
Email	contact@lafeuillaie.com	Email	closdelavigneronne@gmail.com
Web	www.lafeuillaie.com	Web	www.leclosdelavigneronne.com

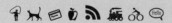

Entry 302   Map 5

Entry 303   Map 5

Loire Valley

Moulin Guillard

Just outside the village of Subligny, not far from Sancerre, is an idyllic blue-shuttered mill where flour was once produced. Now it is a fascinating B&B. Dorothée, a cultured woman who once ran a bookshop in Paris, divides her time between her exquisite garden of rare plants and her guests. She offers you a smallish, softly serene double upstairs, and an enchanting two-bedroom suite across the way, with a sitting room and a piano you may play. In summer you breakfast between the two, in an open barn overlooking the stream and Dorothée's several breeds of free-roaming hen. Dinners are superb.

Loire Valley

Domaine du Château de Moison

A creamy château set in lush lawns, shaded by tall trees and given a lavish renovation by the owner's talented designer daughter Adèle de La Palme. In the dining room find a full size stag of reclaimed wood twinned with an 18th-century hunting tapestry. The bedrooms, boldly themed around the graphics of artist Grau, have generous beds and state of the art gleaming bathrooms. Breakfast on the terrace or in the airy conservatory. Feel at home in the elegant salons, play the concert piano, watch the giant TV or wander the acres of garden. Book a meal with Bruno and discover his fine wines. This gem deserves more than an overnight stay.

Rooms	1 double: €95.
	1 suite for 4: €95.
Meals	Dinner €26. Wine from €18.
Closed	Rarely.

Rooms	4 doubles: €140–€200.
	1 family room for 4: €230–€260.
Meals	Dinner with coffee, €30–€35;
	children €10. Restaurants 18km.
Closed	Rarely.

	Dorothée Malinge
	Moulin Guillard,
	18260 Subligny,
	Cher
Tel	+33 (0)2 48 73 70 49
Mobile	+33 (0)6 61 71 15 30
Email	malinge.annig@orange.fr

	Bruno de La Palme
	Domaine du Château de Moison,
	18380 Ivoy le Pré,
	Cher
Mobile	+33 (0)6 20 65 03 83
Email	bdelapalme@gmail.com

Entry 304   Map 5

Entry 305   Map 5

La Verrerie

Deep countryside, fine people, fantastic bedrooms. In a pretty outbuilding, one of the doubles, with a green iron bedhead, old tiled floor and Provençal quilt, looks onto the garden from the ground floor; the suite's twin has the same tiles underfoot, beams overhead and high wooden beds with an inviting mix of white covers and red quilts. The Count and Countess, who manage forests, farm and hunt, enjoy doing B&B, they are charming and thoroughly hospitable. If you would like to dine in, you will join them for dinner in the main house. Members of the family run a vineyard in Provence, so try their wine.

Minimum stay: 2 nights at weekends.

Les Aubuées

In a peaceful street overlooking lush meadows, sheltered by old walls and surrounded by trees, is an 1850s maison de maître, a Belle Époque residence; the first view takes your breath away. Little Toto and Chopin wag their welcome, followed by smiling Pascale. In big bedrooms on the first floor, wood, linen, silk and cotton blend with antique pieces and a luxurious modern feel pervades. Borrow the bikes, visit Sancerre and the cathedral at Bourges, return to a secluded courtyard and a delicious pool. Breakfast, served under the Napoleonic chandelier, is divine: Pascale, warm hostess, is a skilled pastry chef.

Rooms	2 doubles: €77-€112. 1 suite for 4: €101-€151. Singles €71-€106. Extra bed/sofabed available €25 per person per night.
Meals	Dinner with wine, €20-€30. Guest kitchen. Restaurants 10km.
Closed	Rarely.

Rooms	1 suite for 2, 1 suite for 4: €89-€137. Singles €89.
Meals	Restaurant 5km.
Closed	Rarely.

	Étienne & Marie de Saporta La Verrerie, 18380 Ivoy le Pré, Cher
Tel	+33 (0)2 48 58 90 86
Email	m.desaporta@wanadoo.fr
Web	www.laverreriedivoy.com

	Pascale & Benoît Portier Les Aubuées, 51 route de Montcorneau, 18500 Mehun sur Yèvre, Cher
Tel	+33 (0)2 48 57 08 24
Email	les.aubuees@gmail.com
Web	www.lesaubuees.fr/

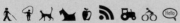

Entry 306   Map 5

Entry 307   Map 10

Domaine de l'Ermitage

Ten minutes from the delights of café-chic Bourges, this articulate husband-and-wife team run their beef and cereals farm and Menetou-Salon vineyards (tastings arranged), make their own jam and still have time for their guests. Vivacious and casually elegant, Laurence runs an intelligent, welcoming house. The big, simple yet stylishly attractive bedrooms of her 18th-century farmhouse are of pleasing proportions, one (the least grand) up a steep tower stair, the rest full of light and views over the graceful park. Guests may use the discreet pool at pre-arranged times.

Rooms	2 doubles, 1 twin: €81–€92.
	1 triple: €117.
	1 quadruple: €147.
Meals	Restaurants in village.
Closed	Rarely.

Laurence & Géraud de La Farge
Domaine de l'Ermitage,
18500 Berry Bouy,
Cher
Tel +33 (0)2 48 26 87 46
Mobile +33 (0)6 64 77 87 46
Email domaine-ermitage@wanadoo.fr
Web www.hotes-ermitage.com

Entry 308   Map 10

Les Bonnets Rouges

Cross the garden courtyard to the ancient, peaceful coaching inn where Stendhal once laid his head. Beyond the breakfast room, where 15th-century timbers, wraparound oak panels and stone alcoves dance in mixed-up glory for breakfast amid Turkish rugs, is the staircase up. Three bedrooms, wonderfully quaint and nicely tatty, have antique beds (one a four-poster), new mattresses, hanging rails, perhaps a roll top bath. Up steeper, narrower stairs, a pretty attic double has festoons of beams and the loo behind a curtain. Your charming host, Olivier, lives just across the courtyard. Sleep among angels beneath Bourges' unsurpassed cathedral.

Rooms	2 doubles: €72–€78.
	2 suites for 3-4: €80–€110.
	Extra bed €20.
Meals	Restaurants within walking distance.
Closed	Rarely.

Olivier Llopis
Les Bonnets Rouges,
3 rue de la Thaumassière,
18000 Bourges,
Cher
Tel +33 (0)2 48 65 79 92
Email contact@bonnetsrouges-bourges.fr
Web www.bonnetsrouges-bourges.fr

Entry 309   Map 10

Domaine de la Trolière

The beautifully proportioned house in its big shady garden has been in the family for over 200 years. The sitting room is a cool blue-grey symphony, the dining room smart yellow-grey with a rare, remarkable maroon and grey marble table: breakfast is in here, dinner, sometimes en famille, always delicious, is in the big beamed kitchen. Each stylishly comfortable room has individual character and Madame has a fine eye for detail. She is charming, dynamic, casually elegant and has many cats. Visitors have poured praise: "quite the most beautiful house we've ever stayed in", "the evening meals were superb".

Château de la Villette

More pretty 19th-century hunting lodge than grand château, la Villette sits in 40 idyllic acres of parkland, close to a huge spring-fed lake: borrow the row boat and potter. Capable, hospitable, generous Karin – dynamic gardener, fine cook – loves and cares for each inch of the place. A winding staircase leads to a beauty of a bedroom done in Biedermeier style, with a sloping ceiling and serene views; the second room too is seductive. Feather duvets will cosset you, elegant breakfasts and dinners at the convent table will delight you, and nothing is too much trouble for Karin.

Rooms	3 doubles; 1 double with separate wc: €53–€73. Extra bed €10.
Meals	Dinner with wine, €27.
Closed	Rarely.

Rooms	1 double, 1 double with separate bathroom: €90.
Meals	Dinner, with wine, €25.
Closed	Rarely.

	Marie-Claude Dussert Domaine de la Trolière, 18200 Orval, Cher
Tel	+33 (0)2 48 96 47 45
Mobile	+33 (0)6 72 21 59 76
Email	marie-claude.dussert@orange.fr

	Karin Verburgh Château de la Villette, St Août, 36120 Ardentes, Indre
Tel	+33 (0)2 54 36 28 46
Web	www.romantik-destinations.com

Entry 310   Map 10

Entry 311   Map 10

Loire Valley

La Croix Verte

Vincent and Élisabeth's serene home lies plumb in the heart of George Sand country. Linger under lime trees in a secret courtyard garden while relishing a plentiful breakfast; enjoy a dinner of home-grown produce; get cosy in the family sitting room before an open fire. A staging post in the 12th century, La Croix Verte stands in the heart of the village but you won't hear a peep as you slumber under a hand-stitched bedcover; the charming loft bedrooms in natural tones share sofas, books and games. Come for heaps of character, unspoilt countryside, and artist hosts (potter and painter) who are an absolute delight.

Loire Valley

Le Manoir du Menoux

In the heart of a quiet village, through a formal French garden, is a pretty half-timbered house with a Normandy air. Pleasant Marie-Estelle is a straightforward lady with a quiet smile, serving breakfast around a large oak table in the dining room, or outside in summer. Sit listening to the gurgling stream down by the charming summerhouse; in chillier weather, the salons' daybeds make a comfy spot. Up the winding oak staircase are the light and luminous suite 'Diane', southern-coloured 'Manon' gazing over romantic rooftops, and 50s-feel 'Amélie'. Visit snail and chestnut fêtes, and Lake d'Eguzon for nautical things. Lovely.

Rooms	2 doubles, 1 twin: €68. Singles €58. Extra bed/sofabed available €30 per person per night.
Meals	Dinner with wine, €23. Restaurant 1.5km.
Closed	Rarely.

Rooms	2 doubles: €70–€80. 1 suite for 4: €97–€134.
Meals	Dinner €27, maximum 4 people. Restaurant within walking distance.
Closed	Christmas & New Year.

Élisabeth & Vincent Portier
La Croix Verte,
Le Bourg, 12 rue des Maîtres
Sonneurs, 36400 St Chartier,
Indre

Tel   +33 (0)2 54 31 02 71
Email   contact@veportier.com
Web   www.veportier.com

Marie-Estelle Rives
Le Manoir du Menoux,
15 rue Haute, 36200 Le Menoux,
Indre

Tel   +33 (0)2 36 27 91 87
Mobile   +33 (0)6 60 10 20 57
Email   rivesme@wanadoo.fr
Web   www.manoirdumenoux.com

Entry 312   Map 10

Entry 313   Map 9

Loire Valley

Loire Valley

Le Canard au Parapluie Rouge

This pretty 17th-century house has been welcoming guests for most of its history: it was once the Auberge de la Gare; the station has gone but a train occasionally shoots through the sleepy calm. Kathy, from Ohio, and Martin, from Wiltshire, are great fun and will make you feel instantly at home. Each of the sunny little bedrooms has a charm and flavour of its own and the big heavy-beamed living room opens onto an enclosed garden with a well-hidden above-ground pool. Beautiful meals are served in the elegant dining room or out under the trees. Kathy loves cooking and Martin grows the vegetables. It's all absurdly good value.

Domaine du Ris de Feu

No longer part of a defensive frontier of castles, this 15th-century manor and lake is a sanctuary swathed in lush forest. The domain is the pride and joy of Caroline, who runs it to the highest eco and ethical standards, and husband Luc. Artisan builders (still discreetly on site) have restored using natural materials and traditional craft. Your charming fruit loft, on two floors, has oval windows, oak fittings and a wood-burner; upstairs, drift off under organic linen. After breakfast in the old bakery, wander and enjoy, listen to the birdlife, bathe in the lake, hire canoes or bicycles... explore this enchanted kingdom!

Rooms	3 doubles; 1 double with separate bathroom: €58–€85. 1 family room for 3: €58–€85. Extra bed/sofabed available €10 per person per night.
Meals	Dinner with wine, €26.
Closed	Rarely.

Rooms	1 suite for 2: €105–€125.
Meals	Dinner from €35 (not Saturdays). Restaurant 900m.
Closed	Rarely.

Martin & Kathy Missen
Le Canard au Parapluie Rouge,
3 rue des Rollets, 36200 Celon,
Indre

Tel	+33 (0)2 54 25 30 08
Email	info@lecanardbandb.com
Web	lecanardbandb.com

Luc & Caroline Fontaine
Domaine du Ris de Feu,
36370 Chalais,
Indre

Tel	+33 (0)2 54 37 87 73
Email	contact@lerisdefeu.fr
Web	www.lerisdefeu.fr

Entry 314   Map 9

Entry 315   Map 9

Saint Victor La Grand' Maison

The 16th-century château bursts into view from its wooded hilltop, tall turrets and ivy-clad façade towering over the river Anglin. You can saunter down here past the pool and picnic on organic pâté under a 400-year-old oak; just water, trees and birdsong. Inside, read by the fire, tinkle on the baby grand, retire to bed. Deeply comfortable rooms in warm reds, blues and pastels have museum-worthy antiques, plush fabrics, gilt portraits, book-lined walls. Hugely friendly, Madame offers tastings, courses and talks by local savants – and there are gîtes in the grounds. "Simply a delight" says our inspector, "for anybody at all."

Pets by arrangement.

Château de la Celle Guenand

In the heart of an old Touraine village, four hectares of delightful walled park and a fairytale castle that dates from 1442. It's large but not palatial, grand but not ornate, and refreshingly unstuffy. Much is being updated, everything is charming, and Stephen is putting all his energies into his new project. You get top mattresses on king-size beds, bedrooms with beautifully proportioned windows (cool conservative shades for the newest) and delicious quince jams at breakfast. After dinner: brocade sofas in faded reds, books to browse and a piano to play. All this, châteaux by the hatful, and the Brenne National Park.

Children over 6 welcome. Pets by arrangement.

Rooms	1 double: €130. 1 suite for 2: €150; rooms can interconnect to form a suite for 4: €200.
Meals	Dinner €20. Wine €8–€20. Restaurant 1.5km.
Closed	14 November to 17 February.

Rooms	4 doubles: €100–€165. 1 family room for 5: €160–€180.
Meals	Hosted dinner, 4 courses with wine, €48; children over 16, €30; under 16, €20. Restaurant in village.
Closed	9 October to 20 May.

Marie Rouet Grandclément
Saint Victor La Grand' Maison,
36300 Ingrandes,
Indre

Tel	+33 (0)2 54 37 46 55
Mobile	+33 (0)6 03 81 51 37
Email	marie@saintvictorlagrandmaison.fr
Web	www.saintvictorlagrandmaison.fr

Stephen Palluel
Château de la Celle Guenand,
14 rue du Château,
37350 La Celle Guenand,
Indre-et-Loire

Tel	+33 (0)2 47 94 93 61
Mobile	+33 (0)6 76 23 74 77
Email	stephane@chateaucelleguenand.com
Web	www.chateaucelleguenand.biz

Le Clos de Ligré

This elegant country house sings in a subtle harmony of traditional charm and contemporary chic under Martine's modern touch. Sponged walls, creamy beams and eye-catching fabrics breathe new life into rooms with old tiled floors and stone fireplaces, and the doubles in the attic are great, with views over the huge garden. Windows are flung open to let in the light and the stresses of city living are forgotten in cheerful, easy conversations with your hostess, who joins guests for candlelit dinners. Bookcases, baby grand, buffet breakfasts at the oval table, a barn for barbecues, a pool for the energetic… delightful.

Rooms	3 doubles: €110.
Meals	Dinner with wine, €35.
Closed	Rarely.

	Martine Descamps
	Le Clos de Ligré,
	Le Rouilly,
	37500 Ligré,
	Indre-et-Loire
Tel	+33 (0)2 47 93 95 59
Email	mdescamps@club-internet.fr
Web	www.le-clos-de-ligre.com

Entry 318   Map 9

La Closerie Saint Martin

Katharina, Marcel and Fado the dog offer a tranquil retreat in their historic home, once part of the local monastery. In a wine-growing hamlet, five peaceful rooms from classic to contemporary, four-poster to panelled chalet-style, all mellow colours and white linen, period pieces and cosy fabrics. Bathrooms are fresh and modern. Bountiful breakfasts with home-made cake, yoghurt and fresh fruit are taken at one table in the airy dining room. Markets and châteaux are nearby; rent a bike or walk the Nature Park; read a book, visit the vegetable garden. Eat out or in: dinners start with a drink in the impressive wine cellar.

Rooms	4 doubles, 1 twin/double: €80–€100. Discount for stays of 2+ nights. Extra bed/sofabed available €25 per person per night.
Meals	Dinner with wine, apéritif & coffee, €30. Restaurants 10km.
Closed	Rarely.

	Katharina Hirt
	La Closerie Saint Martin,
	6 rue du Prieure,
	Les Roches Saint Paul, 37500 Ligré,
	Indre-et-Loire
Tel	+33 (0)2 47 58 17 24
Email	info@lacloseriesaintmartin.fr
Web	www.lacloseriesaintmartin.fr

Entry 319   Map 9

Loire Valley

Domaine de Beauséjour

Dug into the hillside with the forest behind and a panorama of vines in front, this wine-grower's manor successfully pretends it was built in the 1800s. Venerable oak beams and stone cut by troglodyte masons create a mood of stylish rusticity. Bedrooms are charming, the suite in the main house, the other two in the romantic poolside tower. Find carved bedheads, old prints, vases of fresh and artificial flowers, elegant bathrooms. Your vivacious hostess helps her son run the family wine estate and will arrange a tasting for guests. Picnic in the conservatory or in one of the caves overlooking the valley.

Minimum stay: 2 nights.

Rooms	2 doubles: €70-€90.
	1 suite for 3-4: €120.
Meals	Restaurants 5km.
Closed	Rarely.

Marie-Claude Chauveau
Domaine de Beauséjour,
37220 Panzoult,
Indre-et-Loire

Tel	+33 (0)2 47 58 64 64
Mobile	+33 (0)6 86 97 03 40
Email	info@domainedebeausejour.com
Web	www.domainedebeausejour.com

Entry 320   Map 9

Loire Valley

La Baumoderie

Anne designed interiors in Paris, Jean-François managed hotels, now they do B&B from their imaginatively restored farmhouse on the top of a hill. Lively, charming people, they serve excellent French dinners in a modern chandelier'd conservatory and give guests big rustic-elegant rooms: one cool and spacious on the ground floor (with just French windows) and a suite at the top of an outside stone stair; there's a stunning 'cabane' with a shower on the veranda. The large garden and wild flower meadow and Jeremy Fisher-like pond blend into the landscape, the small village is up the road, and peace reigns supreme.

Rooms	1 double with separate shower & wc: €100-€125.
	1 suite for 2 with separate shower & wc: €135-€150.
Meals	Lunch and dinner with wine, €35.
	Restaurant 4km.
Closed	Rarely.

Anne Tardits
La Baumoderie,
17 rue d'Étilly,
37220 Panzoult,
Indre-et-Loire

Mobile	+33 (0)6 08 78 00 73
Email	anne@labaumoderie.fr
Web	www.labaumoderie.fr

Entry 321   Map 9

Le Clos Chavigny

Through the impressive carriage door you wash up at this long, extremely attractive house, the impeccably restored wing of these listed 17th-century buildings. Step inside to find a magnificent salon, billiard and dining rooms, and a charming 'library' for bookish nights in. Big sophisticated bedrooms have canopied beds beneath soaring timbers, fine period furniture, rich fabrics and art. The gardens are box hedged and rose bordered, with a pool to the side, and the Loire's pretty rolling countryside and glorious châteaux lie at your feet. A tranquil place with warm and welcoming hosts.

Over 12s welcome.

La Chancellerie

Bernard and Claire have a real sense of hospitality and love their charming old manor house, backed by trees and lawns, fronted by pretty parterres. Talented musicians, they host concerts and masterclasses too (note the five pianos!). Bedrooms lie in the more humble wing but one of the family suites is in the house – large and lofty with a splendid stone fireplace. All is immaculate, the food is delicious, there are wine tastings in the cellars (the best local bottles) and beautiful Chinon is a 15-minute drive. Swim in the nearby river or in your friendly hosts' pool; hire canoes and float down the Vienne.

Parking on-site.

Rooms	3 doubles: €130–€150.
	1 suite for 4: €150–€200.
Meals	Dinner with wine, from €40.
	Restaurants 10km.
Closed	Rarely.

Rooms	3 doubles: €95–€115.
	2 suites for 2-5: €110–€305.
	Dogs welcome, €5 per day.
Meals	Dinner with wine, €22–€35.
	Restaurants 1km.
Closed	Rarely.

	Moha Oulad
	Le Clos Chavigny,
	3 rue de la Rouillère, 37500 Lerné,
	Indre-et-Loire
Tel	+33 (0)2 47 93 94 72
Mobile	+33 (0)6 83 10 46 64
Email	closchavigny@gmail.com
Web	www.lecloschavigny.com

	Claire & Bertrand Pelourdeau
	La Chancellerie,
	37420 Huismes,
	Indre-et-Loire
Tel	+33 (0)2 47 95 46 76
Mobile	+33 (0)6 60 89 43 23
Email	info@lachancellerie.com
Web	www.lachancellerie.com

Loire Valley

Manoir de la Touche

Longing for your own miniature Loire château? Here it is, a stone's throw from Azay-le-Rideau, though infinitely more comfortable having been renovated to the highest environmental standards. Alain is a relaxed, congenial and helpful host, the simply elegant bedrooms are big, stylish and uncluttered, bathrooms smartly contemporary. The whole place is beautifully furnished and decorated, with lots of gleaming oak for a perfect château atmosphere. The best châteaux and vineyards of Touraine are close by, while at home there's a piano and superb games room, and a covered pool in the grounds. A wonderful spot from which to explore.

Rooms	2 doubles: €110–€155.
	2 suites for 5: €120–€195.
	Extra bed €20–€30.
Meals	Restaurants 1.5km.
Closed	Rarely.

Alain Patrice
Manoir de la Touche,
24 rue du Vieux Chêne,
37190 Cheillé,
Indre-et-Loire
Mobile   +33 (0)6 08 64 42 51
Email   apatrice37@orange.fr

Entry 324   Map 4

Loire Valley

Le Chat Courant

A handsome 18th-century family house on the river Cher just opposite Villandry and with its own lovely garden (whose birdsong drowns out occasional train noise). Bedrooms are pretty and stylish: the double in the converted cottage opens to the swimming pool, the family room in the main house has fine antique furniture. Éric – who is also a keen photographer – has created garden enchantment here with old species of apple trees, a walled vegetable garden, a wisteria-clad pergola, a formal boxed flower garden, and a semi-wild garden beyond, all surrounded by woodland and pasture where the family's horses peacefully graze.

Minimum stay: 2 nights in high season. Pets by arrangement.

Rooms	1 double: €78–€85.
	1 family room for 5: €110–€180.
Meals	Restaurant 5-minutes drive.
Closed	Rarely.

Éric Gaudouin
Le Chat Courant,
37510 Villandry,
Indre-et-Loire
Tel   +33 (0)2 47 50 06 94
Mobile   +33 (0)6 37 83 21 78
Email   infos@le-chat-courant.com
Web   www.le-chat-courant.com

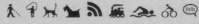

Entry 325   Map 4

Loire Valley

Loire Valley

Château du Vau

At the end of a long bumpy drive is a house of great character run with good humour: delightful philosopher Bruno has turned his family château into a stylish refuge for travellers. Two large, light bedrooms have been redecorated with seagrass and family memorabilia round splendid brass bedsteads; one remains, very comfortably, in its traditional, distinguished garb. And then there are the beautifully crafted treehouses: 'Oriental' in the oak tree, 'African' in the cedar, breakfast hampers delivered at the end of a rope… Dinners showcase estate produce. There's a fine pool, and a golf course bang opposite.

Château de l'Hérissaudière

You could get used to country-house living here, French-style. Madame, charming, cultured, welcomes you as family. Wrapped in 18 acres of parkland, the manor is all light, elegance, bold paintings and fresh flowers. Relax in the sunny salon or the splendid library. Bedrooms are spacious, gracious and subtly themed, Empire perhaps, or rich Louis XV. Bathrooms have the original tiling and marble floors. Tuck into a gourmet breakfast while Madame recommends local restaurants for dinner. Ping-pong and pool are in the grounds, with wild cyclamen and giant sequoias, and the old chapel has become a summer kitchen.

Minimum stay: 2 nights in high season. Pets by arrangement.

Rooms	3 doubles: €130.	
	2 treehouses for 2: €140.	
Meals	Dinner with wine, €42.	
	Summer buffets in garden €26.	
Closed	Rarely.	

Rooms	2 doubles: €110-€140.
	3 suites for 2-5: €130-€150.
	Extra bed/sofabed available €20 per person per night.
Meals	Summer kitchen. Restaurant 3km.
Closed	14 November to 1 April.

Bruno Clément
Château du Vau,
37510 Ballan Miré,
Indre-et-Loire
Tel   +33 (0)2 47 67 84 04
Email info@chateau-du-vau.com
Web   www.chateau-du-vau.com

Claudine Detilleux
Château de l'Hérissaudière,
37230 Pernay,
Indre-et-Loire
Tel   +33 (0)2 47 55 95 28
Mobile +33 (0)6 03 22 34 45
Email   lherissaudiere@gmail.com
Web   www.herissaudiere.com

Entry 326   Map 4

Entry 327   Map 4

Loire Valley

La Louisière

Simplicity, character and a marvellous welcome make La Louisière special. Madame delights in her role as hostess; Monsieur, who once rode the horse-drawn combine, tends his many roses, and his paintings of the countryside line the walls. A caring and unpretentious couple, both are active in their community. The traditional bedrooms have well-chosen colour schemes and sparkling bathrooms; touches of fun, too. Surrounded by chestnut trees, the farmhouse backs onto the gardens of the château and is wonderfully quiet. Tennis, bikes, tractors, horses to ride and an old-fashioned playground – it's bliss for children.

Rooms	1 twin: €55-€60.
	1 suite for 5, 1 triple: €55-€60.
Meals	Auberge 800m (Tuesday/Thursday only & Friday lunch). Restaurants 10km.
Closed	Rarely.

Andrée Campion
La Louisière,
37360 Beaumont la Ronce,
Indre-et-Loire

Tel	+33 (0)2 47 24 42 24
Mobile	+33 (0)6 78 36 64 69
Email	andree.campion@orange.fr
Web	http://louisiere.racan.org/

Entry 328   Map 4

Loire Valley

La Falotière

A cave suite! Hewn long ago into the rock beside a bell-topped presbytery, deliciously cool and light, it's a spacious retreat. Step from private courtyard to sitting room with big fireplace and old bread oven, smart wicker chairs, red lamps, tiled floors. Burrow through to a cushioned, red-carpeted bedroom sculpted into whitewashed rock; soak in a theatrical free-standing bath. Locals and walkers, your delightful hosts serve home-laid eggs at breakfast, enjoy sharing their lovely shady garden and this intriguing town, wedged in a gully ten minutes from Tours amid the Loire's vineyards and châteaux. Private, unique, fantastic.

Rooms	1 suite for 2: €150.
Meals	Restaurant 150m.
Closed	Rarely.

Dominique & Jean-Pierre Danderieux
La Falotière,
51 rue du Docteur Lebled,
37210 Rochecorbon,
Indre-et-Loire

Mobile	+33 (0)6 50 65 41 49
Email	jpdanderieux@gmail.com
Web	www.falotiere.com

Entry 329   Map 4

Bagatelle

A graceful 18th-century house in a charming setting close to the famous white wine vineyards of Vouvray. Bertrand and Anne are well-travelled and love literature – the bedrooms are named after the novels of Balzac. Choose between rooms in the house or memorable ones carved into the stone cliff outside: all are filled with interesting pictures, maps and objects; all have comfortable beds and good linen. Wake to breakfast in the dining room or outside in the sunshine – freshly-squeezed juice, homemade cake and jams, local hams and cheeses. Wander the pretty garden, laze in the large pool, or strike out on an adventure.

Château de Nazelles

A charming 16th-century manor house in the centre of the village with a shady courtyard and a winding track leading to woodlands and vineyards. House and garden are an exuberant mix of formal and informal, contemporary and traditional. Steps and pathways entice you through a series of 'secret' gardens, doorways cut in high hedges offer intriguing glimpses of the Loire valley. Rooms are a delight, furnished with simple understated elegance to fully show off the character of the house and the breakfast room is serene with a low, beamed ceiling. Great breakfasts, delightful hosts; even the pool is special.

Rooms	1 double: €90–€96.
	2 suites for 2-3,
	2 suites for 2-4: €100–€140.
Meals	Restaurants 15-minute walk.
Closed	Mid-November to mid-February.

Rooms	4 doubles: €115–€150.
	2 suites for 4: €260–€300.
Meals	Summer kitchen. Restaurants 3km.
Closed	Rarely.

	Anne & Bertrand Chandouineau
	Bagatelle,
	77 rue du Petit Coteau,
	37210 Vouvray,
	Indre-et-Loire
Tel	+33 (0)2 47 27 04 43
Mobile	+33 (0)6 71 76 35 26
Email	contact@bagatelle-chambresdhotes.fr
Web	www.bagatelle-chambresdhotes.fr/?lg=en

	Véronique & Olivier Fructus
	Château de Nazelles,
	16 rue Tue-La-Soif,
	37530 Nazelles,
	Indre-et-Loire
Tel	+33 (0)2 47 30 53 79
Email	info@chateau-nazelles.com
Web	www.chateau-nazelles.com

Entry 330   Map 4   Entry 331   Map 4

Loire Valley

Château de Pintray

Instant charm at the end of the long leafy avenue. This intimate château glows with personality and peculiarity yet this is no museum-piece: delightful Anne looks after the B&B while Jean Christophe produces some of the region's best sweet and dry white wines; enjoy the tastings. Stuffed full of character, bedrooms have super comfy beds on carpeted floors and bathrooms big old roll top tubs and walk-in showers. Tuck in to a splendid breakfast at the convivial table – alongside the Guignol puppet theatre! – before setting off for the great châteaux: Chenonceau, Amboise, Villandry and Azay le Rideau, all within an hour's drive.

Rooms	2 doubles: €115.
	1 family room for 4: €115-€165.
Meals	Restaurant 2km.
Closed	Rarely.

Anne Ricou & Jean Christophe Rault
Château de Pintray,
RD 283, Lussault sur Loire,
37400 Amboise,
Indre-et-Loire

Tel	+33 (0)2 47 23 22 84
Email	marius.rault@wanadoo.fr
Web	www.chateau-de-pintray.com

Entry 332   Map 4

Loire Valley

Le Clos de Fontenay

Sweep up the wooded drive to the formal garden to be greeted by Madame, or one of her grown-up children brushing up their English… and know you have entered an enchanting place. The graceful château sits in wooded splendour on the banks of the Cher – and you can see it the river from the suitably châteauesque bedrooms. Breakfast well on a wisteria-shaded terrace by the pool, or in the elegant dining room where you can tuck into a rather fine dinner too. Borrow bikes (masses to see within pedalling distance), play billiards in the fab games room or just have a wander: it's the most relaxed of places.

Minimum stay: 2 nights at weekends.

Rooms	2 doubles with separate bathroom,
	2 twin/doubles: €90-€148.
	Extra beds €30.
	Cot & highchair free of charge.
Meals	Restaurants 5km.
Closed	Rarely.

Nathalie Carli
Le Clos de Fontenay,
Château de Fontenay, 5 Fontenay,
37150 Bléré,
Indre-et-Loire

Tel	+33 (0)2 47 57 12 74t
Mobile	+33 (0)6 07 34 48 32
Email	contact@leclosdefontenay.fr
Web	www.leclosdefontenay.com

Entry 333   Map 4

Loire Valley

Loire Valley

Manoir de Chaix

Up a quiet lane, embraced by woodland and fields, an exceedingly fine manor house with dovecot, orchard, barn, pool and flourishing potager. Friendly Dominique welcomes you in, and treats you to a wonderful table d'hôtes. Spacious beamed bedrooms – four reached via a stone turret stair – are full of traditional comfort, and the dining room is inviting, with blazing logs, light-flooded windows and a great big convivial table. This is the Loire and there are châteaux by the hatful: Chenonceau, Loches, Amboise, Azay le Rideau, Villandry. A great find, and good value.

Cèdre et Charme

A treat! Lively, intelligent conversation, good food and music in elegant surroundings. The du Garreaus love sharing their fine 19th-century townhouse with its big bosky garden, and helping guests discover the riches of Touraine and the Loire Valley. Bright, serenely stylish bedrooms, with excellent bedding and bathrooms, are a seamless blend of period and modern (two inter-connect). The table – outdoors or in – is beautifully dressed for friendly meals focused on regional and homemade food. Children can eat separately and romp safely; there's an enticing, enclosed pool to look forward to – after a châteaux-cycling day?

Rooms	4 doubles, 2 twins: €80-€95. 1 family room for 4: €120. 1 triple: €100-€112. Extra bed/sofabed available €25 per person per night.	Rooms	2 doubles, 3 twin/doubles: €115-€125. Extra bed/sofabed available €20-€30 per person per night.
Meals	Dinner with wine, €30. Restaurants 5km.	Meals	Dinner with wine, €20-€30.
Closed	Rarely.	Closed	Rarely.

	Dominique Casaromani-Fillon Manoir de Chaix, Lieu dit Chaix, 37320 Truyes, Indre-et-Loire		**Anne du Garreau** Cèdre et Charme, 17 Grand Rue, 37320 Saint Branchs, Indre-et-Loire
Tel	+33 (0)2 47 43 42 73	Mobile	+33 (0)6 32 15 19 31
Email	manoirdechaix@sfr.fr	Email	contact@cedre-et-charme.fr
Web	www.manoir-de-chaix.com	Web	www.cedre-et-charme.fr

Loire Valley

Moulin de la Follaine

A smart metal gate opens to courtyard and garden beyond: Follaine is a deeply serene place. Ornamental geese adorn the lake, the tended garden has places to linger, colourful bedrooms have antique furniture, fabulous mattresses and lake views; one opens to the garden. Upstairs is a lovely light sitting room – and a guest fridge for picnics in the garden. Amazingly, the old milling machinery in the breakfast area still works – ask and Monsieur will turn it on for you; there are relics from the old hunting days, too. Your hosts, once in the hotel trade, know the area intimately and are utterly charming.

Rooms	1 double: €75-€80.
	2 suites for 4: €80-€120.
Meals	Bar-restaurant 800m; choice in
	Loches.
Closed	November – March.

Danie Lignelet
Moulin de la Follaine,
2 chemin du Moulin,
37310 Azay sur Indre,
Indre-et-Loire
Tel   +33 (0)2 47 92 57 91
Email   moulindelafollaine@wanadoo.fr
Web   www.moulindefollaine.com

Entry 336   Map 4

Loire Valley

Logis de la Fouettiere

A 19th-century farmhouse near the national forest of Loches filled with glorious colour, eclectic art and interesting furniture. Warm, well-travelled owners, Patricia and Henry, give you sumptuous bedrooms in bold hues with lively fabrics and wallpapers. You breakfast on homemade croissants and pains aux raisins at the sociable kitchen table, or linger outside on warmer days. Meander the winding streets of medieval Montrésor, visit the châteaux of the Loire, taste Cheverny wines. Return to a seat in the garden, or deep purple armchairs and plenty of books on art and design in the living room. Do eat in! Henry makes the best pizzas.

Babies under 2 and over 15s welcome. Pets by arrangement.

Rooms	1 double; 1 double with separate
	bathroom & wc: €95.
Meals	Dinner €32. Restaurants 3km.
Closed	15 November to 15 April.

Henry & Patricia Arnould
Logis de la Fouettiere,
Lieu-dit La Fouettiere,
37460 Chemille sur Indrois,
Indre-et-Loire
Mobile +33 (0)6 09 10 76 18
Email   logisdelafouettiere@gmail.com
Web   www.logisdelafouettiere.com

Entry 337   Map 9

Loire Valley

Loire Valley

Le Moutier

This fine traditional townhouse hides behind vast cedars on the edge of the village. Behind its walls lie warmth, exuberance, good humour, windows flung open to let in light and fresh air, and Jean-Lou's vibrant paintings. All feels friendly and unpretentious: a den-like sitting room, a comfy leather sofa, wonderful books, an open fire. Two bedrooms are in the main house, two are accessed via the studio, heaving with paintings and brushes. All this and a charming garden, throngs of fruit trees, a few loitering hens and, best of all, table d'hôtes at which food and wine flow. B&B at its best.

La Roseraie de Vrigny

White shutters, beams, old stones, comfortable bedrooms, organic potager, communal breakfasts and generous hosts – quintessential Sawday's. Rosalind, musician and philosopher, and John understand what B&B is all about and treat their guests as friends; sup with them on fine French food in the candlelit dining room and you will be charmed. The garden is entrancing too, all rambling roses, contemplative spots, even a little corner that is forever Scotland (like your hosts) and a Chinese bridge across a weeping-willow'd stream. Perfectly restful and welcoming after a day contemplating the glories of Chenonceau!

Wine tours available.

Rooms	4 doubles: €80. Singles €70. Extra bed/sofabed available €20 per person per night.
Meals	Dinner with wine, €30.
Closed	Rarely.

Rooms	1 double, 1 double with separate bathroom: €74. 1 family room for 4: €78-€122. 1 cottage for 2: €77-€120. Singles €68. Extra bed/sofabed available €23 per person per night.
Meals	Dinner €32; children under 12 €18. Restaurant 1km.
Closed	Rarely.

Martine & Jean-Lou Coursaget
Le Moutier,
13 rue de la République,
41110 Mareuil sur Cher,
Loir-et-Cher
Tel +33 (0)2 54 75 20 48
Email lemoutier.coursaget@wanadoo.fr
Web www.chambresdhotesdumoutier.com

Rosalind Rawnsley
La Roseraie de Vrigny,
3 rue du Ruisseau,
41400 St Georges sur Cher,
Loir-et-Cher
Tel +33 (0)2 54 32 85 50
Mobile +33 (0)7 60 45 99 14
Email rosalind.rawnsley@gmail.com
Web www.laroseraiedevrigny.com

Entry 338   Map 4

Entry 339   Map 4

La Folie Saint Julien

The three buildings are classic Loire Valley; the well-tended garden, its pool-in-a-barn cleverly fitted into an 18th-century wine tank, and the soft new décor – lovely bedrooms and bathrooms – bring a sense of ease and elegance. And Madame is a wonderful hostess; add her culinary prowess and you have a travelling gourmet's treat. Breakfast is the freshest imaginable with marvellous pastries (Madame took a course…). Then walk it off exploring the glorious châteaux. You can book dinner, and they will love you if you drive a vintage car. For wine buffs, cyclists, château-lovers, here is a touch of luxury in a sea of vineyards.

Parking on-site.

Les Loges de St Eloi

A large and impressive conversion of a 19th-century barn which hides behind tall gates in a small country town. Walk in to a lofty living space with a roomy table for breakfast and a seating area to one side; if you can't face going out for supper you can have cheese and *antipasti* here. Patricia and David, both interior designers, give you a visual feast too – the decoration is unique, flamboyant and reflects the fact they've travelled far and wide. Bedrooms have sober stone walls, perfect antiques, lovely textiles; bathrooms are glamorous affairs. The veranda is a fine spot from which to admire the clever garden with pool.

Minimum stay: 2 nights in high season & public holidays.

Rooms	3 doubles: €105–€125. 1 suite for 2, 1 suite for 4: €145–€230. Cot & sofabed available.		Rooms	4 doubles: €140–€160. Extra bed available €27 per person per night. Baby €10 per night.
Meals	Dinner, 4 courses, with apéritif & wine, €30. Restaurants 2km.		Meals	Light supper €12–€15. Restaurants 2-minute walk.
Closed	Rarely.		Closed	Rarely.

	Christine Sensenbrenner La Folie Saint Julien, 8 route de La Vallée, 41400 Saint-Julien de Chédon, Loir-et-Cher
Tel	+33 (0)2 54 32 71 08
Mobile	+33 (0)6 99 13 13 80
Email	contact@lafoliesaintjulien.com
Web	www.lafoliesaintjulien.com

	Patricia & David Jaep–Morley Les Loges de St Eloi, 11 rue des Fourneaux, 41400 Pontlevoy, Loir-et-Cher
Mobile	+33 (0)6 37 18 92 75
Email	leslogesdesainteloi@gmail.com
Web	www.leslogessainteloi.com

Entry 340   Map 4

Entry 341   Map 4

La Ferme des Bordes

Quirky and whimsical round the edges, artistic, gritty and charming in a rustic farm-y way, it's a collector's paradise and a housemaid's hell. Bright whatnots and treasures (some really good) pack this solid old guest farmhouse with its heavy wooden beams, ancient furniture and a real feel of long-ago France. Dinner, lots of it homegrown, is French-farm style with award-winning wines. You'll find more china in the pretty bedrooms, lace in the spotless bathrooms, prints and pictures in the common rooms. Your lovely hosts are warm and friendly. Outside, it's dogs and cats, a big wild garden and long farmland views.

Parking on-site.

La Cave Margot

The approach is pretty, along a green open valley, the family is charming, and the house is an immaculate longère. As for the bedrooms, they are large, inviting and contemporary, with original features and superb bathrooms. Two open to gardens and terrace, the third is up an outside stair, dotted with objects from exotic travels and overlooking an ancient walnut tree. For families, couples and seekers of peace: billiards, books, a warming wood-burner for chilly nights. Table d'hôtes is great fun and dinners are delivered with enthusiasm and imagination; Nathalie grows organic vegetables for savoury crumbles and Nicolas loves his wines.

Minimum stay: 2 nights at weekends & in high season.

Rooms	2 doubles: €64.
	2 suites for 4: €128.
	1 triple: €96. Extra bed €32.
Meals	Dinner with wine, €30;
	children €12. Restaurants 4km.
Closed	December – January.

Rooms	1 double: €70-€80.
	1 suite for 3, 1 suite for 5: €90-€95.
	Extra bed/sofabed available €20 per
	person per night.
Meals	Dinner, with apéritif, €20-€30.
	Restaurant 12km.
Closed	Rarely.

Jean-Philippe Werner
La Ferme des Bordes,
8 les Bordes, 41400 Pontlevoy,
Loir-et-Cher

Tel	+33 (0)2 54 32 51 08
Mobile	+33 (0)6 81 01 85 58
Email	werner.jeanphilippe@orange.fr
Web	www.la-ferme-des-bordes.net

Nathalie & Nicolas Leal
La Cave Margot,
41360 Lunay,
Loir-et-Cher

Tel	+33 (0)2 54 72 09 53
Email	info@lacavemargot.fr
Web	www.lacavemargot.fr

Entry 342   Map 4

Entry 343   Map 4

Loire Valley

Les Chambres Saint Martin

How lovely to stay in this ancient stone presbytery – one wall shared with the church – at the very top of the village of Chailles. Rooms are a delightful mix of old and new, intimate and quietly elegant, with good art and bursts of eccentricity in the form of bold lighting and wacky colours. Beds are deeply comfortable, bathrooms sleek with fluffy towels and posh lotions. You breakfast convivially on great cakes and juices, and all of Madame's food is fresh, local, homegrown and homemade. Take along one of her picnics as you visit vineyards and royal châteaux, then return to a delicious dinner – special diets are no bother – and lounge in the lovely garden.

Free parking available.

Rooms	3 doubles: €96–€130.
Meals	Dinner with wine, €25.
	Light dinner €15. Picnic €7.
	Restaurants 7km.
Closed	Rarely.

Marie-Luce Pradines
Les Chambres Saint Martin,
29 rue de l'Église,
41120 Chailles,
Loir-et-Cher

Tel	+33 (0)2 54 74 79 57
Email	contact@leschambressaintmartin.com
Web	www.leschambressaintmartin.com

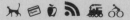

Entry 344 Map 4

Loire Valley

Château de Nanteuil

Revered grand-mère's house has faded charm but no châteauesque style or opulence: a few crumbly bits outside, frescoes and trunks in the hall, antlers in the dining room, floral wallpapers, large wardrobes and marble fireplaces in the bedrooms. These are light-filled and unashamedly old-fashioned but there's soul; bathrooms are time-warp 70s; river-water murmurs below your window. Most of all, you'll enjoy Frédéric – he's refreshingly unfussy, occasionally mercurial and serves you excellent organic dinners; asparagus in season, baked fillet of perch: he really cares about food. In summer sit on the terrace by the river.

Rooms	2 doubles: €80–€95.
	2 family rooms for 4: €80.
	Extra person €20.
Meals	Dinner with wine, €30.
Closed	Rarely.

Frédéric Théry
Château de Nanteuil,
16 rue Nanteuil,
41350 Huisseau sur Cosson,
Loir-et-Cher

Tel	+33 (0)2 54 42 61 98
Mobile	+33 (0)6 88 83 79 84
Email	contact@chateau-nanteuil.com
Web	www.chateau-nanteuil.com

Entry 345 Map 4

Les Grotteaux

Such a beautiful sight as you first glimpse this 17th-century château in its parkland setting. The du Halgouet family admired it for more than a decade before buying it and bringing it energetically back to life. Now, there are lofty reception rooms with painted panels, extraordinary ceilings and pretty antiques, plus a fine ceramic chimney to admire as you breakfast at a large table on local specialities. One bedroom has recently rediscovered 'grisaille' frescoes, the suite has river views, all have stunning bathrooms and super comfy beds with artisan made duvets and pillows. A fabulous pool, woods carpeted with cyclamen.

Over 12s welcome.

La Villa Médicis

Why the Italian name, the Italianate look? Queen Marie de Médicis used to take the waters here in the 17th century: the fine garden still has a hot spring and the Loire flows regally past behind the huge old trees. Muriel, a flower-loving perfectionist (artificial blooms as well as fresh), has let loose her decorative flair on the interior. It is unmistakably yet adventurously French in its splash of colours, lush fabrics and fine details. Fine antiques and brass beds grace some rooms, while the suite is a great 1930s surprise with a super-smart bathroom. You are wonderfully well looked after in this elegant and stylish house.

Rooms	3 doubles: €260-€280. 1 suite for 2: €350-€380.
Meals	Restaurants 5-minute drive.
Closed	Mid-December to mid-January.

Rooms	2 twins: €69. 1 suite for 2: €99. 1 triple: €83.
Meals	Dinner with wine, €32.
Closed	In winter, except by arrangement.

	Gaël du Halgouet
	Les Grotteaux,
	41350 Huisseau sur Cosson,
	Loir-et-Cher
Tel	+33 (0)2 54 52 01 43
Mobile	+33 (0)6 24 38 04 96
Email	gaelduhalgouet@gmail.com
Web	www.lesgrotteaux.wordpress.com

	Muriel Cabin-Saint-Marcel
	La Villa Médicis,
	Macé,
	41000 St Denis sur Loire,
	Loir-et-Cher
Tel	+33 (0)2 54 74 46 38
Email	medicis.bienvenue@wanadoo.fr
Web	www.lavillamedicis.com

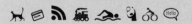

Entry 346   Map 4

Entry 347   Map 4

Château de la Rue

This 1810 'Directoire' mansion, approached via a grand avenue of trees, is lived in and loved by adorable Madame, who has been doing B&B for years. The croissants are home baked, the fruits are from the orchard – a historic walled beauty – the bedrooms are handsome ('Mme de Segur' the smallest, 'Cassandre' the most luxurious) and the furniture, all antique with the exception of some comfortable sofas, look as if it has been here forever. The Château de Chambord is close but best of all, you can cycle along the river to Blois (restaurants, market, château): the Loire flows at the end of the park.

La Gaucherie

A talented hostess, a beautifully restored farmhouse, a serene chic décor, a magical spot. The grassy garden leads seamlessly to woodland; there's a pond, a lovely orchard, and quiet spots for contemplation. Gentle Aurélia swapped New York for the forests of the Solonge, and loves light and simplicity. Fabulous bedrooms – and a 'restaurant' – lie in the converted stables and barn, with a wood-burning stove and red sofas; floors are terracotta or seagrass, bathrooms are mosaic'd. Rejoice in ponies and hens for the children, home-produced lamb, a lake with boat, marvellous breakfasts and a discreet, fenced pool.

Rooms	3 doubles: €120–€180. 2 suites for 4: €250.
Meals	Dinner with wine, €39 Restaurants 2km.
Closed	January/February.

Rooms	2 doubles, 1 twin/double: €90–€105. 2 suites for 4: €135–€185. Extra bed/sofabed available €25 per person per night. Cot €15 per night.
Meals	Dinner €32.
Closed	Mid-January to mid-February.

	Véronique de Caix
	Château de la Rue,
	41500 Cour-sur-Loire,
	Loir-et-Cher
Tel	+33 (0)2 54 46 82 47
Email	chateaudelarue@wanadoo.fr
Web	www.chateaudelarue.com

	Aurélia Curnin
	La Gaucherie,
	Route de Méry, Dep 76,
	41320 Langon,
	Loir-et-Cher
Tel	+33 (0)2 54 96 42 23
Mobile	+33 (0)6 88 80 45 93
Email	lagaucherie@wanadoo.fr
Web	www.lagaucherie.com

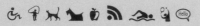

Entry 348   Map 4

Entry 349   Map 5

Le Bouchot

Come not for luxury but for deep country authenticity – and to make friends with a generous, charming, free-thinking family who gave up Paris for this lush corner of France. They have restored, renovated and eco-converted a run-down farm, insulated it with hemp, wattle and daub, then added wood-burning stoves, organic breakfasts... and cats, dogs, horses, hens, donkeys. Family rooms in outbuildings round the courtyard are wood-clad with sloping ceilings, rudimentary furnishings, mix and match bed linen, the odd rug. Dinner is in the kitchen diner – or the barns when there are campers. A place for new horizons.

Rooms	2 family rooms for 3, 1 family room for 4, 1 family room for 5: €70.
Meals	Dinner with wine, €25. Restaurant 2km.
Closed	Rarely.

Anne & Jean-Philippe Beau-Douëzy
Le Bouchot,
Route de Chaon,
41300 Pierrefitte sur Sauldre,
Loir-et-Cher

Tel	+33 (0)2 54 88 01 00
Mobile	+33 (0)6 71 57 61 26
Email	contact@lebouchot.net
Web	www.lebouchot.net

Entry 350   Map 5

Photo: Chez Vallee,
entry 362

Poitou – Charentes

Château de la Roche Martel

At the apex of three provinces, a sensational launch pad for Anjou, Touraine and Poitou. There's character and history in spades (Henry III is buried here), mullioned windows, a rare covered wooden gallery, a horse in the paddock, century old trees. And now, delightful new owners, she a Polish picture restorer, he an expert on Plantagenet history. Bedrooms glow with gorgeous fabrics and tadelakt walls, the larger double with a four-poster and fine stone fireplace, the smaller in a pretty round tower. All feels generous, the bathrooms are splendid (one with a rare antique wc) and salons face north and south – take your pick!

Minimum stay: 2 nights November-February.

Château de La Plante

You'll be charmed by this unpretentious stone manor looking proudly over farmland to the wooded Vienne valley. It has been in Françoise's family forever and she and Patrick tend it with loving care, as they do their guests. Period elegance drifts through rooms where the family grew up, leaving canopied beds, parquet floors and the odd empty picture frame in bedrooms named after great-grandmothers. Serenity reigns supreme; breakfast is in the old music room, a fittingly classic cream-blue affair. Join your hosts for an apéritif on the balustraded terrace or under the spreading lime tree. If houses could sing, this one surely would.

Rooms	1 double: €120. 1 family room for 3: €140-€165. 1 single: €90. Extra bed €25.
Meals	Restaurant 6km.
Closed	Rarely.

Rooms	2 doubles, 1 twin/double: €100-€120. 1 suite for 4 with bath & separate wc: €150. Children's triple room: €60-€80.
Meals	Restaurants 10-minute drive.
Closed	Rarely.

Alicja & Dominique
de Cornulier Lucinière
Château de la Roche Martel,
Lieu-dit la Roche Marteau,
86120 Roiffé, Vienne
Tel   +33 (0)5 49 22 36 31
Mobile +33 (0)6 83 43 46 34
Email   larochemartel@orange.fr
Web   www.larochemartel.com

Patrick & Françoise Dandurand
Château de La Plante,
86540 Thuré,
Vienne
Tel   +33 (0)5 49 93 86 28
Email patrick.dandurand@orange.fr
Web   www.chateaudelaplante.fr

Entry 351   Map 9

Entry 352   Map 9

Château de Labarom

A great couple in their genuine family château of fading grandeur; mainly 17th century, it has a properly aged face. From the dramatic hall up the superbly bannistered staircase, you reach the salon gallery that runs majestically through the house. Here you may sit, read, dream of benevolent ghosts. Bedrooms burst with personality and wonderful old beds. Madame's hand-painted tiles adorn a shower, her laughter accompanies your breakfast (organic garden fruits and four sorts of jam); Monsieur tends his trees, aided by Hermes the dog – he's a fount of local wisdom. A warm, wonderful, authentic place, and Michelin stars five miles away.

La Roseraie

Country B&B with one foot in the town: Neuville is a stroll. Warm and generous, Heather and Michael live in an elegant townhouse in four enclosed acres with orchard, vegetable garden and two rows of vines. The sitting area is cosy, the pool is fabulous, the bedrooms are immaculate, restful and calm: seagrass floors, white tub chairs, a carved bedhead, a balcony here, a garden patio there. Put the world to rights over Heather's delicious dinner served at the big table, or under the pergola in summer: gîte and B&B guests combine. Doves coo, Jack Russells frolic, Poitiers is the shortest drive.

Pets by arrangement.

Rooms	2 doubles, 1 twin: €85–€90.
Meals	Auberge nearby; restaurants 3–8km.
Closed	Rarely.

Rooms	3 doubles: €68–€95.
	2 family rooms for 4–5: €120–€160.
Meals	Dinner with wine, €28.
Closed	Rarely.

Éric & Henriette Le Gallais
Château de Labarom,
Route de Thurageau,
86380 Cheneché,
Vienne

Tel	+33 (0)5 49 51 24 22
Mobile	+33 (0)6 83 57 68 14
Email	labarom@labarom.com
Web	www.labarom.com

Michael & Heather Lavender
La Roseraie,
78 rue Armand Caillard,
86170 Neuville de Poitou,
Vienne

Tel	+33 (0)5 49 54 16 72
Email	heather@laroseraiefrance.fr
Web	www.laroseraiefrance.fr

Le Chai de Villiers

A lovely, quiet house in a peaceful part of France, it used to be the winery for the village château next door. The owners have one end of the long low building, you have the other with a bright, light sitting/breakfast room done in soft beige, cream and grey tones. All the chairs and sofas have been refurbished by clever upholsterer Martine: she also runs a workshop every week. Not a wrinkle disturbs the carefully matched, airy bedrooms. In the garden, olive and palm trees screen the saltwater pool – another successful exotic blend. A restful place, with listed St Savin to visit and Marais Poitevin, the 'Green Venice'.

Chat Noir Chambre d'Hôtes

On the edge of a hamlet amidst rolling valleys, well travelled Chris and Michelle's eclectically furnished home oozes character from every stone and quirky corner, from the burgeoning library with log stove to the exposed stone walls, timber beams and elegant French beds in the bedrooms. One of the bathrooms is a few steps along the hall. Tuck into omelettes for breakfast at the kitchen table, snooze in a hammock in the tiered garden, take a dip in the pool or a soak in the hot tub. Markets, shops and restaurants are 10 minutes drive away, and Montmorillon, Poitiers and Limoges are all within striking distance.

Rooms	2 doubles: €70-€100.
Meals	Restaurants 50m. Platter on arrival on arrangement available, with wine, €23.
Closed	Rarely.

Rooms	1 double; 1 double with separate bathroom: €55-€60.
Meals	Dinner, 3-4 courses with wine, €25. Restaurants 15-minute drive.
Closed	End of October to beginning April.

	Martine Dereume
	Le Chai de Villiers,
	2 rue Champ Parmant,
	86190 Villiers,
	Vienne
Mobile	+33 (0)6 27 93 64 77
Email	chambresdhotespoitiers@gmail.com
Web	www.chambredhotepoitiers.com

	Chris & Michelle Burns
	Chat Noir Chambre d'Hôtes,
	Les Rechers,
	86250 Genouille,
	Vienne
Mobile	+44 (0)7714 980001
Email	chatnoir86250@gmail.com
Web	www.chatnoir86.com

Wisteria House

A bright white table greets you, topped with books and info, and teas and coffees to the side – and Judy and Peter, full of generosity and good humour, proud of their finely restored barn. Grazing cows, farmland, more barns: the setting is green and deliciously peaceful. Tucked under the eaves, the en suite shower rooms are as fresh and charming as the bedrooms themselves, and the treats continue at table… what could be nicer than to be served a beautiful dinner under a wisteria-strewn pergola on a warm southern night? Ancient Angoulême is an easy drive, bustling market town Chasseneuil is even closer.

Rooms	2 doubles, 1 twin: €60. Singles €40.
Meals	Dinner, 4 courses with apéritif & wine, €32; Monday, Wednesday & Saturday only.
Closed	Rarely.

Judy Hemsworth
Wisteria House,
La Chaume,
16450 St Laurent de Ceris,
Charente

Tel	+33 (0)5 45 84 07 61
Mobile	+33 (0)6 04 47 81 24
Email	pj@thewisterias.com
Web	www.thewisterias.com

Le Bourg

Stone cottages, nodding hollyhocks, ducks in the lane: Mareuil epitomises rural France, and the house sits in its heart. Arrive to a sweeping drive, an immaculate pool, a grand façade and Vanessa, who has travelled the world. After a final posting in Paris she landed in sunny Charente, and is very happy. Bedrooms are bright, airy and comfortable, with cosy bathrooms; dinners, in the ample dining room, are gastronomic, cosmopolitan, entertaining and preceded by pineau de Charente. You are surrounded by sunflowers and vines and Cognac is close. Friendly, interesting, great fun.

Rooms	3 twin/doubles: €95.
Meals	Dinner with wine, from €32.
Closed	Rarely.

Vanessa Bennett-Dixon
Le Bourg,
16170 Mareuil,
Charente

Tel	+33 (0)5 45 66 29 75
Email	lebourg-charente@wanadoo.fr
Web	www.lebourg-charente.com

Le Chiron

The big old well-lived-in house is all chandeliers, ceiling roses and heavy dark furniture. The Toile de Jouy triple has a rustic elegance, La Rose is… pink. Bathrooms are more functional than luxurious but with so much natural beauty to hand who wants to stay in anyway? Madame's regional cooking is a treat, served in a conservatory big enough for many. Genuinely welcoming, your farmer hosts stay and chat (in French, mostly!) when they can. They'll also show you the fascinating old cognac still. Big, off the beaten track and great for families (they run a campsite next door).

Le Logis du Paradis

Mellow stones, chunky beams, sensuous fabrics… there's a timeless feel to the Logis, with 18th-century buildings embracing a magnificent oval courtyard. In big luxurious bedrooms you snuggle down in superbly comfortable king-size beds under white linen… and wake in anticipation of a delicious breakfast. There's a pool in the aromatic garden, books on the landings, a tea and coffee kitchen, a bar in the former distillery shared with the other guests. Sally's generous table features market-fresh local produce, fine wines, and a glass of the neighbour's superb XO Cognac to finish with. Highly professional.

Rooms	2 doubles, 1 twin: €50.
	1 family room for 4: €80.
	2 triples: €65.
Meals	Dinner with apéritif & wine, €20.
Closed	Rarely.

Rooms	5 doubles: €110–€150.
Meals	Lunch €19. Dinner €39.
	Wine from €12.50.
	Restaurant 4km.
Closed	Mid-January to end February.

Micheline & Jacky Chainier
Le Chiron,
14 rue Haute,
16130 Salles d'Angles,
Charente

Tel	+33 (0)5 45 83 72 79
Email	jacky.chainier@orange.fr

Sally Brimblecombe
Le Logis du Paradis,
La Magdeleine,
16300 Criteuil la Magdeleine,
Charente

Tel	+33 (0)5 45 35 39 43
Email	info@logisduparadis.com
Web	www.logisduparadis.com

Entry 359   Map 9

Entry 360   Map 9

Le Chatelard

This is a gem of a place to stay, both grand and intimate. Béatrice inherited the exquisitely French neo-gothic château and she lovingly protects it from the worst of modernisation (though the hurricane took its toll and trees have had to be replanted). Sleep between antique linen sheets, sit in handsome old chairs and be charmed by a bedroom in a tower. The sitting room has that unusual quirk, a window over the fireplace, the dining room a panelled ceiling studded with plates. Béatrice, a teacher, and Christopher, a lecturer in philosophy, are interesting, cultured hosts who enjoy eating with their guests.

Chez Vallee

A fine old house with wellbeing at its warm heart. Amanda's passionate about yoga, Ayurveda and living well and the Grahams chose this idyllic rural setting, among Cognac vines, to realise her dream retreat; her massages alone are worth the detour... A yoga podium takes centre stage in the establishing garden. Indoors they've retained the handsome bones of the building and furnishings reflect their world travels and taste for contemporary art, design and comfort. You've a choice of generous, traditional and healthy meals – nutri-bullets, seasonal fruit and vegetarian dishes a speciality. Come for a course or simply to unwind.

Minimum stay: 2 nights. Parking on-site.

Rooms	1 double, 1 double with separate wc, 1 twin with separate wc: €60–€70. 1 family room for 6 with separate wc: €80–€120. Extra bed €10. Singles €50.
Meals	Dinner with wine, €25. Restaurant 1km.
Closed	Rarely.

Rooms	3 doubles: €90–€110.
Meals	Dinner, 3 courses with wine, €25. Restaurants 15-minute drive.
Closed	November – March.

	Béatrice de Castelbajac & Christopher Macann Le Chatelard, 16480 Passirac, Charente
Tel	+33 (0)5 45 98 71 03
Email	c.macann@wanadoo.fr
Web	www.chateaudepassirac.jimdo.com

	Amanda Graham Chez Vallee, 17500 St Germain de Vibrac, Charente-Maritime
Mobile	+33 (0)6 40 33 23 82
Email	praanawellness@gmail.com
Web	www.praanawellness.com

Entry 361 Map 9

Entry 362 Map 8

Domaine du Meunier

A lovely, friendly house built in 1893 and renovated perfectly. Find a living room with a library and a piano, a dining room and a games room. Bedrooms are calm and serene, breakfast is a feast with coddled eggs from the family's hens; dinner (twice a week in high season) is lively! The outbuildings have become gîtes, the 'Pinball Hall' hosts events, and the family live in the old mill. Stroll through the walled garden, let the children splash in the pool, doze in an antique deckchair; at high tide you can swim or sail. Views are gentle, while the nearby harbour, pretty with sailing boats, joins the port to the Gironde.

Château de la Tillade

It's clear that Michel and Solange like people: they immediately put you at ease in their comfortable home. The château sits at the top of an avenue of lime trees; the vineyards have produced grapes for cognac and pineau for two centuries. Solange holds painting courses; her artistic flair is reflected in her love of fabrics, and the comfortable bedrooms are marvellously individual, each like a page out of Michel's memory book, steeped in family history. Meals around the family table are a delight with conversation in English or French; lavish, but without stuffiness. A rare opportunity to get to know a pair of charming French aristocrats.

Rooms	3 doubles, 2 twins: €70.
Meals	Dinner €25, twice weekly in high season. Restaurants 50m.
Closed	Rarely.

Rooms	1 twin: €100–€130. 2 family rooms for 4, 1 family room for 4 with separate wc: €100–€130. Extra bed/sofabed available €25 per person per night.
Meals	Dinner €40. Restaurant 12km.
Closed	Rarely.

Ariane & Coen Ter Kuile
Domaine du Meunier,
36 quai de L'Estuaire,
17120 Mortagne sur Gironde,
Charente-Maritime
Tel   +33 (0)5 46 97 75 10
Email info@domainedumeunier.com
Web   www.domainedumeunier.com

Vicomte & Vicomtesse Michel de Salvert
Château de la Tillade,
Gémozac,
17260 Saint Simon de Pellouaille,
Charente-Maritime
Tel   +33 (0)5 46 90 00 20
Email contact@la-tillade.com
Web   www.la-tillade.com

La Rotonde

Stupendously confident, with priceless river views, this city mansion seems to ride the whole rich story of lovely old Saintes. Soft blue river light hovers into high bourgeois rooms to stroke the warm panelling, marble fireplaces, perfect parquet. Double glazing, yes, but ask for a room at the back, away from river and busy road. The Rougers love renovating and Marie-Laure, calm and talented, has her own sensitive way with classic French furnishings: feminine yet not frilly, rich yet gentle. Superb (antique) linen and bathrooms, too, breakfasts with views and always that elegance.

La Porte Rouge

Central, cobbled, car-free Saintes – perfect for Francophiles. Do arrange a meal here at one big table (herbs from the walled garden). Cooking comes high on well-travelled (American) Jim and Monique's list of passions; history and art too – their relaxed, typically French home (a hotel since the 16th-century) is full to bursting with beautiful antiques from different countries. Quiet, comfortable bedrooms on the second floor have linen from Italy, beams, white stone walls, original wood and parquet floors, and modern bathrooms with antique tubs. Take a trip on the Charente which runs through this fine town.

Rooms	3 doubles, 1 twin with kitchenette: €100.
	1 family room for 4: €100.
Meals	Restaurants in town centre.
Closed	Rarely.

Rooms	2 doubles; 1 twin sharing bathroom with suite: €95-€105.
	1 suite for 4: €145-€175
	Singles €85-€95.
	Child bed €6 per night. Cot available.
Meals	Dinner, 4 courses with wine, coffee & apéritif, €26; children €12.
	Restaurant 2-minute walk.
Closed	Rarely.

Marie-Laure Rouger
La Rotonde,
2 rue Monconseil,
17100 Saintes,
Charente-Maritime

Mobile   +33 (0)6 87 51 70 92
Email   laure@laboutiquedelarotonde.com
Web   www.laboutiquedelarotonde.com

Monique Potel
La Porte Rouge,
15 rue des Jacobins,
17100 Saintes,
Charente-Maritime

Tel   +33 (0)5 46 90 46 71
Email   monique.potel@la-porte-rouge.com
Web   www.la-porte-rouge.com

Logis de l'Astrée

Along the rustic track to a long, low nobleman's house walled behind vines, and sweet Sophie to welcome you with a glass of their wine. All is beautiful inside and flooded with light: lofty ceiling beams painted white, 17th-century terracotta looking like new. Elegant beds are topped with blankets and sheets; two rooms have kitchenettes, one opens to the garden. A stone fireplace stacked with logs dominates the irresistible salon, and home-grown grape juices join homemade jams at the table. Explore the pretty Coran valley and the river on foot or by bike, and visit historic Saintes with its amphitheatre and cathedrals.

Minimum stay: 2 nights at weekends & in high season.

Le Logis du Port Paradis

Seafood is fresh from the Atlantic, the palm-ringed pool shimmers and five light-filled rooms exude your hosts' love of the sea. Clustered round a family home a short drive from Royan's sandy beaches, the nicely independent rooms and family suites have terraces, gleaming showers, ingenious headboards (sail canvas, slate, terracotta), a seaside feel. If you're lucky, Monsieur will cook – tuna carpaccio, fresh sole, gratin aux fraises – joining guests at one long table overlooking the pool; as Madame shares stories of oyster farming. Plump down afterwards on cherry sofas or step out to the flower garden for fresh air and stars.

Rooms	2 doubles with separate wc: €115–€130. 1 suite for 4 with separate wc: €130–€240. 1 studio for 2 with separate wc: €130–€145. Singles €105–€120. Extra bed/sofabed available €29 per person per night.	Rooms	3 doubles: €70–€75. 2 suites for 4: €92–€132. Extra bed/sofabed available €20 per person per night.
Meals	Occasional dinner with wine, €29. Restaurants 5-minute walk.	Meals	Dinner with wine, €32. Restaurants 3km.
Closed	3 November to 31 March.	Closed	Rarely.

	Sophie Boutinet Mangeart Logis de l'Astrée, Le Logis, 17770 Saint Bris de Bois, Charente-Maritime		Nadine Bauve Le Logis du Port Paradis, 12 route du Port Paradis, 17600 Nieulle sur Seudre, Charente-Maritime
Tel	+33 (0)5 46 93 44 07	Tel	+33 (0)5 46 85 37 38
Email	smangeart@terre-net.fr	Mobile	+33 (0)6 09 71 64 84
Web	www.logis-astree.fr	Email	contact@portparadis.com
		Web	www.portparadis.com

Entry 367   Map 8   Entry 368   Map 8

Vents et marées Ile d'Oléron

Hidden down narrow cobbled streets are these light and bright rooms surrounded by shared gardens filled with fig, mimosa and roses. Madame Geffroy, a Paris stylist, has given them a New England beach feel with jaunty stripes, old shutters as mirrors, surf boards and ships' flags on panelled walls, smart new bathrooms with walk-in showers and pebbled floors. Breakfast on homemade jams, freshly-baked artisan bread and galettes charentaises under a wooden pergola or around Madame's kitchen table. Golden sands and the Atlantic are a five minute stroll: hire bikes locally or take a boat to bustling La Rochelle or neighbouring islands.

Minimum stay: 2 nights July / August. Family room can be rented by the week. Parking on-site.

La Tillaie

Renovated with great care by Olivier and Christophe, this three-storey maison is filled with special touches; furniture old and new, family heirlooms, an open fire, even a jacuzzi and sauna. Spacious bedrooms have garden views and are thoughtfully decorated with interesting wallpaper and rugs; sparkling en suites are equally snazzy. Start your day with a breakfast of fresh pastries, cakes and jams – in the dining room or outside on the decking – before heading out to visit a nearby château or seaside town. Stroll to a nearby restaurant for dinner, or ask charming Olivier – a former chef – to cook you something special.

Parking on-site.

Rooms	2 doubles, 1 twin: €95.
	1 family room for 4: €120-€180.
	Cot available.
Meals	Restaurants 5-minute walk.
Closed	Mid-November to March.

Rooms	4 doubles: €80-€120. Extra
	bed/sofabed available €15.
Meals	Dinner with wine, €25.
	Restaurants 2-minute walk.
Closed	Rarely.

Marie Geffroy
Vents et marées Ile d'Oléron,
6 rue du Centre La Biroire,
17310 Saint Pierre d'Oléron,
Charente-Maritime
Mobile +33 (0)6 86 88 73 94
Email marie.geffroy75@gmail.com
Web www.chambre-hote-ile-oleron.fr/ index.php

Olivier Rotensztajn
La Tillaie,
28 rue du Vieux Pont,
17250 Pont l'Abbé d'Arnoult,
Charente-Maritime
Mobile +33 (0)6 15 24 71 03
Email latillaie@gmail.com

Entry 369   Map 8

Entry 370   Map 8

Palmier Sur Cour

A handsome townhouse in the heart of the historic town with an understated, calm interior. Find period details, deep skirtings, fireplaces, cornices and a light-flooded stone staircase with iron balustrading. Three lovely lofty bedrooms are decorated in classic French style with a mix of antiques and prettily dressed beds. Catherine and Eric give you homemade breakfasts of fresh fruit salad, cakes, yogurts and jams at one big table; in summer you spill onto the terrace. Beaches and seafood beckon and the port of Rochefort (that lies within the charmed triangle of La Rochelle, Saintes and Royan) is fascinating.

Minimum stay: 2 nights.

Château de Champdolent

On the edge of a village in a pastoral landscape is an 11th-century manor, an 18th-century farmhouse, and a keep, its outline majestic in the setting sun. You sleep under beams in rooms elegant and simple, the largest with its own kitchen area for making drinks, and sitting room with designer chairs and huge sofas. Rifle through art books in the library, repair to the guard room with armchairs and immense chimney. Dinner? Enjoy Line's tarte tatin and the best foie gras in France. The place is amazing and the charming owners (he a sculptor and food producer, she a lover of philosophy) relate the history with relish.

Parking on-site.

Rooms	1 double: €84–€102.
	1 family room for 3, 1 family room for 4: €110–€135.
	Reduced rate for single occupancy.
Meals	Guest kitchenette. Restaurants within walking distance.
Closed	Rarely.

Rooms	2 doubles: €80.
	1 apartment for 2–3: €120.
Meals	Dinner €27. Wine list €10–€40.
	Restaurants 10-minute drive.
Closed	Rarely.

Catherine & Eric Malingrey
Palmier Sur Cour,
55 rue de la République,
17300 Rochefort,
Charente-Maritime

Tel	+33 (0)5 46 89 72 55
Mobile	+33 (0)6 70 76 41 91
Email	contact@palmiersurcour.com
Web	www.palmiersurcour.com

Line & Dominique Cozic
Château de Champdolent,
3 rue de la Charente,
17430 Champdolent,
Charente-Maritime

Tel	+33 (0)5 46 82 96 07
Email	d.cozic@gmail.com
Web	www.chateaudechampdolent.fr

Entry 371 Map 8

Entry 372 Map 8

Les Hortensias

Behind its modest, wisteria-covered mask, this 17th-century former wine-grower's house hides a charming interior – and a magnificent garden that flows through orchard to topiary, a delight in every season. Soft duck-egg colours and rich trimmings make this a warm and safe haven, light airy bedrooms are immaculate and unpretentious (one with its original stone sink, another with a pretty French pink décor), the bathrooms are luxurious, the walls burst with art and the welcome is gracious, warm and friendly. Superb value with a good restaurant a mile or so away. It's a treat to stay here.

L'Etoile du Port

Built in 1633, this mellow-stone former cognac store is part of a terrace on the banks of the languid Boutonne. Here lives Clare, full of life, with a love of people and an eye for detail: cotton buds in bathrooms, honey from the market, umbrellas by the door! All is tranquil and delightful inside, from the first-floor salon with its gorgeous grand fireplace and inviting cream sofas, to the bedrooms with their delicious pale-stone walls; there's also a tip-top guest kitchen. Atlantic beaches are a 40-minute drive, restaurants are a stroll, and a children's park and café lie on the other side of the river.

Pets by arrangement.

Rooms	2 doubles: €65.
	1 triple: €72. Extra bed €20.
Meals	Summer kitchen.
	Restaurant in village, 1.5km.
Closed	Christmas & 1 January.

Rooms	3 doubles: €70–€75.
	1 suite for 4: €80–€120.
	Singles €65–€75. Cot €10.
	Extra bed €20.
Meals	Guest kitchen.
	Restaurant 10-minute walk.
Closed	Rarely.

Marie-Thérèse Jacques
Les Hortensias,
16 rue des Sablières,
17380 Archingeay,
Charente-Maritime
Tel   +33 (0)5 46 97 85 70
Email   jpmt.jacques@wanadoo.fr
Web   www.chambres-hotes-hortensias.com

Clare Pickering
L'Etoile du Port,
14 quai de Bernouet,
17400 Saint Jean d'Angely,
Charente-Maritime
Tel   +33 (0)5 46 32 08 93
Email   etoileduport@gmail.com
Web   www.letoileduport.com

Entry 373   Map 8

Entry 374   Map 8

Les Grands Vents

Close to a village in the heart of cognac country, beside a sleepy road, is a big old farmhouse with simple limewashed walls and a French country décor. Warm enthusiastic Virginie has an interiors boutique in town, and Philippe is a cabinet-maker. Guests have their own entrance and breakfast/living room, and use of the summer kitchen too – make yourselves at home! Bedrooms, both with lovely garden views, are big and fresh and catch the morning or evening sun. There's a lush pool surrounded by velvet greenery, and a covered terrace for simple summer breakfasts. Great value.

Pets by arrangement.

Le Clos de la Garenne

Charming owners and animals everywhere, from boxer dog to donkey to hens! Brigitte and Patrick gave up telecommunications for their dream of the country and the result is this heart-warming, small-village B&B. Avid collectors, they have decorated their roomy 16th-century house with eclectic flair, and old and new rub shoulders merrily; discover doll's house furniture and French cartoon characters, old armoires and antique treasures. Harmony breathes from walls and woodwork, your hosts are endlessly thoughtful, food is slow, exotic, organic (and delicious), and families are truly welcome.

Minimum stay: 2 nights in high season.

Rooms	1 suite for 4: €70 €115.
	1 family room for 3: €70-€95.
	Extra bed €20.
Meals	Restaurants in Surgères, 9km.
Closed	Rarely.

Rooms	2 doubles: €78-€88.
	1 suite for 6: €108 €178.
	1 cottage for 5: €88-€138.
	Singles €68. Extra bed/sofabed
	available €20 per person per night.
Meals	Dinner with wine, €27;
	children over 12, €22;
	children under 12, €12.
Closed	January/February.

Virginie Truong Grandon
Les Grands Vents,
17380 Chervettes,
Charente-Maritime
Tel   +33 (0)5 46 35 92 21
Mobile   +33 (0)6 07 96 68 73
Email   adaunis@orange.fr
Web   www.les-grands-vents.com

Brigitte & Patrick François
Le Clos de la Garenne,
9 rue de la Garenne,
17700 Puyravault,
Charente-Maritime
Tel   +33 (0)5 46 35 47 71
Email   info@closdelagarenne.com
Web   www.closdelagarenne.com

Entry 375   Map 8

Entry 376   Map 8

Poitou – Charentes

La Grande Barbotière

Between the fruit trees a hammock sways, breakfast is served next to a sparkling pool and sculpted chickens peck. Tucked behind gates (child-safe) in the heart of a busy village is a maison de maître of elegance and charm. Your hosts (she half Belgian, he from Yorkshire) have a wicked sense of humour and have created a luxurious and eclectic décor – gazelle antlers, pebbled showers, delicious French linen – for suites with private terraces. Table tennis, croquet, bicycles, toys, jasmine and, everywhere, that spirit-lifting light that you find on this cherished stretch of coastline.

Minimum stay: 2 nights. Children under 4 welcome.

Rooms	1 suite for 3, 1 suite for 5: €95–€270. Cot & sofabed available.
Meals	Restaurants 4km.
Closed	Rarely.

Christopher & Jacqui McLean May
La Grande Barbotière,
10 rue du Marais Doux,
17220 St Vivien,
Charente-Maritime
Tel   +33 (0)5 46 43 76 14
Mobile   +33 (0)6 43 12 11 04
Email   info@mcleanmay.com
Web   www.lagrandebarbotiere.com

Entry 377   Map 8

Poitou – Charentes

Eden Ouest

This fabulous building, built in 1745, stands in the old heart of La Rochelle. An immense amount of thought has gone into its renovation, and manager Lise is brimming with ideas as to how they can go the extra mile. Sweep up grand stairs to a marble fireplace and muted grey walls, a long polished dining table and a rococo-esque chandelier. Bedrooms are colour coordinated right down to the paintings; most have sofabeds for children, all but one have bath tubs crafted from wood, and one bathroom's doors open to a patio and salty sea air. Tread the ancient cobbles, sample the local apéritifs, catch a boat to the marvellous Ile de Ré.

Rooms	4 doubles: €125–€255. 1 suite for 2: €170–€255. Extra bed €25. Cot & high chair available.
Meals	Restaurants within walking distance.
Closed	Rarely.

**Bertrand Patoureau &
Lise Humeau**
Eden Ouest,
33 rue Thiers,
17000 La Rochelle,
Charente-Maritime
Mobile   +33 (0)6 82 62 68 97
Email   contact@edenouest.com
Web   www.edenouest.com

Entry 378   Map 8

Entre Hôtes

A ten-minute walk from the charming, bustling harbour of La Rochelle is an 18th-century merchant's house with an immaculate décor and a secret garden. Olivier and Sabine live on the top floor and look after you exceedingly well. Bedrooms and bathrooms are large and luxurious – polished floors, perfect beds, a pleasing, neutral palette. We particularly liked the wine 'cave' bedroom at the end of the garden: secluded, vaulted, lit with a warm glow and blessed with a sun terrace. Breakfast, served at small tables in an L-shaped living space, is a treat, and if the sun shines, you spill into the garden.

Maison des Algues

In a residential area, behind private gates on the outskirts of Rivedoux Plage, is a single-storey hotel, whitewashed, shuttered and impeccably maintained. Nothing is too much trouble for Christian and Jocelyne, who will pick you up from the airport and insist on giving you the best: white towels for the bathroom, coloured towels for the pool, pâtisseries for tea. Bedrooms open to a wicker-chaired terrace and are roomy, restful and flooded with light. Spin off on a bike (there are ten, all free) and acquaint yourself with the island – the whitewashed houses of La Flotte, the fabulous white sands, the chic shops of St Martin.

Minimum stay: 2 nights in high season.

Rooms	5 doubles: €108–€178. Extra bed €25.
Meals	Restaurants 5-minute walk.
Closed	Rarely.

Rooms	3 doubles: €125–€215. 2 suites for 2: €125–€215. 2 of the doubles interconnect.
Meals	Restaurants within walking distance. Guest kitchen.
Closed	Rarely.

Sabine & Olivier Durand-Robaux
Entre Hôtes,
8 rue Réaumur,
17000 La Rochelle,
Charente-Maritime
Tel   +33 (0)5 16 85 93 33
Email   contact@entre-hotes.com
Web   www.entre-hotes.com/fr

Christian & Jocelyne Gatta-Boucard
Maison des Algues,
147 rue des Algues,
17940 Rivedoux (Ile de Ré),
Charente-Maritime
Tel   +33 (0)5 46 68 01 23
Mobile   +33 (0)6 88 48 35 80
Email   information@maison-des-algues.com
Web   www.maison-des-algues.com

Un Banc Au Soleil

Only birds and bells break the bubble around this handsome B&B, set in quiet gardens near Marsilly port. The old stables of Stéphane's family home are transformed: soaring beams, elegant stone, huge terrace doors, a window to the cellar... You can slip into the pool after a day on the beach or brew a coffee and sit by the wood-burner flipping through magazines. At night, find snowy linen, original art, perhaps an antique desk or African carving. And in the morning, a homemade feast with traditional breads, tarts and more; nothing is any trouble for sweet Corinne. Hike or cycle coastal paths, golf, sail, visit historic Rochefort or La Rochelle...

Minimum stay: 2 nights July-October.

À l'Ombre du Figuier

A rural idyll, wrapped in birdsong. The old farmhouse, lovingly restored and decorated, is simple and pristine; its carpeted rooms, under eaves and polished to perfection, overlook a pretty garden where you may picnic. Your hosts are an interesting couple of anglophiles. Thoughtful, stylish Madame serves generous breakfasts of homemade jams, organic breads, cheeses and cereals under the fig tree in summer. Monsieur teaches engineering in beautiful La Rochelle; follow his suggestions and discover its lesser-known treasures. Luscious lawns are bordered by well-stocked beds. Great value.

Rooms	5 doubles: €85-€118. Extra bed €28.
Meals	Restaurants within walking distance.
Closed	Rarely.

Rooms	1 double: €71-€99. 1 family room for 4: €101-€159. Extra beds available.
Meals	Guest kitchen. Restaurant within walking distance. Auberge 3km.
Closed	Rarely.

	Stéphane & Corinne Lassegue Un Banc Au Soleil, 25 quater Rue du Port, 17137 Marsilly, Charente-Maritime
Mobile	+33 (0)6 24 96 82 70
Email	contact@unbancausoleil.com
Web	www.unbancausoleil.com

	Marie-Christine & Jean-François Prou À l'Ombre du Figuier, 43 rue du Marais, 17230 Longèves, Charente-Maritime
Tel	+33 (0)5 46 37 11 15
Mobile	+33 (0)6 79 35 55 12
Email	mcprou17@gmail.com
Web	www.alombredufiguier.com

Entry 381   Map 8

Entry 382   Map 8

Le Logis de Bellevue

You're within strolling distance of one of the prettiest towns in the Marais Poitevin. The blue-shuttered lodge has been transformed by this happy, hospitable British couple into a colourful home with the guest suite on the first floor: white walled, wooden floored, clean-limbed and spotless. The garden is immaculate too, with lawns and colourful borders, croquet, table tennis and (shared with gîtes) super pool. Garden fruits make an appearance at breakfast in homemade juices and jams; clever Marylyn even makes brioche. Dinner might include goat's cheese from the area and lamb from the farmer next door. A treat.

Bois Bourdet

A Charentaise farmhouse steeped in character, with hens in the gardens, two barns for self-catering and enchanting bedrooms for B&B guests. A family live here so it's ideal for children, with ropes, slides, swings, toys, and Monsieur a marvellous chef. There's a pool surrounded by lavender, a sitting room just for guests and a kitchen opening to a patio (with bedrooms above) and home-grown produce in the garden for every guest to enjoy. Hire a traditional punt or cycle along the canals; this is the 'Green Venice' of France, the Marais Poitevin. Handmade soaps, bikes to borrow, cookery courses to book into… Bois Bourdet is a gem.

Rooms	1 suite for 4: €115–€220. Singles €90–€105.
Meals	Dinner with wine, €40; children €20. Restaurants 5-minute walk.
Closed	1 January to 31 March; 1 October to 31 December.

Rooms	1 double: €70–€80. 1 family room for 3: €70–€80.
Meals	Dinner, 4 courses, €35; children €15. Restaurants 6km. Guest kitchen,
Closed	Rarely.

	Marylyn & Anthony Kusmirek
	Le Logis de Bellevue,
	55 route de Benet,
	79510 Coulon,
	Deux Sèvres
Tel	+33 (0)5 49 76 75 45
Email	kusmirek@orange.fr
Web	www.lelogisdebellevue.com

	Xavier & Stéphanie Trouillet
	Bois Bourdet,
	Lieu-Dit Bois Bourdet,
	79800 Souvigné,
	Deux Sèvres
Tel	+33 (0)5 49 34 57 99
Email	info@boisbourdet.com
Web	www.boisbourdet.com

Entry 383   Map 8

Entry 384   Map 9

Château Pont Jarno

An elegant 1860s château in a small valley, hidden from the nearby village and surrounded by parkland. Debbie and Colin, refugees from Glasgow, have nurtured it back to life and somehow found time to open up a nursery business too. Rooms are grandly proportioned with tall windows, oak panelling and tapestries in the entrance hall, a beautiful wooden fireplace in the vast drawing room. Tuck in to boiled eggs and home-squeezed juice at the big dining room table; if you're lucky Debbie will treat you to her *cullen skink* at supper. Sleep serenely in exuberant bedrooms with gorgeous views. Explore the countryside and castles.

Over 12s welcome.

Rooms	2 doubles: €130.
Meals	Dinner, 3 courses with coffee, €30.
	Restaurants 5-minute drive.
Closed	Christmas.

	Debbie McIsaac
	Château Pont Jarno,
	Les Groseillers, 79220 Cours,
	Deux Sèvres
Tel	+33 (0)5 49 25 74 06
Email	debbie@chateaujarno.fr
Web	www.chateaujarno.fr

Aquitaine

Château l'Hospital

Vineyards surround the Duhamels' restored 15th-century Girondine home and Bruno is keen to show you around and share his passion for their organically produced Côtes de Bourg wines. He's also in charge of breakfasts — honey, fresh orange juice, homemade brioche and jams — served indoors or on the terrace, with uninterrupted views. Dinner, with terroir wine of course, can be arranged; perhaps after visiting Bordeaux, 30 minutes south. Bedrooms are spotless and spacious — no frills, no surprises! — with gleaming new floors and windows, and modern bathrooms. It's peaceful here, with lovely walks through the vines.

Clos Marcamps

A super-stylish makeover by the de Gamas who moved here from Paris with their young children. All is pale and lovely, clear and uncluttered — designed to enhance the elegant proportions of this handsome Chartreuse house. You eat — superbly and seasonally — in the main house. You sleep in beautifully compact rooms in the converted barns. Each has its own entrance and is on two levels with beds upstairs. Bathrooms are sleek, with walk-in showers; one a spa bath. Roam the grounds; there's a wow of a pool, swings and table tennis; stroll through the vines; book beauty treatments, or baby-sitting, and head for Bordeaux. Smart.

Rooms	1 double: €79-€89.
	1 suite for 2: €79-€89.
	Singles €69-€72. Extra person €10
Meals	Dinner with wine, €25-€35.
	Children's meal available.
Closed	15 September to 15 October.

Rooms	2 doubles: €95-€250.
	3 suites for 2-3: €110-€170.
Meals	Dinner €35. Restaurant 7km.
Closed	Rarely.

Christine & Bruno Duhamel
Château l'Hospital,
33710 Saint Trojan,
Gironde
Tel +33 (0)5 57 64 33 60
Email alvitis@wanadoo.fr
Web www.alvitis.fr

Alexandre da Gama
Clos Marcamps,
2 chemin des Carièrres,
33710 Prignac et Marcamps,
Gironde
Tel +33 (0)5 57 58 57 09
Email contact@closmarcamps.fr
Web www.closmarcamps.fr

Manoir d'Astrée

In the gentle folds of Bordeaux sits this 1766 house half way up a hill, with views across vineyards – swoop through electronic gates to find owner Béatrice who gives you a comfortable shared sitting room and four private-feeling bedrooms. There are three on the ground floor and one upstairs, all with a Gustavian flavour and extremely plush; sleep peacefully in beautifully dressed beds, pad around serious bathrooms with soft robes and pebble flooring. Breakfast (outside on balmy days) on local jams, honey and fresh pastries from the village baker. Splash in the pool, wander the grounds, visit vineyards, discover Perigueux. Restful.

Minimum stay: 2 nights; 3 nights in high season.

L'Esprit des Chartrons

A delicious vintage townhouse in chic Chartrons, metres from the Garonne quays where Bordeaux's bourgeoisie once traded: 21st-century design blends with wine-soaked history. Playful bedrooms are named after famous local writers: glamorous 'Montaigne' with bubble tub; red-brick, industrial-style 'Montesquieu'; light-filled 'Mauriac'. There are private terraces for tête-à-têtes, swish Italian bathrooms for pampering, a leafy sun terrace and a stylish stove-warmed salon for breakfast (crisp pastries, real hot chocolate). On a quiet lane, with covered parking, yet a stroll from restaurant-lined streets and World Heritage sites.

Rooms	3 twin/doubles: €115-€150. 1 suite for 2-4: €140-€200. Extra bed/sofabed available €20-€70 per person per night.
Meals	Restaurant 2km.
Closed	Rarely.

Rooms	2 doubles, 1 twin/double: €115-€155. Singles €105-€135.
Meals	Restaurants nearby.
Closed	Rarely.

	Béatrice Rengner Manoir d'Astrée, Lieu dit Pelet, 33240 Lugon et l'Ile du Carnay, Gironde
Tel	+33 (0)5 57 25 24 25
Mobile	+33 (0)6 73 33 90 56
Email	contact@manoirdastree-bordeaux.com
Web	www.manoirdastree-bordeaux.com

	Brigitte Gourlat L'Esprit des Chartrons, 17 bis rue Borie, 33300 Bordeaux, Gironde
Tel	+33 (0)5 56 51 65 87
Mobile	+33 (0)6 82 20 20 67
Email	brigitte.gourlat@gmail.com
Web	www.lespritdeschartrons.fr

Entry 388   Map 9

Entry 389   Map 8

Aquitaine

15 Cours de Verdun

Sleep like kings in the heart of lovely Bordeaux. Climb the monumental staircase to your suite in a private mansion. It's a festival of pictures, colours and textures. There's so much to look at that it's hard to close your eyes. Vibrant Emmanuelle lives on the same floor, loves her city and will tell you all about its treasures and stories when she brings copious breakfast to your baroque-modern sitting room. Enjoy the high ceilings, original panelling and antiques, the superb bedding and fabrics. The big bedroom is exquisite but the elegant tall windows are single-glazed... A rare treat of a B&B.

Rooms	1 suite for 4: €160–€240.
Meals	Restaurants 2-minute walk.
Closed	Rarely.

Emmanuelle Robine
15 Cours de Verdun,
33000 Bordeaux,
Gironde

Mobile +33 (0)6 08 73 28 59
Email touna33@gmail.com

Entry 390   Map 8

Aquitaine

L'Arène Bordeaux

Within strolling distance of the most beautiful spots in Bordeaux is this elegant townhouse in a residential street. Handsome colours and discreet décor blend with herringbone parquet, cosy shared spaces are classically furnished, the Roman arena views are stunning. Lofty and evocatively named bedrooms ('Margaux', 'St Émilion') have sumptuous beds, accent chairs or three-piece suites, espresso machines, iPod docks and chic bathrooms in grey slate. Your friendly hosts offer wine in the garden on arrival, homemade jams at breakfast and all their best tips. Markets, antiques, boutiques, bistros and bars lie at your feet.

Minimum stay: 2 nights at weekends. Please check owner's website for availability and offers.

Rooms	5 twin/doubles, 2 rooms interconnect: €95–€200. Singles €100–€190. Extra bed/sofabed available €30 per person per night.
Meals	Restaurants 3-minute walk.
Closed	Rarely.

Jean Marie Terroine
L'Arène Bordeaux,
29 rue Émile Fourcand,
33000 Bordeaux,
Gironde

Tel +33 (0)5 56 52 05 89
Mobile +33 (0)6 16 06 48 31
Email larenebordeaux@gmail.com
Web www.larenebordeaux.com/Reservez

Entry 391   Map 8

Ecolodge des Chartrons

A many-splendoured delight: city-centre and eco-friendly, with lovely materials and the warmth of simplicity. Your relaxed and friendly hosts have put their earth-saving principles to work, stripping the wonderful wide floorboards, insulating with cork and wool, fitting solar water heating and sun pipes to hyper-modern shower rooms, organic linen and blankets to beds and providing all-organic breakfasts. At the bottom of this quiet road flows the Garonne where cafés, shops and galleries teem in converted warehouses (English wine merchants traded here 300 years ago) and a mirror fountain baffles the mind.

83 rue de Patay

Martine may have just one room but she's used to making guests feel welcome: she owns a restaurant in the middle of the old town. Le Loup has been serving local specialities since 1932: you will probably want to pay a visit. This old stone townhouse is a welcome retreat after days visiting the city (ten minutes by tram) or those renowned vineyards. Martine has given it a light modern touch which works well. Your cosy little bedroom is approached up a curved stone staircase and you have the floor to yourselves. It overlooks a small courtyard garden and has a desk and other pieces stencilled by a friend.

Rooms	2 doubles, 2 twin/doubles: €120–€142. 1 triple: €160–€181. Singles €108–€125. Extra bed/sofabed available €32 per person per night.
Meals	Restaurants within walking distance.
Closed	Rarely.

Rooms	1 twin/double: €70.
Meals	Martine's restaurant 'Le Loup' near Cathedral.
Closed	Rarely.

Véronique Daudin
Ecolodge des Chartrons,
23 rue Raze,
33000 Bordeaux,
Gironde
Tel   +33 (0)5 56 81 49 13
Mobile   +33 (0)6 99 29 33 00
Email   veronique@ecolodgedeschartrons.com
Web   www.ecolodgedeschartrons.com

Martine Peiffer
83 rue de Patay,
33000 Bordeaux,
Gironde
Tel   +33 (0)5 56 99 41 74
Mobile   +33 (0)6 19 81 22 81
Email   mpeifferma95@numericable.fr
Web   www.lapetitepause33.wordpress.com

Entry 392   Map 8

Entry 393   Map 8

La Forge

Overlooking vines once worked by the blacksmith's horse is an unforgettable house. Carol fell in love with France many years ago, then married a French man, Bruno. Since when they have been serving breakfasts under the cherry trees (home honey, eggs, bread, fruits, jams). The place is resplendent with modern art, family antiques, fresh flowers. Tables are laden with books, sofas demand you unwind, beds have vintage linen and the bunk bedroom is a child's dream. Do visit their farm: hens, meadows, paths, cookery classes in a 14th-century water mill. They'll also give you a free pass to a private turquoise blue lake for swimming.

Self-catering also available in cottage.

Château de Castelneau

A heavenly 14th-century château with Provençal towers. Behind: a shuttered 17th-century façade, a courtyard with outbuildings and an avenue lined with young trees. All around: hectares of vines. The de Roquefeuils are a warm, intelligent, enthusiastic couple, working their socks off to make the estate pay (the claret is delicious). Bedrooms are simple, comfortable, traditional – and there's a landing with videos for early risers. Downstairs: stone flags, rugs, books, paintings, eclectic aristocratic furnishings, and breakfasts generous and delicious. Enjoy the sunny pool and take a tour of the cellars. Outstanding.

Rooms	1 double, 1 twin/double sharing bathroom with single & bunk room: €85-€95. 1 suite for 3: €95. 1 single sharing bathroom: €65. 1 bunk room for 4 sharing bathroom: €60-€120. Extra child's bed €30.	Rooms	2 twin/doubles: €130-€210. 1 annexe for 2: €130-€210.
		Meals	Restaurants 2km.
		Closed	1 November to 28 February.
Meals	Restaurants 8km.		
Closed	Rarely.		

	Carol de Montrichard Dalléas La Forge, 26 route du Moulin Neuf, 33750 St Quentin de Baron, Gironde		**Loïc & Diane de Roquefeuil** Château de Castelneau, 8 route de Breuil, Lieu-dit Châteauneuf, 33670 Saint Léon, Gironde
Tel	+33 (0)5 57 24 18 54		
Mobile	+33 (0)6 31 85 65 20	Tel	+33 (0)5 56 23 47 01
Email	whatscookinginfrance@gmail.com	Email	dianederoquefeuil@gmail.com
Web	www.whatscookinginfrance. wordpress.com	Web	www.chateaudecastelneau.com

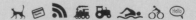

Entry 394   Map 9

Entry 395   Map 9

Domaine de l'Espelette

Take a picnic to the stream, stroll down the avenue into the village, let the children frolic, swim in the shaded pool. This long house, tucked into the hillside and overlooking the Romanesque church, dates from the 15th century. Unearth a treasure or two in the sitting room and library shared with the owners: books, magazines, paintings. Bedrooms are reassuringly chintzy, bathrooms generously marble. Madame is happy to serve breakfast until two o'clock; in such a haven she's used to guests oversleeping and the thick walls will ensure you won't hear a murmur from the grandchildren playing upstairs.

Minimum stay: 2 nights. Over 12s welcome.

Rooms	2 twin/doubles: €100-€150.
Meals	Restaurant 1.5km.
Closed	15 August & December/January.

	Silvia Prevost
	Domaine de l'Espelette,
	Route de Chaumont,
	33550 Haux,
	Gironde
Tel	+33 (0)5 56 23 37 36
Mobile	+33 (0)6 63 82 01 78
Email	contact@domainedelespelette.com
Web	www.domainedelespelette.com

Entry 396   Map 8

Peyraguey Maison Rouge

Born and raised amid the Sauternes' vine-clothed hills and châteaux, the Belangers know Bordeaux wines intimately. Monsieur may offer a tasting on your second night in this authentic old wine-grower's house; for deeper insights, book an œnology course (min. 4). Tour châteaux, kayak down the Ciron, follow Bordeaux's wine trail past the 12 top Grands Crus Classés and St Émilion. Return to a dip in the pool, a game of ping-pong, grilled duck in the village auberge and a book by the fire in the elegant sitting room where wine scenes dot warm stone walls and champagne-coloured curtains glimmer. A genuine French vineyard stay.

Rooms	2 doubles, 1 twin: €82-€119.
	Singles €87-€119.
Meals	Restaurants 2km.
Closed	14 November to 23 March.

	Annick & Jean-Claude Belanger
	Peyraguey Maison Rouge,
	33210 Bommes Sauternes,
	Gironde
Tel	+33 (0)5 57 31 07 55
Email	contact@peyraguey-sauternes.com
Web	www.peyraguey-sauternes.com

Entry 397   Map 9

Aquitaine

Chambres d'Hôtes Janoutic

Charming Jean-Pierre finds the finest organic produce for his table. From croissants to charcuterie, 'poulets fermier' to orchard jams (apricot, blackcurrant, redcurrant, fig), it sounds delicious. This is a well-restored old farmhouse in the hamlet of Janoutic, two miles from the motorway, a great little stopover between Bordeaux and Toulouse. We like the two bright, carpeted bedrooms upstairs best, their rustic rafters hung with tobacco leaves in memory of old farming days; all have big walk-in showers. There's more: leather sofas and a great log fire; a wild garden with an aviary and a pool for newts and birds.

Advance booking required: 24-48 hours.

Aquitaine

La Girarde

In gentle countryside of wooded valleys near pretty Ste Foy la Grande, this smartly renovated farmhouse has its origins in the wine industry; St Émilion lives and breathes wine. You will be impeccably looked after by lovely, relaxed, fuss-free owners Trish and Mark, who give you serene rooms in classical-chic style – heated stone floors, designer fabrics, African art, touches of tartan from home. All the bedrooms, upstairs and down, have big beds and super bathrooms, and dinners are delicious. Outside: a lovely terrace, a park-like garden edged with cedars and weeping willows, a heated saltwater pool. Gorgeous!

Rooms	2 doubles: €70.
	1 family room for 3: €70-€90.
	Singles €60. Extra bed €20.
	Cot available.
Meals	Dinner €28; children under 12, €19.
Closed	Rarely.

Rooms	2 doubles, 2 twin/doubles: €115-€130.
	Extra bed/sofabed available €30 per person per night.
Meals	Dinner €30; children over 7, €15; children under 7, €7. Wine €15-€45.
Closed	Rarely.

Jean-Pierre Doebele
Chambres d'Hôtes Janoutic,
2 Le Tach,
33124 Aillas,
Gironde
Mobile +33 (0)6 81 97 02 92
Email jpdoebel@club-internet.fr
Web www.chambresdhotesjanoutic.com

Trish Tyler
La Girarde,
33220 St Quentin de Caplong,
Gironde
Tel +33 (0)5 57 41 02 68
Mobile +33 (0)6 76 07 97 43
Email bienvenue@lagirarde.com
Web www.lagirarde.com

Entry 398   Map 9

Entry 399   Map 9

Aquitaine

Château de Carbonneau

Big château bedrooms bedecked in soft linens with splashes of splendid detail, a fine old bed in the 'Peony' room, huge bathrooms done with rich tiles – here is a self-assured family house where quality is fresh, history stalks and there's plenty of space for guests. Visit Wilfrid's winery and taste the talent handed down by his forebears. Jacquie, a relaxed dynamic New Zealander, provides tasty alternatives to the ubiquitous duck cuisine, has a relaxed approach to dining and has now opened a salon de thé; a dab hand at interiors, she has also cultivated a luminescent, airy guest sitting room near the orangery.

Rooms	2 doubles, 3 twin/doubles: €105–€145. Singles €95–€135. Extra bed/sofabed available €25 per person per night. Dinner, B&B €30 extra per person.
Meals	Dinner €30. Wine €8–€20.
Closed	1 November to 28 February.

Jacquie & Wilfrid Franc de Ferrière
Château de Carbonneau,
33890 Pessac sur Dordogne,
Gironde

Tel	+33 (0)5 57 47 46 46
Mobile	+33 (0)6 83 30 14 35
Email	carbonneau@orange.fr
Web	www.chateau-carbonneau.com

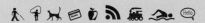

Entry 400   Map 9

Aquitaine

Domaine de Polus

Waves of vines surround St Émilion, horses graze the field, a shaded terrace overlooks the large heated saltwater pool. The Fergusons have lovingly renovated the former chai for the sole use of guests, Alex's interior design experience producing a gorgeously stylish retreat with its own sitting room, English furniture, French fabrics and subtle paints. There's homemade cake for tea and a choice of local wines as apéritifs. The dawn-facing double has a balcony down to the pool, showers are luxuriously new. After self-service breakfast, you can cycle all the way to magnificent Bordeaux, or hire a canoe and explore the Dordogne River.

Minimum stay: 2 nights.

Rooms	1 double, 1 twin: £130–£140. Extra bed/sofabed available £30 per person per night.
Meals	Dinner €30. Wine from €15. Restaurants 1km.
Closed	Rarely.

Alexandra & Dominic Ferguson
Domaine de Polus,
33420 St Vincent de Pertignas,
Gironde

Tel	+33 (0)5 57 50 22 03
Mobile	+44 (0)7803 434619
Email	mrsaferguson@btinternet.com
Web	www.depolus.blogspot.com

Entry 401   Map 9

Aquitaine

Château Claud-Bellevue

On the edge of a sleepy village, a 17th-century priory with a lych gate to the church. Mellow stone walls are lapped by groomed lawns and gravel paths; a central fountain plays; beyond are 10 hectares of vines. Your hosts, new to chambres d'hôtes and full of plans, give you an effusive welcome and delicious air-conditioned rooms: gilt-edged prints on rustic walls and goosedown as soft as a cloud. The treats continue at table with food from their son, a three Michelin-starred chef; expect cheeses, fruits, charcuterie and homemade breads, granola and conserves. Take a private tour of their own château, discover the wines of St Émilion.

Minimum stay: 2 nights.

Rooms	2 doubles, 1 twin/double: €135–€150.
Meals	Light dinner with wine, €40.
	Afternoon tea included.
	Restaurants 3km.
	Private kitchen for guests.
Closed	Rarely.

Ana Bockmeulen
Château Claud-Bellevue,
31 le Bourg,
33350 Belvès de Castillon,
Gironde

Tel	+33 (0)5 57 49 48 23
Email	abockmeulen@mac.com
Web	www.chateauclaudbellevue.com

Entry 402   Map 9

Aquitaine

The Old Bakery

A place of rest for weary travellers in the Dordogne, simple and green with a wood stove in the snug and full English or continental breakfast each morning. Owner Louis has opened up this old baker's building, so that the sitting room and kitchen flow into one – and out through terrace doors to the lush garden. You can wander among the fruit trees or lie in the shade of an old pine, soaking up the peace of this hamlet near the market town of Montpon Ménestérol. Artworks, vintage furniture and objets will keep you intrigued, and you wake on a handmade mattress to see the sun rise over the vegetable patch.

Minimum stay: 2 nights at weekends.

Rooms	1 double: €65–€75.
Meals	Dinner & picnics available.
Closed	Rarely.

Lou O'Leary
The Old Bakery,
29 rue Jean Monnet,
24700 Montpon Ménésterol,
Dordogne

Tel	+33 (0)5 53 82 34 59
Email	louoldbakery@icloud.com
Web	www.oldbakeryfrance.co.uk

Entry 403   Map 9

Aquitaine

Aquitaine

La Boissière

In a bucolic valley in the Périgord Vert, a stately B&B bordering village and fields. Built in the 18th-century, the beautiful house sits in immaculate lawns shaded by lime trees; the silence is blissful. Delightful Caroline and Dominique have expertly converted an annexe to create three elegant, spacious rooms. Finely-dressed beds, antiques and contemporary bathrooms add charm and comfort. Terracotta-floored 'Agapanthe' opens onto the garden, while 'Escallonia' has extra space for a child or two. Breakfast on brioche and homemade jam in the soothing dining room, take a dip in the pool, or hire kayaks to paddle down the Dronne.

Pauliac

The exuberant hillside garden, full of blossom and bamboo, has gorgeous views of sunflowers and an overflowing stone plunge pool. John and Jane's talents are a restful atmosphere, great dinners, and interiors that are a brilliant marriage of cottage simplicity and sparks from African throws and contemporary paintings. Beautiful bedrooms have a separate entrance. Delightful, energetic Jane offers superb, imaginative food in the sun-splashed veranda with its all-season views, or the bright, rustic dining room with roaring log fire – and early suppers for children. Lovely people in a tranquil view-drenched spot.

Rooms	1 double, 1 twin/double: €95–€105. 1 suite for 3: €105. Extra bed €30.	Rooms	2 doubles, 1 twin: €65–€85. 1 suite for 4: €85–€110.
Meals	Restaurants 3km.	Meals	Dinner €25. Wine €10.
Closed	1 December to 28 February.	Closed	Rarely.

	Caroline de Mercey La Boissière, Le Bourg, 24350 Grand Brassac, Dordogne		Jane & John Edwards Pauliac, Celles, 24600 Ribérac, Dordogne
Tel	+33 (0)5 53 91 14 51	Tel	+33 (0)5 53 90 32 50
Email	ddemercey@hotmail.fr	Mobile	+33 (0)6 88 13 06 27
Web	www.laboissiere-grandbrassac.com/ ?lang=en	Email	info@pauliac.fr
		Web	www.pauliac.fr

Entry 404   Map 9

Entry 405   Map 9

Briançon

The 14th-century walnut mill is a house full of art, riches and light, and the English garden, blessed with a burbling brook, is resplendent with rare plants. Inside, sofas wear colourful throws, boho-stylish bedrooms burst with personality and shower rooms have retro touches. Dinners at the big old country table sound enticing: wines from Michael's cellar, produce from Katie's potager, herbs scattered with studied abandon, and plenty for vegetarians. Katie and Michael, from London, have created a sophisticated yet laid-back home – and two heated, saltwater swimming pools!

Pets by arrangement.

Manoir Camélia

A 19th-century wisteria-covered granite manor with red pantile roof and sky blue shuttered windows on the edge of a pretty Dordogne village. Ex-firefighter Steve and his wife Gill love to share their home, complete with two cats, chickens in the garden and, if you choose to eat in, fresh veg from the allotment for dinner. Bedrooms are in soft pastels with garden views, bathrooms are fresh and modern. Breakfasts of homemade yoghurt and honey from Steve's bees set you up for a day in the surrounding Parc Naturel Regional. Walk, cycle, visit the preserved wartime village of Oradour-sur-Glane, or just stay in and chill.

Parking on-site.

Rooms	3 doubles; 2 twins, sharing bathroom: €85–€150.
Meals	Dinner €35. Restaurant 2km.
Closed	December – March.

Rooms	2 doubles: €75–€85.
Meals	Dinner, 2 courses with wine & coffee €23; not Thursday or July/August. Restaurants 1km.
Closed	Rarely.

	Katie Armitage
	Briançon,
	24320 Verteillac,
	Dordogne
Tel	+33 (0)5 53 91 38 40
Email	katie@elliottarmitage.com
Web	www.brianconlespace.com

	Stephen Holmes
	Manoir Camélia,
	Chez Gonaud,
	24360 Champniers-et-Reilhac,
	Dordogne
Tel	+33 (0)5 53 56 47 31
Email	steveandgillholmes@gmail.com
Web	www.manoircamelia.com

Alzzzzace

Abeille & Abeille à la Ferme de Miel

Who hasn't dreamt of sleeping in a beehive at one point or other? Oh, maybe it's just me. Well anyway, now you can at our latest discovery, Abeille & Abeille. Nectar farmers, Bee and Buzz, have lifted the lid of their amazing home – a modernist masterpiece where identical, hexagonal rooms, dripping in gold, have a sweet charm. Buzz stays in and drones on a bit while busy sister Bee, clad antennae to toe in black and gold velvet, goes out and about, stocking up on supplies. If you're not good with crowds, then possibly this place isn't for you but if you love a buzzy atmosphere and a chance to see the queen, you've struck gold.

Direct Beeseyjet flights every day.

Rooms	100,000 singles; no bathrooms: don't get stung.
Meals	Honey for breakfast, lunch & tea.
Closed	Heaven help us if it ever is.

Bee & Buzz Pétale
Abeille & Abeille à la Ferme de Miel,
Rue de la Fleur,
BUZZ1E Pollèn

Tel	Just give them a buzz
Email	abeille@beeonholiday.com
Web	www.beeonholiday.com

Aquitaine

Château de Villars

View the château from a teak pool lounger, iced drink in hand: views swoop to forests as far as the eye can see, there's comfort in abundance and superb attention to detail. Light pours into this 1860s building, where hosts invite you to enjoy library, sitting room, gym, massage salon and grand terrace, and bedrooms are immaculate. Tucked between trees, the splendid summerhouse is ideal for self-caterers, as is the 18th-century village townhouse. There's a long banqueting table for breakfast, dinner (good value) is served with homegrown delights from the kitchen garden and lots of local produce.

Minimum stay: 2 nights.

Rooms	5 doubles: €95–€145. 2 houses for 4: €695–€1,395.
Meals	Dinner €32–€36. Wine €11–€35. Restaurant on site or 2-minute walk.
Closed	November to mid-April.

Bill Davies & Kevin Saunders
Château de Villars,
Près de la Cure, 24530 Villars,
Dordogne

Tel	+33 (0)5 53 03 41 58
Mobile	+33 (0)6 83 26 03 95
Email	chateauvillars@aol.com
Web	www.gofranceholiday.com

Le Chatenet

Brantôme has layers of history. The grand Benedictine abbey, carved out at the bottom of the cliffs, overlooks the river Dronne, and just up the road, a perfect distance from hustle and bustle, is this Périgord-style stone house built at the end of the 17th century. Jane and William are super hosts and give you big rooms with stunning fabric on the walls, billiards in the games room, swimming pool, breakfast eggs and milk from the nearby farm. Canoe the rivers, explore grottoes, sit on the veranda and follow the sun as it sets over walnut trees and green valleys. The town is a ten-minute stroll – don't miss the Friday market.

Auberge de Castel-Merle

High above the valley of the Vézère is an atmospheric inn where a Templar castle once stood; views from the terrace are peerless. It's been in Anita's family for generations, she and Christopher love the place and have renovated the buildings with great care, keeping the traditional look, and using walnut wood from their own land to restore bed heads and doors. Pastel, pelmets and painted flowers on the walls clothe the dining room; modest bedrooms have beams, stone walls and wooden floors; shower rooms are compact. Some rooms overlook the courtyard, others the woods. Walk to the hamlet, hike through the forests. Great value.

Rooms	3 twin/doubles: €135-€160. 2 suites for 2: €175-€220. Extra bed €25.
Meals	Dinner from €30. Wine from €25. Restaurant 1km.
Closed	Mid-October to mid-April.

Rooms	7 doubles, 1 twin: €77-€85.
Meals	Wine €9-€28. Picnics available on request. Restaurants 10-minute walk.
Closed	10 October to 1 April.

Jane & William Laxton
Le Chatenet,
Lieu-dit Le Chatenet,
24310 Brantôme,
Dordogne
Tel   +33 (0)5 53 05 81 08
Email   lechatenet@gmail.com
Web   www.lechatenet.com

Anita Castanet & Christopher Millinship
Auberge de Castel-Merle,
24290 Sergeac,
Dordogne
Tel   +33 (0)5 53 50 70 08
Email   hotelcastelmerle@yahoo.fr
Web   www.hotelcastelmerle.com

Entry 410   Map 9

Entry 411   Map 9

Aux Fontaines d'Eyvigues

No wonder this happy young family loves welcoming guests: their big stone house is in a beautiful spot, hugged by wooded hills and a semi-wild flower meadow with a swimming pool. Cleverly restored and romantic for two, the bedroom has a claw-foot bath behind a head-height wall and a wood-burner by the soft purple bed. You can join in family dinners around the kitchen table — food is local but influenced by Jean-Yves' Moroccan origins — and enjoy breakfast in the garden. Whether on foot, in a canoe, by (hired) bike or whizzing down a zipline, the northern Dordogne is a playground for couples seeking peace and adventure.

Le Clos des Sources

Birdsong, a frog chorus, the murmur of springs: the rest is silence in these splendid gardens, a labour of love for owner Monique, a joy for her guests, who have private access. Looking down on this happy valley is a cluster of apricot-hued limestone buildings. Rooms – sleek and contemporary, mixing dressed stone with rag-rolled walls – are in the apex of the old barn; each has its own terrace fragrant with lavender and wisteria. Walk over wobbly stone to the shabby chic salon and dining room, where breakfast is served on English bone china. For dinner, Monique plunders her garden to produce regional specialities. A delight in the Dordogne!

Rooms	1 double: €75-€95.
	Child's bed available.
Meals	Dinner with wine, €25.
	Restaurants 1km.
Closed	Rarely.

Rooms	2 doubles: €75-€95.
	1 suite for 2: €95-€115.
Meals	Dinner €25.
	Restaurants 3km.
Closed	Rarely.

Jean-Yves & Cathy Tomas
Aux Fontaines d'Eyvigues,
Lieu dit Eyvigues,
24590 Salignac Eyvigues, Dordogne
Tel +33 (0)5 53 29 04 35
Mobile +33 (0)6 72 61 33 27
Email ctomas446@gmail.com
Web www.auxfontainesdeyvigues.com/figuiers1

Monique Jourdan
Le Clos des Sources,
Rue les Crochets,
24200 Vitrac,
Dordogne
Tel +33 (0)5 53 29 67 93
Mobile +33 (0)6 82 14 57 76
Email jardinleclosdessources@yahoo.fr

Les Chambres de la Voie Verte

Steps curl up and around the old stone walls and lead to four rooms, each delightful, each with its own outside entrance. Find soft purples, greens, greys, rose reds, comfortable new beds and state-of-the-art bathrooms with walk-in showers. From the top floor, views stretch over the town's Perigordian rooftops, to Montfort château beyond. Enjoy breakfast off white Limoges china at the long table in the house next door (and on the terrace on warm days). The friendly owners also run the bar and florist's on either side; extrovert Madame revels in her projects. The old railway track for cycling to Sarlat and Souillac is near.

Minimum stay: 2 nights in high season.

Rooms	2 doubles, 2 twins: €77–€87. Extra bed/sofabed available €22 per person per night.
Meals	Restaurants in town.
Closed	Rarely.

Annie Boyer
Les Chambres de la Voie Verte,
24200 Carsac Aillac,
Dordogne
Mobile +33 (0)6 70 09 38 95
Email annie.boyer43@orange.fr
Web www.chambres-de-la-voie-verte.com

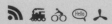

Entry 415   Map 9

La Guérinière

Once a charterhouse in private parkland, this big, good-looking Perigord house, on a hill facing Domme, is a tribute to the rich sober taste of the area. Inside reflects outside: the same dark timbers against pale stone. The feel is warmly authentic and the owners have redecorated the bedrooms most charmingly, gradually replacing the modern furniture with country antiques. They used to run a restaurant; now there's a big candlelit table for guests and you may find more gourmets in the beamed dining room (outsiders are occasionally allowed in). Outside: palm trees and pool. A gem.

Rooms	2 doubles, 2 twin/doubles: €90–€105. 1 triple: €130–€140. 1 family room for 3-4: €155–€170.
Meals	Dinner €28. Wine from €20.
Closed	November – March.

Brigitte & Christophe Demassougne
La Guérinière,
Baccas, 24250 Cénac & St Julien,
Dordogne
Tel +33 (0)5 53 29 91 97
Email contact@la-gueriniere-dordogne.com
Web www.la-gueriniere-dordogne.com

Entry 416   Map 9

La Source

You're just off the heavily-beaten tourist track with passionate owners who are experts on their patch and can help you avoid the crowds. Your B&B rooms — sprung mattresses, muted colours, lots of pictures, tiled bathrooms with views — and a 'salon littéraire' stuffed with books and games, are opposite their house. Breakfasts of homemade breads, pastries and jams are at one table on the terrace, or in the dining room. The road next to you is busy, but quietens down at night, you're near to all the Dordogne has to offer (boating, walking, cycling) yet away from Sarlat, and dinner is bursting with regional produce.

Minimum stay: 2 nights.

Par La Rivière

Sophisticated simplicity in deep countryside, down by the river Dordogne. Light rooms and lovely breakfasts in the beautifully converted barn extension of Canadian Allison and Reg's farmhouse are just great. The first floor's a huge, beamed, open-plan space, with the ultra-modern bathroom up on a platform and the calm, comfortable sleeping and sitting area — with slipper bath — below. The similarly stylish ground floor has a separate sitting room and terrace overlooking the big garden and its lawns, mature trees and a central swimming pool. And, coming soon, the two-storey Bakehouse. Relax, join the canoeists, walk Murphy the wolfhound.

Minimum stay: 2 nights.

Rooms	3 doubles: €80–€90. 1 family room for 4 with separate wc: €155–€165 Cot available.		Rooms	1 double: €175. 2 suites for 2: €175.
Meals	Dinner, 3 courses, €25. Wine €18–€28. Restaurants 4km.		Meals	Restaurants 4km.
Closed	1 October to 27 April.		Closed	December – March.

	Eloy Casanova & Jean-Pierre Fauvet La Source, Lieu Dit Le Coudert, 24250 Saint Cybranet, Dordogne			**Reginald & Allison Ashby** Par La Rivière, Le Port de St Julien, 24250 Cenac et St Julien, Dordogne
Mobile	+33 (0)6 12 58 38 53		Mobile	+33 (0)7 86 49 18 61
Email	lasource-perigord@hotmail.fr		Email	ajmacinnes@hotmail.com
Web	www.lasource-perigordnoir.fr		Web	www.parlariviere.com

Entry 417   Map 9 Entry 418   Map 9

Manoir de la Malartrie

On the banks of the Dordogne river, a beautifully restored 19th-century manor house with luxurious rooms and a cosy, beamed gîte. Surrounded by fragrant Mediterranean gardens planted with lavender and rosemary, this is an idyllic retreat. Inside, charming Ouafaa has blended Moroccan style with Edwardian elegance. Sleep in sumptuous bedrooms furnished with antiques; eat Franco-Moroccan meals made with fresh veg from the potager in the magnificent salon. There's a sleek pool and you can watch boats sail by as you picnic in the grounds. Explore grand châteaux or stroll to pretty La Roque-Gageac for shops and restaurants.

Minimum stay: 3 nights. Heated pool available May-October.

Les Hauts de Saint Vincent

Your delightful hosts have combined the best of modern design with old French charm and travellers' treasures to create a thoughtful elegance and different moods in each room. Fabulous views top it all off and help to make this handsome 17th-century house special. Bedrooms full of light, originality and comfort lead to excellent newly-done bathrooms; the living and dining rooms breathe the simplicity and warmth of glowing wood against old stone; breakfast is on the terrace where eyes sweep out to the river and Josephine Baker's château. Take the children to see Castelnaud's giant catapults and improbable armour; book early for Lascaux.

Rooms	4 doubles: €110–€160. 1 suite for 4: €200–€260. 1 apartment for 2-4: €140–€260. Sofabeds available €30 per night.	Rooms	4 doubles: €110–€140. 1 triple: €120–€160. €10 deduction per night from 3 night stay. Singles €110–€130.
Meals	Dinner with wine & appetizer, €50. Available for groups of 8 or more. Restaurants 5-minute walk.	Meals	Dinner, 4 courses with wine, €30. Restaurants 2km.
Closed	Mid-December to mid-March (except pre-booked Christmas parties).	Closed	Rarely.

	Ouafaa Diebolt-Balbal Manoir de la Malartrie, La Malartrie, 24220 Vezac, Dordogne		**Fabrice & Stephanie Berbessou** Les Hauts de Saint Vincent, Le Pech, 24220 Saint-Vincent-de-Cosse, Dordogne
Tel	+33 (0)5 53 29 03 51	Mobile	+33 (0)6 08 21 19 10
Email	lamalartrie@orange.fr	Email	contact@leshautsdesaintvincent.com
Web	www.manoir-lamalartrie.com	Web	leshautsdesaintvincent.com

Manoir de la Brunie

An elegant village manor in a glorious setting: the views are stupendous. The owners live in Paris but the genial manager will introduce you to a fine living room full of warm bright colours overlooking a sweeping lawn (play the piano, browse the books) and excellent bedrooms. The tower suite and small double have a modern feel, the other rooms, huge and high-ceilinged, are more classical; all have subtle colours, new wood floors, space for armchairs and sofas, and good lighting. Breakfasts are fresh, bathrooms delightful... there's a heated pool shared with gîte guests, a river beach nearby, riding next door.

Château de la Bourlie – Les Bories

Delicious breakfast is delivered by tractor in a basket – to your private tobacco barn on a dreamy estate. After which it's a gentle stroll to the fortified château with its 'jardin remarquable', its potager and pool. Lovely Lucy lives on site and welcomes you into a funky-urban space, all white and flooded with light from glazed barn doors at either end. Polished concrete floors run throughout, there's an Italian 50s sofa, a sleek cooking unit, a great oak table, stunning shower, vast lofty bedroom with a curtain-hung bed – and pallet mattresses for a couple of friends. Car-free, nature-steeped, hilltop heaven.

Rooms	3 doubles, 1 twin/double: €75–€110. 1 suite for 4: €125–€140. Extra bed €17.
Meals	Dinner with wine, €27.
Closed	December/January.

Rooms	1 barn for 2-4: €200.
Meals	Private kitchenette. Restaurants 5-10km.
Closed	Rarely.

Joyce Villemur
Manoir de la Brunie,
La Brunie,
24220 Le Coux & Bigaroque,
Dordogne
Tel   +33 (0)5 53 31 95 62
Email hervelynecagniet24@gmail.com
Web   www.manoirdelabrunie.com

Lucy Williams
Château de la Bourlie – Les Bories,
24480 Urval,
Dordogne
Mobile +33 (0)6 18 72 05 74
Email   contact@chateaudelabourlie.com
Web   www.chateaudelabourlie.com/
les-bories.html

Entry 421   Map 9

Entry 422   Map 9

Maison Oléa

High in the hills, on the rustic-suburban outskirts of Le Bugue, is a hospitable house, designed and built expressly for B&B. Roses billow around the infinity pool, views pour over the valley, and children are free to roam. The house hums with people, the owners are delightful and the bedrooms, four with terraces and one on the ground floor, are filled with light and decorated with flair; big bathrooms have a Mediterranean theme. This is the Dordogne, and hosted dinners – fun affairs – flourish truffles, duck and Perigordian treats, as well as fruit and veg from the great gardens.

Minimum stay: 4 nights in high season.

Le Moulin Neuf

Robert's greeting is the first line of an ode to hospitality written in warm stone in breathtaking gardens, set to the tune of the mill stream. Immaculate rooms in the guest barn are comfortingly filled with good beds and fresh flowers, bathrooms are sheer luxury, and views sweep over the lawns. Wake up to a royal breakfast of breads, croissants, pâtisseries, homemade jams, fruits and tiny cheeses served on white tablecloths on the vine-shaded veranda. All is beautifully, lovingly tended by Robert. His two happy rescue dogs will make friends with yours; find your own special spot in the gardens.

Children over 10 welcome. Minimum stay: three nights in winter. Pets by arrangement only.

Rooms	2 twin/doubles: €75–€105. 1 family room for 3; 2 family rooms for 4: €85–€105.	Rooms	2 doubles, 1 twin/double: €93–€97. 1 suite for 2: €93–€97. 1 family room for 3: €123. Singles €82.60–€86.60.
Meals	Dinner with wine, €35-38. Restaurants 3km.	Meals	Restaurant in Paunat, 1km.
Closed	15 December to 15 January.	Closed	Rarely.

	Murielle Nardou Maison Oléa, La Combe de Leygue, 24260 Le Bugue, Dordogne		**Robert Chappell** Le Moulin Neuf, Paunat, 24510 Ste Alvère, Dordogne
Tel	+33 (0)5 53 08 48 93	Tel	+33 (0)5 53 63 30 18
Email	info@olea-dordogne.com	Email	moulin-neuf@usa.net
Web	www.olea-dordogne.com	Web	www.the-moulin-neuf.com

Manoir de Beauregard

Artist and interior designer, Angela, welcomes guests to her beautifully restored 17th-century house set in 40 acres of landscaped gardens with grass paths and wide views. Inside is filled with taste and passion: discover antiques, French and Italian painted furniture, bedrooms with hand carved four-poster beds, embroidered linen sheets and limewashed beams. Splash in the pool in summer, warm yourself by a big log fire on chilly days with tea and homemade cakes. On Fridays, Angela may cook you a candlelit dinner using local, seasonal ingredients: duck, wild mushrooms, foie gras or truffles, with excellent Bergerac wine.

Rooms	3 doubles: €110–€160.
Meals	Cooked breakfast €8.
	Afternoon tea €5.
	Dinner, 4 courses, with wine, from €35.
	Restaurant 1.5km.
Closed	Rarely.

	Angela Meunier
	Manoir de Beauregard,
	Le Grand But,
	24140 Clermont de Beauregard,
	Dordogne
Tel	+33 (0)5 53 81 66 97
Email	manoirbeauregard@gmail.com
Web	www.manoirbeauregard.com

Entry 425　Map 9

Le Bourdil Blanc

Jane is a perfectionist, and that extends to her chef's 'îles flottantes', should you be inspired to book dinner one night. She also spoils you with luscious fresh fruit at breakfast – and interesting, compelling conversation. Her beloved house is glorious with soft spaces, antiques and fine fabrics, modern shower rooms and old beams, kilims on parquet floors and open log fires. The super great garden has tennis, a big heated pool and all the secret corners you could wish for. Come for a week to ride horses, learn French or trawl the wonders of the Dordogne. Or just for a night before flying from nearby Bergerac.

Rooms	2 doubles, 2 twins: €70–€90.
	Pigeonnier: 1 double, 1 twin,
	sharing bath: €70–€90.
Meals	Dinner €20.
Closed	July/August; November – March.

	Jane Hanslip
	Le Bourdil Blanc,
	24520 Saint Sauveur de Bergerac,
	Dordogne
Mobile	+33 (0)6 32 62 43 15/
	+44 (0)7768 747610
Email	jhanslip@aol.com
Web	www.bourdilblanc.com

Entry 426　Map 9

La Ferme de la Rivière

The busy auberge sits surrounded by fields in a hamlet near the river Dordogne. The Archer family honour tradition; he is a poultry breeder, she is an industrious (decidedly non-vegetarian) cook and the recipes for handcrafting pâtés and foie gras are their heirlooms. Readers talk of fabulous meals and delicious apéritifs. The honey stones of the building are impeccably pointed and cleaned, bedrooms are spotless though dark, shower rooms are large and pristine and there's a delightful, very French dining room with an open fire. Good for families (a climbing frame in the garden) – and brilliant value.

Chartreuse le Cariol

Arrive at Irene and Marthijn's 12th-century estate house and you will likely hear the buzz of conversation around a laden table. A friendly, creative place – with Marthijn's art and sculptures brightening the fresh, eclectic rooms. A boutique vibe pervades: dark walls, floors and sofas; super-modern lighting; Indian grilles; a glass-topped stone table. Cosy bedrooms (one a generous family size) are on the ground floor, or downstairs by the wine cellar and sauna. There's a terrace with open views, a large pool with pool house and fire and your hosts will gladly point you to cultural events in nearby Beaumont and Bergerac.

Minimum stay: 2 nights; 3 nights in high season. Pets by arrangement.

Rooms	1 double: €59.
	1 triple: €59-€72.
Meals	Dinner with wine, €21.50.
Closed	November – February.

Rooms	1 family room for 4: €225.
	1 family room for 5: €325.
	Extra bed/sofabed available €39 per person per night.
Meals	Dinner, 4 courses with wine, €34.50 (July/August). Restaurants 7km.
Closed	Rarely.

	Marie-Thérèse & Jean-Michel Archer
	La Ferme de la Rivière,
	24520 St Agne,
	Dordogne
Tel	+33 (0)5 53 23 22 26
Email	archer.marietherese@wanadoo.fr
Web	www.lafermedelariviere.com

	Irene de Groot
	Chartreuse le Cariol,
	Le Cariol, 24440 Naussannes,
	Dordogne
Tel	+33 (0)5 53 63 97 07
Email	lecariol@icloud.com
Web	www.lecariol.com

Château Gauthié

Outside a perfect bastide village, here is château B&B run with warmth and energy. Stéphane cooks brilliantly and loves wine; Florence is enormous fun, a breath of fresh air. Restful, light-filled, traditional bedrooms have white bathrooms. An infinity pool overlooks the lake below, above it perches the rustic-modern treehouse, its balcony gazing over meadows and cows, its mother tree thrusting two branches through the floor. Solar-lit paths lead you down through the trees at night, a breakfast basket is winched up in the morning. Later... play badminton, fish in the lake, spin off on a bike, bask in the hot tub.

Minimum stay: 2 nights; 7 nights in treehouses in summer.

Labarthe

At the end of a track lined with cherry trees, surrounded by vineyards and sunflowers, is a blue-shuttered house with far-reaching views; take a book to the garden and dream. There's no traffic to disturb the peace, just the odd splash from the pool which you are most welcome to share. Jeanette and Richard have taken the leap, to leave the UK for the Lot-et-Garonne and open up a B&B. Bedrooms are spotless and sweet; bathrooms are new; dinner includes local wines. Little Duras (two kilometres away) has restaurants, a bar, a market and a château on top of the hill – and if you're feeling lively you can kayak down the river Dordogne.

Rooms	3 doubles, 1 twin: €90–€115.
	1 treehouse for 2: €130–€175.
	1 treehouse for 5: €1,050–€1,540.
Meals	Dinner, 4 courses with wine, €40.
	Wine €15–€50.
Closed	Mid-November to March.

Rooms	4 doubles: €70–€78.
Meals	Dinner, 3 courses with wine, €30.
	Vegetarian meals available.
	Restaurants 2km.
Closed	Rarely.

	Florence & Stéphane Desmette
	Château Gauthié,
	24560 Issigeac Monmarvès,
	Dordogne
Tel	+33 (0)5 53 27 30 33
Email	chateau.gauthie@laposte.net
Web	www.chateaugauthie.com

	Richard & Jeanette Hyde
	Labarthe,
	47120 Duras,
	Lot-et-Garonne
Tel	+33 (0)5 53 89 77 58
Email	Hideawayfrance@gmail.com
Web	www.hideawayfrance.co.uk

Entry 429   Map 9

Entry 430   Map 9

Manoir Laurette B&B

Lora has filled her light-drenched 200-year old home with curios, artwork and furniture collected on her travels and it all works magically. Bedrooms are large and bright and have antique furniture; bathrooms are brand spanking new, two have roll tops. You can breakfast in bed or in the garden underneath the shade of the walnut tree: smoothies, granola, local honey, bacon sarnies, delicious buttermilk pancakes, proper coffee... You're slap bang in the middle of wine-tasting country, the steepled church in Lorette is a two-minute walk and for trips out sup champagne and oysters in Arcachon or hang out in trendy Cap Ferret.

Pets by arrangement.

Rooms	4 doubles, 1 twin: €85–€115.
Meals	Restaurants 3km.
Closed	Rarely.

Lora Munro
Manoir Laurette B&B,
Lorette Ouest,
47180 St Martin Petit,
Lot-et-Garonne
Mobile +44 (0)7957 662008
Email hello@manoirlaurette.com
Web www.manoirlaurette.com

Entry 431 Map 9

Domaine du Moulin de Labique

Soay sheep on the drive, ducks on the pond, goats in the greenhouse and food *à la grand-mère*. Shutters are painted with *bleu de pastel* from the Gers and the 13th-century interiors have lost none of their charm. In house and outbuildings there are chunky beams, seagrass on ancient tiles, vintage iron bedsteads, antique mirrors, and wallpapers flower-sprigged in raspberry, jade and green. Outside are old French roses and young alleys of trees, a bamboo-fringed stream, a restaurant in the stables, an exquisite pool. Wonderful hosts, the Bruxellois owners loved this place for years; now they are its best ambassadors.

Rooms	3 doubles, 2 twins: €110–€140.
	1 suite for 4: €199.
	Dinner, B&B €83–€99 per person.
Meals	Dinner €31. Wine €16–€30.
Closed	Rarely.

Patrick & Christine Hendricx
Domaine du Moulin de Labique,
Saint Vivien,
47210 Villeréal,
Lot-et-Garonne
Tel +33 (0)5 53 01 63 90
Email moulin-de-labique@wanadoo.fr
Web www.moulin-de-labique.net

Entry 432 Map 9

Domaine de Rambeau

Handsome and enticing, this 18th-century manor house is perched on a hillside with views of silken wheat fields and distant valleys. But feast your eyes on the star of the show: an all-bells-and-whistles pool. Inside: an air of decadent splendour – even a knight in armour – where all is tasteful, relaxed and spacious in sitting, dining and bedrooms – just watch out for some low beams (and ask for an extra single if you need one). There's lovely artisan bread and homemade jams for breakfast, scrumptious dinners from generous owners and acres of parkland to mosey around – home to a huge and friendly black pig.

Manoir Beaujoly

The medieval manor surveys fertile land rich in tales of knights and kings: a stunning hilltop setting. Horses graze, quails potter and guests gather by the pool in a ruined granary to barbecue trout from the river or duck from the market. The cool, thick-walled building wears its no-frills minimalism well: rough stone, hefty beams, a roll top bath, canvas wardrobes, ancient bullet holes… and 'open' bathrooms behind screens. There's a great fire in the monastic sitting room where delightful Dutch-German host serves breakfasts of cheese and charcuterie. Rampage, like those medieval Templars, across glorious 'French Tuscany'.

Minimum stay: 3 nights.

Rooms	4 doubles: €100. Extra bed €20.
Meals	Breakfast €10.
	Dinner, 3 courses with wine, €25.
	Restaurant 4km.
Closed	Rarely.

Rooms	5 doubles: €110.
Meals	Restaurants 4km.
Closed	Rarely.

	Kim Reeves
	Domaine de Rambeau,
	Lieu dit Rambeau,
	47260 Castelmoron sur Lot,
	Lot-et-Garonne
Tel	+33 (0)5 53 79 38 43
Mobile	+33 (0)6 13 95 39 52
Email	reeves.kim@hotmail.fr
Web	www.domainederambeau.com

	Lana Elise Siebelink
	Manoir Beaujoly,
	47340 Hautefage la Tour,
	Lot-et-Garonne
Tel	+33 (0)5 53 01 52 51
Mobile	+31 (0)6 28 12 64 76
Email	be@beaujoly.com
Web	www.beaujoly.com

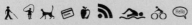

Entry 433   Map 14

Entry 434   Map 14

Domaine de Pine

Hidden among sunflower fields is a well-proportioned and delightful hotel, an intimate haven run by charming English hosts. Convivial meals are served on fine white linen on a summer terrace with stunning panoramic views, beamy bedrooms are mostly large, light and elegant in whites and creams, and bathrooms sport fluffy robes. Springtime calls for lazing on loungers by the walled pool, happy hour is between five and six. For winter: a fitness room, a roaring fire, a candlelit supper in a blue and white dining room. Step out for music festivals and markets – or stay put and explore. Brilliant.

Pets by arrangement.

Le Domaine de l'Escuderia

Monsieur milks 100 Friesian cows, Madame breeds horses happily. Their maison de maître was a wreck in storm-torn woodland before they rolled up their sleeves. Now it has country-pretty rooms with iron four-posters and massage showers, a modern guest kitchen, sofas on the veranda, a bubbling hot tub… one extravagance in an eco-friendly restoration. Breakfast on farm milk and homemade flan, borrow bikes for a spin down to Lac Biscarosse, tempt the ponies with a carrot, jog around sprawling grounds and unkempt woods – or kite-surf off Atlantic beaches, half an hour away. Country fun for all the family.

Rooms	3 doubles, 2 interconnect: €99-€235. 1 suite for 4: €145-€190. Singles €79-€149. Extra bed/sofabed available €15 per person per night. Dinner, B&B from €115 for 1; from €180 for 2.
Meals	Lunch & dinner from €35. Restaurants 2-minute drive.
Closed	Rarely.

Rooms	3 doubles: €66-€140. 1 family room for 5: €91-€157. Extra beds available.
Meals	Guest kitchen. Restaurant 3km.
Closed	Rarely.

Marcus & Cathy Becker
Domaine de Pine,
47470 Blaymont,
Lot-et-Garonne

Tel	+33 (0)5 53 66 44 93
Mobile	+44 (0)7055 393015
Email	email@ddpine.com
Web	www.domainedepine.com

Emmanuelle Gallouet
Le Domaine de l'Escuderia,
Route de Blaise,
40160 Parentis en Born,
Landes

Mobile	+33 (0)6 61 42 58 83
Email	contact@lescuderia.com
Web	www.lescuderia.com

Domaine de Sengresse

In the undiscovered Landes, two hours from Spain, a remote and ravishing 17th-century domaine. A solid stone house, a cathedral-like barn, an elegant pool, red squirrels in luscious acres and a 'petite maison' whose bread oven served the area's farms: such are the riches in store. A Godin stove and six-oven Aga feed today's guests in gourmet style from a wonderful array of homemade produce, the rooms are bathed in light and everything sparkles, from the luxurious bedrooms with their calming colours to the library brimful of books. More country hotel than B&B, run by the loveliest people.

Pets by arrangement.

Villa etcheBri

A tee's throw from surfing beaches, fringed by pines in the smart enclave of Chiberta, is a serene, secluded, 1960s villa. Here live Brigitte and her adorable bulldog Icarc, happily sharing their home with guests. The setting is lovely: bamboos and palms on lawns, exotic plants in pots, and two ground-floor suites opening to a decked terrace and a fabulous pool. Bedrooms are clean, contemporary and restful in white, with splashes of sunshine from fabrics and towels. Bathrooms are… flawless! Walk to bars, restaurants, beaches, golf; set off for the lovely towns of Biarritz and Bayonne.

Parking on-site.

Rooms	3 doubles, 2 twins: €115-€135. 1 house for 2-6: €100-€165. Singles €110-€135. Extra bed/sofabed available €25 per person per night.
Meals	Dinner with wine, from €35.
Closed	Rarely.

Rooms	3 doubles: €110-€185. 2 suites for 4: €190-€330. Extra bed available.
Meals	Restaurants 5-minute drive.
Closed	Rarely.

	Michèle, Rob McLusky & Sasha Ibbotson Domaine de Sengresse, Route de Gouts, 40250 Souprosse, Landes
Tel	+33 (0)5 58 97 78 34
Email	sengresse@hotmail.fr
Web	www.sengresse.com

	Brigitte Wallon – Van de Velde Villa etcheBri, 9 avenue de la Forêt, 64600 Anglet, Pyrénées-Atlantiques
Mobile	+33 (0)6 73 53 36 48
Email	etchebri@gmail.com
Web	www.etchebri.fr

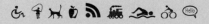

Entry 437 Map 13

Entry 439 Map 13

Les Volets Bleus

High in these ancient hills stands a beautiful new farmhouse built with old Basque materials. Chic, clever Marie has made a perfect creation. The décor has been meticulously studied, a magical effect achieved. Through the double-arch door, a flagged entrance hall, then a terrace with charming rattan chairs. Up stone staircases are bedrooms in restful colours with wood or tiled floors, gilt mirrors, embroidered sheets, ancestral paintings; exquisite bathrooms have iron towel rails and aromatic oils. Marie is an accomplished gardener so retreat to her garden for a read or a swim — or lounge in the salon on deep sofas. Heaven.

Rooms	2 doubles, 1 twin: £125–£180. 2 suites: £155–£191. Extra bed/sofabed available €30 per person per night.
Meals	Restaurants 1.5km.
Closed	November – March.

Marie de Lapasse
Les Volets Bleus,
Chemin Etchegaraya,
64200 Arcangues,
Pyrénées-Atlantiques

Tel	+33 (0)6 07 69 03 85
Email	maisonlesvoletsbleus@wanadoo.fr
Web	www.lesvoletsbleus.fr

Entry 440   Map 13

La Bergerie d'Anne-Marie

Basque houses have a charm all of their own. This one is steeped in green hills and its views are panoramic, with thrilling sightings of the sea. Bruno, once a magazine photographer in Paris, knows and loves his neck of the woods and looks after guests with aplomb; his table d'hôtes is a delight. Bedrooms have the same fabulous views, the 'Squirrel Room', with mirrors and Louis XVI pieces, the most pleasing to the eye. The suite is ideal for a family, with interlinking rooms and a gorgeous old bath down four stairs. Cruise the coastal road, hop into Spain, return to an apéritif on the intimate terrace.

Minimum stay: 2 nights.

Rooms	1 double: €90–€140. 1 suite for 3 with separate bathroom: €185. Pets €20.
Meals	Dinner with wine, €32. Restaurant 1km.
Closed	November.

Bruno Krassinine
La Bergerie d'Anne-Marie,
Chemin de Goyetchea 1285,
La Croix des Bouquets,
64122 Urrugne,
Pyrénées-Atlantiques

Tel	+33 (0)5 59 20 79 44
Email	bkrassinine@free.fr
Web	www.labergeriedannemarie.venez.fr

Entry 441   Map 13

Ferme Elhorga

Unwind here with truly gracious hosts, a beautiful house with spoiling bedrooms and bathrooms, delightful views, a drinks menu (with little apéro plates) and lawns which swoop down to a sparkling pool. Plenty of space and lots of hidden seating areas give you privacy – sneak off with your breakfast if you want: a gourmand affair with local charcuterie, brebis cheese, eggs to boil, a pâtisserie of the day and as much coffee and tea as you want – all day! A little kitchen is yours, there's a large living room filled with quirky brocantes, comfy sofas and leather armchairs, bikes are yours to borrow and the area has much to explore. Restful.

Bidachuna

The electronic gate clicks behind you and 29 hectares of forested peacefulness are yours – with wildlife. Open wide your beautiful curtains next morning and you may see deer feeding; lift your eyes to feast on long vistas to the Pyrenean foothills; trot downstairs to the earthly feast that is Basque breakfast; fall asleep to the hoot of the owl. Shyly attentive, Isabelle manages all this impeccably and keeps a refined house where everything gleams; floors are chestnut, bathrooms are marble, family antiques are perfect. Pop off to lovely St Jean de Luz for lunch or dinner, return to this manicured haven and blissful cosseting.

Rooms	4 doubles: €90-€190.
	1 suite for 2: €150-€220.
	Extra bed €30-€50.
Meals	Dinner €19. Guest kitchen & BBQ.
	Restaurants 1km.
Closed	15 November to 1 March.

Rooms	2 doubles, 1 twin: €125.
	Singles €115.
Meals	Restaurant 6km.
Closed	Mid-November to mid-March.

	Julie Despons
	Ferme Elhorga,
	Chemin d'Elhorga,
	64310 St Pée sur Nivelle,
	Pyrénées-Atlantiques
Mobile	+33 (0)6 08 68 13 30
Email	contact@elhorga.com
Web	www.elhorga.com

	Isabelle Ormazabal
	Bidachuna,
	Route D3, Lieu dit Otsanz,
	64310 St Pée sur Nivelle,
	Pyrénées-Atlantiques
Tel	+33 (0)5 59 54 56 22
Email	isabelleormazabal@gmail.com
Web	www.bidachuna.fr

Entry 442   Map 13

Entry 443   Map 13

Dominxenea

You're well looked after here by bubbly Madame, steeped as she is in the Basque tradition of hospitality. The house is listed: find ox-blood red shutters and door, a courtyard garden and wide views of the mountains. You breakfast in the dining room or on the terrace; what could be nicer than a just-baked croissant and a fresh fruit salad surrounded only by views and birdsong. This is a gentle, quiet place – not for those seeking thrills. Bedrooms are old-fashioned and flowery with balconies; beds have thick mattresses and embroidered pillow cases, bathrooms are clean and comfortable. Hop on the petit train for even more views.

Maison Marchand

A lovely face among all the lovely faces of this listed village, the 16th-century Basque farmhouse, resuscitated by its delightful French/Irish owners, is run with well-organised informality. Dinners are lively; local dishes are excellent. Discreetly luxurious bedrooms (each with its own sitting area and terrace) have beams, exposed wafer bricks, thoughtful extras. Summer breakfast is on the covered terrace in the beautiful walled garden with peaceful reading spots and three friendly cats. Your hosts delight in sharing their culture of pelote basque, rugby, real tennis, horses… and their passion for all things Basque.

Minimum stay: 2 nights in high season.

Rooms	3 twin/doubles: €55-€75. Extra bed €15.
Meals	Restaurants 10-minute walk.
Closed	1 November to 31 March.

Rooms	2 doubles: €75-€85. 1 family room for 4: €75-€125. Extra bed/sofabed available €25 per person per night.
Meals	Dinner with wine, €25.
Closed	1 November to 31 March.

Laurence & Jean Baptiste Fagoaga
Dominxenea,
Quartier Ihalar,
64310 Sare,
Pyrénées-Atlantiques
Tel   +33 (0)5 59 54 20 46
Email   hotel@arraya.com
Web   www.dominxenea.fr/

Valerie & Gilbert Foix
Maison Marchand,
64240 La Bastide Clairence,
Pyrénées-Atlantiques
Tel   +33 (0)5 59 29 18 27
Mobile   +33 (0)6 82 78 50 95
Email   maison.marchand@wanadoo.fr
Web   pagesperso-orange.fr/
         maison.marchand

Entry 444   Map 13

Entry 445   Map 13

La Closerie du Guilhat

Through the iron gates, up the tree-lined drive to an astonishing kingdom of plants of all shapes and sizes: a hidden garden of exotica. Weave your way through magnolias and rhododendrons, bananas and bamboos to secret benches for reading and the Pyrénées as a backdrop. A delight for all ages! To the sturdy and spotless Béarn house with its solid old furniture Marie-Christine – a genuine and generous host – has added her own decorative touches. Table tennis is shared with gîte guests, dinners are delicious. The other-worldliness is restorative yet the spa town of Salies is a pedal away.

La Bergerie

Through ancient woods and unspoilt farmland you wind your way up to little Montestrucq, to a farm half a mile from the church, steeped in ancient character. Now, in the former bergerie, are sheepskin-strewn sofas, standing timbers, a huge open fire and, upstairs, bedrooms charming and cosy... Irish bed linen, pure wool carpets, Italian walk-in showers. Cassoulets, piperades, fondues, wild boar: Didier loves his 'cuisine gourmande' and sources with gusto; Sabine is full of smiles. The house faces south, the pool is inviting, and views soar over the hills to the majestic Pyrénées.

Heated swimming pool.

Rooms	1 double, 1 twin: €60-€66.
	1 suite for 3-4: €74-€88.
Meals	Dinner €22. Wine from €16
Closed	Rarely.

Rooms	2 doubles; 1 twin with separate
	bathroom: €78-€98.
	Extra bed/sofabed available €20 per
	person per night.
Meals	Lunch €18. Dinner €29.
	Gastronomic dinner €38.50.
	Non-alcoholic drinks
	complimentary.
	Restaurants 10km.
Closed	Rarely.

	Marie-Christine Potiron
	La Closerie du Guilhat,
	64270 Salies de Béarn,
	Pyrénées-Atlantiques
Tel	+33 (0)5 59 38 08 80
Email	guilhat@club-internet.fr
Web	www.closerieduguilhat.com

	Sabine & Didier Meyer
	La Bergerie, 2 chemin de Lhostebielh,
	64300 Montestrucq,
	Pyrénées-Atlantiques
Tel	+33 (0)5 59 38 63 76
Mobile	+33 (0)6 14 83 53 24
Email	sabine.meyer3@orange.fr
Web	www.sites.google.com/site/
	labergeriebearn/

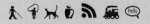

Entry 446   Map 13

Entry 447   Map 13

La Bastide Estratte

In six remote hectares of woodland with Pyrenean peaks beyond, a solid slate-roofed farmhouse. Enter the wide stone arch into a beautiful balcony-fringed, flagstoned courtyard: sip a cappuccino among ornamental acers, japonicas, box hedges as Virginia creeper winds its way over the walls. Inside, a patina of olives, pale greys and ecru provides a studied canvas for polished floors, white sofas, porcelain in bookcases, fine fittings and herbal prints. Lovely Chantale, at ease in six languages, helps with Jurançon wine routes, restaurants (a new one close by) and walks. If it's all too cool, bask in the jacuzzi.

Minimum stay: 2 nights.

Clos Mirabel

Fifteen minutes from city lights, yet surrounded by vineyards. French-Canadian André is a retired diplomat, Ann worked in travel, Emily goes to the village school. They fell in love with Clos Mirabel eleven years ago, now they delightedly welcome guests. The 18th-century manor is flanked by a winery and gatehouse; the interiors are light, airy and restful, their gracious proportions enhanced by Ann's elegant eye. A spiral staircase links the Gustavian apartment's three levels, there's a pool terrace with breathtaking Pyrenean views and breakfast honey comes from André's bees. Outstanding.

Pets by arrangement.

Rooms	3 doubles: €85. Singles €75. Extra bed €30.
Meals	Restaurant 1km.
Closed	Rarely.

Rooms	3 doubles: €95–€159. 1 apartment for 4–6 with kitchen: €85–€217. Extra bed €35.
Meals	Restaurants 3km.
Closed	Rarely.

Chantale Albert
La Bastide Estratte,
Quartier St Michel, Chemin de Bas
Afittes, 64360 Lucq de Béarn,
Pyrénées-Atlantiques

Tel	+33 (0)5 59 34 32 45
Mobile	+33 (0)6 22 64 16 55
Email	chantale.albert@nordnet.fr
Web	www.labastide-estratte.com

Ann Kenny & André Péloquin
Clos Mirabel,
276 av des Frères Barthélémy,
Jurançon, 64110 Pau,
Pyrénées-Atlantiques

Tel	+33 (0)5 59 06 32 83
Mobile	+33 (0)6 79 59 04 91
Email	info@closmirabel.com
Web	www.closmirabel.com

Entry 448   Map 13

Entry 449   Map 13

Limousin

Château du Fraisse

After 800 years of family and estate symbiosis, Le Fraisse is a living history book, mainly a rustic-grand Renaissance gem by the great Serlio — pale limestone, discreetly elegant portico, Henry II staircase and an astonishing fireplace in the vast drawing room. Your cultured hosts, two generations now, will greet you with warmth, happily tell you about house and history and show you to your room: fine furniture, paintings and prints, traditional furnishings; one bathroom has a fragment of a 16th-century fresco. If you return late at night you must climb the steep old spiral stair to your room as the main door is locked.

Château Ribagnac

Patrick and Colette are intelligent, thoughtful and enthusiastic, and their château, built in 1647, is an absolute treat. Grand fireplaces, original features, rugs on oak floors, superb new bathrooms (one loo in its turret): the conversion is authentic, not luxurious but elegantly comfortable. Ask for a lighter room with views over park and lake. Outside: a children's play area, an organic kitchen garden, a heated pool, an orchard you can enjoy… tranquillity and views. The local meat is succulent, there is a deep commitment. Conversation flows with the wine.

Minimum stay: 2 nights in high season.

Rooms	1 double, 1 twin: €90–€100.
	1 suite for 3,
	1 suite for 4: €135–€150.
Meals	Restaurants 6km.
Closed	Mid-December to mid-January.

Rooms	4 suites for 2: €100–€160.
Meals	Dinner with wine, €45.
Closed	Christmas.

	Marquis & Marquise des Monstiers Mérinville
	Château du Fraisse,
	Le Fraisse, 87330 Nouic,
	Haute-Vienne
Tel	+33 (0)5 55 68 32 68
Email	infos@chateau-du-fraisse.com
Web	www.chateau-du-fraisse.com

	Patrick & Colette Bergot
	Château Ribagnac,
	87400 St Martin Terressus,
	Haute-Vienne
Tel	+33 (0)5 55 39 77 91
Mobile	+33 (0)6 85 40 45 99
Email	reservations@chateauribagnac.com
Web	www.chateauribagnac.com

Entry 450   Map 9

Entry 451   Map 9

Limousin

Limousin

Le Jardin des Lys

A handsome house in the heart of a bustling medieval town. From an impressive hall, a twisting staircase leads to big balconied bedrooms with windows overlooking the church; rich colours and baroque wallpapers are the backdrop for fireplaces and leather chairs; tea trays and pillow bonbons complete the elegant scene; bathrooms are immaculate. You breakfast on compotes and fresh bread in an airy dining room with Louis XIV tables and chairs. Your discreet hosts leave you to your own devices with a handy entry code. Stroll to restaurants, public garden, museum, buy Limousin chocolates from the Chartier family's tiny shop.

Les Drouilles Bleues

High on a granite hill, with views to swell your heart, the low stone house and its greenly rocky garden creak with age and history. As does the whole region. Paul and Maïthé, a most intelligent and attentive couple, take their hosting to heart, greeting with homemade treats, revelling in – and joining – the people who gather at their convivial and tasty dinner table. In converted outbuildings, handsome bedrooms large (the suite) and smaller, are simple, a touch old-fashioned and done with care and soft colours. All have working fireplaces, sleeping quarters on mezzanines, good shower rooms. Deeply, discreetly, welcoming.

Rooms	2 doubles, 2 twin/doubles: €89–€99. 1 suite for 4: €119. Singles €89. Extra bed/sofabed available €15 per person per night.
Meals	Cold meats & cheese platter €20. Wine €15. Restaurants 50m.
Closed	Rarely.

Rooms	2 doubles: €70–€94. 1 suite for 5: €94–€160. Dinner, B&B €99–€135 per person. Extra bed/sofabed available €15 per person per night.
Meals	Dinner with wine, €26; children under 12, €15.
Closed	Rarely.

Joël Chartier
Le Jardin des Lys,
3 place de la Collégiale,
87400 Saint Léonard de Noblat,
Haute-Vienne
Tel   +33 (0)5 55 56 63 39
Email   le-jardin-des-lys@orange.fr
Web   www.le-jardin-des-lys.com

Maïthé & Paul de Bettignies
Les Drouilles Bleues,
La Drouille,
87800 St Hilaire les Places,
Haute-Vienne
Tel   +33 (0)5 55 58 21 26
Email   lesdrouillesbleues@gmail.com
Web   drouillesbleues.free.fr

Entry 452   Map 9

Entry 453   Map 9

Limousin

Au Fil du Temps

This handsome 1930s Deco-style house in central Chalûs makes an ideal stop en route to the Atlantic coast. The kind, attentive Antonaccios have designed an inviting ground floor guest room, in white and gentle colours with striped and toile de Jouy fabrics, in what was once the doctor's surgery. The tiled bathroom with walk-in shower is behind a partition wall; the loo's separate. And you've a cosy sitting area with sofa bed and brick fireplace. Breakfast's in the main house, where light floods in on period décor lifted by some nicely quirky touches. There's a heated pool in the garden and restaurants a short stroll away.

Covered parking available.

Limousin

La Residence Limousin

On the quiet fringes of St Yrieix la Perche's medieval quarter, a formal town-house exterior conceals a scene of fin de siècle opulence. From the dining room's pink Murano chandelier to the comfortable bedrooms' bold feature walls and rich fabrics, kind and friendly Patti and Dave have really put their stamp on this house. Pristine bathrooms are ultra-modern and gleaming white, stocked with top end potions. You have the run of the peaceful and pretty walled garden with burgeoning potager too. Fuelled by your fresh and plentiful breakfast, you'll be more than ready to launch yourself into France's lake district.

Children over 8 welcome.

Rooms	1 suite for 2-4: €80-€108. Singles €80. Babes in arms free of charge.
Meals	Restaurants 1-minute walk.
Closed	Rarely.

Rooms	3 doubles: €75-€90.
Meals	Dinner, 4 courses with wine, €25. Restaurant 2-minute walk.
Closed	Rarely.

Sandrine Antonaccio
Au Fil du Temps,
41 rue Salardine,
87230 Chalûs,
Haute-Vienne
Tel   +33 (0)5 55 55 95 99
Mobile +33 (0)6 76 17 25 84
Email   sandrine.antonaccio@gmail.com

Patti Atwood
La Residence Limousin,
5 place President Magnaud,
87500 Saint Yrieix la Perche,
Haute-Vienne
Tel   +33 (0)5 55 58 94 48
Email laresidencelimousin@gmail.com
Web   www.laresidencelimousin.com

Entry 454   Map 9

Entry 455   Map 9

Moulin de Marsaguet

The nicest people, they have done just enough to this proud old building so it looks as it did 200 years ago when it forged cannon balls. The farm is relaxed and natural, the bedrooms quaint, they have ducks and animals (including Lusitanian horses), three teenagers and a super potager, and make pâtés and 'confits' by the great mill pond, hanging the hams over the magnificent hearth in their big stone sitting room with its old-fashioned sofa. Relish the drive up past tree-framed lake (boating possible) and stone outbuildings and the prospect of dining on home-grown ingredients.

Pets by arrangement only.

Art de Vivre

In glorious Treignac, a family of Dutch francophiles are living their dream in a brilliant mix of urban cool and country charm. Their laidback yet savvy hospitality promises relaxation and interesting encounters. Han and Yvon are professional cooks so people also come for their refined modern take on local food. The terraced garden with its discreet pool is delightful, the interior comes with white walls and warm wood, the bedrooms are trimmed with smart slate grey and pretty floral quilts while painted retro wardrobes add charm. There's a good sitting room, a library with books and games – and so much to explore outside.

Minimum stay: 2 nights.

Rooms	3 twin/doubles: €60.
Meals	Dinner with wine, €22.
	Restaurant 3km.
Closed	November to mid-April.

Rooms	4 doubles: €65–€95.
	1 suite for 6: €175–€200.
	Extra bed/sofabed available €35 per
	person per night.
Meals	Dinner with wine, €27.50.
	Restaurant 10-minute walk.
Closed	November – March.

Valérie & Renaud Gizardin
Moulin de Marsaguet,
87500 Coussac Bonneval,
Haute-Vienne

Tel   +33 (0)5 55 75 28 29
Mobile +33 (0)6 26 16 34 47
Email   renaudvalerie.gizardin@orange.fr
Web   www.moulin-marsaguet.com

Yvon Merks & Han Sluis
Art de Vivre,
3 rue Soulanche,
19260 Treignac,
Corrèze

Tel   +33 (0)5 87 52 13 99
Mobile +31 (0)6 23 23 71 39
Email   info@artdevivre-treignac.eu
Web   www.artdevivre-treignac.eu

Limousin

Maison Grandchamp

In an historic town, be welcomed by a charming, cultured couple to a 400-year-old house of fascinating origins. Thrill to Marielle's tales: her ancestors built and extended the house, their portraits hang in the panelled drawing room; find time for François' knowledge of history, geography and the environment. Up the elegant spiral stairs, bedrooms are in proper but unpompous château style, big, soft and quiet. Breakfast is in the beamy 16th-century dining room, or by the kitchen fire, or in the terraced garden overlooking jumbled rooftops, or in the luminous veranda. Then explore glorious Corrèze.

Rooms	2 twin/doubles; 1 twin/double with separate bathroom: €80–€90. Extra bed €25. Overflow room for 2 available.
Meals	Dinner with apéritif & wine, €29–€32. Restaurants within walking distance.
Closed	January – March.

Marielle & François Teyssier
Maison Grandchamp,
9 place des Pénitents,
19260 Treignac,
Corrèze

Tel	+33 (0)5 55 98 10 69
Mobile	+33 (0)6 59 05 09 46
Email	teyssier.marielle@wanadoo.fr
Web	www.hotesgrandchamp.com

Entry 458   Map 10

Limousin

La Pissarelle

In a green and lovely corner of France, discover the wee hamlet where Annie's family have always farmed. Here she and Wolfgang, (he worked with NATO and speaks impeccable English), have returned to renovate a highly personal, treasure-filled farmhouse with a cosily simple 'Petite Maison' for guests just across the patio. Having lived all over the world, they adore having visitors at their table in the former cattle byre or in the new veranda – and hope you might park your horses in their field. Before the vast ex-château fireplace, you will be regaled with tales of local life and exotic lands. A fascinating couple.

Rooms	1 cottage for 4: €60–€150. Extra single available.
Meals	Lunch, 2 courses, €15. Dinner with wine, €28. Picnic €10. Restaurant 7km.
Closed	Rarely.

Wolfgang & Annie Oelsner
La Pissarelle,
La Clupte,
23430 Châtelus le Marcheix,
Creuse

Tel	+33 (0)5 55 64 30 58
Mobile	+33 (0)6 73 00 26 68
Email	lapissarelle@gmail.com
Web	www.lapissarelle.com

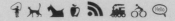

Entry 459   Map 9

La Bourge

Suzie's artistry makes this fine house especially warm and charming. Built around 1900 as a summer retreat for Parisians, now almost hidden by wisteria, it sits back from the road near the town centre. Light, lovely rooms are in gentle colours with fireplaces, Venetian mirrors, 18th-century armchairs, kilims, candlesticks and hat blocks; one bathroom has a claw foot bath, another a huge walk in shower; the 60s-inspired beamy loft room is fun and family-friendly. Breakfasts are at one table in the dining room or outside – the terrace shared by the pretty 50s-style lunch and tea room – and market fresh dinners are often meat-free.

On-street parking.

Maison Numéro Neuf

Lisa and Duncan from England have embraced life in southern La Souterraine. She is the least ruffled, most contented of chefs; he serves wines with finesse; both love house, children, guests, and their secret garden with hens. Now, at last, the renovation of the former residence of the Marquis de Valady is complete. So much to enjoy: the fine proportions, the sweeping balustrade, the antique mirrors, the crystal-drop chandeliers, the pale walls, the glowing parquet… and superb breakfasts and dinners. If Lisa pops a hot water bottle into your bed it will be encased in white linen: the hospitality here is exceptional.

Rooms	1 double; 2 doubles each with separate bathroom: €65–€85. 1 apartment for 4: €120.
Meals	Dinner, 4 courses, €25. Restaurants 1-minute walk.
Closed	Rarely.

Rooms	2 doubles; 1 twin sharing shower with single: €65–€115. Singles €45–€85. Dinner, B&B €57–€109 per person. Extra bed/sofabed available €25–€35 per person per night. Extra 2 rooms available.
Meals	Dinner €22–€45. Wine €18.
Closed	Rarely.

	Susie Casson La Bourge, 56 rue du Pont de la Gartempe, 23240 Le Grand Bourg, Creuse
Tel	+33 (0)5 87 56 13 78
Email	susiecasson@hotmail.co.uk
Web	www.chezlabourge.com

	Duncan & Lisa Rowney Maison Numéro Neuf, Rue Serpente, 23300 La Souterraine, Creuse
Tel	+33 (0)5 55 63 43 35
Email	reservations@maisonnumeroneuf.com
Web	www.maisonnumeroneuf.com

Auvergne

Auvergne

Auvergne

Manoir du Mortier

A hilltop manoir surrounded by 50 hectares of remote oak forest… Sumptuously restored by vivacious Catherine, the interiors are straight out of a design book. Her inherited antiques, vintage finds and fresh fabrics make every corner a treat for the eye. Sleep in the tower with its door on to the swimming pool, or choose the square tower suite for a family: white-clad beds, soft *boutis* and traditional toile de Jouy. Big bathrooms, down winding staircases, have walk-in Italian showers. Convivial breakfasts are served at the large round table in the lofty dining room. Ramble on forest paths, explore on horseback, linger by the pool.

Parking on-site.

Château de Clusors

Atop a hill, this small château has gazed on untouched countryside since the 14th century. Steeped in history (Henri is full of stories; Madame de Montespan once stayed here), the place is still a working farm: friendly and down-to-earth, Madame manages a herd of Charolais cows. Up the spiral stone stair are big bedrooms with fine furniture and excellent modern bathrooms; breakfast is set before family portraits and a bookcase stocked with leather-bound tomes. Outside: a large garden with orchard and pool; rest in the shade of a lime tree and admire the magnificent view. Wonderfully, authentically French.

Rooms	1 double; 2 twin/doubles: €75–€150. 1 suite for 5: €190–€220. Extra bed/sofabed available €25 per person per night. Cots available.
Meals	Dinner, 3 courses with wine & coffee, €32. Restaurants 5–10km.
Closed	8 January to end of March.

Rooms	2 triples: €105. Extra bed €20.
Meals	Cold meats and vegetable platter €10. Restaurants 1km.
Closed	Rarely.

	Catherine Greninger
	Manoir du Mortier,
	Le Mortier,
	03360 Meaulne,
	Allier
Mobile	+33 (0)6 30 34 06 40
Email	manoirdumortier@yahoo.fr
Web	www.manoirdumortier.fr

	Christine & Henri Thieulin
	Château de Clusors,
	03210 St Menoux,
	Allier
Tel	+33 (0)4 70 43 94 69
Mobile	+33 (0)6 70 79 27 75
Email	henri.thieulin@orange.fr
Web	www.chateaudeclusors.com

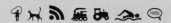

Entry 462   Map 10

Entry 463   Map 10

Domaine d'Aigrepont

Madame greets you warmly outside the original 1640s manor that her ancestors built overlooking the Allier valley. Round a grassy courtyard, the manor, chapel and handsome guest wing float in a sea of terraced gardens surging with lavender, jasmine, roses, vines and a pool. Named after family heroes, bedrooms breathe authenticity with high beams, beautiful antiques, oriental rugs, fireplaces, snow-white linen and new bathrooms, one with a bulls-eye window to the courtyard. Breakfast on homemade brioche, dive into the valley for walks, gardens, vineyards and thermal baths, then off to Moulins for dinner.

Château du Ludaix

Pure château with a touch of humour, Ludaix is glamorous, dramatic and utterly welcoming. David and Stephanie have boundless energy, love people (they run a training company) and lavish care on house and guests. David is exploring the archives ("Ludaix is a living history book"), rebuilding the ancient waterworks and shady walks in the wood. Stephanie's talent cossets the rich warm rooms with English and French antiques ancient and modern, myriad hats, clocks and costumes, the odd tented ceiling. Gorgeous rooms, imaginative bathrooms, delicious food, great conversation – and lots more…

Rooms	1 double, 1 twin/double, 1 twin: €120-€130. Singles €120.
Meals	Catered meals available. Restaurant 5km.
Closed	October – April.

Rooms	2 suites for 2, 1 suite for 3, 1 suite for 4: €120-€180. Whole house available.
Meals	Dinner, 4 courses with wine, €40.
Closed	Rarely.

Édith de Contenson
Domaine d'Aigrepont,
Aigrepont,
03000 Bressolles,
Allier
Mobile   +33 (0)6 80 05 51 02
Email   postmaster@chambres-d-hotes-
          en-bourbonnais.com
Web   www.aigrepont.com

David Morton & Stephanie Holland
Château du Ludaix,
Rue du Ludaix,
03420 Marcillat en Combraille,
Allier
Tel   +33 (0)4 70 51 62 32
Mobile   +44 (0)7739 431918
Email   stephanie@rapport-online.com
Web   www.chateauduludaix.com

Entry 464   Map 10

Entry 465   Map 10

La Maison des Collines Autour

Pascal teaches and tends the veg patch, Evelyne is an artist with a proper sense of colour and texture. Both hugely enjoyed doing up the barn beside their house, and now love sharing local lore and swapping stories with B&B guests (in English), though the barn is separate from their house. The rather disparate exterior belies the warmth and liveliness of the eco-friendly materials and fabrics used inside, the new bedding and smart bathrooms, and the cosy comfort of the wood burner. There's space and softness in the living rooms, lots of peaceful garden — and so much to discover beyond. Remarkable value and so welcoming.

Parking on-site.

Les Eydieux

At the northern tip of the Auvergne Volcanoes Regional Park are these two guest suites, perfect for a total escape — it's around 7 miles to shops and restaurants (and 15 miles out of season). Artistic and chatty Marie-Claire and her husband Cyr have painstakingly renovated their old farm buildings: exposed stone walls, ceilings open to the rafters and hand-picked furniture set the tone, complemented by modern bathrooms. Breakfast of fresh fruit, jams and bread sets you up for walking, swimming or visiting châteaux. Return to a jacuzzi bath and a vegetarian dinner, or rustle up supper in the communal kitchen. Rural bliss!

Parking on-site.

Rooms	3 twin/doubles: €52–€59. Extra bed/sofabed available €14 per person per night.
Meals	Dinner with wine, €25; children 11-16, €15; children under 11, €10. Restaurants 5-minute walk.
Closed	15 December to 1 January.

Rooms	1 suite for 4, 1 suite for 5: €135–€240. Extra bed €35.
Meals	Restaurants 10km. Guest kitchen.
Closed	Rarely.

	Evelyne Dauvergne La Maison des Collines Autour, Le Pouthier, 03300 La Chapelle, Allier
Tel	+33 (0)4 70 41 82 20
Email	evdauv@aol.com
Web	www.la-maison-des-collines-autour.fr

	Marie-Claire Mercier Les Eydieux, 63410 Saint Angel, Puy-de-Dôme
Tel	+33 (0)4 73 86 91 95
Email	leseydieux@orange.fr
Web	www.leseydieux.com

Manoir de la Manantie

Passionate about regional gastronomy – do eat with them, it's a real treat – Véronique and Guillaume quit Paris to pour their talents into this fine neoclassical manor. They've done it up to the nines, from the grand entrance with its volcanic stone stair, smart in crisp red, to the big, super-modern bathrooms. Grand, high-ceilinged bedrooms (the suite is vast), are full of light and antique furniture. The woodwork alone is worth a visit, so too is the English gentleman's room, with its head-high hog-roasting fireplace. Walk into Lezoux, stroll in the park and enjoy the Auvergne's fabulous Regional Parks – and cheese.

Minimum stay: 2 night; 3 nights in high season.

Château de Vaulx

A jewel in the forest, a fairytale haven. Creak along the parquet, swan around the salon… sleep in one tower, wash in another. It's been in the family for 800 years, and traditional rooms have furnishings worthy of the troubadours who sang here. It's an adorable château owned by an adorable pair who welcome you like long lost friends. Philippe and Martine are nurturing the castle as their parents did, with joy – and updating a bit. Breakfast on brioche, yogurt, eggs, cheese, and honey from their hives, stroll from peaceful lawn to sweeping view, settle in to sociable dinners at the delicious, candlelit table.

Arrivals from 5pm.

Rooms	2 doubles: €105-€145.
	2 suites for 3: €125-€145.
	1 apartment for 5: €125-€270.
	Extra bed/sofabed available in the suites €30 per person per night.
Meals	Dinner €17-€27;
	children under 8, €13;
	children under 13, €20.
	Wines €15-€35.
Closed	Rarely.

Rooms	2 doubles: €80-€100.
	1 family room for 3: €100-€130.
	Extra bed/sofabed available €30 per person per night.
Meals	Dinner with wine, €30.
Closed	November – April.

Véronique Vernat-Rossi
Manoir de la Manantie,
Rue Georges Clémenceau,
63190 Lezoux,
Puy-de-Dôme

Tel	+33 (0)4 44 05 21 46
Email	veronique@manoir-manantie.fr
Web	www.manoir-manantie.fr

Guy & Régine Dumas de Vaulx,
Philippe & Martine Vast
Château de Vaulx,
63120 Ste Agathe,
Puy-de-Dôme

Tel	+33 (0)4 73 51 50 55
Mobile	+33 (0)6 42 01 11 94
Email	ph.vast@orange.fr
Web	www.chateaudevaulx.net

Domaine de Gaudon – Le Château

Tranquil and unexpected: smart new Medici urns outside, 19th-century splendour within, glossy oak panelling, fine stucco, original glowing blue paint. Alain and Monique, generous and attentive, have created a setting of astonishing brass, gilt and quilted glamour for their polished French antiques. A fabulous wellness centre and buzzing, trilling, wooded and watery grounds. Bedrooms are extravagant; bathrooms splendidly classical. Breakfasts dazzle: Auvergne ham, baked apple, homemade nut cake, honey and jams in the Salon Bleu (coffered timber ceiling, great timber fireplace, wooden chandelier).

Chez Helen

Montpeyroux is a beautifully revived medieval hilltop village and the Pittmans' house, full of quirks, brocante and family warmth, has a bowl-over view. Sun floods the taupe-cosy bedroom; your sitting room lies cool and restful in the vaulted former wine store. Helen happily shares her knowledge of her adopted region with you over breakfast here or on the terrace; Kevin works in town and is here in the evenings. Charming and relaxed, they love life here. You have a little terrace and private entrance. The village has excellent eateries, from crêpes to creative gourmet. Do stay, there's masses to see and do.

Rooms	3 doubles, 1 twin: €120.	Rooms	1 suite for 2: €85–€95.
	1 suite for 2: €140.	Meals	Restaurants 3-minute walk.
	Extra bed €25.	Closed	Rarely.
Meals	Supper trays available.		
	Restaurant 4km.		
Closed	Rarely.		

	Alain & Monique Bozzo		**Helen Pittman**
	Domaine de Gaudon – Le Château,		Chez Helen,
	63520 Ceilloux,		Montée du Guetteur,
	Puy-de-Dôme		63114 Montpeyroux, Puy-de-Dôme
Tel	+33 (0)4 73 70 76 25	Tel	+33 (0)4 73 89 93 28
Email	domainedegaudon@wanadoo.fr	Mobile	+33 (0)6 81 13 28 23
Web	www.domainedegaudon.fr	Email	helen.t.pittman@gmail.com
		Web	www.facebook.com/
			ChezHelenMontpeyroux/

Château Royal de Saint-Saturnin

A volcanic region is the perfect cradle for this magnificently turreted and castellated fortress, high on the forested fringes of one of France's most beautiful villages. A stone spiral, worn with age and history, leads to five swish bedrooms in the oldest wing. The Louis XIII suite, its bathroom tucked into a tower, spans the castle's width; views are to tumbling rooftops and gardens and parkland behind. The vaulted dining room, decked with gleaming coppers, is the background for relaxed breakfast spreads, and your hosts are friendly and well-travelled. Once owned by Catherine de' Medici, now open to the public.

Les Frênes

Perched above Saint Nectaire, the old farmhouse has stupendous views from its hillside garden of the romanesque jewel below and woods and mountains soaring beyond. Monique, chatty and knowledgeable, enthuses her guests with descriptions of the Auvergne in perfect English. She doesn't pretend to offer luxury, just the cosy comfort of a real home. You stay in an attached one-bedroom cottage with a shower and kitchen area downstairs. Breakfast is in Monique and Daniel's vaulted dining room, full of exposed beams and stone; eat copiously and enjoy the humour, zest and kindness of a couple who were born to hospitality. Astonishing value.

Private parking available.

Rooms	2 doubles: €205–€270.
	2 suites for 2-3, 1 suite for 2-5:
	€250–€290. Extra bed/sofabed
	available €20 per person per night.
Meals	Breakfast €15. Restaurant 0.5km.
Closed	11 November to 20 March.

Rooms	1 cottage for 2: €60.
Meals	Restaurants in St Nectaire, 2km.
Closed	Rarely.

	Emmanuel & Christine Pénicaud
	Château Royal de Saint-Saturnin,
	Place de l'Ormeau,
	63450 Saint Saturnin,
	Puy-de-Dôme
Tel	+33 (0)4 73 39 39 64
Email	contact@chateaudesaintsaturnin.com
Web	www.chateaudesaintsaturnin.com

	Monique Deforge
	Les Frênes,
	Sailles,
	63710 St Nectaire,
	Puy-de-Dôme
Tel	+33 (0)4 73 88 40 08
Email	daniel.deforge@orange.fr
Web	pagesperso-orange.fr/deforge/lesfrenes

Entry 472 Map 10

Entry 473 Map 10

La Closerie de Manou

The rambling old house sits solid among the ancient volcanoes of Auvergne where great rivers rise and water is pure (it's in the taps here). There's a fine garden for games, a family-sized dining table before the great fireplace and a mixed bag of friendly armchairs guarded by a beautiful Alsatian stove in the salon. The décor is properly, comfortably rustic, bedrooms are lightly floral, no bows or furbelows, just pretty warmth and good shower rooms. Maryvonne, intelligent and chatty, knows and loves the Auvergne in depth and serves a scrumptious breakfast. A great find for walkers.

Minimum stay: 2 nights July/August.

Maison d'Hôtes de Charme La Fournio

The approach is mysterious and magical, the views to the Auvergne are spectacular, and your host likes nothing better than to share with you his enchanting home. Cherrywood glows with beeswax, copper pots shine, 18th-century floor boards creak and gorgeous old roses grow around the door. Albert is also a passionate cook, of local sausages and Cantal cheeses, homemade jams and tasty fruit purées. Listen to birds – and cow bells – from the garden, discover lovely Argentat on the Dordogne, settle in with cards by the wood-burner, retire to delicious beds dressed in hand-embroidered linen. Exquisite!

Rooms	1 twin/double: €85–€90.
	1 suite for 3,
	1 family room for 3: €85–€130.
	Extra bed €30.
	Whole house available.
Meals	Restaurant in village, 300m.
Closed	Mid-October to March.

Rooms	1 double: €95.
	1 family room for 3: €80–€110.
	1 cottage for 3: €95–€145.
	Singles €75–€90.
	Extra bed/sofabed available €20 per person per night. Cot available.
Meals	Dinner with wine, €23.
	Restaurants 2km & 7km.
Closed	Rarely.

Françoise & Maryvonne Larcher
La Closerie de Manou,
Le Genestoux, 63240 Le Mont Dore,
Puy-de-Dôme
Tel   +33 (0)4 73 65 26 81
Mobile +33 (0)6 08 54 50 16
Email lacloseriedemanou@orange.fr
Web   www.lacloseriedemanou.com

Albert Marc Charles
Maison d'Hôtes de Charme La Fournio,
Escladines, 15700 Chaussenac,
Cantal
Tel   +33 (0)4 71 69 02 68
Mobile +33 (0)6 81 34 91 70
Email albert.charles@wanadoo.fr
Web   www.lafournio.fr

La Roussière

Not another house in sight, just the Cantal hills and a chattering stream. Your hosts did a lot of the huge restoration of their harmonious house themselves. Christian, a genius at woodwork, made the panelled interior and staircase – pure Auvergne – from reclaimed timber, built the chalet-style bedrooms for Brigitte to furnish, so comfortably, and add old armoires, ancient ceiling hooks… Beds are excellent, meals 'en famille' are a delight: great food, good wine, water from the spring. Be calmed by a serene, rustic elegance. There's an organic vegetable garden, green rolling acres – a haven for wildlife, and for you. Glorious.

Minimum stay: 2 nights.

Château de Lescure

At the head of a long shapely valley stands this 18th-century château guarded by an atmospheric 11th-century keep where bedrooms are steeply, sensationally 'gothic' or French château in style. In the big inglenook dining hall, eco-committed Sophie – she's a carriage driver too – serves home-smoked ham, her own organic veg and fruit. Michel's passions are heritage conservation and blazing trails across the hills straight from the door. They are bilingual hosts who may invite you to join in bread-making, cooking, wide-ranging conversation and visiting their medieval garden… Stunning views, absolute peace, an inimitable welcome.

Rooms	2 doubles: €80–€100. 1 suite for 2-3, 1 suite for 3-4: €100–€160. Extra bed/sofabed available €25 per person per night.
Meals	Dinner with wine, €24–€28.
Closed	Rarely.

Rooms	1 twin, 1 double with separate shower, 1 double with separate shower downstairs: €90. Extra bed €30.
Meals	Dinner with wine, €28; children under 14, €15; under 5 free.
Closed	15 November to 31 March.

	Christian Grégoir & Brigitte Renard La Roussière, 15800 St Clément, Cantal
Tel	+33 (0)4 71 49 67 34
Email	info@laroussiere.fr
Web	www.laroussiere.fr

	Michel Couillaud & Phoebe Sophie Verhulst Château de Lescure, 15230 St Martin Sous Vigouroux, Cantal
Tel	+33 (0)4 71 73 40 91
Email	michel.couillaud@orange.fr
Web	www.chateaudelescure.com

Entry 476   Map 10

Entry 477   Map 10

Les Pierres d'Antan

Friendly Pascale and Serge go the extra mile – an extra 10 miles, to be precise: the distance they're happy to travel to deliver a picnic! A stay with them is full of little touches, such as Pascale's jam and cakes and lifts into Saugues with its natural outdoor pool. Wonderfully remote, their granite farmhouse sits at the end of a lane in a small hamlet between the mountains and the Gorges of the Haut-Allier. Expect stone walls and handsome wood in the bedrooms, sleek bathrooms, and convivial meals around a large table in the former barn. Walk, cycle, ride and visit beautiful Le Puy en Velay less than an hour away.

Gîte du Tapissier

At the top of a twisty mineral village, the big black farmhouse is dated 1490-1575. Sensitively renovated by this welcoming, dynamic family (she does yoga, he does upholstery – superbly), any gloom wafting from the great stones vanishes before Sylvie's use of colour. The Blue room is… streaky blue, its floor like roiling magma, its superb shower done in multi-hued volcanic stone from Brazil, its big balcony a treat; the more traditional Gîte room has a kitchen/diner and a terrace onto fields and volcanoes – whence the black stone; breakfast in the family kitchen showcases local produce. Then visit spectacular Polignac – and more.

Rooms	2 doubles: €69-€92.
	1 triple: €102.
	Child bed €17.
Meals	Dinner, 4 courses, €26.50;
	children €12. Restaurants 7km.
Closed	Rarely.

Rooms	1 double with wc on floor below:
	€77-€87.
	1 family room for 3 with separate
	wc: €107-€127.
	1 dovecote for 2: €77-€87.
Meals	Auberge 15-minute walk; choice in
	Le Puy 7-minute drive.
Closed	November – March.

	Pascale Pays
	Les Pierres d'Antan,
	Le Mazel,
	43170 Venteuges,
	Haute-Loire
Tel	+33 (0)4 71 76 06 94
Email	pascalepays@hotmail.fr
Web	www.lespierresdantan.fr

	Philippe & Sylvie Pubellier
	Gîte du Tapissier,
	Cheyrac, 43000 Polignac,
	Haute-Loire
Tel	+33 (0)4 71 02 56 42
Mobile	+33 (0)6 26 21 59 70
Email	pubellier@orange.fr
Web	www.pubellierphilippe.fr

La Maison sous les Étoiles

Between stream and river, in a remote hamlet guarded by stands of giant pine, it has a touch of Hansel and Gretel under the brilliant stars. Behind those stone walls all is light and cosy, boards are bleached, the open fire blazes, the cheery pine table smiles up, rooms are excellent. Your charming hosts love their antique-furnished farmhouse and their adopted region. Walk or ride in glory – gather berries or mushrooms as you go; visit medieval towns (La Chaise-Dieu is renowned for its sacred music). In a lovely part of rural France, you will find character, comfort and a really genuine welcome. And Christiane loves to cook.

Pets by arrangement.

La Souraïade

You dream of B&B just for two? (Though you can share with two others.) Remote rural France? Woods, wildlife and clear pure air? Seek no more. Above the glittering Allier (great kayaking), among a web of hiking paths, a tiny Auvergnat hamlet holds this expertly renovated cliffside house, decorated in gentle grey and taupe with finely sewn old lace (all Joëlle's work) and plenty of country antiques. Your big raftered room is pretty, cosy and private, breakfast – in the big open-fired kitchen or on the terrace – is a feast (sweet or savoury – you choose) and your hosts the easiest, most generous people you can hope for.

Rooms	1 double: €75. 1 suite for 4: €75-€130. Singles €75. Dinner, B&B €67 per person.		Rooms	1 family room for 2-4: €115. Extra person €20 per night. Children under 6 stay free.
Meals	Dinner with wine, €30; children €15. Restaurants 7km.		Meals	Light supper with wine, €15
Closed	Rarely.		Closed	Rarely.

	Christiane Serre La Maison sous les Étoiles, Hierbettes, 43160 Sembadel, Haute-Loire		Joëlle & Michel Gagnon La Souraïade, Pruneyrolles, 43380 Villeneuve d'Allier, Haute-Loire
Tel	+33 (0)4 71 57 60 91	Tel	+33 (0)4 71 74 71 73
Email	m.etoiles@free.fr	Email	jo.gagnon2@orange.fr
Web	www.maison-etoiles.fr	Web	www.emerenciane.wix.com/ la-souraiade

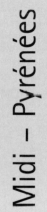

Midi – Pyrénées

La Bruyle

Charming and stylish – Franck and Pascale were born to run a B&B. On hand with creative apéritifs and inspired ideas for exploring the Dordogne, they make their home a pleasure to visit. Local artisans helped them transform the 18th-century house into a chic retreat, restoring ancient beams and flagstones. Outside, sage green shutters add a cheery flash of colour to the mellow stone façade and there's a fruit tree filled garden with a pool. Inside, country décor reigns; four immaculate en suite rooms have pretty linen, oak floors and bucolic views. Locally sourced breakfasts of farm eggs, homemade cake and jams are superb.

Meet & Cook: cookery classes available; enquire with owners.

Moulin du Goth

The 13th-century mill – imaginatively restored by its Australian owners – guards a garden of rare peace and beauty. Find a mill pond, home to wildlife and flashing kingfishers, willows, lawns and garden sculptures. Coral is kind, dedicated, full of fun, Bill's life stories make for fascinating conversation, and big, dramatically raftered rooms have decorative iron beds and touches of old-world charm. Occasionally dinners are served in the stunning vaulted dining room (its arrow slit intact) or in the garden on the terrace within sound of the tinkling stream. Readers adore this place.

Children over 5 welcome. Pets by arrangement.

Rooms	4 doubles: €80–€115. Extra bed €15 for children under 5.		Rooms	1 double: €90–€100. 1 suite: €90–€185.
Meals	Dinner with wine, €30. Restaurants 4km.		Meals	Dinner with wine, €27–€31. Restaurants 3km.
Closed	Rarely.		Closed	Rarely.

Pascale Brunet & Franck Leroy
La Bruyle,
Lieu-dit Colonjac,
46110 Saint-Michel-de-Bannières,
Lot

Tel   +33 (0)5 65 37 48 03
Email   contact@labruyle.com
Web   www.labruyle.com

Coral Heath-Kauffman
Moulin du Goth,
46600 Creysse,
Lot

Tel   +33 (0)5 65 32 26 04
Mobile   +33 (0)6 98 63 41 80
Email   coral.heath@orange.fr
Web   www.moulindugoth.com

Le Moulin de Latreille

The mill is 13th century and Cistercian, the owners are talented and attentive, the setting is magical. Kingfishers and wild orchids, herons, hammocks and happy dogs... and it is just as wonderful inside. Furniture has been renovated and painted, books peep from alcoves, bathrooms are delightful, and you get a little guest sitting room with a wood-burner. Down its own bumpy track from the village, with timeless views of cliffs, woods and weir, let the chorus of birdsong and the rush of the millrace wash over you; they even generate their own electricity. Heaven in Quercy.

Minimum stay: 2 nights.

Moulin de Fresquet

On the edge of Gramat, down a private drive, a gorgeous old mill and a big welcome from a hospitable couple. Cushioned loungers furnish sloping lawns down to the stream, the water flows beneath your feet and you'll relax the second you arrive. Warm inviting bedrooms, four reached down a spiral stair, and most opening to the garden, are distinguished by taffeta curtains and fine tapestries; the more private suite lies in a charming outbuilding. Gardens are a treat – a charming collection of rare ducks wander through the grounds. The region is much loved, but please note, the surroundings whilst beautiful are not suitable for small children.

Rooms	2 doubles: €95.
Meals	Dinner with wine, €38. Light lunches & picnics available. Restaurant in village.
Closed	December – February.

Rooms	1 double, 2 twin/doubles: €83–€119. 2 suites for 2: €119–€144
Meals	Restaurants 800m
Closed	1 November to 30 April.

	Giles & Fi Stonor Le Moulin de Latreille, Calès, 46350 Payrac, Lot
Tel	+33 (0)5 65 41 91 83
Email	gilesetfi@gmail.com
Web	www.moulindelatreille.com

	Gérard & Claude Ramelot Moulin de Fresquet, 46500 Gramat, Lot
Tel	+33 (0)5 65 38 70 60
Email	info@moulindefresquet.com
Web	www.moulindefresquet.com

Entry 484   Map 9   Entry 485   Map 9

Domaine de Labarthe

These vital, welcoming, interesting people, who are in the wine trade and grow walnuts, have turned one wing of the handsome old family house into elegant B&B rooms, two in subtle designer colours, one in traditional cosy French style. The two-storey pigeonnier would be perfect for a small family. Laurence's dinners alone are worth the visit, then there's the fine pool on the olive-studded terrace, the rose garden and Italianate formality rolling past walnut groves to the Lot countryside, gastronomy and wine, old villages and unmissable Cahors. Such wealth.

Minimum stay: 2 nights; 3 in high season. Pets by arrangement.

Téranga

This happy, secluded house is charged with childhood memories. Agnès, vivacious ex-English teacher, and Francis, wine-lover and retired architect, have filled the rooms with Senegalese touches and take immense pleasure in welcoming guests. Bedrooms have wooden floors and ethnic hangings, the gardens hide a delicious pool and the long vine-strewn veranda is the perfect spot for breakfast gâteaux and jams. Discover restaurants in old Pradines, history in lovely Cahors (a short drive), and the river Lot for watery adventures.

Minimum stay: 2 nights.

Rooms	2 doubles, 3 twin/doubles: €135-€145. 1 suite for 2-3 with kitchenette: €160. Extra bed €30 for children under 13.	Rooms	2 doubles: €74-€79. Singles €65-€69.
Meals	Occasional dinner, 3 courses, €32.	Meals	Restaurants 5-minute drive.
Closed	Rarely.	Closed	November – March.

Laurence & Guillaume Bardin
Domaine de Labarthe,
46090 Espère,
Lot
Tel   +33 (0)5 65 30 92 34
Email   contact@domaine-de-labarthe.com
Web   www.domainedelabarthe.com

Agnès & Francis Sevrin-Cance
Téranga,
303 av Adeline Cubaynes,
46090 Pradines,
Lot
Tel   +33 (0)5 65 35 20 51
Email   chambres.teranga@orange.fr
Web   www.chambresteranga.com

Mas de Garrigue

Match natural Irish hospitality with the personality of a many-layered French house and you have a marriage made in heaven. Steve raises two fine black pigs in the kitchen garden each year which Sarah transforms into terrines – delicious served with their own onion or fig conserves: they care deeply about their food and its sourcing. The big, unusual house has an elegance all its own: vast rooms, supremely beamed and raftered, are furnished with quiet taste, Irish antiques and the occasional contemporary flourish; beds are the best you've ever slept in, each bathroom a poem. They are a lovely, witty couple, generous to a fault.

Children over 10 welcome.

Rooms	3 doubles, 1 twin: €110–€150. Singles €110–€120.
Meals	Dinner, 4 courses with wine, €37; Monday & Thursday only.
Closed	4 October to 31 March.

Sarah Lloyd & Steven Allen
Mas de Garrigue,
La Garrigue,
46160 Calvignac,
Lot
Tel   +33 (0)5 65 53 93 31
Email   info@masdegarrigue.com
Web   www.masdegarrigue.com

Entry 488   Map 10

La Vayssade

Sociable foodies will love it here: Hélène and Emmanuel shop in the market every day and enjoy an ever-changing menu with their guests at a huge table, outside on the terrace on fine evenings. You'll sleep well in large bedrooms (some upstairs, some down) with old beams, exposed stone, dreamy beds and compact bathrooms. A large living room has floor to ceiling arched windows at one end, wonky beams, paintings by Hélène's mother and a comfy sofa area. This is truffle country so enjoy the Tuesday afternoon market in winter – or stay put and wander at will through the pretty garden, have a float in the pool or the hot tub with views.

Rooms	4 twin/doubles: €92–€110. 1 suite for 4: €165–€192. Sofabed available in all rooms.
Meals	Dinner with wine, €32. Restaurants 1km.
Closed	Rarely.

Famille Baysse
La Vayssade,
205 chemin de La Vayssade,
46230 Lalbenque,
Lot
Tel   +33 (0)5 65 24 31 51
Email   contact@lavayssade.com
Web   www.lavayssade.com

Entry 489   Map 14

Les Chimères

In a wonderful hilltop village is a big old house with a painted wrought-iron gate and matching shutters – inside and out oozes character and history. Find magazines, books, paintings, antiques, playing cards, flowers, pottery on dressers, cats on chairs and a huge fireplace in the kitchen where lovely Lisanne creates great meals and breakfasts to remember (breads, brioche, fruits, yogurts, cheese, ham and divine jams). Big bedrooms, reached via 12th-century stone stairs, are equally charming. Bathrooms are luxurious, bathrobes are colourful, there are fans, books and irons – and gorgeous views from garden and house.

Rooms	2 doubles: €70–€80. Singles €60. Cot available.
Meals	Dinner with wine, €27; children under 12, €12. Restaurants within walking distance.
Closed	Rarely.

Lisanne Ashton
Les Chimères,
23 av Louis Bessières,
82240 Puylaroque,
Tarn-et-Garonne

Tel	+33 (0)5 63 31 25 71
Email	aux-chimeres@orange.fr
Web	www.aux-chimeres.com

Entry 490   Map 14

Le Cheval Blanc

A super B&B in the heart of a beautiful medieval town and more than just a place to stay. You'll meet Peter (a self-confessed bike fanatic who runs local cycling holidays) and Natalie, a passionate cook who runs workshops and gives you sociable breakfasts round the dining room table and locally-sourced vegetarian dinners influenced by her world travels – vegan and gluten-free too. Bedrooms are cool in the summer months, beds are truly comfortable with Egyptian cotton sheets, bathrooms are spotless. You can tumble out to art galleries, restaurants and shops, or sign up for cycling here:

Minimum stay: 2 nights. No parking available.

Rooms	2 twin/doubles: €70–€100. 1 family room for 4: €80–€120. Extra beds available. Whole house available as self-catered.
Meals	Dinner, 3 courses with wine, €25. Restaurants 1-minute walk.
Closed	Christmas.

Peter & Natalie Quaife
Le Cheval Blanc,
3 rue Droite,
82140 St Antonin-Noble-Val,
Tarn-et-Garonne

Tel	+33 (0)5 63 02 23 88
Email	info@lechevalblanc.net
Web	www.lechevalblanc.net

Entry 491   Map 14

Au Château

A beguiling mix of grandeur and informality. The house is filled with light and life, thanks to this young Anglo-French family. Softly contemporary bedrooms, two in a separate building, are airy spaces that mix the best of modern with the loveliest of traditional: pale beams and white plaster walls, bold colours, luxurious silks, elegant antiques. There's a country-style breakfast room and a fully equipped kitchen so you can make your own suppers – then eat al fresco on the terrace. Visit historic towns, explore the Canal du Midi, let the kids roam free in the garden, stroll the charming village.

Tondes

Warm country people, the Sellars left Sussex for a small farm in deepest France to run a flock of indigenous milking sheep the natural way: no pesticides, no heavy machines, animals roaming free. Their recipe for a simple rewarding life includes receiving guests happily under the beams, by the wood burning stove, in pretty-coloured, country-furnished rooms with super walk-in showers. While Julie creates homemade marvels from her farmhouse kitchen – most of what you eat has been harvested from the garden or the farm – you can relax on the terrace with a home – brewed sun-downer and admire it all. A slice of rural bliss.

Rooms	1 double: €70-€75.
	2 suites for 2-3: €90-€95.
	1 family room for 4: €130-€140.
	1 triple: €80-€105.
Meals	Restaurants within walking distance. Guest kitchen.
Closed	Rarely.

Rooms	1 double: €58.
	1 family room for 4: €58-€98.
	Singles €42.
Meals	Dinner with wine, €25.
Closed	Rarely.

	Kathrin Barker
	Au Château,
	1 bd des Fossés de Raoul,
	82210 St Nicolas de la Grave,
	Tarn-et-Garonne
Tel	+33 (0)5 63 95 96 82
Email	kathrin.barker@sfr.fr
Web	www.au-chateau-stn.com

	Julie & Mark Sellars
	Tondes,
	82400 Castelsagrat,
	Tarn-et-Garonne
Tel	+33 (0)5 63 94 52 13
Email	juliedsellars@gmail.com
Web	www.allezatondes.com

Entry 492   Map 14

Entry 493   Map 14

Le Petit Feuillant

Magret de canard, beans from the garden, wines from the Côtes de Gascogne, melons from over the hill: table d'hôtes (and lots of French guests) is pure pleasure for David and Vikki. In a hilltop, out-of-the-way village, this well-restored house and barn, with its several terraces and outstanding views, has become a B&B of huge comfort and charm. Find old stone walls and tiled floors, whitewashed beams and weather-worn shutters, soft colours and uncluttered spaces, and homemade croissants for breakfast. Foodies come for the cookery courses, astronomers for the night skies. Great value.

Minimum stay: 2 nights July / August.

La Lumiane

Step off the narrow street to discover a delightful sweet-smelling garden and its pool. Friendly, vivacious Mireille and charming English Stuart run this gracious house with enthusiasm for their new life and the guests it brings. Up the stunning stone staircase, bedrooms breathe tradition old fireplaces and antiques; rooms in big the garden wing are less grand, more contemporary. All have an uncluttered mix of florals and stripes (due to put on modern style very soon). In winter, eat well in the formal dining room or on the terrace by candlelight, wake to the sound of the church bells. Much authenticity and charm.

Rooms	3 doubles: €60-€90.
	1 family room for 5: €70-€130.
	1 triple: €80-€100.
	1 cottage for 2: €60-€90.
Meals	Dinner with wine, €25.
	Auberge within walking distance.
Closed	Rarely.

Rooms	5 doubles: €68-€73.
Meals	Dinner with wine, €26;
	not high season.
	Restaurant 50m.
Closed	Rarely.

David & Vikki Chance
Le Petit Feuillant,
82120 Gramont,
Tarn-et-Garonne
Tel +33 (0)5 63 32 58 78
Email david.chance@neuf.fr
Web www.gasconcook.co.uk/
accommodation-in-france

Mireille Mabilat & Stuart Simkins
La Lumiane,
Grande Rue,
32310 St Puy,
Gers
Tel +33 (0)5 62 28 95 95
Email info@lalumiane.com
Web www.lalumiane.com

Entry 494   Map 14

Entry 495   Map 14

Le Biau

Inventive artisans have done a fine job renovating the cut stone, half timbering and imposing doorways of this grand old vigneron's house (with barns), in three tranquil hectares of very gently sloping land. Your relaxed hosts left Hong Kong for the Gers and welcome guests with genuine warmth. Bedrooms are lavish with oriental touches, bathrooms (half classic, half rustic) are indulging, and the salon, with wood-burner and white sofas, is the hub of the house. Fran and Ray are creating a garden full of surprising corners – an idyllic backdrop for chargrilled peppers straight from the plot, magret of duck, almond and plum tart…. delicious!

Le Bernussan

At the end of a country lane lies Harriette's traditional, pale yellow fairytale house in a spacious garden with fruit trees, hammocks and terrapins in the pond. Enthusiastic Phoenix the dog may greet you and all-day teas, toast and other treats are on-hand for a quick pick-me-up. Bright bedrooms with garden views have smart bathrooms with walk-in showers, while downstairs is full of cosy comforts: log stoves, exposed beams, sumptuous rugs on tiled floors. For breakfast, pastries, muesli and fresh fruit from the garden. Shops and restaurants are six miles away, and markets, mountains, lakes and kayaking are all within reach.

Parking on-site. Over 14s welcome.

Rooms	2 doubles; 1 double with separate bathroom: €70–€110. 1 suite for 2: €90–€110. €10 discount for bookings of 2+ nights. Extra bed/sofabed available €20 per person per night.
Meals	Dinner with wine, €35.
Closed	1 November to 1 March.

Rooms	2 doubles with separate showers: €85.
Meals	Occasional dinner available on request. Restaurants 9km.
Closed	November – April.

	Ray & Fran Atkinson
	Le Biau,
	32190 Lannepax,
	Gers
Tel	+33 (0)5 62 06 47 61
Email	rayatkinson2010@hotmail.com
Web	www.lebiau.com

	Harriette Smart
	Le Bernussan,
	32190 Demu,
	Gers
Tel	+33 (0)9 82 12 94 65
Mobile	+44 (0)7805 797384
Email	lebernussan@gmail.com

Laouarde

In rolling Armagnac country: a former wine estate, an 1823 house with watchtower views. Simon and Catherine swapped London for warm limestone and blue shutters, beautiful sash windows and oak parquet, and 25 acres of meadows, orchards and peace. Wonderful breakfasts (compotes from the garden, delectable croissants) are taken by the open fire or on the pool terrace, and Simon's dinners are mouthwatering. Up the beeswax-polished stair are delicious bedrooms full of personality, from country-pretty to elegant Bourbon. Read, listen to music, take an apéritif in the walled courtyard, explore this amazing region.

Rooms	1 twin: €85–€110.
	2 suites for 2: €95–€120.
	1 single: €55–€65.
Meals	Dinner €35 (Sunday-Wednesday).
	Restaurants 1km.
Closed	November – April, except by
	arrangement.

Simon & Catherine Butterworth
Laouarde,
32190 Vic Fezensac,
Gers

Tel	+33 (0)5 62 63 13 44
Email	info@laouarde.co.uk
Web	www.laouarde.com

La Raillère

It's deeply peaceful here among vines in rolling Gers countryside – great for walking and cycling. Charming owners Amanda and Colin have breathed new life into the rustic frame of their old wine farm, and the feel is homely with some grand family château pieces, roaming dogs and cats, horses in the fields. Bedrooms have rugs on wooden floors, smart wallpapers and super-comfy big beds: one four-poster, one with wrought iron bedstead. Light bathrooms are impressive. They've also created a pretty courtyard and garden, shaded by ancient oaks. Most of the food is home-grown and breakfasts are delicious – try the fig, plum and peach jam.

Parking on-site. Minimum stay: 2 nights.

Rooms	1 double; 1 double with
	interconnecting child's room with
	cot and child's bed: €85–€120.
	Extra bed/sofabed available £45–£60
	per person per night. Cot €50–€65.
Meals	Dinner with wine, €30.
	Lunch or picnic available.
	Restaurants 10-minute drive.
Closed	Rarely.

Amanda Soden
La Raillère,
32360 Jegun,
Gers

Tel	+33 (0)5 62 58 33 54
Email	french.forsythe@btconnect.com

Domaine de Peyloubère

The waterfall, the wild orchids, the pool, the painted ladies, the super food – there's no other place like it. Years ago Theresa and her late husband fell for this big romantic house, its wildlife-rich domaine and its centuries-old cedars; the enthusiasm remains undiminished, the sensitive restoration shows in every room. But the sober buildings don't prepare you for the explosion inside… late 19th-century painter Mario Cavaglieri spread his love of form and colour over ceilings and doors. Now 'his' suite has vast space, fine antiques, a dream of a bathroom, dazzling murals. Heaven for children – or an anniversary treat.

Le Relais de Saux

High on a hill facing dazzling Pyrenean peaks, the house still has a few unregenerate arrow slits, left over from sterner days. You come in through the multi-coloured garden that spreads across lawns and terraces with corners for reading or painting. Bernard knows the area thoroughly and can guide you to fine walks, climbs or visits. Return to deep armchairs in the dark and timeworn salon with its garden view (some traffic hum outside). Bedrooms with carpeted bathrooms are in the same traditional, elegant mood with draped bedheads, darkish plush or flock-papered walls and an air of faded glory. Nip to Lourdes but watch the road.

Rooms	2 suites for 2: €85–€120. Dinner, B&B extra €30–€40 per person.
Meals	Dinner with wine, €30.
Closed	Rarely.

Rooms	3 doubles, 2 twin/doubles: €96–€103.
Meals	Restaurant 2km.
Closed	Occasionally.

Theresa Martin
Domaine de Peyloubère,
32550 Pavie,
Gers
Tel   +33 (0)5 62 05 74 97
Email   martin@peyloubere.com
Web   www.peyloubere.com

Bernard Hères
Le Relais de Saux,
Route de Tarbes,
Le Hameau de Saux, 65100 Lourdes,
Hautes-Pyrénées
Tel   +33 (0)5 62 94 29 61
Email   contacts@lourdes-relais.com
Web   www.lourdes-relais.com

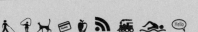

Eth Berye Petit

Beauty, harmony, tranquillity... all who stay, long to return. The grand old village maison de maître, in Henri's family for centuries, opens to soft green rolling meadows and the majestic Pyrénées – the finest view in all France! Basque-born Ione, graceful and gracious mother of two, ushers you up the venerable stair to wonderful warm bedrooms in pastel hues – one with a balcony – and luscious beds wrapped in antique linen. The living room, where a fire roars and a fine dinner is served on winter weekends, is a delight to come home to after a day's skiing or hiking. For summer? A dreamy garden. Exceptional.

Minimum stay: 3 nights in high season.

Rooms	2 doubles, 1 twin: €75. Singles €65-€70.
Meals	Dinner with wine, €23. Auberge 100m.
Closed	24 December to 2 January.

Henri & Ione Vielle
Eth Berye Petit,
15 route de Vielle,
65400 Beaucens,
Hautes-Pyrénées

Tel	+33 (0)5 62 97 90 02
Email	contact@beryepetit.com
Web	www.beryepetit.com

Entry 502   Map 14

Ancienne Poste Avajan

By the side of the winding village road find this renovated lodge with a deck and child-friendly garden – perfect for nursing weary limbs with a sundowner – James is generous with the booze! He makes this place buzz and is an outward bound professional par excellence so you're in safe hands. Fuel up on porridge, eggs, scrumptious croissants, then head off. Summer or winter the Pyrénées are a joy – you can take part in any activity imaginable. Return to bedrooms (about to have a makeover) with thick duvets and spotless shower rooms, a big dining/sitting room with leather sofas, a roaring wood-burner, games and a big screen for DVDs.

Rooms	2 doubles, 1 twin, 2 triples; 1 bunk room for 2: €90-€110; half-board price €197-€265. All rooms only available on half-board basis with activity package. Winter price: €799-€899 per person per week.
Meals	Half-board: breakfast, dinner with wine & coffee. Restaurants 9km.
Closed	Rarely.

James Dealtry
Ancienne Poste Avajan,
65240 Avajan,
Hautes-Pyrénées

Tel	+33 (0)5 62 40 53 17
Mobile	+33 (0)6 09 49 73 80
Email	james@ancienneposteavajan.com
Web	www.ancienneposteavajan.com

Entry 503   Map 14

Domaine de Jean-Pierre

Madame is gracefully down to earth and her house and garden an oasis of calm where you may share her delight in playing the piano or golf (3km) and possibly make a lifelong friend. Built in Napoleon's time, her house has an elegant hall, big airy bedrooms and great bathrooms, while fine furniture and laundered linen reflect her pride in her ancestral home – a combination of uncluttered space and character. The huge triple has space to waltz in and the smallest bathroom; the colours chosen are peaceful and harmonious; the garden is a treat; and breakfast comes with an array of honeys and civilised conversation. Great value.

Bed in Bellongue

The village farmhouse, big and beautiful with a deep-pitch roof, stands peacefully by the side of the stream. Here live two horses, 24 chickens, one delightful dog and Marion and Michel, full of love and life. The décor, in-your-face modern, stands in stark contrast to the big old fireplace and ancient beams and stones, and bedrooms are in similar vein, one on the ground floor and with a balcony that runs the length of the bathroom and opens off it. Marion grows everything organically, and dinner, enjoyed at a table lined with white fabric-clothed chairs, is exactly what's wanted after serious hikes in the Haut-Couserans.

Rooms	2 doubles: €70. 1 triple: €80.	Rooms	1 double with separate wc: €60. 2 family rooms for 3: €65-€70. Singles €50. Extra bed/sofabed available €15 per person per night.
Meals	Restaurants 3km.	Meals	Dinner €22. Restaurant 5km.
Closed	Rarely.	Closed	Rarely.

Marie-Sabine Colombier
Domaine de Jean-Pierre,
20 route de Villeneuve,
65300 Pinas,
Hautes-Pyrénées
Tel   +33 (0)5 62 98 15 08
Mobile   +33 (0)6 84 57 15 69
Email   mariec@domainedejeanpierre.com
Web   www.domainedejeanpierre.com

Marion Dupuy
Bed in Bellongue,
Chemin du Viellot,
09800 Aucazein,
Ariège
Tel   +33 (0)5 81 15 72 55
Email   bedinbellongue@gmail.com
Web   www.bedinbellongue.fr

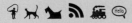

Entry 504   Map 14   Entry 505   Map 14

La Genade

Up in her beloved mountains with the wild streams splashing and an unbroken view of 13th-century Lordat, Meredith loves sharing her heaven. A passionate climber, skier and cyclist, she rebuilt a ruined auberge; old stones and new wood, craggy beams, precious furniture and a cheery fire make it rustic, warm and elegant. Under truly American care, rooms have fine linens, oriental rugs and books. The welcome is genuine, breakfast is fresh and generous, dinners are animated and delicious. Walkers and cyclists should stay a week, and there's a repair room specially for bikes. Remarkable value.

Minimum stay: 2 nights; 1 for cyclists.

Impasse du Temple

Breakfast among the remains of a Protestant chapel, sleep in a townhouse, one of a terrace built in 1758; John and Lee-Anne are its second owners. Delightful, humorous Australians, they have restored their elegant mansion and are very much part of the community. Graciously high ceilings, a sweeping spiral staircase, lovely great windows in an oasis of ancient, stream-kissed oaks… arrive as strangers, leave as friends. The food is fantastic and the pastel-shaded bedrooms are generous, with just enough antiques; one even has the vast original claw-footed bath. The attention to detail is exceptional and readers sing their praises.

Rooms	2 doubles, 1 twin: €60–€70. Extra bed €10.
Meals	Dinner with wine, €23–€30.
Closed	Occasionally.

Rooms	2 doubles: €80–€90. 1 suite for 4: €125–€130. 2 triples: €100–€105.
Meals	Dinner €25. Wine €9–€20. Restaurant nearby.
Closed	Rarely.

Meredith Dickinson
La Genade,
La route des Corniches, 09250 Axiat,
Ariège

Tel	+33 (0)5 61 05 51 54
Mobile	+33 (0)7 87 45 33 26
Email	meredith.dickinson@orange.fr
Web	www.chambre-dhote-pyrenees-lagenade.com

John & Lee-Anne Furness
Impasse du Temple,
09600 Léran,
Ariège

Tel	+33 (0)5 61 01 50 02
Mobile	+33 (0)6 88 19 49 22
Email	john.furness@wanadoo.fr
Web	www.chezfurness.com

La Ferme de Boyer

Your hosts, friendly, humorous, great fun, have filled the big rambling farmhouse with polished mahogany and family memorabilia. He was once a helicopter engineer and loves classic cars, she is a Cordon Bleu cook; both have designed furniture for first-class hotels and worked for hotels in Paris. Now they do sparkling B&B! The blue-shuttered exterior is prettier than a picture while bedrooms are sunny and charming, more English than French. The garden has pastoral views down to a rare weeping beech, and Harriet's dinners are convivial and delicious. Mirepoix, once an important cathedral town, is just down the road.

Rooms	1 double, 1 twin: €65–€80.
	1 family room for 4 with sitting room & kitchenette: €50–€80.
Meals	Dinner with wine, €30.
Closed	Rarely.

Robert & Harriet Stow
La Ferme de Boyer,
09500 Coutens – Mirepoix,
Ariège
Tel   +33 (0)5 61 68 93 41
Mobile   +33 (0)6 22 04 05 84
Email   ferme.boyer@gmail.com
Web   www.fermeboyer.iowners.net

Chaumarty

Head up, up to a hilltop farmhouse with panoramic views to the Pyrénées and a lovely family who've spent 12 years fixing up their eco-friendly home. It's all hemp, lime, wood and terracotta, solar energy, a natural swimming 'bassin', horses, a donkey, a sand pit and a swing for your kids to share with theirs... such fun. Inside are two big, beamed guest rooms with country antiques, good beds and walk-in ochre showers. Sink into an easy chair by the wood-burner and browse books that reveal a passion for all things bio... as do family dinners with Italian-Swiss Stefano and Violaine from Bordeaux. Great value, too.

Rooms	1 double: €65–€75.
	1 family room for 4: €105–€115.
Meals	Dinner with wine, €22.
	Restaurant 5km.
Closed	Rarely.

Violaine & Stefano Comolli
Chaumarty,
31550 Gaillac-Toulza,
Haute-Garonne
Tel   +33 (0)5 61 08 68 64
Email   chaumarty@free.fr
Web   www.chaumarty.com

Midi – Pyrénées

Les Pesques

Surrounded by rolling farmland, at the end of a quiet lane, a gorgeous old manor house in a luxuriant garden – a happy place and home. Brigitte has decorated in peaceful good taste and all is charmingly cluttered, each country antique the right one. Now the stable has been transformed into the prettiest, airiest country bedroom you have ever seen, all soft grey-blues with white linens and touches of red, and a window onto the field where the hens and horse run. It's a joyful house where Brigitte concocts delicious dinners with vegetables from the potager and has a brocante shop in the garden. All the bedrooms are dreamy.

Midi – Pyrénées

La Maison du Lac

This grand 1800 Gascogne house, with its yellowy ochre façade, was saved from ruin by the Charons, then faithfully restored and now shared with you! French and English antiques meet textiles from North Africa and you can laze here all day until evening cocktails. You have the salon – once the kitchen – with its wide stone hearth and billiard table. Oak floored rooms are elegant; twin beds can be added to the open-plan suite for a family. You can breakfast on the terrace, in the summer dining room or by the pool facing the lake. Nicole is a talented cook and does noon-time grillades, and dinner on the south-facing terrace.

Rooms	1 double, 1 twin: €67.
	1 family room for 3: €67-€87.
Meals	Dinner with wine, €22.
Closed	Rarely.

Rooms	1 double: €90-€100.
	1 suite for 2: €110-€130.
	Extra bed/sofabed available €20 per person per night.
Meals	Dinner with wine, €30.
	Restaurant 2km.
Closed	1 November to 1 April.

	Brigitte & Bruno Lebris
	Les Pesques,
	31220 Palaminy,
	Haute-Garonne
Tel	+33 (0)5 61 97 59 28
Email	reserve@les-pesques.com
Web	www.les-pesques.com

	Patrick & Nicole Charon
	La Maison du Lac,
	Lieu dit Michalet,
	31350 Boulogne sur Gesse,
	Haute-Garonne
Tel	+33 (0)5 61 88 92 16
Email	nicole.charon@hotmail.fr
Web	www.lamaisondulacgascogne.com

Entry 510   Map 14

Entry 511   Map 14

Le Clos du Cèdre

Just 15 minutes from Toulouse city centre a grassy shrubby garden spreads its arms. Ideal for children to run, roll and hide in, it has two superb cedars and a curly pool with a quaint Hansel and Gretel pool house designed by Françoise. She welcomes you with energetic enthusiasm to her big 18th-century farmhouse, its family-elegant high-windowed drawing room, a grand gentleman farmer's double bedroom and a more cottagey twin room, both big, independent and comfortable. Her breakfast is the star turn: maybe crêpes, cake or clafoutis, on a table decorated with flowers and imagination. And she's great fun.

Le Moulin Pastelier

Meals are 'en famille' – four courses and delicious – and breakfasts include homemade muffins. Donna and Chris are great hosts, love to cook, and know the best secret places to visit. This fabulous house, a woad mill many centuries ago, has big windows to pull in the light and views that sail across rolling fields to the Pyrenees. Boutique bedrooms feed off a shared guest space (dining table, sofas, log-burner, books) which opens to the garden and landscaped pool. Cycle along the Canal du Midi, visit the bastide town of St Felix, and return to cool colours, sophisticated bathrooms, luxurious beds, and a choice of pillows!

Children over 10 welcome.

Rooms	1 double, 1 twin: €85–€95. Extra bed €35.
Meals	Restaurant in village.
Closed	Rarely.

Rooms	2 doubles, 2 twin/doubles: €80–€95. Extra bed available in one room.
Meals	Dinner, 4 courses with apéritif & wine, €30. Restaurants 15-minute drive.
Closed	Mid-November to Easter.

	Françoise Martin Le Clos du Cèdre, 130 chemin de Tournefeuille, 31000 Toulouse, Haute-Garonne
Tel	+33 (0)5 61 86 63 09
Email	closducedre@orange.fr
Web	www.closducedre.fr/en/

	Donna Orchard Le Moulin Pastelier, Rue du Château, 31540 Belesta en Lauragais, Haute-Garonne
Tel	+33 (0)5 61 83 52 19
Email	donna@lemoulinpastelier.com
Web	www.lemoulinpastelier.com

Entry 512   Map 14

Entry 513   Map 15

La Ferme d'en Pécoul

Wrap yourself in the natural warmth of this Lauragais farmhouse. Talented Élisabeth makes jams, jellies and liqueurs, pâté, confit and foie gras, keeps hens and is wonderfully kind. The first floor is lined with new wood, there's an airy guest sitting room with beams and blue sofas, and two comfortable bedrooms with tiny showers. Summer meals are outside on the terrace, enjoyed with your host. Exquisite medieval Caraman (once rich from the dye woad) is just down the road; Toulouse, 'The Pink City', is a short drive. One dog, two cats, a tended potager and fields as far as the eye can see... Great value.

Minimum stay: 2 nights weekends & summer holidays.

Hôtel Cuq en Terrasses

Philippe and Andonis gave up good jobs in Paris to buy this 18th-century presbytery after falling in love with the region. Perched in mouthwatering gardens on the side of a hill, the multi-level mellow stone edifice looks – and is – utterly inviting. All the rooms have original terracotta floors, hand-finished plaster, exposed beams. Evening meals, on the terrace in summer, are a delight for eye and palate: something different each day, fresh from the market, beautifully balanced by wines from the region. Guests are full of praise, for the food and the gardens, the pool and waterfall, the blissful views, the wonderful hosts.

Children over 10 welcome.

Rooms	2 doubles: €50. Singles €41. Dinner, B&B €56 per person. Extra bed/sofabed available €16 per person per night. Single child's room available.	Rooms	3 doubles, 2 twin/doubles: €85–€165. Dinner, B&B €92–€128 per person. Extra bed/sofabed available €20 per person per night.
Meals	Dinner with wine, €19–€30.	Meals	Snacks available. Hosted dinner €38; book ahead. Wine €16–€25.
Closed	Rarely.	Closed	21 October to 21 April.

	Élisabeth Messal La Ferme d'en Pécoul, 31460 Cambiac, Haute-Garonne		Philippe Gallice & Andonis Vassalos Hôtel Cuq en Terrasses, Cuq le Château, 81470 Cuq Toulza, Tarn
Tel	+33 (0)5 61 83 16 13		
Mobile	+33 (0)6 78 13 18 07	Tel	+33 (0)5 63 82 54 00
Email	enpecoul@wanadoo.fr	Email	cuq-en-terrasses@wanadoo.fr
Web	pagesperso-orange.fr/enpecoul	Web	www.cuqenterrasses.com

La Villa de Mazamet & Le Petit Spa

A 'coup de foudre' caused Mark and Peter to buy this grand 1930s house in walled gardens, a few minutes' walk from the market town of Mazamet. Renovation revealed large light interiors of wood-panelled walls, parquet floors and sweeping windows. Furnished with modern elegance, the ground floor invites relaxation in comfy sofas or quiet corners. Bedrooms, with sumptuous beds and fine linen, are calmly luxurious; bathrooms are Art Deco gems. Your hosts are interesting, relaxed and well-travelled, meals in the restaurant are gastronomic. Ideal for Carcassonne, Albi and all those medieval villages.

Minimum stay: 2 nights. Over 14s welcome. Public transport 200m.

Domaine d'en Naudet

Superb in every way, and such a sense of space! The domaine, surrounded by a patchwork-quilt countryside, was donated by Henri IV to a hunting crony in 1545 it was in a parlous state when Éliane and Jean fell for it. They have achieved miracles. A converted barn/stable block reveals four vast and beautiful bedrooms (two with private wicker-chaired terraces), sensuous bathrooms and a stunning open-plan breakfast/sitting room. In the grounds, masses for children and energetic adults, while the slothful may bask by the pool. Markets, history and beauty surround you, and Éliane is a lovely and attentive hostess.

Minimum stay: 2 nights July/August.

Rooms	3 doubles, 2 twin/doubles: €110–€190. Whole property available for exclusive use.
Meals	Dinner €35. Wines from €14.
Closed	November – March.

Rooms	2 doubles, 2 twins: €95.
Meals	Guest kitchen. Restaurant 3km.
Closed	Rarely.

Peter Friend & Mark Barber
La Villa de Mazamet & Le Petit Spa,
4 rue Pasteur,
81200 Mazamet,
Tarn
Tel   +33 (0)5 63 97 90 33
Mobile   +33 (0)6 25 50 56 91
Email   info@villademazamet.com
Web   www.villademazamet.com

Éliane & Jean Barcellini
Domaine d'en Naudet,
81220 Teyssode,
Tarn
Tel   +33 (0)5 63 70 50 59
Mobile   +33 (0)6 07 17 66 08
Email   contact@domainenaudet.com
Web   www.domainenaudet.com

Combettes

Come for an absolutely fabulous French bourgeois experience: a wide 16th century stone staircase, deeply worn, high ceilings, southern colours, loads of stairs, interesting objets at every turn. Add the owners' passion for Napoleon III furniture, oil paintings and ornate mirrors and the mood, more formal than family, is unmistakably French. Bedrooms, some with rooftop views, are traditional and very comfortable; breakfast is served overlooking the old part of Gaillac. A treat to be in the heart of town, with utterly French people. Madame is a darling and it's excellent value for money.

Rooms	3 doubles, 1 twin: €60.
	1 suite for 2: €75-€80.
	Singles €45.
Meals	Restaurants 30m.
Closed	Rarely.

Lucile & Marie-Pierre Pinon
Combettes,
8 place St Michel,
81600 Gaillac,
Tarn

Tel	+33 (0)5 63 57 61 48
Email	contact@combettesgaillac.com
Web	www.combettesgaillac.com

Entry 518   Map 15

Mas de Sudre

George and Pippa are ideal B&B folk — relaxed, good-natured, enthusiastic about their corner of France, generous-spirited and adding lots of extras to make you comfortable. Set in rolling vineyards and farmland, Sudre is a warm friendly house with beautiful furniture, shelves full of books, big inviting bedrooms and a very lovely garden full of sunny/shady fragrant corners in which you can sleep off delicious breakfast. The more energetic may leap to the pool, boules, bikes or several sorts of tennis and you are genuinely encouraged to treat the house as your own. French guests adore this very British B&B.

Rooms	2 doubles, 1 twin: €80.
Meals	Restaurants nearby.
Closed	Rarely.

Pippa & George Richmond-Brown
Mas de Sudre,
81600 Gaillac,
Tarn

Tel	+33 (0)5 63 41 01 32
Email	masdesudre@wanadoo.fr
Web	www.masdesudre.fr

Entry 519   Map 15

Le Domaine de Perches

Sheltered below the country lane, the 17th-century pale-stone building faces south, revelling in its fruitful valley. Inside: a club-like morning room, a library with a classical fireplace, a white-furnished salon in the old winery. Dip into the pool hiding below the terrace; dream under a willow by the lily pond. Bedroom moods vary: mushroom shades here, ivories and greys there; a draped bed head, a claw foot tub, immaculate lighting. Monsieur is passionate about architecture and design and his lovingly collected paintings and antiques add sparkle to the sobriety. A very beautiful place. The table d'hôtes looks outstanding.

Minimum stay: 2 nights in high season. Pets by arrangement €15 per night.

Les Vents Bleus

Gaillac vineyards surround this old wine master's house – the definition of relaxed French country chic, with a decorative smattering of foreign pieces. Florence and Olivier are delightfully attentive and want you to love this rich, rural area as much as they do. Calm rooms charm with church views, high, beamed ceilings, stone and light-painted walls, linen cushions and canopies. Breakfasts – dinners too in summer – are memorable, out under the rambling vine shelters. And it's simply lovely, after a spin on a bike, to plunge into the sparkling pool to gentle cooing from the pigeonnier. Cordes is close.

Rooms	1 double, 1 twin/double: €150–€165. 1 suite for 2: €185–€205.
Meals	Dinner with wine, €50. Restaurants nearby.
Closed	Rarely.

Rooms	3 doubles: €100–€110. 1 family room for 5: €130–€160. 1 triple: €120–€130.
Meals	Dinner €30; children under 12, €15. July & August twice a week only. Platter €18. Restaurants 5km.
Closed	End December to end March.

M. Guyomarch
Le Domaine de Perches,
Perches, 2083 Route de Laborie,
81600 Gaillac,
Tarn
Tel   +33 (0)5 63 56 58 24
Mobile   +33 (0)6 08 88 19 29
Email   domainedeperches@orange.fr
Web   www.domainedeperches.com

Florence & Olivier Tracou
Les Vents Bleus,
Route de Caussade,
81170 Donnazac,
Tarn
Tel   +33 (0)5 63 56 86 11
Mobile   +33 (0)7 81 60 74 60
Email   contact@lesventsbleus.com
Web   www.lesventsbleus.com

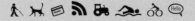

Entry 520   Map 15

Entry 521   Map 15

Maison 28

A fresh, serene room in the cobbled medieval bastide village of Cordes. It's on the ground floor, has its own entrance, an inviting wrought iron bed, a country wardrobe and modern shower room. There's a pleasingly bohemian feel to the Thackers' renovation of their medieval townhouse and they are the most engaging hosts; they sparkle when they talk about their love of cooking and passion for the local ingredients they use to create Mediterranean/Middle Eastern dishes for guests. Views are magnificent from the small pool you're welcome to use after a day exploring – perhaps the Gaillac vineyards or the World Heritage city of Albi.

Domaine du Buc

Bright, smiling Brigitte is proud of her lovely 17th-century domaine, in the family for 100 years. An imposing stone staircase leads to wonderful big bedrooms with original parquet and grand mirrors, period beds, subtle paint finishes and 19th-century papers, and quirky treasures discovered in the attic: sepia photographs, antique bonnets, vintage suitcases. Showers are top-range Italian and the old arched billiards room makes a perfect salon. It's unusually, richly authentic, the breakfasts are locally sourced and delicious and you are eight miles from the city of Albi, a World Heritage Site. A huge treat.

Minimum stay: 2 nights July/August.

Rooms	1 double: €100–€125.
Meals	Dinner, 4 courses with wine, €40.
	Restaurants 10-minute walk.
Closed	October – April.

Rooms	3 twin/doubles: €120–€150.
	Extra rooms available.
Meals	Restaurant 1.5km. Guest kitchen.
Closed	December to mid-March.

Gilles Thacker
Maison 28,
B&B in Cordes,
28 rue des Tisserands,
81170 Cordes sur Ciel,
Tarn

Tel	+33 (0)5 63 45 03 25
Email	gilles812@yahoo.com
Web	www.maison28cordes.com

Brigitte Lesage
Domaine du Buc,
Route de Lagrave,
81150 Marssac sur Tarn,
Tarn

Tel	+33 (0)5 63 55 40 06
Mobile	+33 (0)6 70 14 96 47
Email	contact@domainedubuc.com
Web	www.domainedubuc.com

Château Touny les Roses

If you're on the trail of Toulouse-Lautrec, this pretty estate in seven verdant hectares is right up your rue. Inside, art prevails: the hall and scarlet breakfast room display eclectic modern works, big bedrooms evoke Mondrian or the Moulin Rouge. The verdant grounds are no less inspiring – 300 roses bloom in the formal garden, there's woodland to explore and a private jetty on the Tarn. You're 15 minutes from medieval Albi: if you want to roam, bikes and kayaks are available – but with fishing, badminton, pétanque, a pool and BBQ on hand, it's easy to stay put. In summer friendly Thierry and Sophie serve breakfast in the garden and can organise dinner.

Parking on-site.

Clos Saint Blaise

Magali and Guilhem now call this noble abode home – a charming pair of Anglophiles with a young family and two friendly dogs. Expect a very warm welcome. Inside, ancestral furniture is laced with brocante treasures, and the two doubles, both en suite, have high ceilings, big windows and a quirky, nautical theme inspired by Lapérouse (ask Guilhem!) A comfortable lounge has leather couches and glass tables. Breakfast is a feast of handpicked local goodies served under the giant wisteria, or in the glass veranda. Wander under ancient oaks in the grounds, float in the pool, and discover historic Albi, home to Toulouse-Lautrec.

Parking on-site.

Rooms	2 doubles: €104–€144.
	2 suites for 4: €140–€177.
	Extra bed available.
Meals	Dinner, 4 courses with wine, €29.
	Cold plate with wine, €23.
	Restaurants 1km.
Closed	Rarely.

Rooms	2 doubles: €90–€100. Extra bed
	available €10 per child per night.
Meals	Restaurants 7km.
Closed	Rarely.

Sophie & Thierry Bosschaert
Château Touny les Roses,
32 chemin de Touny,
81150 Lagrave,
Tarn
Tel   +33 (0)5 63 57 90 90
Email   thierry@touny.fr
Web   www.tounylesroses.com

Magali & Guilhem Bertrand
Clos Saint Blaise,
Chemin de Saint Blaise,
81000 Albi,
Tarn
Mobile   +33 (0)6 80 00 50 07
Email   clossaintblaise@orange.fr
Web   www.clossaintblaise.fr

Villa Caroline

Right in the centre of ancient Albi, down a tiny side street, young enthusiastic owners Patricia and Mario have created a fresh and appealing refuge replete with character. The airy, inviting bedrooms with white-washed floorboards swathed in pale rugs feature carefully chosen brocante furniture that's both practical and beautiful to look at. Bathrooms are ultra modern and also chock full of style. Breakfast on the terrace on sunny days and drink in those amazing vistas of the city's stunning medieval cathedral. Whatever you need, from shops to cafés, restaurants and galleries are right on your doorstep – Albi is all yours!

Nichoir

A pastoral paradise that your hosts share by filming wildlife at night and showing guests, especially children, the footage. They have restored their rambling farmhouse for family-friendly living with lots of books, games and space, comfortable and super adaptable sleeping arrangements. And moreover… an old bread oven and forge untouched since their last use, a well that still provides water for the lovely garden, a great softie Newfoundland, good dinners in the big guest living room. Views are magnificent, the loudest noise is the frogs on the pond, Simon and Noella, endlessly thoughtful, will give you a memorable time.

Pets by arrangement.

Rooms	1 double: €80–€110.
	1 suite for 3: €80–€140.
	1 family room for 4: €80–€150.
Meals	Restaurants 2-minute walk.
Closed	Rarely.

Rooms	1 double with separate bathroom: €65–€105.
	1 apartment for 3: €75–€115.
	Dinner, B&B €62 per person.
	Extra bed/sofabed available €15–€25 per person per night.
Meals	Dinner with wine, coffee & apéritif, €25. Light supper €12.50
	Vegetarian dishes available.
Closed	Rarely.

Mario Lapuente Ballén
Villa Caroline,
16 rue de l'Equerre,
81000 Albi,
Tarn
Mobile +33 (0)7 83 95 22 70
Email villacaroline.vc@gmail.com
Web www.villacaroline-albi.com

Simon & Noella Mauger
Nichoir,
Le Bruel,
81340 Lacapelle Pinet,
Tarn
Tel +33 (0)5 63 54 31 75
Email simon.mauger@sho-shin.net
Web www.lebruel.net

Midi – Pyrénées

La Barthe

Your Anglo-French hosts in their converted farmhouse welcome guests as friends. The pastel-painted, stencilled rooms are smallish but beds are good, the hospitality is wonderful and it's a deliciously secluded place; take a dip in the raised pool or set off into the country on foot or by bike. The Wises grow their own vegetables and summer apéritifs are hosted on the terrace overlooking the lovely Tarn valley, in a largely undiscovered part of France where birds, bees and sheep serenade you. Watch the farmers milking for roquefort and don't miss Albi, with its huge and magnificent cathedral – it's no distance at all.

Pets by arrangement.

Rooms	1 double: €54–€60.
	1 family room for 4: €90.
Meals	Dinner with wine, €22.
Closed	Rarely.

Michèle & Michael Wise
La Barthe,
81430 Villefranche d'Albigeois,
Tarn

Tel	+33 (0)5 63 55 96 21
Email	labarthe@chezwise.com
Web	www.chezwise.com

Entry 528   Map 15

Midi – Pyrénées

Le Gouty

A lovely old farmhouse on two levels, a terrace at the back for meals (lots of produce from sweet neighbours) and the dreamiest sunsets and views – Phillipe and Lynda, embarking on a new life in France, love the house, the community and the region. Guest bedrooms, each in a renovated farm building, have chestnut floors and reclaimed beams, the showers are super-large, and one bedroom has its own terrace – raise a glass to the view. You are in heart of the sparsely populated Aveyron – 'la France profonde.' Homemade yogurt and fig jam at breakfast, apple juice from the village and wonderful walks from the door.

Rooms	2 doubles: €60. Singles €58.
Meals	Dinner €25. Restaurant 10km.
Closed	Rarely.

Phillipe & Lynda Denny
Le Gouty,
12380 Pousthomy,
Aveyron

Tel	+33 (0)5 65 49 40 31
Mobile	+33 (0)6 42 48 47 58
Email	le.gouty@nordnet.fr
Web	legouty.webplus.net

Entry 529   Map 15

Le Couvent

Louise couldn't be kinder and there's a mellow, bohemian feel to her former convent home. She's carefully mixed finds from her global travels with antiques, brocante and modern pieces and the result is charming. Peaceful, comfortable bedrooms have practical showers and lovely valley views over the pretty village. Breakfast under the pergola, in the nooked and crannied garden, or in the sunny salon. And do arrange to have homemade dinner too. Wander down for a dip in the river, the dogs may come with you; visit Lautrec's magical Château du Bosc, Albi and Cordes; relax – to birdsong or to the crackling logs of a winter fire.

Minimum stay: 2 nights. Parking on-site.

Rooms	1 double, 1 twin: €65–€75.
	1 triple: €65–€75. Extra bed €15.
Meals	Dinner, 4 courses with wine, €20.
	Restaurants 10km.
Closed	Rarely.

Louise Flynn
Le Couvent,
12800 St Just sur Viaur,
Aveyron
Tel +33 (0)5 65 72 06 00
Email louise@lecouventfrance.com
Web lecouventfrance.com

Entry 530   Map 15

L'Ancienne Maison du Notaire

You are in Najac, one of the most gorgeous villages in France, with an amazing mishmash of medieval streets and a castle on a hill: architectural gems at every turn. Summer hubbub does not penetrate this house's thick walls, and Hugh promises parking outside (a bonus!). He and Meg, friendly and generous, offer guests a big, airy, well-furnished bedroom upstairs, with a fabulous bed and a sofa to lounge on, or a super suite/apartment in the West Wing with your own sitting room. Bathe in the river, dine at the rustic L'Oustal del Barry, stroll the Sunday market, come home to crisp linen, WiFi and books.

Minimum stay: 2 nights in double; 3 nights in apartment.

Rooms	1 double: €75–€85.
	1 apartment for 2: €80–€90.
Meals	Restaurants 500m.
Closed	February.

Meg & Hugh Macdonald
L'Ancienne Maison du Notaire,
1 rue Saint Barthélémy,
12270 Najac,
Aveyron
Tel +33 (0)5 65 65 77 86
Email hugh.macdonald@outlook.fr
Web www.lamaisondunotaire.com

Entry 531   Map 15

La Braguèse

Come to discover a gloriously remote spot in deep rural France; to meet charming Sheena whose love of France embraces fine cooking and a deep knowledge of French wine; to enjoy a fascinating mix of hefty 200-year-old rural architecture and exquisite antiques: in all cases, La Braguèse will delight you. Plus sweet comfy rooms in the converted barn, a suntrap of a stone-walled pool, outdoor breakfast and dinner and a plunging view onto an utterly romantic weeping willow pond. There are stunning walks, ancient towns, painted caves and myriad other things to see and do. An enchantment.

Over 12s welcome.

Chambres d'Hôtes Les Brunes

Swish through large wooden gates into a central courtyard and garden filled with birdsong to find lovely Monique and her 18th-century family home, complete with tower. Bedrooms are up the spiral stone tower staircase which oozes atmosphere; all are a good size ('Le Clos' is enormous) and filled with beautiful things. Antiques, beams, rugs, gilt mirrors and soft colours give an uncluttered, elegant feel; bathrooms are luxurious, views from all are lovely. You breakfast on homemade cake, farm butter and fruit salad in the handsome farmhouse kitchen.

Minimum stay: 2 nights in high season.

Rooms	2 twin/doubles: €60-€65.
Meals	Dinner with wine, €30.
	Restaurants 3km.
Closed	1 December to 6 February.

Rooms	2 doubles, 2 twins: €92-€158.
	Discounted rates for longer stays.
	Extra bed/sofabed available
	€30-€34 per person per night.
Meals	Guest kitchenette. Restaurant 5km.
Closed	Rarely.

	Sheena Gilmour
	La Braguèse,
	12270 Lunac,
	Aveyron
Tel	+33 (0)5 65 81 19 62
Email	davidgilmour22@gmail.com

	Monique Philipponnat-David
	Chambres d'Hôtes Les Brunes,
	Hameau les Brunes,
	12340 Bozouls,
	Aveyron
Tel	+33 (0)5 65 48 50 11
Mobile	+33 (0)6 80 07 95 96
Email	lesbrunes@wanadoo.fr
Web	www.lesbrunes.com

Entry 532   Map 15   Entry 533   Map 10

Languedoc – Roussillon

Languedoc – Roussillon

Gîte San Feliu

Climb the cliff face and burst into the wide Cerdagne valley. This family-friendly guesthouse is perfect for lovers of nature and the simple life. The garden has hide-and-seek paths, herbs for Anne's dinners, shady seats, swings and a barbecue. There's storage for wet clothes and a guest kitchen. In winter, curl up on a sofa by the sitting room fire while the children explore the toy box. Simple bedrooms are light and bright, each with a modern shower up an internal stair. Walk, cycle, ski to your heart's content; ride the Little Yellow Train, dip into hot-spring baths: a place for a wonderful, convivial holiday.

Parking on-site; also secure bike & ski storage.

Rooms	4 doubles: €102–€106.
	2 family rooms for 3,
	5 family rooms for 4,
	2 family rooms for 5: €78–€154.
Meals	Dinner €23; children €8.
	Packed lunch €12.
	Restaurants 2km.
Closed	November.

	Anne Constantin
	Gîte San Feliu,
	Voie communale Carretera d'Eina,
	66800 Llo,
	Pyrénées-Orientales
Mobile	+33 (0)6 21 61 50 59
Email	gitedello@orange.fr
Web	www.gite-de-llo.com

Entry 534   Map 15

Languedoc – Roussillon

Castell Rose

A beautiful, pink marble gentleman's house in its own parkland on the edge of a very pretty town between the sea and the mountains; the views are superb. Evelyne and Alex are both charming and give you large graceful bedrooms with calm colour schemes, good linen, tip-top bathrooms and elegant antiques. After a good breakfast, wander through the flourishing garden with its ancient olive trees to find a spot beside the lily pond, or just float in the pool. It's a five-minute stroll to village life, or take the Little Yellow Train up the mountain from Villefranche for more amazing views.

Rooms	3 doubles, 1 twin: €85–€99.
	1 family room for 4: €119–€139.
Meals	Restaurant 500m.
Closed	Rarely.

	Evelyne & Alex Waldvogel
	Castell Rose,
	Chemin de la Litera,
	66500 Prades,
	Pyrénées-Orientales
Tel	+33 (0)4 68 96 07 57
Email	castellroseprades@gmail.com
Web	www.castellrose-prades.com

Entry 535   Map 15

Maison Prades

Informal, vibrant and fun is this peaceful townhouse with big sunshiney rooms. Already well-integrated into the community, the charming new owners – Robson Brazilian, Benoît Belgian – are super well-travelled and following their dream: to run a laid-back but stylish B&B. They've opened up the garden, pruned back the trees, introduced teak tables for breakfast and loungers for leisure. Original features have been restored, wooden floors uncovered, bedrooms refurbished and the whole house handsomely revived. Robson is a keen cook and table d'hôte dinners have an international flavour – as well as being fun!

Minimum stay: 2 nights July/August. Free secure parking.

Casa-tena

Ardent globetrotters Gil and René love to welcome guests to their typical French villa surrounded by lovingly tended gardens, the ideal base for discovering the area. Antiques, an eye-catching range of paintings and calming hues create an air of timeless comfort throughout. Bedrooms are elegant with king-size beds and neat shower rooms tucked discreetly into corners; two also have balconies overlooking the garden. Breakfast on the terrace (don't miss Gil's jams!) and spend days exploring the mountains and coast, or lazing with a book in the shade of the olive trees. Handy shops and restaurants are just a ten minute walk away.

Rooms	2 doubles, 2 twin/doubles: €65-€80. 1 triple: €80-€85. Singles €55-€80. Extra bed/sofabed available €15 per person per night.
Meals	Dinner, with wine €30; Monday & Wednesday only. Restaurants 5-minute walk.
Closed	5 November to 31 December.

Rooms	3 doubles: €80-€90. Extra bed available €20.
Meals	Restaurants 10-minute walk.
Closed	January – March.

	Robson Santana Maison Prades, 51 av du Général de Gaulle, 66500 Prades, Pyrénées-Orientales
Tel	+33 (0)4 68 05 74 27
Mobile	+33 (0)6 19 01 27 86
Email	info.maisonprades@gmail.com
Web	www.maisonprades.com

	Gil Tena Casa-tena, 25 rue de l'Oasis, 66690 Sorède, Pyrénées-Orientales
Mobile	+33 (0)6 31 91 10 13
Email	sorede.bb@gmail.com
Web	www.casa-tena.fr

Entry 536   Map 15

Entry 537   Map 15

Castell de Blés

At the end of a country lane, through orchards of apricot and peach, is this: a 19th-century villa shaded by ancient planes, with a balustrade terrace and immaculate outbuildings. Inside all is stately, calm and impeccably put together by Aurélie. She and Frédéric are a talented pair, and delightful with it, giving you apéritifs on arrival and big, stylish, uncluttered bedrooms – three facing a sea of green grazed by white horses. Dogs doze, cicadas hum, hens cluck in the paddocks. Families will sigh over the palm-fringed pool and the two-bedroom suite, and everyone will love the breakfasts, fun, elegant, sociable, at the long white table.

Parking available on-site.

Clos des Aspres

Meet the guests over breakfast at the long table (Emmanuel's cakes are delicious) or by the pool with a view of Mont Canigou, and relax to the cooing of the doves. The old Catalan farmhouse is surrounded by its vineyards, there's a special building for weddings, seminars, yoga, and bedrooms and bathrooms are bright, contemporary, full of personality, with patio doors to the gardens – a delight. Visit magical Collioure by the sea, take the Little Yellow Train into the Pyrénées, return to wine cocktails as the sun goes down. An exceptional place: immaculate, uplifting, and run by the nicest people.

Minimum stay: 3 nights in high season.

Rooms	4 doubles: €75–€120.
	1 suite for 3: €115–€155.
	Extra bed €15. Cot available.
Meals	Restaurants 4km.
Closed	Rarely.

Rooms	3 doubles: €95–€135.
	1 family room for 4: €160–€185.
	1 triple: €110–€160.
	Extra bed/sofabed available €25 per person per night.
Meals	Occasional dinner with wine, €28.
	Restaurants 2km.
Closed	Rarely.

Aurélie Prudhomme
Castell de Blés
Domaine Castell de Blés,
66740 Saint Génis des Fontaines,
Pyrénées-Orientales
Mobile +33 (0)6 51 04 59 58
Email contact@castelldebles.fr
Web www.castelldebles.fr

Pierre & Emmanuel Ortal
Clos des Aspres,
Domaine de la Camomille,
66560 Ortaffa,
Pyrénées-Orientales
Tel +33 (0)4 68 95 70 74
Email contact@closdesaspres.com
Web www.closdesaspres.com

Entry 538   Map 15

Entry 539   Map 15

Château d'Ortaffa

Medieval Ortaffa sits in a pocket of sunshine between the Pyrénées and the lively port of Collioure, and this big old winemaker's château perches on its fortified walls. Breakfast on the terrace comes with a stunning tableau of mountains and sea with village rooftops tumbling below. Slip into a beautifully restored house whose elegant, pastel-shaded library and guest rooms display your hosts' love of antiques and fine art: your room may have Picasso prints, quirky graffiti, bookshelves, an antique child's bed, remnants of the former chapel… Roll down to the port for seafood, slide south along the coast to Spain.

Minimum stay: 2 nights on weekdays. Pets by arrangement.

Domaine de Mas Bazan

Twenty minutes from the border is an 1890s Catalan farmhouse fronted by plane trees and surrounded by vines. Chickens, goats, and delightful Nelly and Géraud greet you. Enter directly into the living room with fireplace, large table and comfortable chairs; here you can buy wines from the vineyard and homemade jams. Bedrooms have views over parkland, brightly coloured bedspreads and antiques; bathrooms are modern and mostly have a proper bath. Wake to breakfasts of home-baked breads, homemade cakes, cheeses and eggs, stay in for dinner – even Sunday lunch. Bask by a pretty pool, visit beaches, borrow a bike and explore.

Parking on-site.

Rooms	2 doubles: €110–€130. 1 suite for 2-3, 1 suite for 2-5: €110–€130. Extra bed/sofabed available €30 per person per night.
Meals	Restaurant in village.
Closed	Rarely.

Rooms	4 doubles: €57. 1 family room for 5: €100. Singles €36–€75. Extra bed/sofabed available €10–€15 per person per night.
Meals	Dinner with wine & coffee, €26. Restaurants 3km.
Closed	Rarely.

Michelle & Alain Batard
Château d'Ortaffa,
8 rue du Château, 66560 Ortaffa,
Pyrénées-Orientales
Mobile +33 (0)6 64 14 53 42
Email   chateau.ortaffa@gmail.com
Web   www.chateau-ortaffa.com

Géraud Boissonnade
Domaine de Mas Bazan,
66200 Alénya,
Pyrénées-Orientales
Tel   +33 (0)4 68 22 98 26
Email   contact@masbazan.fr
Web   www.masbazan.fr

Entry 540   Map 15

Entry 542   Map 15

L'Orangerie

The most charming town with a bustling market, and lovely restaurants... you stay in the heart of it all. Through huge green gates enter a pretty courtyard with flowering pots, the orange tree (as announced) and a true 18th-century maison de maître with original terrazzo floors. Calm and relaxed, Sylvie and Claude offer a charming sitting room with a reading corner and comfy seating, and bright inviting bedrooms, one with a terrace. Breakfast in the dining room or in the courtyard brings seasonal fresh fruits, cake and homemade jams. Dinner can be served here too – in best traditional French style.

La Rassada

In a corner of Corbières where wild orchids flourish and eagles soar stands Philippa's eco-friendly barn. Once used for drying rosemary and thyme, it's now a modern home, open to the rafters with massive windows and heady views. Simple, comfy, contemporary ground-floor rooms with big glass doors open to the garden, while the kitchen opens to the terrace – for breakfasts of brioche, jams, muesli and local yoghurt. Your charming host is a heavenly cook so dinners too are a treat. Perfect for nature-loving families and walkers – and the coast is close. Ask for a picnic and you can be as free as a bird all day.

Minimum stay: 2 nights; 4 nights July/August.

Rooms	4 doubles: €70–€95. Whole house to rent €2,500 per week.
Meals	Dinner with wine, €27.
Closed	Rarely.

Rooms	1 twin/double; 1 double, sharing bathroom with twin/double (let to same party only): €80–€100. Dinner, B&B €65–€75 per person.
Meals	Dinner with wine, €25. Restaurants 15-minute drive.
Closed	1 December to 28 February.

	Sylvie & Claude Poussin
	L'Orangerie,
	3T rue Ludovic Ville,
	66600 Rivesaltes,
	Pyrénées-Orientales
Tel	+33 (0)4 68 73 74 41t
Mobile	+33 (0)6 09 82 75 87
Email	maisonhoteslorangerie@wanadoo.fr
Web	www.maisonhoteslorangerie.com

	Philippa Benson
	La Rassada,
	Route d'Opoul,
	11510 Feuilla,
	Aude
Tel	+33 (0)4 68 42 82 56
Email	philippa@feuillanature.com
Web	www.feuillanature.com

Entry 543   Map 15

Entry 544   Map 15

Le Roc sur l'Orbieu

Hélène has been renovating for 25 years. Full of life and laughter she has achieved marvels, from digging deep finding 900-year-old cobbles to creating terraces dotted with brocante and fuchsia-pink cushions – one with a counter-current swimming pool. Inside: whitewashed stone and antique terracotta, charming beds topped with vintage linen, blissful bathrooms with fluffy white towels, flowered armchairs for aperitifs by the fire. Dinner is at one table and she does it on her own – asparagus with smoked trout, *chevreau* in a herby crust, sorbet de fraises. Breakfasts are divine.

Minimum stay: 2 nights in high season.

La Fargo

An ancient converted forge, an oasis in Corbières countryside. Christophe gives you a large house with a very relaxed vibe and the option to make light meals in a kitchen, order in a chef, be catered for if you are a group of 10, or you can eat out in the village. Bedrooms are large, light and unfussy; bathrooms all have separate loos. You breakfast on homemade jams, fresh bread and viennoiseries from the local bakery. You can birdwatch, walk, fish, explore vineyards, castles, medieval abbeys – or potter in La Fargo's potager and orchard, play the piano, gather some fruit and laze on a wooden lounger. A river swim is heaven.

Parking on-site.

Rooms	3 doubles: €53–€100. 2 family rooms for 4: €70–€100. Extra bed/sofabed available €30 per person per night.
Meals	Dinner with wine, €26–€32. Childrens' meals available. Restaurants 5km.
Closed	Rarely.

Rooms	8 doubles, 2 twins: €120–€150. 2 family rooms for 4: €140–€170. Extra bed €20.
Meals	Breakfast €15. Dinner €30. Restaurants 5km.
Closed	October – April.

Hélène Carreaud
Le Roc sur l'Orbieu,
4 rue des Pavés,
Saint Pierre des Champs,
11220 Lagrasse,
Aude
Tel   +33 (0)4 68 43 39 07
Email   h.carreaud@wanadoo.fr
Web   www.lerocsurlorbieu.com

Christophe & Dominique Morellet
La Fargo,
11220 Saint Pierre des Champs,
Aude
Tel   +33 (0)4 68 43 12 78
Email   contact@lafargo.fr
Web   www.lafargo.fr

Entry 545   Map 15   Entry 546   Map 15

Languedoc – Roussillon

Château Haute-Fontaine

Vineyards crossed with walks circle this sea-breezy château, home to sociable British hosts. Paul and Penny have a small local team and you can explore their garrigue-rich estate, tour the cellars, hear their story. Mingle with guests from the three gîtes – and some snoozing cats; breakfast in a courtyard with clambering jasmine. You sleep in the former grape-pickers' house, up steepish stairs: terracotta tiles, ochre walls and a simple, family feel. Beds are wicker or wrought-iron, shower rooms large and shared; there's a kitchen for twilight feasts and communal sitting room. Walk into the village for dinner; the coast is close.

Self-catering properties also available.

Rooms	2 doubles: €60–€70.
	1 single: €50.
	1 triple: €75.
	All rooms share 2 bathrooms & wcs.
Meals	Breakfast €6. Guest kitchen.
	Restaurant 1km.
Closed	1 September to Easter.

Paul & Penelope Dudson
Château Haute-Fontaine,
Domaine de Java, Prat de Cest,
11100 Bages,
Aude

Tel   +33 (0)4 68 41 03 73
Email   haute-fontaine@wanadoo.fr
Web   www.chateauhautefontaine.com

Entry 547   Map 15

Languedoc – Roussillon

Domaine Michaud

Stylish Jolanda from Holland looks after you beautifully in ancient buildings in a pastoral setting with views of the Pyrénées and mature trees. The big living room has a fireplace, tapestries on the walls, antique furniture and a terrace for breakfast. Dinner (for locals too) is always a surprise and usually a home-grown one; and you can socialise or be private. Bright, lovely bedrooms, some with stone walls, most with views, one in romantic whites, are peaceful. The pool is just below so it may be splashy during the day and there's a self-catering studio-apartment too, in the main house with its own terrace.

Rooms	4 twin/doubles: €125–€175.
	1 apartment for 2: €825–€1,105
	per week. Cot €15.
Meals	Dinner, 3 courses, €30.
	Restaurant 4km.
Closed	Rarely.

Jolanda Danen
Domaine Michaud,
Route de la Malepère, Roullens,
11290 Carcassonne,
Aude

Mobile +33 (0)6 44 29 42 30
Email   info@domainemichaud.eu
Web   www.domainemichaud.eu

Entry 548   Map 15

Camellas-Lloret

The streets are narrow, the approach is charming, and the house, built around a zen-like courtyard with swinging basket chairs and greenery, dates from the early 1700s. Annie is a designer, Colin a chiropractor, and the whole place exudes warmth, serenity and beauty. A wide central staircase ascends in luscious curves as subtle whites and greys create an exquisite backdrop for ornate mouldings and modernist pieces. In the light-filled suite under the eaves, you'll find lovely old tomette floors, and then there's Annie's breakfast, a treat every day, served in the greenhouse or by the little fountain. Exceptional.

Parking is on the square close by.

Château de la Prade

Lost among the cool shadows of tall sunlit trees beside the languid waters of the Canal du Midi is a place of understated elegance and refinement. Sitting in 12 acres, the 19th-century house is more 'domaine' than 'château' – formal hedges, fine trees, ornamental railings – though the vineyards have long gone. George looks after the gardens, Roland and Anas run the B&B: they are kind and discreetly attentive hosts. Dinner is served on beautifully dressed tables, breakfasts are a treat, bedrooms have tall windows, polished floors and an immaculate, uncluttered charm. Half a mile from the road to Carcassonne but so peaceful.

Rooms	2 doubles; 1 double, summer only: €140–€200. 2 family rooms for 4: €140–€180. Singles €120–€140. Extra bed/sofabed available €35 per person per night.
Meals	Restaurants 10km.
Closed	Rarely.

Rooms	4 twin/doubles: €95–€125. Singles €80–€105. Extra bed/sofabed available €25 per person per night.
Meals	Dinner €18–€28. Wine €17–€36.
Closed	Mid-November to mid-March.

Annie Moore
Camellas-Lloret,
4 rue de l'Angle, 11290 Montréal,
Aude
Tel   +33 (0)9 67 00 40 44
Email   annie@camellaslloret.com
Web   www.camellaslloret.com

Roland Kurt & Anas Jarna
Château de la Prade,
11150 Bram,
Aude
Tel   +33 (0)4 68 78 03 99
Email   chateaulaprade@wanadoo.fr
Web   www.chateaulaprade.fr

La Rougeanne

Monique has endless energy and adores people, Paul-André is quiet and charming, together they promise you a wonderful stay. They bought the old wine-grower's estate on the edge of town in a most parlous state – but look at it now! The sitting room is stylish, restful, flooded with light and washed with pearl grey and the bedrooms are quietly luxurious; Monique has a way with interiors. Have breakfast by the lavender in summer, then discover hilltop bastides and the castles of the Cathars… monumental Carcassonne is up the road. Return to a garden within gardens and distant views, an orangery and a pool. Bliss.

Villelongue Côté Jardins

Painters, poets, nature-lovers love this place, where history and romance combine. Dark 16th-century passages and uneven stone floors open into heavily beamed rooms sympathetically revived. Big, simple bedrooms, authentic in their white cotton and old armoires, the more recent on the ground floor, look out to the ancient trees of the park or the great courtyard and ruined Cistercian abbey. Sisters Renée and Claude, warm, knowledgeable, generous, were born here and provide convivial breakfasts and dinners. Wild gardens and duck ponds, lazy cats and lovely walks into the landscape.

Rooms	3 doubles, 1 twin: €110–€130. 1 family room for 4: €110–€190 Singles €100–€120. Extra bed/sofabed available €30 per person per night.
Meals	Restaurants within walking distance
Closed	Rarely.

Rooms	1 double, 1 twin: €70–€80. 1 family room for 3: €70–€83.
Meals	Dinner with wine, €25. Dinner July/August.
Closed	Christmas.

	Monique & Paul-André Glorieux La Rougeanne, 8 allée du Parc, 11170 Moussoulens, Aude
Tel	+33 (0)4 68 24 46 30
Mobile	+33 (0)6 61 94 69 99
Email	info@larougeanne.com
Web	www.larougeanne.com

	Claude Antoine & Renée Marcoul Villelongue Côté Jardins, Lieu-dit Villelongue, 11170 St Martin le Vieil, Aude
Tel	+33 (0)4 68 76 09 03
Email	villelonguecotejardins@gmail.com
Web	www.villelongue-cote-jardin.com

Entry 551 Map 15

Entry 552 Map 15

La Forge de Montolieu

Napoleonic cannonballs were once fashioned in this striking country forge, in a secluded valley where flowers and bird-filled forests give way to waterfalls and trout-rich pools. Later, textiles emerged from its creamy walls… Now home to a charming Franco-American family, it's a wonderful renovation project with four country-pretty bedrooms, new Italian showers and a kitchenette in the guest wing. Charles' photos hint at their passion for the place, and you'll learn more over a lazy brunch, a family supper or five-course dinner – organic with seasonal veg. Walk the dogs through a pocket of woods to book-happy Montolieu.

2 self-catering properties for 4-6 available.

Château de Puichéric

There's a thousand years of history steeped in the tower and walls of this château but much has been altered and rebuilt since: a spectacular 17th-century stone staircase, 18th-century frescoes, Art Deco wallpaper and tiles. When Dominica and Philippe arrived in 2010 they installed a modern heating system with lashings of hot water so now you get deep comfort in an ancient castle. View-filled bedrooms (one looks over the Corbières) are simply but well furnished with original furniture, new mattresses, modern bathrooms. Your generous hosts feed you well: continental breakfast on the terrace, join them for a barbecue supper.

Rooms	2 doubles, 1 twin: €88–€100. 1 triple: €100. Extra bed/sofabed available €22 per person per night.
Meals	Cooked breakfast €5. Dinner €18–€30. Wine from €4–€25. Guest kitchenette. Restaurant 2km.
Closed	Rarely.

Rooms	2 doubles, 1 twin/double: €80–€100. Extra beds/sofabeds €15.
Meals	Dinner €20; children €12. Wine €10.
Closed	Occasionally.

Charles Cowen
La Forge de Montolieu,
Hameau de Franc,
11170 Montolieu,
Aude

Tel	+33 (0)4 68 76 60 53
Email	info@forgedemontolieu.com
Web	www.forgedemontolieu.com

Dominica Teuschl
Château de Puichéric,
2 rue de l'Église,
11700 Puicheric,
Aude

Tel	+33 (0)4 68 75 40 95
Mobile	+33 (0)6 02 33 74 29
Email	contact@chateaudepuicheric.fr
Web	www.chateaudepuicheric.fr

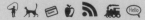

Languedoc – Roussillon

Le Jardin d'Homps

Dutch charm now fills this handsome old townhouse with its impressive panelling and Art Nouveau windows. Gerda and Thomas have made the street-side theirs so you have lofty, uncluttered bedrooms overlooking the informal garden; parquet floors and beautiful large beds. Yours too: the sparkling pool and gentle hammock swinging from a pair of pine trees; the large sitting room – shelves of crime novels, doors onto the terrace; buffet breakfast feasts and friendly, French and Italian-style dinners. Rent bikes or a Canal du Midi barge for the day, sample Minervois wines, delve into things Cathar, return to restful, historic Homps.

Minimum stay: 2 nights in high season.

Rooms	3 twin/doubles: €89–€110. 2 suites for 4: €140–€160.
Meals	Dinner €20–€30. Restaurants 5-minute walk.
Closed	November – April.

Gerda & Thomas Wijnands
Le Jardin d'Homps,
21 grand rue,
11200 Homps,
Aude

Mobile	+33 (0)6 71 89 15 70
Email	contact@jardinhomps.fr
Web	www.jardinhomps.fr

Entry 555   Map 15

Languedoc – Roussillon

La Maison des Rossignols

The village is known for its wine and Romanesque church; get up early on a clear day and you're rewarded with a Pyrenean view. This is an elegant, fresh-painted maison de maître whose warm, kind German owners, well integrated into French life, prepare for you a generous English breakfast (or a French one should you prefer) in a big friendly kitchen with a bright red wall. Immaculate and uncluttered bedrooms off a wide landing have sweeping wooden floors, handsome old pine doors, and space for button-back sofas. After a day out in idyllic Lagrasse or splendid Carcassonne, prepare to be spoiled by Marco's fabulous dinners.

Rooms	3 doubles, 1 twin: €85–€90. Singles €85.
Meals	Dinner with wine, €35. Restaurants 4km.
Closed	1 December to 1 March.

Marco Raumann
La Maison des Rossignols,
7 Traverse du Mourel,
11120 Pouzols-Minervois,
Aude

Mobile	+33 (0)6 32 16 43 13
Email	maison.rossignols@gmail.com
Web	www.chambres-hotes-rossignols.com

Entry 556   Map 15

Languedoc – Roussillon

Languedoc – Roussillon

La Souqueto

In a sweet, sleepy village, a skip from a river you can swim in, is this charming grey-shuttered house. It is owned by two down-to-earth designers in love with the Languedoc, excited to share their new home with guests. Inside: a delicious mix of old and new: tall windows, polished tomettes, a winding stone stair, deep mattresses, big rain showers. Upstairs are the bedrooms, warm, berugged and sprinkled with antiques, and a two-room family suite in the attic, flooded with light and blessed with a little sun terrace. After a sumptuous breakfast, cruise the Canal du Midi – Jon and Mel have their own boat.

Minimum stay: 2 nights.

La Casa Occitane

A fine old townhouse right in the heart of this bustling fishing port, famous for its seafood. Step straight in to a large hallway with a beautiful stone staircase and iron banisters, high limewashed walls hung with large oils of nymphs and shepherds, vibrant colours. Roberto, a charming Italian, and his French wife Peggy can organise wine tastings or visits to local markets and lend you bikes. Sleep well on thick mattresses with snowy linen (two rooms are big enough for a sofabed), wander the pretty garden with pool, take a book to the vast sitting room, eat hearty breakfasts (bacon, eggs, cheese) with freshly-baked bread on the terrace.

Parking on-site.

Rooms	2 doubles; 1 twin with separate bathroom: €85–€95. 1 family room for 4: €140.	Rooms	3 doubles: €100–€160. Extra bed/sofabeds €25 per person per night.
Meals	Restaurants 1-minute walk.	Meals	Restaurants 5-minute walk.
Closed	November – March.	Closed	Rarely.

Jonathan Alport
La Souqueto,
c/o 6 Impasse d'Occitanie,
Mirepeisset, 11120 Narbonne,
Aude

Tel   +33 (0)4 68 70 87 83
Mobile +44 (0)7775 620475
Email info@lasouqueto.com
Web   www.lasouqueto.com

Roberto Aiello
La Casa Occitane,
23 boulevard Lamartine,
34340 Marseillan,
Hérault

Tel   +33 (0)4 67 90 51 09
Mobile +33 (0)6 76 56 66 74
Email contact@lacasaoccitane.com
Web   www.lacasaoccitane.com/en/

Entry 557   Map 15

Entry 558   Map 15

Chai Richard

In an old wine village, tucked behind high walls, is a tranquil, contemporary B&B. A sweet surprise to find, behind big wooden doors, a gravelled courtyard, a small pool and shady trees. Chef Richard from the Savoie cooks in colourful Provençal style, Doreen is from Mauritius, and they love to offer table d'hôtes. On the second floor of this old wine chai, up the lift or the spiralling stair, are bedrooms elegant, uncluttered and spacious, with soft colours and heated, tiled floors, and a great big roof terrace for the suite. Wild-swim in the Salagou lake, canoe on the Hérault, discover fresh seafood in the little harbour of Marseillan.

Les Balcons de Molière

Like Molière, you'll discover the best thing about staying in Mèze's 16th-century auberge is you're never far from beach, wine and a pot of fresh mussels. Lap up the Old Town ambience of family bistros, rooftop views and a maze of narrow streets hung with geraniums; in summer the area fills with festivals. One bedroom is pink, silvery and small, another has a four-poster, and a feast-like breakfast is brought to all. Two rooms have their own terraces; in one, 'Belle du Seigneur', you breakfast grandly in the bathroom! Later, sink into a fireside armchair, and look forward to Corinne's excellent cooking.

Rooms	1 double, 1 twin/double: €80. 1 family room for 4: €100–€140. Singles €65.
Meals	Dinner with wine, €30; children under 12, €15. Restaurant 5km.
Closed	Rarely.

Rooms	1 double; 1 double with spa bath; 1 twin/double with separate wc: €80–€150.
Meals	Gourmet dinner with wine, €40. Tapas with sangria, €25. Restaurants within walking distance.
Closed	Rarely.

Richard Peillot
Chai Richard,
1 rue Despetis,
34810 Pomérols,
Hérault

Mobile +33 (0)6 73 23 41 78
Email lechairichard@gmail.com
Web www.chai-richard.fr

Corinne Briand-Seurat
Les Balcons de Molière,
14 rue des Trois Pigeons,
34140 Mèze,
Hérault

Tel +33 (0)9 53 69 95 96
Email lesbalconsdemoliere@gmail.com
Web www.lesbalconsdemoliere.co

Entry 559 Map 15

Entry 560 Map 15

Meze Maison

The welcoming apéritif sets the tone. Rob left a demanding job to turn this graceful 19th-century merchant's house into an elegant, relaxed home. Stone stairs curve to two floors of bedrooms, soft with silvery colours, chandeliers and chic bathrooms. Balconies with French windows look over the town or gardens of the nearby château. Painted in the subtle hues of Farrow & Ball and beautifully beamed, the open-plan living space is coolly stylish: antique mirrors, books, oversize table lamps. Breakfasts are served at the white dining table. Explore harbours, beaches and Mèze's fish restaurants. Gentle hosts, serene surroundings.

Rooms	3 doubles, 1 twin/double: €95–€180.
Meals	Restaurants within walking distance.
Closed	Rarely.

Rob Budden
Meze Maison,
34140 Mèze,
Hérault

Mobile	+33 (0)6 21 16 43 42
Email	rob@mezemaison.com
Web	www.mezemaison.com

Entry 561   Map 15

La Bergerie de Laval

Keen cyclists and walkers, your kind hosts, Sonia and John, make unwinding easy at their traditionally dressed villa in vineyards two minutes from Pézenas. The pool, jacuzzi, lingering breakfasts (homemade jams, excellent pastries); the smell of Mediterranean plants and a hammock hung between mature pines – all help! As do the quietly decorated ground-floor rooms that come with super bedding, refreshed brocante furniture, parquet floors, good bathrooms and towels. Dine in the village or simply picnic if you've had a big day out: being sporty on Lake Salagou, eating from the Étang de Thau or marketing in medieval St Guilhem.

Minimum stay: 2 nights.

Rooms	1 double; 2 doubles with separate wc: €65–€105.
Meals	Restaurant within walking distance.
Closed	1 December to 28 February.

Sonia & John Potts
La Bergerie de Laval,
21 chemin de Laval,
34120 Tourbes,
Hérault

Tel	+33 (0)4 67 90 77 86
Mobile	+33 (0)6 79 25 85 52
Email	jwh.sj.potts@gmail.com
Web	www.la-bergerie-de-laval.com

Entry 562   Map 15

Villa Juliette

This house, these hosts and Pézenas itself are a treat. Gilles is French and ran the family vineyard for years – he'll give you tasting tips. Ruth is English, an interior architect and talented jam-maker – breakfasts won't disappoint. You share their lovely home in a green part of town, in a beguiling, mature garden with a curvaceous pool. All is elegantly stylish but not too grand. Rooms are quietly, comfortably attractive: softly painted, striped and parquet-floored, park and garden-viewed. Pézenas will absorb you for hours with its brocante, antique and craft shops, its market, music and theatre – and many eateries.

Minimum stay: 2 nights July / August.

Maison Butterfly

Warm and energetic Harriet and her team are passionate about their B&B venture. The mix of French-Trad and Art Deco with an eclectic collection of furniture gives the place huge character. Butterflies throng the flowery garden filled with rare plants near the secluded pool. The house is colourful too – red or vine-leaf walls, patterned sofas – and deeply comfortable. Glamorous bedrooms sport chandeliers, super linen and Impressionist reproductions. The orangery and terrace have spectacular views over vineyards to the distant Pyrénées, beckoning you to the wineries, mountains and sea, and myriad other Languedoc riches.

Parking on-site.

Rooms	2 twin/doubles; 1 twin/double, 1 double, each with separate wc; 1 twin with separate shower & wc: €90–€120. Singles discount €10.	Rooms	3 doubles: €90–€125.
Meals	Restaurants within walking distance.	Meals	Dinner available on request
Closed	December/January.	Closed	Rarely.

Gilles & Ruth de Latude
Villa Juliette,
6 chemin de la Faissine,
34120 Pézenas,
Hérault
Tel   +33 (0)4 67 30 46 25
Email   ruthdelatude@wanadoo.fr
Web   www.villajuliette.fr

Harriet Leavey
Maison Butterfly,
5 route des Lauriers,
34480 Puissalicon,
Hérault
Tel   +33 (0)4 34 58 58 26
Mobile   +33 (0)6 10 53 38 05
Email   maisonbutterfly@gmail.com
Web   www.maisonbutterfly.com

Entry 563   Map 15

Entry 564   Map 15

Maison des Artists

A village house with thoroughly easy-going owners: artist Derek (you'll see his water colours on the walls) and designer Wendy (who organises monthly jazz concerts) have knocked down walls to create lots of light and space. Find high ceilings, terracotta tiles and golden beams – plenty of books, sculptures and rugs create a homely, but not cluttered, feel. Bedrooms have the best linen and are soft and fresh; the bathroom has a power shower and white robes. Pay extra for a generous breakfast at one long table, or sleep in and grab something in the village later. Discover the quiet, fecund garden; cool off in the sparkling pool.

Minimum stay: 3 nights. Parking on site.

Le Manoir

Barbara loves pampering her guests with perfect details. You have a cosy king-size room with an inspired mix of old and new furnishings – a stone basin on a chunk of wild wood and initialled pillows – and a double-aspect living room (fireplace, sofa and glass table) leading out to a big hillside garden (the free-range hens provide your breakfast eggs) and a spot in the sun in the newly-planted citrus courtyard. Enjoy this friendly, generous couple's fine art collection and travellers' tales from afar. Then set out to explore the little towns and natural wonders of the unsung Languedoc – and return to a dip in your hosts' hidden pool.

Minimum stay: 2 nights.

Rooms	1 double: €85-€100. 1 triple sharing bathroom with double, let to same party only: €75-€90. Extra double bed €40. Cot available. Dog €10 per week.
Meals	Breakfast €8. Restaurants 5-minute walk.
Closed	Rarely.

Rooms	1 suite for 2: €90-€150. Dinner, B&B €85 per person.
Meals	Dinner with apéritif and wine, €35.
Closed	Rarely.

Wendy Ogg
Maison des Artists,
Chemin des Baraques,
34480 Laurens,
Hérault

Tel   +33 (0)4 67 31 30 15
Email   wendy@corkeogg.com

Barbara Simpson-Birks
Le Manoir, Le Grand Hermitage,
Chemin de la Faïence Villeneuvette,
34800 Clermont l'Hérault,
Hérault

Tel   +33 (0)4 67 96 62 31
Mobile   +33 (0)7 71 01 48 84
Email   sunfor300days@gmail.com
Web   www.legrandhermitage.com

Domaine de Pélican

In summer, vignerons drop by for Monday tastings – followed by a special dinner: book to join in. This eco-leaning wine estate has a mulberry-lined drive and a real family atmosphere: he is quiet and gentle, she energetic and charming. In the old barn, bedrooms have soft-coloured walls, some beds on mezzanines (no windows but glazed doors), pretty shower rooms. Old honey-coloured beams protect the dining room – a dream that gives onto the terrace and rows of vines beyond. Cool off in the saltwater pool, or wild-swim in the river Hérault. Ideal for those interested in good wine, peacefulness and proper French country cuisine.

Castle Cottage

On the edge of unspoilt woodland, in a garden full of trees and colour where 23 tortoises roam (no touching please)… it's hard to believe you're a tram ride from Montpellier. The house is recent, the vegetation lush, the tempting pool (mind the alarm) set among atmospheric stone 'ruins'. In the house are small but comfortable beds in pretty rooms (shuttered in summer) full of family pieces and colour, a good shower room and doors to the terrace. Outside is a sweet little independent 'studio' for two. Your exuberant, dynamic hostess loves this place passionately, her garden is an oasis even in winter and the beach is nearby.

Minimum stay: 2 nights at weekends.

Rooms	1 double; 1 double, 1 twin, each with extra fold-out bed: €80–€90. 1 suite for 4: €80–€90. Extra beds available.	Rooms	1 double: €128 (April-Sept only). 1 suite for 2-4: €102–€216. 1 studio for 2: €150–€180. Children under 5 free. Extra bed €32.
Meals	Dinner with wine, €28. Restaurant in village.	Meals	Restaurants in Montpellier, 3km.
Closed	Rarely.	Closed	Rarely.

	Isabelle & Baudouin Thillaye du Boullay Domaine de Pélican, 34150 Gignac, Hérault		Dominique Cailleau Castle Cottage, 289 chemin de la Rocheuse, 34170 Castelnau le Lez, Hérault
Tel	+33 (0)4 67 57 68 92	Tel	+33 (0)4 67 72 63 08
Email	domaine-de-pelican@wanadoo.fr	Mobile	+33 (0)6 75 50 41 50
Web	www.domainedepelican.fr	Email	castlecottage@free.fr
		Web	www.castlecottage-chambresdhotes.com

Hôtel de l'Orange

A touch of 'la vieille France' in this enchanting town set on the Vidourle. Thomas and Liz are breathing new life into their fine house which stands on the hill under the château and has gorgeous views. Pick up a book from the large hallway, tinkle on the piano in the drawing room, find a shady spot in the front garden. Breakfast is out here on balmy days: fresh breads, fromage blanc, home-squeezed juice, local honey, an eclectic mix of china from the antique market. Sometimes they do dinner, so do ask. Explore vineyards, visit the wonderful Camargue, pick up some food at the Saturday market for a 'Table du Marche' back here.

Parking on-site.

Bed and Art

It's an old house in a little market town. Step off the narrow street to her simple, direct welcome and hosted by unusual, interesting Corinne her stone-vaulted world. Up a spiral stair lined with tapestries and smelling of waxed stone lie two attractive rooms. Expect fine old doors and a newly-revived Bechstein: you can tell that an artist and an art historian live here, it has huge visual appeal and music is vital to them. The patio, source of light and greenery, and the open breakfast barn are hung with Régis' paintings and there's a terrace on the roof, too. Don't miss Calvisson's Sunday market.

Minimum stay: 2 nights July/August.

Rooms	3 doubles: €95–€140. 2 suites for 2: €110–€160. Singles €95–€115	Rooms	2 doubles: €68–€70.
Meals	Occasional group dinner with wine, €45. Restaurants 3-minute walk.	Meals	Dinner with wine, €25. Restaurant in Calvisson.
Closed	Rarely.	Closed	Rarely.

Tom & Liz Banfield
Hôtel de l'Orange,
7 rue de Baumes,
30250 Sommières,
Gard
Tel   +33 (0)4 66 77 79 94
Email liz@hoteldelorange.com
Web   www.hoteldelorange.com

Régis & Corinne Burckel de Tell
Bed and Art,
48 Grand Rue,
30420 Calvisson,
Gard
Tel   +33 (0)4 66 01 23 91
Email bedandart@gmail.com
Web   www.bed-and-art.com

Entry 569   Map 16

Entry 570   Map 16

Languedoc – Roussillon

Habanera

The owners – artists, perfectionists – love nothing more than to share with guests their passion for the Camargue, and the treasures of Arles and Nîmes. Birdwatching, riding, fishing, archaeology… they can recommend the best tours and the best people. As for the house, its sleepy village façade is deceptive: in reality it is immense, with high ceilings, tall windows and a stunning courtyard garden. Walls are subtly limewashed, linen is hand monogrammed, toiletries are très chic, and the suite, spacious and serene, has its own boudoir. For breakfast? Fruit smoothies, Fougasse d'Aigue Morte pastries, homemade crème caramels.

Minimum stay: 2 nights.

Rooms	3 doubles: €95.
	1 suite for 2-3: €135.
Meals	Restaurant in village, 200m.
Closed	Rarely.

Michel Joassard
Habanera,
65 rue de la Poste,
30640 Beauvoisin,
Gard

Tel	+33 (0)4 66 57 58 46
Email	reservation@habanera.fr
Web	www.habanera.fr

Entry 571   Map 16

Languedoc – Roussillon

La Claire Demeure

Surrounded by great plane trees that have never been pruned, a charming southern home. The stone vaulted salon bears witness to the days of the Knights Templar; the sofas are comfy, the fireplace glows in winter, the piano (not grand) is ready to play. Kind Claire, friendly and refined, gives you elegant bedrooms with flagged floors and high windows, fine linen, fresh flowers, a sprinkling of antiques – and simple generous family suppers enhanced by her husband's wines. He knows all about Gigondas and Châteauneuf-du-Pape so don't miss the vineyards. This is a wonderful area where markets, cafés and galleries abound.

Rooms	2 doubles: €65-€88.
	Singles €60-€83.
	Extra bed/sofabed available
	€15-€20 per person per night.
Meals	Dinner with wine, €15.
	Restaurants 10km.
Closed	Mid-November to mid-March.

Claire Granier
La Claire Demeure,
1424 route de Jonquières,
30490 Montfrin,
Gard

Tel	+33 (0)4 66 37 72 48
Mobile	+33 (0)6 74 50 86 84
Email	claire.tytgat@wanadoo.fr
Web	www.laclairedemeure.com

Entry 572   Map 16

Maison Orsini

This medieval house, overlooking the walled City of Avignon (splash out on a terrace room with a view) is the former palace of Cardinal Orsini. Rich in decorative tiles, steep narrow stairs and 14th-century timbers, it has been in the family for three generations. Today the owners live over the road but are hugely helpful and on the spot for breakfast, served in an atmospheric, vaulted chapter house at one big table; all is delicious. Xavier is an artist who runs workshops on site; splendid suites combine modern art with country antiques and chandeliers. The grassed grounds are beautiful – there's even a pool.

Pont d'Ardèche

An ancestor built this fine fortified farmhouse 220 years ago; it stands by the Ardèche with its own small beach. Inside: a cavernous hall, a stone stair lined with portraits, and fresh simple bedrooms above, saved from austerity by Ghislaine's painted furniture and friezes. The glorious park – old plane trees, hidden deckchairs – invites lingerers, there's a lovely pool shared with gîte guests, and summer dinners can be enjoyed the other side of the river at their son's 'guinguette' (grilled meats, delicious salads). Pierre can accompany you on canoe trips: your sociable hosts enjoy all their guests.

Rooms	1 double: €130–€170.
	2 suites for 2-4: €150–€310.
	Extra beds available.
Meals	Restaurant 3km.
Closed	Rarely.

Rooms	1 double: €70.
	2 family rooms for 4: €70–€90.
	1 triple: €80–€95.
	Child under 10, €10. Extra bed
	available €15 per person per night.
Meals	Guest kitchen.
	Dinner with wine, €25.
Closed	Rarely.

	Anne-Marie & Xavier Peltier
	Maison Orsini,
	Montée de la Tour,
	30400 Villeneuve-les-Avignon,
	Gard
Mobile	+33 (0)6 82 27 65 94
Email	maisonorsini@gmail.com
Web	www.maisonorsini.com

	Ghislaine & Pierre de Verduzan
	Pont d'Ardèche,
	30130 Pont St Esprit,
	Gard
Tel	+33 (0)4 66 39 29 80
Email	pontdardeche@orange.fr
Web	www.pont-dardeche.com

La Maison Papillons

Overlooking a tiny hamlet on the borders of the Gard and the Ardèche is a multi-levelled hillside farmhouse, a heavenly B&B. Welcome to a home of hand-woven rugs on polished concrete floors, upcycled rustic doors and Italian walk-in showers. Not only is the house beautiful, it is run by Caroline and Olivier, warm, delightful hosts, passionate about art, sustainability and nature. The suite, beneath the family house, comes with its own patio, so start the day in the sun and feast on fruits, pancakes and homemade granola. Discover the Pont d'Arc, laze by the pool, hike or bike through lavender fields with Oliver – your enthusiastic guide.

Demeure Monte Arena

Towering over the village, by the castle, this handsome 17th-century townhouse mixes history and modernity with panache. Vaulted ceilings and flagged floors sit with modern art and black leather. Bedrooms are huge, spread between the two towers. Colours are soft, bedlinens crisp, fine antiques nudge funky lights, bold rugs are spread on ancient tiles. Two rooms are duplex with stunning staircases. All have views over the courtyard garden. Breakfast – organic and homemade – is here or in the vaulted dining hall; dinners, too. Nîmes and Avignon are close or relax in the garden with its scents, secluded corners, and secret jacuzzi.

Rooms	1 suite: €145–€155.
Meals	Restaurants 10-minute drive.
Closed	Rarely.

Rooms	2 doubles: €102–€165. 2 suites for 2-3, 1 suite for 2-5: €156–€300. 10% discount for 2 nights or more; 15% discount from 3 nights. Extra bed/sofabed available €25 per person per night.
Meals	Dinner, 4 courses with apéritif, wine & coffee, €50. Restaurants 10-minute walk.
Closed	Rarely.

Caroline Girault de Burlet
La Maison Papillons,
Hameau de Monteil,
30630 Montclus,
Gard
Mobile +33 (0)6 20 46 80 05
Email contact@lamaisonpapillons.fr
Web www.lamaisonpapillons.fr

Martine Julia
Demeure Monte Arena,
6 place de la Plaine,
Montaren & St Médiers,
30700 Uzès,
Gard
Tel +33 (0)4 66 03 25 24
Email info@monte-arena.com
Web www.monte-arena.com

Entry 575   Map 16

Entry 576   Map 16

L'Espérou

Imagine a fine old house with mullioned windows in a golden hamlet five minutes from Uzès. Delight in paintings, portraits, carpets, mirrors, and a fine collection of hats up the wide stone stairs to grandly beautiful bedrooms. The rooms overlook lush lawns, white roses and southern pines: an oasis with an elegant pool and loungers awaiting apéritifs. Your hosts, passionate about baroque music, opera and treasured old things, offer you lovely lazy breakfasts on immaculate china and an indulging bathroom with Christian Dior towels. For Provençal magic, explore the shops, galleries and market of Uzès.

Mas Vacquières

Thomas and Miriam have restored these lovely 18th-century buildings with pretty Dutch simplicity, white walls a perfect foil for southern-toned fabrics in outlying bedrooms reached by steep stone stairs. Mulberry trees where silkworms once fed still flower; the little vaulted room is intimate and alcoved, the big soft salon a delight. Tables on the enchantingly flowered terrace under leafy trees and a lawn sloping down to the stream make perfect spots for silent gazing; the table d'hôtes is superb. Enjoy the pool, sheltered in its roofless barn… it's all so relaxed you can stay all day.

Over 12s welcome. Pets by arrangement.

Rooms	2 doubles, sharing bathroom, let to same party only: €140-€240. Rooms can interconnect to form suite.
Meals	Restaurants nearby.
Closed	Rarely.

Rooms	2 doubles, 1 twin/double: €95-€150.
Meals	Dinner €35.
Closed	Rarely.

	Jacques Cauvin
	L'Espérou,
	Hameau St Médiers,
	30700 Montaren & St Médiers,
	Gard
Tel	+33 (0)4 66 63 14 73
Mobile	+33 (0)6 64 14 48 89
Email	contact@lesperou.com
Web	www.lesperou.com

	Thomas & Miriam van Dijke
	Mas Vacquières,
	Hameau de Vacquières,
	30580 St Just & Vacquières,
	Gard
Tel	+33 (0)4 66 83 70 75
Email	info@masvac.com
Web	www.masvac.com

Le Mas du Figuier

This vast silk farm stands among fig orchards beneath medieval Vézénobres. The interior is big and generous too, as is the welcome from Valérie and Gilles. A lively, broad-minded couple, they happily share their passions for wine, food and jazz. Valérie cooks brilliantly, often with figs, and Gilles knows all about the local wines. Bedrooms are roomy, peaceful and uncluttered, with gentle fabrics, windows to orchards or the garden and colourful bathrooms. Beautifully presented, breakfast is fresh and unhurried. Lounge by the pool in the enchanting garden, walk up (three minutes) to the listed village, explore the Cévennes and Provence.

Mas Suéjol

You are tucked away in the hills with Jean-Pierre and Patrick, charming and warm, who ask only that you feel at home. Thick stone walls surround you, fine plants in vast pots sit at the entrance, views soar and the air is filled with birdsong. You breakfast at a long oak table or on the terrace in the sun: breads, homemade jams, yogurt, fruit, all organic or local. Take a book from the bursting library and settle down for a read here, or by the pool on a colourful lounger. Bedrooms are filled with characterful brocantes, bathrooms are beautifully designed with bamboo towels. Tempting to stay put but there's lots to do round and about.

Parking on-site.

Rooms	2 doubles: €100–€135.
	1 family room for 5: €165–€180.
	Extra bed €30.
Meals	Dinner, 2-3 courses with wine,
	€25–€30.
	Restaurants 3-minute walk.
Closed	November & January/February.

Rooms	1 double: €64–€129.
	3 family rooms for 4: €54–€129.
	Extra bed/sofabed available
	€10–€28 per person per night.
	Self-catering option available.
Meals	Restaurants 3km.
Closed	Rarely.

Valérie Savary
Le Mas du Figuier,
110 chemin Souville,
30360 Vézénobres,
Gard
Mobile +33 (0)6 09 40 61 74
Email   le.mas.dufiguier@hotmail.fr
Web   www.lemasdufiguier.fr

Jean-Pierre Samama
Mas Suéjol,
1405 chemin du Fraisal,
30140 Anduze,
Gard
Tel   +33 (0)4 66 60 92 55
Email   suejol@gmail.com
Web   www.suejol.com

Château Massal

The château façade flanks the road and the many-terraced garden rambles behind, with views across river and red-roofed town. Up a stone spiral are big beautiful bedrooms with a château feel. Warm, deep colours, walnut parquet and quirky touches set off family furniture to perfection; one room has a bathroom in the tower, another houses an ancient grand piano. Madame, one of an old French silk family who have been here for several generations, is as elegant and charming as her home. She will tell you all the best places to go, after sociable breakfast around the big dining room table. Enchanting!

Rooms	4 doubles: €68–€98. Child's bed available.
Meals	Restaurant 5km.
Closed	Mid-November to March.

Françoise & Marie-Emmanuelle du Luc
Château Massal,
Bez & Esparon,
30120 Le Vigan,
Gard
Tel   +33 (0)4 67 81 07 60
Email   francoiseduluc@gmail.com
Web   www.cevennes-massal.com

La Villa des Claux

Christian and Muriel, the soul of hospitality, will pamper you with bathrobes for the pool and hot tub and their home-made apéritif if you choose to dine in. Theirs is a big modern house with lots of family furniture and mementoes and a good garden where you can play pétanque or just lounge under the oaks. The bedrooms, each with its own 'front door' and patio, have different moods: traditional French — think stone walls and family antiques — in the oldest, hyper-contemporary black and white and silver in the newest, quiet classic in the third. There are electric bikes for exploring the Cévennes, and do ask for Muriel's fine picnic hamper.

Please check owner's website for availability.

Rooms	3 doubles: €89–€109. Electric bikes available: €18 per day; €120 per week.
Meals	Dinner €27.50. Picnic hamper for 2, €25. Restaurants 3km.
Closed	19 September to 24 April.

Christian Cintre
La Villa des Claux,
5 chemin des Claux,
30960 Les Mages,
Gard
Tel   +33 (0)4 66 30 44 76
Email   contact@lavilladesclaux.com
Web   www.lavilladesclaux.com

Transgardon en Cévennes

A light-filled valley and utter solitude. Eco-minded Pascal and Frédérique fell in love with this remote hamlet, then restored the main house and a pretty stone cottage with three, very private, bedrooms, all with their own entrance. Find gorgeous linen, gleaming antique furniture, good bathrooms. Wander up the path and over a bridge to the welcoming main house for a hunker by the stove, breakfasts of homemade brioches and honey from their bees, or a divine supper of local meat and home grown veg. Swim in the stream under the old bridge (catch a trout in the rockpool?). Hike, cycle, explore… or do nothing.

La Source de Castagnols

Here, in deepest France, clinging to a Cévennes hillside, is this ruined stone farm rebuilt by your amazing eco-hosts, Henk-Jan, architect and carpenter extraordinaire, and Marjoleine, decorator and great cook. Their commitment to nature, their hamlet and house is impressive. In a huddle of stable, piggery, and chestnut dryer, the warm woody interior embraces you: rafters, panelling and floors, ingenious shutters and ladders are all hand-made from reclaimed local timber, the shelves are sparkling slices of local stone and the beds are superb. Peace is total, harmony reigns. Walk with a donkey, return for good food.

Rooms	3 twin/doubles, 1 with extra bed on mezzanine: €105–€110. Singles €90. Under 5s free. Extra bed €25. Discounted rates for stays of 4+ nights (Jun–Aug) & 5+ nights (Sept–Dec).	Rooms	5 twin/doubles: €84–€94. Extra bed & cot available.
Meals	Dinner with wine, €28. Restaurants 6km.	Meals	Dinner, 3 courses with wine, €25; not Friday. Restaurants 10km.
Closed	Rarely.	Closed	15 October to 1 May.

Frédérique & Pascal Mathis
Transgardon en Cévennes,
Transgardon,
48240 St Privat de Vallongue,
Lozère
Tel   +33 (0)4 34 25 90 23
Email transgardon@transgardon.fr
Web   www.transgardon.fr

Marjoleine & Henk-Jan Spruijt
La Source de Castagnols,
Lieu dit Castagnols,
48220 Vialas,
Lozère
Tel   +33 (0)4 66 41 05 79
Email info@castagnols.com
Web   www.castagnols.com

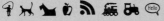

Rhône Valley – Alps

Château de Balazuc

A remarkable wow of a place. An imposing 11th-century château, above the Ardèche river and the tiny higgledy village of Balazuc, with inspired 'ancient meets modern' interior design. The warmly friendly Lemaires – multilingual former journalists – invite you to mingle at evening drinks; superb breakfasts are sociable too, in the vaulted dining room or on the view-filled terrace. Choose from hugely comfortable, radically different rooms – Moroccan touches, balconies, chain mail… sleep to the sound of owls and the river. Visit the Chauvet-Pont d'Arc cave – the oldest art gallery on earth, go canoeing, walking, cycling. Fabulous.

Over 15s welcome.

Château Clément

On a wooded hill this ornate 19th-century château is both luxurious eco-hotel and family home. An extraordinary wooden staircase sweeps you up to airy bedrooms of understated elegance with original glowing parquet, antiques, tall views to gardens and the undulating Ardèche. The apartment is a must for families. Magnificent new garden-level rooms in exciting contemporary style have private terraces. Marie-Antoinette, her family and her team are as welcoming as can be, grow their own fruit and veg and give you fabulous breakfasts. Wander the rose-strewn garden to find a shady spot, drift in the south-facing pool.

Minimum stay: 2 nights in high season. Pets by arrangement.

Rooms	4 doubles: €140–€180.
Meals	Restaurants within walking distance.
Closed	December/January.

Rooms	2 doubles: €180–€230.
	2 suites for 2,
	1 suite for 6: €230–€600.
	1 apartment for 4, 1 apartment for 10: €2,000–€4,000 per week.
	Singles €135–€250.
	Extra bed/sofabed available €50 per person per night.
Meals	Restaurants 5-minute walk.
Closed	Mid-November to mid-March.

Luc & Florence Lemaire
Château de Balazuc,
07120 Balazuc,
Ardèche

Tel	+33 (0)9 51 39 92 11
Mobile	+33 (0)6 07 16 66 58
Email	contact@chateaudebalazuc.com
Web	www.chateaudebalazuc.com

Marie-Antoinette Rojon
Château Clément,
La Châtaigneraie,
07600 Vals les Bains,
Ardèche

Tel	+33 (0)4 75 87 40 13
Mobile	+33 (0)6 72 75 03 36
Email	contact@chateauclement.com
Web	www.chateauclement.com

L'Angelot

The approach is magical, winding through the gorges of the Ardèche, to lovely hilltop Antraigues and an 18th-century farmhouse full of paintings. Ilse and Fons have acres of chestnut forest, there's a circular walk to a medieval castle... and you come home to big rustic bedrooms, peaceful, private and charmingly furnished: simple natural fabrics, perhaps an old door for a bedhead. The house is on many levels, with a cool pool for aching limbs, a stream below and plenty of tranquil corners. Homemade jams and local honey for breakfast, and hosts without a whiff of pretension: walkers adore it.

Minimum stay: 2 nights; 3 nights in high season.

Château de Fontblachère

Framed by a forested valley and mountainous horizons, this 17th-century château marries Provençal peace with deep comfort and style. Eric greets you in a courtyard whose manicured hedges and white roses dissolve into parkland: a panoramic pool, Japanese fish pond, tennis court, jacuzzi... Under vaulted ceilings are more treats: a log fire, piano, candles, art, and Turkish cushions in the orangery where you may dine on iced melon soup and quail. Sprightly Eric cooks, serves, pours and chats all the while. Immaculate rooms have space for families and the valley cries out for walking, riding and fishing in the Rhône.

Rooms	2 family rooms for 3: €80–€125. Extra person €25.
Meals	Restaurants 1km.
Closed	Rarely.

Rooms	2 doubles: €115. 1 family room for 3, 1 family room for 4, 1 family room for 5: €150–€255.
Meals	Dinner with wine, €35. Restaurants 3km.
Closed	16 September to 14 June.

	Ilse & Fons Jaspers-Janssens L'Angelot, Ranc au Ranc, 07530 Antraigues sur Volane, Ardèche
Tel	+33 (0)4 75 88 24 55
Email	info@langelot.com
Web	www.langelot.com

	Bernard Liaudois & Eric Dussiot Château de Fontblachère, 07210 St Lager Bressac, Ardèche
Mobile	+33 (0)6 11 18 23 83
Email	chateau@fontblachere.com
Web	www.chateau-fontblachere.com

Entry 587   Map 11

Entry 588   Map 11

La Moutière

Surrounded by gorgeous gardens, the bastide sits large and square amid old outbuildings concealing perfectly converted gîtes. Bare stone façades and limestone trims under a Provençal roof set the tone for simple, fresh, uncluttered interiors: new limestone floors, white furniture, neutral tones and flashes of unexpected colour. Bedding is sumptuous, bathrooms fashionably funky, views from the beautiful pale blue pool glide pleasingly over rows of poplars and fields of lavender. Your wonderfully exuberant Belgian hostess gives convivial weekly dinner parties under the chestnut trees during high season. Divine.

Pets by arrangement.

Mas de l'Adret

Pure Provence, the acres of lavender, the sea of hills rolling across to Mont Ventoux, the handsome ochre house. Inside, your charming and attentive Luxembourgeois hosts have created a stylish modern surprise of black leather and steel, quirky art and superb bathrooms. Deeply comfortable rooms are sober, uncluttered and each named for a Romina Ressia photograph. The seclusion and peace wash over you, flowers scent the air, the new view-drenched pool and outside jacuzzi are heated… Breakfast-brunch, at separate tables, is a feast. Then walk in wild nature, visit Provence, eat, drink and be merry. Could this be paradise?

Parking on-site.

Rooms	4 twin/doubles: €125-€135.
Meals	Dinner €40. Guest kitchen.
	Restaurant 3km.
Closed	Rarely.

Rooms	4 doubles: €90-€210.
	1 family room for 4: €190-€240.
Meals	Dinner, 4 courses, €30.
	Restaurants 5-minute drive.
Closed	January/February.

Françoise Lefebvre
La Moutière,
Quartier Moutière,
26230 Colonzelle,
Drôme

Tel   +33 (0)4 75 46 26 88
Mobile   +33 (0)6 76 94 90 25
Email   lamoutiere@gmail.com
Web   www.lamoutiere.com

Patrick & Françoise Meisch-Seyll
Mas de l'Adret,
2000 chemin de l'Adret,
26770 Roche-Saint-Secret-Béconne,
Drôme

Mobile   +33 (0)6 43 81 94 28
Email   mail@mas-ladret.com
Web   www.mas-ladret.com

La Ferme du Rastel

B&B with a difference. In a beautifully renovated old stone farmhouse in countryside just a 15-minute stroll from the village of Bourdeaux. Sleek, uncluttered modern rooms: blonde wood in beams, boards and furnishings; white and apparent stone walls; calm, comfortable designer furniture, and high-spec shower rooms (one tub). The difference is that your friendly hosts (who live on the top floor) prepare breakfasts and dinners but otherwise give you the run of the house, including two kitchens – a boon and fun for the sociable. There's also a dormitory for kids, a good-sized swimming pool and an establishing garden. Great.

Minimum stay: 2 nights in high season.

Chambres d'Hôtes Morin Salomé

A feast of colour and art, surrounded by breathtaking views, the Morin house is a visual treat, and is owned by a charming couple. He has created the windows and ironwork of the pergolas, she has tiled, fresco'd and frieze'd bathrooms, bedrooms and kitchen, with skill and imagination. Bedrooms are all river-side, brilliantly done, and fun. Dine on the terrace at one long table amongst a fabulous collection of pots and clambering plants, with the magnificent cliff beyond and rushing river sounds. A second terrace with ponds and goldfish almost drips over the river – the perfect solace. Tons to do nearby. Stunning.

Rooms	2 doubles: €100–€120.
	Extra bed/sofabed available.
Meals	Dinner, 4 courses, €25;
	children €10–€15. Guest kitchens.
Closed	Rarely.

Rooms	2 doubles: €80.
	2 family rooms for 4: €80–€90.
	1 triple: €80.
	Stays of 2+ nights: €70–€80.
Meals	Dinner with wine, €27.50.
	Restaurant 5-minute walk.
Closed	Rarely.

	Camille Barbeyrac
	La Ferme du Rastel,
	Le Rastel,
	26460 Bourdeaux,
	Drôme
Mobile	+33 (0)6 59 23 00 34
Email	lafermedurastel@gmail.com
Web	www.lafermedurastel.com

	Frédéric & Salomé Morin
	Chambres d'Hôtes Morin Salomé,
	34 rue Faubourg du Temple,
	26340 Saillans, Drôme
Tel	+33 (0)4 75 21 43 95
Mobile	+33 (0)6 14 18 75 89
Email	morin-salome@orange.fr
Web	www.chambres-hotes-morin-salome.fr

Entry 591   Map 11

Entry 592   Map 11

Les Marais

Opt for the simple country life at this friendly farm, which has been in the family for over 100 years and has returned to organic methods. A couple of horses, a few hens, and, when there's a full house, beautiful meals of regional recipes served family-style, with homemade chestnut cake and 'vin de noix' apéritif. Monsieur collects old farming artefacts and Madame, although busy, always finds time for a chat. The bedrooms are in a separate wing with varnished ceilings, antique beds, some florals; baths are old-fashioned pink, new showers delight Americans. At the foot of the Vercors range, French charm, utter peace.

Rooms	1 double, 1 twin: €55–€60.
	1 family room for 4: €98.
	1 triple: €70.
Meals	Dinner with wine, €18; not Sundays.
Closed	Rarely.

Christiane & Jean-Pierre Imbert
Les Marais,
285 route des Massouillards,
26300 Charpey,
Drôme

Tel	+33 (0)4 75 47 03 50
Mobile	+33 (0)6 27 32 23 65
Email	imbert.jean-pierre@wanadoo.fr
Web	pagesperso-orange.fr/les-marais

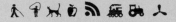

Clos de la Sauvagine

A modern-traditional hillside house with owners who go above and beyond for their guests; literally, a breath of fresh air. Once you've trekked and climbed all you can, come home to cosy pine-clad bedrooms with plump duvets and soft lighting – in the main house or in the chalet. The intricate, sloping garden glows with flowers, trees, vegetables, birds, little winding pathways and views to die for; sip wine on the terrace, flip open a book. Henri and Janine, both incredibly kind and generous, share their homely open-plan living area with you. An immaculate, pampering, very beautiful place – and Henri designed the house.

Children over 10 welcome.

Rooms	1 double with separate wc: €120.
	1 cottage for 4: €120–€180.
	Singles €90.
Meals	Dinner €30. Restaurant 10km.
Closed	15 September to 30 April.

Janine & Henri Bonneville
Clos de la Sauvagine,
La Chapelle,
38650 Château Bernard,
Isère

Tel	+33 (0)4 76 34 00 84
Mobile	+33 (0)6 08 60 18 61
Email	henribonneville@orange.fr
Web	www.closdelasauvagine.com

Château de Pâquier

Old, mighty, atmospheric — yet so homely. Enormous rooms, high heavy-beamed ceilings, large windows with sensational valley views; terraced gardens and animals; impressive bedrooms (handsome wardrobes, underfloor heating) up an ancient spiral staircase that sets the imagination reeling. Twice a week Hélène prepares dinner for guests in her modernised 17th-century tower kitchen (wood-fired range, stone sink, cobbled floor) where she makes her bread, honey, jams and walnut apéritif. Jacques and their daughter run an auberge next door — so do eat there too. And drink wine from the Rossis' own vineyard near Montpellier.

Longeville

There is a gentle elegance about this house and the people who live in it, including three sleek cats and two friendly dogs. Of Scots and Irish origin, the Barrs also give you run of the pretty garden with swimming pool. Their love for this 1750s farmhouse shows in their artistic touch with decorating, their mix of old and modern furniture, their gorgeous big bedrooms done in soft pale colours that leave space for the views that rush in from the hills. A high place of comfort and civilised contact where dinner in the airy white living room is a chance to get to know your kind, laid-back hosts more fully.

Rooms	3 twin/doubles: €86–€106.
	2 family rooms for 5: €90–€150.
Meals	Dinner with wine, €16–€27.
Closed	Rarely.

Rooms	2 twin/doubles: €50–€90.
Meals	Dinner with wine, €25.
Closed	Rarely.

Jacques & Hélène Rossi
Château de Pâquier,
Chemin du Château,
38650 St Martin de la Cluze,
Isère

Tel   +33 (0)4 76 72 77 33
Email   chateau.de.paquier@free.fr
Web   www.chateaudepaquier.fr

Mary & Greig Barr
Longeville,
5 Longeville,
38300 Succieu,
Isère

Tel   +33 (0)4 74 27 94 07
Mobile   +33 (0)6 87 47 59 46
Email   mary.barr@wanadoo.fr

Entry 595   Map 11

Entry 596   Map 11

Le Traversoud

Rooms are named after painters; lovely 'Cézanne' lies under the eaves on the top floor. Nathalie, warm, bright and amusing, and attentive Pascal welcome you to their farmhouse, guide you up the outside stairs to colourful, comfortable bedrooms and spotless shower rooms (a sauna, too) and treat you to some of the best home cooking in France, served at a long table; even the brioche is homemade. The garden overflows with grass and trees, crickets chirrup, the Bernese Mountain dog bounds, the donkeys graze and the exuberant courtyard is a safe space for your children to join theirs. Wonderful, informal B&B.

Les Hautes Bruyères

Once settled on this wooded hilltop in restfully subdued, country-smart comfort, you can't imagine that super-urban Lyon is only 10 minutes away. Karine's converted farm buildings are sophisticated yet simple – and so is she, with a genuine interest in other people and a flair for interiors. With 2,000 years of European history in its bones and a solid reputation for good food, Lyon has myriad treasures to see and taste. After a day of discovery (or work) in the city or the countryside, relax in the green and birdsung garden or the elegant Italianate pool area. Tomorrow there will be delicious breakfast in the 'auberge' dayroom.

Rooms	1 twin: €60.
	1 family room for 3,
	1 family room for 4: €76-€92.
	Children under 10 €10.
Meals	Dinner with wine, €25.
Closed	Rarely.

Rooms	2 doubles, 1 twin/double: €145-€250.
	2 suites for 4: €175-€280.
	Extra bed €35.
Meals	Bocuse cookery school in village:
	weekday bookings.
	Lyon centre 6km.
	Guest kitchen for light
	preparations.
Closed	Rarely.

Nathalie & Pascal Deroi
Le Traversoud,
484 chemin Sous l'École,
38110 Faverges de la Tour,
Isère

Tel	+33 (0)4 74 83 90 40
Mobile	+33 (0)6 07 11 99 42
Email	deroi.traversoud@orange.fr
Web	www.le-traversoud.com

Karine Laurent
Les Hautes Bruyères,
5 chemin des Hautes Bruyères,
Écully, 69130 Lyon,
Rhône

Tel	+33 (0)4 78 35 52 38
Mobile	+33 (0)6 08 48 69 50
Email	contact@lhb-hote.fr
Web	www.lhb-hote.fr

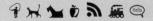

Château de Chambost

It takes little to imagine the owners' aristocratic ancestors residing in this rural, 16th-century hillside château. Traditional going on lavish, it's still fit for Lyonnais elite, its five bedrooms decked out in toile de Jouy and period furniture; one's still adorned with original 1850s parrot-flocked wallpaper. In the basement lies another gem: a striking umbrella-vaulted dining room, where vivacious hostess Véronique serves homemade apéritifs and beef reared on the château's estate. The cows have bagged most of the garden, but guests can retire to the elegant sitting room to plan countryside forays beyond.

La Croix de Saburin

Close to the autoroute, yet with to-die-for views – they soar over vineyards to Mounts Brouilly and Blanc. Built in regional style against the hillside is this very French, contemporary-smart house. Sociable and perfectionist, Monique and Jean-Michel began B&B when they retired; small pretty bedrooms have chalky mango-wood tables, sparkling bathrooms, glorious views. Guests are spoilt with the salon: tea-making kit and plenty of books. Rare birds, orchids and butterflies dwell in the valley below; cycling, wine tasting and Lyon are close by. Dine with the family on salade Lyonnaise and chicken in champagne. Intimate and stunning.

Rooms	2 doubles, 1 twin: €90–€100.
	1 family room for 3: €115.
Meals	Dinner with wine, €30.
	Restaurant 15km.
Closed	Rarely.

Rooms	1 double: €72.
	1 family room for 3: €72–€90.
Meals	Dinner with wine, €25.
Closed	Rarely.

	Vivien & Véronique de Lescure
	Château de Chambost,
	69770 Chambost Longessaigne,
	Rhône
Tel	+33 (0)4 74 26 37 49
Mobile	+33 (0)6 30 52 04 84
Email	infos@chateaudechambost.com
Web	www.chateaudechambost.com

	Jean-Michel & Monique Legat
	La Croix de Saburin,
	Saburin,
	69430 Quincié en Beaujolais,
	Rhône
Tel	+33 (0)4 74 69 02 82
Mobile	+33 (0)6 08 50 19 03
Email	jean-michel.legat@orange.fr
Web	lacroixdesaburin.free.fr

Château de Briante

This exotic-looking château – all glowing-pink stone and striking towers – in baize-green parkland is grand with a laidback touch. Rooms in the Tuscan-style wing mix original features – polished floors and wood panelling – with cool furnishings – vintage chairs and modern art. Sleek in silvers and coffees, all have green views; two have sun-drenched balconies. Breakfast on local cheese and hams, then slip through French windows to stroll the parkland – with its rose-decked orangerie – explore the vineyards or laze by the pool. Young winemakers Lauren and her husband are passionate about their estate. You will taste, learn and be charmed.

Pets welcome, ask in advance.

Les Pasquiers

Come to meet Marylène and Guillaume in their beautiful home in a wine-country village. Oriental rugs and fine antiques rub shoulders with contemporary art, and gorgeous books lie around for everyone to peruse. There's a grand piano in the drawing room, heaps of CDs, bedrooms are sunny, beds have beautiful linen, new bathrooms are on their way and the garden is divine – languid terraces, organic potager, summerhouse, pool. Marylène loves to cook, and great dinners are shared 'en famille'. One of the best – and surprisingly close to the autoroute.

Rooms	3 doubles: €150–€160. Extra bed/sofabed available €20 per person per night. Cot available.
Meals	Restaurant 1.5km.
Closed	3-24 January.

Rooms	1 twin/double; can interconnect with family room: €90. 1 suite for 4, 1 family room for 5: €90–€150. Extra bed available.
Meals	Dinner with wine, €33; children €12–€28; children under 7 free. Restaurants 6km.
Closed	Christmas, New Year & 1-19 August.

Lauren Schneider
Château de Briante,
810 route de Briante,
69220 Saint Lager,
Rhône

Mobile   +33 (0)6 83 31 28 50
Email   lfaupin@gmail.com
Web   www.domainedebriante.fr

Marylène & Guillaume Peyraverney
Les Pasquiers,
69220 Lancié,
Rhône

Tel   +33 (0)4 74 69 86 33
Mobile   +33 (0)6 83 19 01 37
Email   lespasquiers@orange.fr
Web   www.lespasquiers.com

Entry 601   Map 11

Entry 602   Map 11

Maison d'hôtes de La Verrière

Hugging the edge of a beautiful valley in Beaujolais, the high views from nearly every room of this serenely secluded family home are magnificent. Whether waking in your quirky country bedroom, meeting guests at the breakfast table (sampling yogurt cake and nine homemade jams) or swimming in the natural salt pool among wild mountain flowers, the valley is always there – particularly beautiful in autumn. Grégoire's guided walks start from the house. Both he and Christine love having guests to stay, and their French cuisine is so good (never the same dish twice) there's no reason to dine anywhere else.

Rooms	3 twin/doubles: €82-€92. 1 triple: €98. 1 quadruple: €118-€128. Singles €68. Extra bed/sofabed available €18 per person per night.
Meals	Dinner with wine, €28. Restaurant 15km.
Closed	Rarely.

Christine Gesse & Grégoire Lamy
Maison d'hôtes de La Verrière,
69430 Les Ardillats,
Rhône
Tel   +33 (0)4 74 04 71 46
Email   christine.gesse@orange.fr
Web   www.alaverriere.com

Entry 603   Map 11

Domaine de la Chapelle de Vâtre

The Wilson's estate centres on the 17th-century Romanesque chapel, whose bell is rung once a year to mark the end of the harvest. Beamed, terracotta tiled, simply stylish twin rooms are in two separate, stone buildings. Ground floor 'Fleurie', the lightest, has a walk-in shower. Brightly painted 'St Veran', the biggest with light airy bathroom, and smaller 'St Amour', with mini shower room, have hill views. Across the way the breakfast/tasting room has separate tables and Christine is flexible over times. Drink in views of the Haut Beaujolais from the lovely infinity pool, tour the winery and sample the produce.

Cot available. Parking on-site.

Rooms	3 twin/doubles: €65-€105. Extra bed €15.
Meals	Restaurants 5-minute drive.
Closed	Rarely.

Christine Wilson
Domaine de la Chapelle de Vâtre,
Lieu Dit Les Bourbons,
69840 Jullié,
Rhône
Tel   +33 (0)4 74 04 43 57
Email   vatre@wanadoo.fr
Web   www.vatre.com

Entry 604   Map 11

Domaine du Fontenay

Huge care has been taken by these owners to make guests comfortable and well-informed. Simon's lifelong ambition was to become a wine-maker in France, now his wines are highly regarded; enjoy the tastings in the cellar. In a separate building are four super bedrooms with excellent mattresses, big showers, rugs on old terracotta tiles and astonishing views from this hilltop site; and each bedroom has an excellent folder with all the local info. In summer, breakfast is served at check-clothed tables on the big terrace. This is a great area for good-value gourmet restaurants so enjoy them – and ask about 'La Route Magique!'

Château de Tanay

Surrounded by flat lands, a magnificent château in acres of parkland with pool. Inside is equally splendid. A sleek modern décor illuminates fine stonework and medieval beams, there's a games room for children, a grand piano for musicians and a convivial dining table; in summer, take breakfast by the moat beneath the willow. Spend the day in charming old Lyon or treat the family to the Parc des Oiseaux... return for a château tour with your hosts, trot off for dinner at the local pizzeria. Big tasteful bedrooms lie in the courtyard stables but the suite is in the château itself – with an amazing massage bath.

Rooms	1 suite for 2, 2 suites for 4: €80-€100. 1 triple: €80-€90. Cot available free of charge.
Meals	Kitchen available. Restaurant nearby.
Closed	Rarely.

Rooms	4 twin/doubles: €95-€130. 1 suite for 4: €160-€200. Extra bed available.
Meals	Restaurant 100m.
Closed	October – April.

Simon & Isabelle Hawkins
Domaine du Fontenay,
Fontenay,
42155 Villemontais,
Loire

Tel   +33 (0)4 77 63 12 22
Mobile   +33 (0)6 81 03 30 33
Email   info@domainedufontenay.com
Web   www.domainedufontenay.com

Benoît Haym
Château de Tanay,
Chemin de Tanay,
St Didier de Formans,
Ain

Mobile   +33 (0)9 53 36 87 42
Email   info@chateau-tanay.com
Web   www.chateau-tanay.com

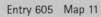

Entry 605   Map 11

Entry 606   Map 11

Château de Marmont

An amazing avenue of plane trees delivers you to an authentic 'time warp' château experience – and private access directly onto the second hole: bring the golf clubs! Madame, a classical historian, is a joy, and her house as colourful as she. Find polished family heirlooms, original wallpapers, a billiard room you can use. Up the grand stairs are bedrooms with books and fresh flowers; one has a bathroom with a claw foot bath and trompe-l'œil walls. Breakfasts are in the orangery or by the fire: classical music plays, the candle is lit, the coffee is hot, the oranges and the squeezer are to hand and the homemade jam is delicious.

Ferme de Pérignat

Kind and enthusiastic Parisians, Caroline and Jean-Robert, have done a grand job restoring this characterful 15th-century farm. The timbered stone and brick walls of the farmhouse peep out from a terracotta-tiled roof topped by a rare minaret-shaped Saracen chimney. Two comfortable beamed bedrooms, each with their own stylish modern bathroom, are prettily furnished with brocante bits and bobs. Breakfast in the stately hall or outside where tumbling rose bushes surround the fish-filled pond. There's a gentle Yorkie in residence and it's very dog friendly here. Foodies will head for gastronomic bliss in La Bresse.

Parking on-site.

Rooms	1 double: €95.
	1 suite for 3–5: €160.
Meals	Restaurant 3km.
Closed	Rarely.

Rooms	1 double: €115–€120.
	1 suite for 2: €100–€115. Cot €15.
	Extra bed €25.
Meals	Dinner, 4 courses with apéritif, €30;
	children €15–€20.
Closed	Rarely.

Geneviève Guido-Alhéritière
Château de Marmont,
2043 route de Condeissiat,
01960 St André sur Vieux Jonc,
Ain
Tel   +33 (0)4 74 52 79 74
Web   www.chateau-marmont.info

Caroline Fabre
Ferme de Pérignat,
Hameau de Pérignat,
01190 St Étienne sur Reyssouze,
Ain
Mobile   +33 (0)6 33 01 30 69
Email   cf01190@gmail.com
Web   www.fermedeperignat.fr

Entry 607   Map 11

Entry 608   Map 11

Château des Allues

A breathtaking setting for an atmospheric château, 13th century and facing the mountains. There's an incredible feeling of openness and space, and a house party feel when you stay. Stéphane's warm personality gives the place soul; Didier is charming; dinners are innovative and delicious and vegetables are from the potager – a glory. Inside: flowers, paintings, sculptures, quirky-chic antiques, music classical and modern, and comforting old-style suites with huge walk-in wardrobes and tip-top bathrooms. Climb snow-topped peaks, collapse by the pool, visit the Château de Miolans. Breakfast will set you up for a hearty day out.

Chalet Savoie Faire

At the top of a winding road find seriously good hiking and cycling in clear mountain air – and behind the façade of this old Savoyard farmhouse is a luxurious B&B. Friendly owners Hugh and Nikki – she runs wonderful cookery courses – have put everything into the renovation and each room has charming touches. The intimate dining room is chandelier-hung and atmospheric, although outdoor meals are on the terrace; the sitting room has a toasty fire and a rug to snuggle toes in; the bedrooms are a delight, especially the first-floor family suite with chunky-chic furniture from old timbers; bathrooms are a wow. People return over and over again.

Minimum stay: 2 nights.

Rooms	2 doubles: €140–€165. 1 suite for 2, 2 suites for 4: €150–€240. Cot available.
Meals	Dinner with wine, €48. Restaurants 5-minute drive.
Closed	3 weeks in December.

Rooms	1 double, 1 double with extra bunk room for children, 1 twin/double, 1 twin with separate bathroom: €110–€150. Whole house available (B&B) €2,700–€3,000 per week.
Meals	Dinner, 3 courses with apéritif, wine, coffee or tea, €35. Restaurant 1km.
Closed	Rarely.

	Stéphane Vandeville Château des Allues, 73250 Saint Pierre d'Albigny, Savoie
Email	info@chateaudesallues.com
Web	www.chateaudesallues.com

	Nikki Shields-Quinn Chalet Savoie Faire, Fontaines-Naves, 73260 La Léchère, Savoie
Tel	+33 (0)4 79 24 54 28
Mobile	+33 (0)7 71 60 50 48
Email	nikki@chaletsavoiefaire.com
Web	www.chaletsavoiefaire.com

Entry 609   Map 12

Entry 610   Map 12

Maison Coutin

In summer it's all flowers, birds and rushing streams; the balconies bloom, the garden is exuberant. Your friendly, sporty hosts have known the valley all their lives, have three children and will be helpful with yours. View-filled bedrooms are traditionally dark-beamed and attractively, imaginatively furnished. Delicious, mostly organic, food is cooked in the wood-fired oven (including the bread), the vegetables are home-grown, the eggs are from the hens, and there's a dayroom with a fridge. Great value and a deeply eco-friendly ethos.

Minimum stay: 3 nights; 4 nights on weekdays; 7 in high season. Pets by arrangement.

Chalet Colinn

Mylène and Elizabeth love the outdoors, hence their five-year fight to reincarnate a fallen ruin as a luxury mountain retreat. Join them for gourmet dinner under soaring, raftered ceilings in the grand living space which hovers above Tignes dam. Or soak in the terrace hot tub under the stars; there's a sauna too. Urban rusticity, mountain chic: the place reeks Italian style yet is impossibly hidden in this tiny hamlet. For daytime adventure: the slopes at Val d'Isère, or Tignes, or the Vanoise park. Just ask Elizabeth, off-piste skier extraordinaire.

Rooms	3 family suites for 3-5: €70-€145. Singles €45. Dinner, B&B €54-€66 per person. Extra bed/sofabed available €25 per person per night. Winter: €320-€358 per person per week.
Meals	Dinner €22; children €9-€17.
Closed	Rarely.

Rooms	3 twin/doubles: €120. 2 triples: €180. Winter: dinner, B&B €120-€280 per person per night (2-night minimum).
Meals	Dinner €35. Wine from €13.
Closed	Rarely.

	Claude Coutin & Franck Chenal Maison Coutin, Chemin de la Fruitière, 73210 Peisey Nancroix, Savoie
Tel	+33 (0)4 79 07 93 05
Mobile	+33 (0)6 14 11 54 65
Email	maison-coutin@orange.fr
Web	www.maison-coutin.fr

	Elizabeth Chabert & Mylène Charrière Chalet Colinn, Le Franchet de Tignes, BP 125, 73150 Val d'Isère, Savoie
Tel	+33 (0)4 79 06 26 99
Email	contact@chaletcolinn.com
Web	www.chaletcolinn.com

La Touvière

Mountains march past Mont Blanc and over into Italy, cows graze in the foreground, the place is perfect for exploring this walkers' paradise. Myriam, bubbly and easy, adores having guests with everyone joining in the lively, light-hearted family atmosphere. In the typical old unsmart farmhouse, the cosy family room is the hub of life. Marcel is part-time home improver, part-time farmer (just a few cows now). One room has a properly snowy valley view, the other overlooks the owners' second chalet, let as a gîte; both are a decent size, simple but not basic, while shower rooms are spotless. Remarkable value.

Rooms	2 doubles: €60.
Meals	Restaurant 3km.
Closed	Rarely.

	Marcel & Myriam Marin-Cudraz
	La Touvière,
	73590 Flumet,
	Savoie
Tel	+33 (0)4 79 31 70 11
Email	marcel.marin-cudraz@wanadoo.fr
Web	www.touviere.fr

Entry 613 Map 12

Les Racines

Screened by trees, with the lake in front and mountains rearing beyond, this house is in a silent green world. Unexpectedly modern – dramatic sloping roofs, large windows – inside all is light and uncluttered. A large living area is coolly furnished with leather sofas on tiled floors; glass encased stove for chillier days. Bedrooms are stylishly simple with polished wood floors, white walls and balconies. Anglo-Russian couple, Stanley and Vera – early rat-race retirees – love sharing their peaceful spot: go cycling, swimming, or take the lakeside path to Annecy. Return to drinks on the terrace, and the sound of birdsong.

Rooms	1 double; 1 double with separate bathroom: €120–€160. Extra bed/sofabed available €20 per person per night. Whole house for 8 available in summer, €3,500–€4,750 per week.
Meals	Restaurants 15-minute walk.
Closed	Rarely.

	Vera Root
	Les Racines,
	567 Allée le Beau,
	74410 Saint-Jorioz,
	Haute-Savoie
Tel	+33 (0)4 50 23 00 56
Mobile	+33 (0)6 44 92 35 34
Email	chezlesracines@gmail.com
Web	www.chezlesracines.com

Entry 614 Map 12

Maison La Cerisaie

This lovely green-shuttered 1830s chalet has been part of the community for years; today it shines. No short cuts have been taken by generous hosts Sally-Anne and Simon (ex-Navy) who delight in providing the best. Start the day with breakfast at a time to suit you (fresh croissants, local jams, Nespresso coffee, Pukka teas), plunge into mountain adventures, return to a hot tub in the garden and supper at the auberge. Or eat in: the food is varied and delicious. Warm, woody, clean-cut bedrooms wait on the first floor, one with an extra sofabed, two with the views, all with bathrobes and toasty bathroom floors.

Minimum stay: 2 nights.

Chalet APASSION

Perched on the mountainside above the lovely old resort of Samoëns, a luxurious, new-build pine chalet; one of four, settled quietly down a private lane. Majestic views stretch from the terraces and balcony, and a great big cedar hot tub is the perfect place to soak away the day's strain after long summer's days spent biking, hiking or climbing. Glossy bedspreads and scatter cushions finish pristine rooms, while in the open-plan sitting/dining room, plush leather sofas sit in the glow of a real fire. Breakfast is just as relaxed – simply let attentive Vicky and Rob know when you'd like it. Delightful dinners are on request.

Minimum stay: 3 nights.

Rooms	1 double, 2 twin/doubles: €100–€130. 1 family room for 3-4: €100–€130. Winter: €625–€975 per person per week.
Meals	Dinner, 3 courses, with wine, €40.
Closed	Rarely.

Rooms	5 twin/doubles: €138–€161. Winter: €777–€1,323 per person per week.
Meals	Dinner, 2 courses with wine, €36. Restaurants 1km.
Closed	November to mid-December.

Simon & Sally-Anne Airey
Maison La Cerisaie,
Salvagny,
74740 Sixt Fer à Cheval,
Haute-Savoie

Tel   +33 (0)4 50 89 94 78
Email contact@maisonlacerisaie.com
Web   www.maisonlacerisaie.com

Rob & Vicky Tarr
Chalet APASSION,
77 chemin du Battieu, Vercland,
74340 Samoëns,
Haute-Savoie

Tel   +33 (0)4 50 18 68 33
Mobile +33 (0)6 06 70 81 57
Email robandvicky@apassion.com
Web   www.apassion.co.uk

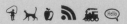

Entry 615   Map 12

Entry 616   Map 12

Chalet Twenty26

With Morzine below and superb peaks above, the Hamblin's chalet is super-stylish and fun. On the deck: a blissful, bubbling, sunken hot tub and a barrel sauna. Indoors: an eye-catching living area with cow-hides, a sleek fireplace, designer seating, an honesty bar, a surround sound music system – downstairs a dedicated cinema. Under the rafters bedrooms are all different, everything top notch; bathrooms chic with fluffy robes. And the food is outstanding; meals on the balcony a treat. As for summer sport: great walking, a well-equipped bike store for cyclists, a nearby water park and swimming complex. A top address!

La Ferme de Margot

A real old farmhouse on the south-facing flank of Morzine with original slates, knobbly beams, and heaps of space. Everything has been beautifully considered by generous English owners (who live downstairs), from the study/snug with its wood-burner to the fabulous living area on the top floor to the media room in between. Imagine silver reindeer heads, a sweeping crushed-velvet sofa, a long matt-white dining table, cowhide wallpaper, a wooden 'sun-beam' ceiling and tartan flourishes. Step out for beautiful mountain and lakeside walks; there's a good golf course ten minutes' away. Return to fabulous food, beers and wines.

Minimum stay: 2 nights in summer.

Rooms	5 twin/doubles: £100–£190. Singles 20% reduction. Cots £5. Extra beds available. Winter: £695–£1,695 per person per week.
Meals	Dinner with wine, £35. Restaurants 15-minute walk.
Closed	Rarely.

Rooms	4 twin/doubles: £120–£150. 1 suite for 4: £150–£200. Winter: £725–£795 per person per week.
Meals	Dinner with wine, €40. Restaurants within walking distance.
Closed	Rarely.

Sarah & Chris Hamblin
Chalet Twenty26,
Route de la Manche,
74110 Morzine, Haute-Savoie
Tel   +44 (0)203 582 6409
Mobile +33 (0)6 35 41 11 02
Email   info@theboutiquechalet.com
Web   www.theboutiquechalet.com/twenty26/

Jane & Stephen Fenlon
La Ferme de Margot,
332 chemin Martenant,
74110 Morzine,
Haute-Savoie
Tel   +33 (0)9 67 01 12 68
Email   hello@grandcruski.com
Web   www.grandcruski.com

Chalet Amuse Bouche

On the edge of an attractive village (1.2km) and close to the resort of Morzine (3km), is a sparkling new chalet run by Lindsay and Steve. Picture windows pull in the views, three bedrooms open to the terrace, two more have private balconies, and the interiors are Alpine and contemporary. Best of all is the food, from Lindsay's breakfast bagels and buns (sticky cinnamon a favourite!) to Steve's delectable dinners (sauces a speciality). For summer: white water rafting, canoeing, climbing and biking. For winter: a free shuttle to the Ardent télécabine and access to the snow-sure Avoriaz, then home to a round of pool, or hot tub and sauna, and a river to sing you to sleep.

Minimum stay: 3 nights.

Chalet Cannelle

The diffuse light of a contemporary chandelier spills onto the white walls of this stylish chalet. Circled by wintry snows or May's wild flowers, in a hamlet just outside Chatel, the lovely old farmhouse has balconies for big windows and stunning views, pine-cosy sleeping quarters, a kids' dorm with its own TV, and a toy-filled mezzanine. Delicious treats (eggs from the hens, truffled pecorino, Lake Geneva trout) flow from the kitchen or the terrace's wood-fired oven. Gather for log fires and nightcaps around the three-beam coffee table as you discuss the exploits of the day. Once in you won't want to leave.

Minimum stay: 2 nights at weekends.

Rooms	1 double, 1 twin/double, 1 twin, 2 family rooms for 4: €100. Whole chalet £2,967 per week.	
Meals	Dinner with wine, €40. Restaurants 1km.	
Closed	30 September to 4 June.	

Rooms	1 double, 2 twin/doubles: €120-€140. 1 family room for 4; 1 quadruple, with children's den: €120-€150. Singles €120. Dinner, B&B €100 per person. Winter: €850-€1,150 per person per week.
Meals	Dinner €40.
Closed	Rarely.

Lindsay Butcher
Chalet Amuse Bouche,
223 chemin sur la Char Montriond,
74110 Morzine,
Haute-Savoie

Tel	+33 (0)9 80 87 42 02
Email	escapetothealps@aol.com
Web	www.escapetothealps.com

Lorraine McDermott
Chalet Cannelle,
Suvay,
74360 Chatel,
Haute-Savoie

Tel	+33 (0)4 50 73 30 97
Email	info@chaletcannelle.co.uk
Web	www.chaletcannelle.co.uk

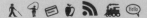

Entre Lac et Montagne

Come to explore gracious, sporty, lakeside Évian – minutes' away. Or head for the mountains – the nearest ski resorts of Bernex and Thollon are a 15-minute drive. And footpaths take off from the door of this well-planned, modernised home above the charming old village of Neuvecelle. The guest wing has a comfortable, lake-view sitting room and each bright bedroom a private balcony or terrace (where you can breakfast): one gazes to Lake Léman, the other is in the pretty garden near the heated pool. The Burtons are keen to share their enthusiasm for this rich area, and to cook – do arrange dinner with them and learn more.

Over 12s welcome.

Rooms	2 doubles: €95.
	Extra sofa bed in guest sitting room €45; available when both rooms booked by same party.
Meals	Dinner with wine, €33.
	Restaurants 5-minute walk.
Closed	Rarely.

Christopher & Christine Burton
Entre Lac et Montagne,
Avenue de Verlagny,
74500 Neuvecelle,
Haute-Savoie

Tel	+33 (0)4 50 84 98 34
Email	oldgranarychrism@aol.com
Web	www.evianchambredhote.com

Entry 621   Map 12

Provence – Alps – Riviera

www.sawdays.co.uk/provence-alps-riviera

La Maison du Bez

An 18th-century farmhouse in a quiet old village by Serre Chevalier with walks from the door. All the B&B rooms are on the second floor: find simple, cool decoration with white walls, some lovely old pieces of furniture, modern showers, good views – most have their own balcony. A big living room downstairs has a comfy seating area with a fireplace and a bar just off it; there's a kids' playroom in the making and a grand terrace outside for a hot chocolate. Tina gives you homebaked bread at breakfast along with organic honey, meats and cheeses. In the garden you'll find Scandinavian style hot tubs and saunas.

Parking on-site.

Chalet Le Pot de Miel

Rebecca and Michel run a charming B&B in the family resort of Montgenèvre, just a kilometre from Italy. Homemade breads, honey from their bees and croissants from the bakery are eaten round a communal table which has stunning mountain views. Dinner is served here too – regional French dishes with a twist. You can ski all day on the pistes (starting from the garden), nip over to Italy, visit the weekday market, cycle in summer. Return to an honesty bar, a very welcoming living room with a beautiful fireplace, TV and billiards in a separate room, indoor and outdoor hot tubs for weary limbs, very comfortable bedrooms with balconies.

Parking available.

Rooms	1 double, 1 twin: €80.
	3 family rooms for 4: €120.
	Dinner, B&B €425–€620 per person per week.
Meals	Restaurants 2-minute walk.
Closed	Rarely.

Rooms	3 doubles: €195–€225.
	1 family room for 3,
	1 family room for 4: €230–€275.
	Singles €110–€195.
	Dinner, B&B €20–€37 per person.
	Extra bed/sofabed available €35 per person per night.
Meals	Dinner with wine, €37; children €20.
	Restaurants 5-minute walk.
Closed	Rarely.

	Tina Isaksson
	La Maison du Bez,
	3 chemin de la Chouchière,
	05240 La Salle les Alpes,
	Hautes-Alpes
Tel	+33 (0)4 92 24 86 96
Email	ski@hoteldubez.com
Web	www.hotel-dubez.com

	Rebecca & Michel Coulliais
	Chalet Le Pot de Miel,
	Hameau de l'Obelisque,
	05100 Montgenèvre,
	Hautes-Alpes
Tel	+33 (0)4 92 21 93 55
Mobile	+33 (0)6 07 87 37 68
Email	lepotdemiel@hotmail.fr
Web	www.lepotdemiel.com

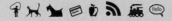

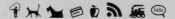

Entry 622   Map 12

Entry 623   Map 12

La Maison du Guil

The 16th-century stone and timber priory, the oldest house in this remote narrow hamlet, has the same glorious views as ever, out over the rooftops to the surrounding peaks. Inside is all stone and timber, too, beautifully architect-renovated and furnished with a cleancut imaginative eye. The big living room has a stunning arched stone ceiling, the perfect foil for high-modern scarlet chairs and table cloths. Delighted with their Alpine venture, the charming new young owners will offer you a big traditional bedroom or a funkier cave-like room with stone nooks for lights and a sunken shower. Superb.

Minimum stay: 3 nights July/August.

Le Jas du Bœuf

In unspoilt Provence, among forests, vineyards and lavender, with the Alps to the east, the Lubéron to the west, the handsome contemporary renovation of the big 18th-century farmhouse suited Jérôme (ex-Parisian) and Dana (he's Canadian) to a T. They hung their modern art collection, laid their lovely carpets and use their bakery-bistro experience to create delicious dinners. Choose plain luxury in the old *jas* or a breathtakingly modern lodge that pulls the outside in (all with their own private entrance). Myriad sports, delightful villages, gardens and markets call you; then chill out by the heated infinity pool or, in the colder months, a roaring indoor fire. Exquisitely minimalist, wonderfully remote, really welcoming.

Rooms	2 doubles: €120-€130.
	2 family rooms for 3: €120-€130.
	Child €45.
Meals	Dinner with apéritif & coffee, €36.
	Wine from €5. Restaurant 3km.
Closed	Rarely.

Rooms	4 doubles: €80-€135.
	Extra bed/sofabed available €30 per
	person per night. Dogs €10 per day.
Meals	Dinner with drinks, €35.
	Summer kitchen.
	Restaurants 3-8km.
Closed	Rarely.

	Tom Van De Velde
	La Maison du Guil,
	La Font, 05600 Eygliers,
	Hautes-Alpes
Tel	+33 (0)4 92 50 16 20
Email	info@lamaisonduguil.com
Web	www.lamaisonduguil.com

	Jérôme Mantel & Dana Silk
	Le Jas du Bœuf,
	Lieu-dit Parrot, 04230 Cruis,
	Alpes-de-Haute-Provence
Tel	+33 (0)4 92 79 01 05
Email	lejasduboeuf@orange.fr
Web	www.lejasduboeuf.fr

Le Clos de Rohan

Cloaked in a remote valley sweet with lavender lies an 18th-century farmhouse with ingeniously restored barns – find lavender stalks in the plaster! Lovely generous rooms have classy bathrooms, iron beds, crisp linen, a patio and terrace each, and views over valley and hills fat with bees. The chic two-storey suite comes with a kitchenette, the other suite is more rustic, and there's a shared living room with a cosy wood-burner. In a courtyard garden heady with blooms breakfast on homemade honey, cherries, plums, and then daydream by the small pool. Provence at its bucolic best.

La Belle Cour

The moment you enter the courtyard you'll feel at home – Angela and Rodney's welcome is cheerful and warm. Their pretty house sits in a bustling village and its décor is traditional and rustic with many shelves of books in different languages, antique furniture and interesting art. Comfortable bedrooms overlook the courtyard and have traditional Provençal fabrics, more books and gleaming furniture. Breakfast is usually taken in the courtyard and includes homemade jams and fresh croissants from the local bakery. You'll be keen to explore wonderful food markets, hike or bike in the Lubéron Natural Park or simply unbend here.

Children over 10 welcome.

Rooms	2 suites for 2: €120–€130. Extra bed/sofabed available €20–€60 per person per night.
Meals	Dinner with wine, €30. Guest kitchen.
Closed	Rarely.

Rooms	2 doubles: €90–€105.
Meals	Restaurants 200m.
Closed	1 November to 16 April.

Françoise Cavallo
Le Clos de Rohan,
04150 Simiane la Rotonde,
Alpes-de-Haute-Provence

Tel	+33 (0)4 92 74 49 42
Mobile	+33 (0)6 20 06 59 76
Email	francoise04.cavallo@gmail.com
Web	www.le-clos-de-rohan.eu

Rodney & Angela Heath
La Belle Cour,
Place Daniel Vigouroux,
04280 Céreste,
Alpes-de-Haute-Provence

Tel	+33 (0)4 92 72 48 76
Email	angela@labellecour.com
Web	www.labellecour.com

Domaine La Parpaille

Recline on a lounger, book a massage or cookery course, enjoy music evenings by the pool, gaze across vineyards to Cucuron. The farm has been in Eve's family for generations and has never looked so dapper. Studiously chic bedrooms are behind the house in barns; find soft blues and mauves with splashes of bright pink, linen curtains, bold art, painted furniture, a Persian carpet on a polished concrete floor, and bathrooms of pure luxury, one with 'his and her' showers. Eve is a keen cook and you dine deliciously in her kitchen or on the flagged terrace. As for medieval Cucuron: Tuesday's market around the spring-fed 'bassin' is a treat.

Rooms	3 doubles; 1 double with separate bathroom: €120–€160. 1 suite for 2: €200.
Meals	Platter €20–€25. Dinner €40; Thursday only.
Closed	Rarely.

Eve Obert Scholefield
Domaine La Parpaille,
Chemin de Blanqui,
84160 Cucuron,
Vaucluse

Mobile	+33 (0)6 75 98 06 70
Email	contact@domaine-la-parpaille.com
Web	www.domaine-la-parpaille.com

La Couleur des Vignes

There's a five-metre-long table for breakfast, a sand pitch for boules, a 20-metre infinity pool for swims, beds brimful of lavender, and unsurpassable views. Marc and Bérénice, warm, welcoming and well-travelled, took early retirement to follow a dream: a house in the sun in Provence. Built on a hillside, it has thick walls, ancient tiles, restored doors, masses of light. The entrance and bedrooms are on the first floor and the living areas (subtle lights, low sofas) are below, opening to delicious lawns and pergola. Imagine limestone floors, pure white bathrooms, neutral colours with accents of rust-red, and galleried suites for families.

Parking on-site.

Rooms	3 twin/doubles: €100–€140. 2 family rooms for 2: €120–€140. Extra bed €30 for children under 12.
Meals	Restaurants 6km.
Closed	16 December to mid-March.

Marc & Bérénice van der Elst
La Couleur des Vignes,
Bonnieux,
Vaucluse

Mobile	+33 (0)6 07 90 07 04/ +33 (0)6 77 85 97 92
Email	lacouleurdesvignes@gmail.com
Web	www.lacouleurdesvignes.com

Le Domaine Saint Jean

With lovely Lubéron views over vineyards and orchards, this sturdy farm centres on a courtyard and its quenching old trough and pump. Thea and Eric came south for warmth and their Provençal project celebrates their care and flair. Thea cooks up a local feast once a week and lays on fine outdoor breakfasts too. Antique dealer Eric's finds add intrigue to calm, clean-lined rooms: white linen and beams, bursts of vibrant fabrics, good new bathrooms. There's a shared pool to plunge in and lounge by, a bar/games/sitting room to retreat to, handy access to kitchens and such a rich area to visit; visual and cultural treats all around.

Smoking permitted in gardens.

Villa Vagabonde

The whole modern, minimalist place, grey and white inside and out, breathes peace and comfort. Relax into Veerle and Wim's dream house. They came from corporate Belgium for a new life, converted an old Provençal farmhouse in the Lubéron Natural Park to sleek purity and opened three fine, light rooms to guests. All is brand new, the stone-walled breakfast terrace, patios and pool are as quiet and delightful as the interior. Under your hosts' welcoming care come and enjoy a thoroughly grownup B&B. Twenty minutes' walk from Gordes and a hop from Aix, Avignon and Arles, Vagabonde is made for lovers of modern style and old Provence.

Minimum stay: 3 nights in high season. Over 16s welcome. Parking on-site.

Rooms	1 double, 1 twin/double: €75-€140. 1 family room for 3, 1 family room for 4: €110-€200.
Meals	Dinner, 3 courses with wine, €30; once a week. Tapas with wine, €15. Restaurants 2km.
Closed	December – February.

Rooms	3 twin/doubles: €135-€165.
Meals	Restaurants 20-minute walk.
Closed	October – March.

Thea Hemery
Le Domaine Saint Jean,
Saint Jean,
84490 Saint Saturnin les Apt,
Vaucluse

Tel +33 (0)4 32 50 10 77
Mobile +33 (0)6 82 92 56 58
Email thea@ledomainesaintjean.com
Web www.ledomainesaintjean.com

Wim & Veerle
Villa Vagabonde,
Chemin des Escortiels,
84220 Gordes,
Vaucluse

Mobile +33 (0)6 42 99 80 32
Email info@villavagabonde.com
Web www.villavagabonde.com

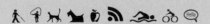

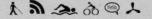

Entry 630   Map 16

Entry 631   Map 16

Maison Noel

Imagine a tiny Provençal village with a sun-dappled café-bar, an excellent auberge, a ruined castle, and a square off which lies Maison Noel. Enchanting, historic, and partially shaded by an old lime tree, it is the home of a charming and well-travelled hostess. The heart of the house is downstairs (open fireplace, country kitchen), the décor is stylish and soothing, and you can spill into a heavenly garden for supper (borrow the barbecue!). A perfect springboard for Provence, with a capacious bed to come home to and your own secluded patio. Artists and romantics will not want to stir.

Minimum stay: 2 nights in high season. Children over 8 welcome.

Sous L'Olivier

Old stonework rules the scene, big arched openings have become dining-room windows, a stone hearth burns immense logs in winter, and all is set round a pretty courtyard. Charming young bon viveur Julien, cooks for you: breakfasts are sumptuous affairs and convivial dinners are worth a serious detour – in summer perhaps a convivial, generous BBQ. Gentle Carole is behind the very fresh, Frenchly decorated bedrooms. Agricultural land is all around, you are close to the Lubéron mountains, the big, child-friendly, saltwater pool is arched with canvas shading and surrounded by giant pots and plants. Lovely people, fabulous food.

Rooms	1 double: €100–€130. Singles €75–€110.
Meals	Restaurant 2-minute walk.
Closed	Rarely.

Rooms	3 doubles: €100. 2 suites for 4: €138. Extra beds available.
Meals	Dinner with wine, €32.
Closed	Easter, bank holidays; 31 October to 1 April.

Trish Michie
Maison Noel,
12 place du Bataillet,
84800 Lagnes,
Vaucluse, Provence
Mobile +33 (0)6 72 45 36 03
Email trishmichie@gmail.com
Web www.come2provence.com

Carole, Julien, Hugo & Clovis Gouin
Sous L'Olivier,
997B, D900,
84800 Lagnes,
Vaucluse
Tel +33 (0)4 90 20 33 90
Email souslolivier@orange.fr
Web www.chambresdhotesprovence.com

La Prévôté

You're on an island, tucked down a network of wiggly streets. Drop your luggage (park nearby), then walk through the ancient stone arch and into a courtyard with convivial tables and shady canopy. Inside, the bar has funky chairs and – quite a talking point – a tributary of the Sorgue running underneath. The hub of this bustling place though is its fabulous 'Maître Restaurateur' restaurant and charming owners Severine and Jean-Marie: locals flock here for their food. Up stone stairs to bedrooms on the first and second floors: colourful and airy, with brocante finds. Browse antique shops in town, and head off to Avignon or Orange.

La Bastide Rose

Once an ancient mill on the river Sorgue, this pink-hued house has a relaxed but regal air. The grounds are huge, with their own island, swimming pool and an orangery where a seasonal breakfast is served. Inside, character abounds. There's a sitting room that was once an ancient kitchen and distinctive bedrooms, one with its own terrace, another with antiques and a sitting room. All have modern bathrooms. The library is stocked with books, and occasional exhibitions are held (almost more hotel than B&B!). Lovely Poppy can point you to the best walks and finest markets, or leave you to linger in this fabulous place.

Minimum stay: 2 nights in high season.

Rooms	2 doubles, 3 twin/doubles: €150–€235. Extra bed/sofabed available €40 per person per night.
Meals	Dinner, 3 courses, €41.
Closed	Rarely.

Rooms	3 twin/doubles, 2 can interconnect: €160–€235. 2 suites for 2: €220–€310. Extra bed/sofabed available €40 per person per night. Pets: €15 per day.
Meals	Breakfast €12–€22. Lunch €25–€30. Dinner €35–€50. Wine €20–€140. Restaurant 7km.
Closed	15 January to 15 March.

Severine Alloin
La Prévôté,
4 rue Jean Jacques Rousseau,
84800 L'Isle sur la Sorgue,
Vaucluse
Tel   +33 (0)4 90 38 57 29
Email contact@la-prevote.fr
Web   www.la-prevote.fr

Poppy Salinger
La Bastide Rose,
99 chemin des Croupières,
84250 Le Thor,
Vaucluse
Tel   +33 (0)4 90 02 14 33
Mobile +33 (0)6 78 43 57 33
Email   contact@bastiderose.com
Web   www.bastiderose.com

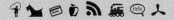

Entry 634   Map 16

Entry 635   Map 16

Château La Roque

Look an eagle in the eye, up here on the edge of the Lubéron; the glorious views still stretch over the tranquil valley. Kind and interesting, Jean can tell you about the golden ratio used to build the castle: bedrooms are huge and comfortable with carefully-chosen antiques, lovely bedding and designer fabrics. One has a deep-coral bed under vaulted ceilings and genuine 13th-century wardrobe doors. Each handsome, roomy bathroom is done with the best fittings. After visiting a pretty Provençal town or famous vineyard (Gigondas, Châteauneuf…), return to a delicious dinner on the vine-dappled terrace or in the garden.

La Nesquière

The gardens alone are worth the detour: trees and greenery galore, riots of roses, all flourishing in a huge many-terraced park by a river. The 18th-century farmhouse harbours a fine collection of antiques – one of Isabelle's passions – tastefully set off by lush indoor greenery and lovely old carpets on ancient tile floors. Softly old-elegant rooms have hand-embroidered fabrics and genuine old linens, including Provençal quilts – truly exquisite – with splashes of red, orange and beige against white backgrounds. Themed weekends, too (cookery, wine, embroidery), and a warm, gracious welcome from Isabelle and her family.

Rooms	2 doubles: €180–€220. 3 suites for 2: €320. Extra bed/sofabed available €35 per person per night. Whole château available on a self-catering basis.
Meals	Breakfast €20. Dinner, 4 courses, €46 (except Sunday & Monday); book ahead. Wine €22–€200.
Closed	Late November to early March. Open New Year.

Rooms	5 twin/doubles: €127–€157.
Meals	Platter available on request.
Closed	Mid-December to mid-January.

Chantal & Jean Tomasino
Château La Roque,
263 chemin du Château,
84210 La Roque sur Pernes,
Vaucluse
Tel +33 (0)4 90 61 68 77
Email chateaularoque@wanadoo.fr
Web www.chateaularoque.com

Isabelle de Maintenant
La Nesquière,
5419 route d'Althen,
84210 Pernes les Fontaines,
Vaucluse
Tel +33 (0)4 90 62 00 16
Mobile +33 (0)6 79 72 43 47
Email lanesquiere@wanadoo.fr
Web www.lanesquiere.com

Provence Alps Riviera

Le Jardin de Mazan

Amidst narrow streets, step through an ancient wooden door into Agnes and Eric's lovingly renovated home. Up the handsome stone staircase to bright bedrooms with garden and village views, furnished with an eclectic mix of antiques – have a soak in the freestanding bath! Bathrooms are smart and fresh. In the shady garden, tuck into a breakfast of homemade seasonal goodies (cherry clafoutis a speciality). Cycle quiet country lanes, visit vineyards, or head for the Sault lavender fields and Lubéron villages. Browse the library or play pool before dining in or out: shops and restaurants are just a few minutes' walk away.

Minimum stay: 3 nights Jul/Aug. Parking on-site.

Châteaux Eydoux

Down a long drive at the end of a country lane lies this handsome building. The home of friendly Guido and Ann, their young son and three dogs, it's peacefully set in 17 acres of gardens and woodland, and has superb views of Mont Ventoux. Oozing style and elegance, from shabby chic to pop art, expect parquet floors, a stone fireplace, light spacious bedrooms, a jacuzzi bath and smart bathrooms. Lavish breakfasts are served in the garden; fresh produce abounds. Wander the grounds, take a dip in the pool, hike the mountains, visit Orange and Avignon, or sample the local wines. It's just a ten-minute drive to shops and restaurants.

Minimum stay: 2 nights; 7 nights Jul/Aug (Fri-Fri). Parking on-site. Cot available.

Rooms	1 double, 2 twin/doubles: €120–€160. Extra bed €30.	Rooms	2 doubles: €125–€140. 2 family rooms for 4: €155–€225. 1 triple: €155. Extra bed €35 per night. Babes in arms free of charge. Cot available.
Meals	Lunch €15. Dinner with wine, €30; children €10. Restaurants 2-minute walk.	Meals	Occasional dinner, 3 courses with wine, €35; children €10. Restaurants 4km.
Closed	Rarely.	Closed	Rarely.

	Eric Duchemin Le Jardin de Mazan, 65 rue des Penitents Noirs, 84380 Mazan, Vaucluse		Ann de Mets Châteaux Eydoux, 673 avenue Général Eydoux, 84870 Loriol du Comtat, Vaucluse
Mobile	+33 (0)6 52 41 02 31	Mobile	+33 (0)7 87 08 53 18
Email	contact@lejardindemazan.com	Email	demetsann26@gmail.com
Web	www.lejardindemazan.com	Web	www.chateau-eydoux.com

Entry 638   Map 16

Entry 639   Map 16

Le Mas de la Pierre du Coq

What's especially nice about this 17th-century farmhouse is that it hasn't been over-prettified. Instead, it has the friendly, informal elegance of a house that's lived in and loved; grey-painted beams, soft stone walls, seductive bathrooms. The Lorenzes loved it the moment they saw it; it reminded gentle Stéphan of the house he grew up in. Bustling Martine starts your day with a terrific breakfast, Stéphan shows you the walks from the door. The gardens, sweet with roses, oleanders and lavender, are shaded by ancient trees and the pool and views are glorious. Stay for as long as you can; book excellent dinners in advance.

Le Mas au Portail Bleu

It's so friendly here you'll feel like you've joined a jolly house party. Monique and Chris welcome you with a glass of wine, serve breakfasts (with home baking) at a shared table on the terrace and arrange barbecues in the large garden. Their light-filled Provençal farmhouse, edged by a canal for easy walks, is elegantly shabby-chic. Large, beamed bedrooms have soft colours, French quilts and views over vines, hills or Mont Ventoux. Bathrooms are crisply modern. There's a sunny open-plan living area (with kitchen) and pool and shady corners in the lavender-filled garden. Explore Avignon and markets; return to a comfortable, sociable home.

Rooms	1 double, 2 twins: €135–€150. 1 suite for 4: €230.
Meals	Dinner with wine, €40.
Closed	Rarely.

Rooms	1 twin/double: €90–€105. 1 suite for 3, 1 suite for 4: €115–€135. Extra person €30. Children under 2 free.
Meals	Restaurants 2km.
Closed	December – Easter.

	Stéphan & Martine Lorenz Le Mas de la Pierre du Coq, 434 chemin de Sauzette, 84810 Aubignan, Vaucluse
Tel	+33 (0)4 90 67 31 64
Mobile	+33 (0)6 76 81 95 09
Email	lorenz.stephane@wanadoo.fr
Web	www.masdelapierreducoq.com

	Monique Tattersall Le Mas au Portail Bleu, Chemin de la Mayolle 102, 84810 Aubignan, Vaucluse
Tel	+33 (0)4 90 62 61 10
Email	Monique.Tattersall@wanadoo.fr
Web	www.mas–au–portail–bleu.com

Villa Noria

The garden sets the scene, a secluded enclave of cedars, palms, roses, lawns, and a saltwater pool with views that sweep over vineyards to mountains. Welcome to an elegant 18th-century house run by the delightful Philippe and Sylvie. Up the stone farmhouse stair are bedrooms decorated in Provençal style, the finest on the first floor. Cool tiles underfoot, beams overhead, beds swathed in white and bathrooms diagonally tiled. You breakfast in a wraparound conservatory, there's a salon with *fauteuils* in red and white checks, and the oval dining table waits beneath a weeping fern: don't miss the hosted dinners! Superb.

Château Juvenal

The château is lived in and loved every day, thanks to Anne-Marie and Bernard, who also produce an award-winning wine and delicious olive oil from their 600 trees. They nurture some superb specimen trees, too, out in the park. The traditional bedrooms with high ceilings and tall windows are all on the first floor and range from cosy to spacious; the sitting and dining rooms sport chandeliers and exquisite furniture. Grab your shopping basket and visit the local market, for the summer kitchen next to the pool. There are wine visits, a pony for the kids, annual tango events, a hammam and two lovely apartments for longer stays.

Rooms	3 doubles, 1 twin: €75-€130. 1 suite for 4: €145-€170. Extra bed €30.
Meals	Hosted dinner with wine, €40. Restaurants 3km.
Closed	Rarely.

Rooms	1 double, 2 twin/doubles: €130–€150. 1 suite for 2-3: €140-€170. 2 apartments for 6: €900-€1,700. Singles €100-€150. Extra bed/sofabed available €40 per person per night.
Meals	Summer kitchen. Hosted dinner with wine, €45, once a week.
Closed	1 November to 11 April.

	Philippe Monti
	Villa Noria,
	4 route de Mazan,
	84330 Modène,
	Vaucluse
Tel	+33 (0)4 90 62 50 66
Email	post@villa-noria.com
Web	www.villa-noria.com

	Anne-Marie & Bernard Forestier
	Château Juvenal,
	120 chemin du Long Serre,
	84330 Saint Hippolyte le Graveyron,
	Vaucluse
Tel	+33 (0)4 90 62 31 76
Mobile	+33 (0)6 07 13 11 47
Email	chateau.juvenal@gmail.com
Web	www.chateaujuvenal.com

Entry 642   Map 16

Entry 643   Map 16

Le Clos Saint Saourde

What a place! Outdoors turns inwards here, spectacularly: many walls, ceilings, even some furniture, are sculpted from solid rock. The décor is minimalist and luxurious with a flurry of natural materials and lots of quirky touches: the wrought-iron lamps and lanterns, the clever lighting, the solar pools. Indulge yourself in a private spa (if you have booked the treehouse) or in a breathtaking grotto bathroom. This lovely couple will tell you all about visits, vineyard tours, activities (fancy rock-climbing, a massage?) and restaurants in their exquisite area. They serve delicious gourmet platters with the right wines.

Rooms	2 doubles: €180–€260.
	3 suites for 2: €220–€420.
	1 treehouse for 2: €370–€470.
	Extra bed €40.
Meals	Gourmet platter with wines, €50.
	Summer kitchen. Restaurant 2km.
Closed	Rarely.

Jérôme & Géraldine Thuillier
Le Clos Saint Saourde,
Route de St Véran,
84190 Beaumes de Venise,
Vaucluse

Tel	+33 (0)4 90 37 35 20
Mobile	+33 (0)6 99 41 44 19
Email	contact@leclossaintsaourde.com
Web	www.leclossaintsaourde.com

Entry 644   Map 16

La Maison des Remparts

Built into the honey-coloured walls of this fortified village, a stylish refuge decorated with a restraint that lets the ancient walls and beams tell their own story. The house is arranged around a secluded courtyard with an azure pool at its centre, overlooked by a big bright living room. Bedrooms are a symphony of pale colours and crisp white linen, elegance and space; unashamedly gorgeous, they have bathrooms to match. Enjoy a madly indulgent breakfast around the oak table in the stone-flagged kitchen, specially set up for guests. The owners don't live here, but bubbly Ludivine makes you feel beautifully at home.

Rooms	2 doubles: €160.
	1 suite for 2: €160–€280.
	1 family room for 3, 1 family room
	for 4: €140–€280. Extra bed €40.
Meals	Guest kitchen. Restaurants within
	walking distance.
Closed	Rarely.

Jérôme & Géraldine Thuillier
La Maison des Remparts,
74 cours Louis Pasteur,
84190 Beaumes de Venise,
Vaucluse

Tel	+33 (0)4 90 37 35 20
Mobile	+33 (0)6 99 41 44 19
Email	contact@leclossaintsaourde.com
Web	www.lamaisondesremparts.com

Entry 645   Map 16

Le Grand Jardin

Robert and Nataliya's home sits snugly amongst the Dentelles de Montmirail in the market town of Lafare. With superb countryside on the doorstep, it's popular with active types. It's also the perfect place to unwind, with five bright rooms, each with a fresh bathroom, garden area and mountain views. Breakfast of fresh croissants, jams and fruit salad is served on the terrace, a riot of colour with its abundance of plants and hanging baskets. Marvel at Mount Ventoux, meander through pretty villages, explore Avignon, sample the Châteauneuf-du-Pape and return to cool off in the pool. Eat in or out: restaurants are close by.

Minimum stay: 2 nights. Parking on-site.

Le Bouquet de Séguret

Fabulous for view hunters. On a clear day you can see all the way to Orange's Roman theatre. Your happy hosts swapped marketing in Utrecht for B&B in Provence and are loving the house they built on the hill, the guests who come to stay, the delicious meals they share. The vine-covered terrace is the ideal shady spot for breakfast and dinner – views shimmer, leaves flutter, warmth pervades – and the pool looks straight up the valley. In a gentle mix of pale cleancut modern décor and happy brocante finds, the big fresh bedrooms have enormous old wardrobe doors, bathrooms are thoroughly up to date, and Provence is at your feet.

Self-catering options also available – please ask owners for details.

Rooms	2 doubles, 2 twins: €98–€120. 1 annexe for 3: €98–€150. Extra bed €30.
Meals	Dinner €29; children €15. Restaurants 2-minute walk.
Closed	1 November to 1 March.

Rooms	3 doubles: €95–€125. 1 family room for 3: €120–€155.
Meals	Dinner with wine, €31.50. Light dinner with wine & coffee, €15. Restaurants within walking distance. Owner organises BBQs, picnics and wine-tasting.
Closed	Rarely.

Nataly Eggens
Le Grand Jardin,
Allée Le Grand Jardin,
84190 Lafare,
Vaucluse
Tel   +33 (0)4 90 62 97 93
Email   legrandjardin@yahoo.com
Web   www.legrandjardin-provence.com

Jos & Ingrid Leijen
Le Bouquet de Séguret,
Route de Sablet, 84110 Séguret,
Vaucluse
Tel   +33 (0)4 90 28 13 83
Mobile   +33 (0)6 18 37 17 13
Email   info@lebouquetdeseguret.com
Web   www.lebouquetdeseguret.com

Annapurna

Perched on the hill – castle above, river below – a fascinating medieval house in the heart of the old town with its steep streets and extraordinary heritage. If you love history and architecture it's a treat to stay, and Martine and Julian, interesting and well-travelled, look after you well. Sleep peacefully in a big bright bedroom with a wooden floor, warm wool rug and long, romantic views. Find a large sitting room with a vaulted ceiling, enjoy generous breakfasts, wander the peaceful garden, walk or cycle endless trails. Below: shops, restaurants, Tuesday market – and one of five remaining Roman bridges in Provence.

L'Évêché

Narrow, cobbled streets lead to this fascinating and beautifully furnished house that was once part of the 17th-century Bishop's Palace. The Verdiers are charming, relaxed, cultured hosts – she a teacher, he an architect/builder. The white walls of the guest sitting room-library are lined with modern art and framed posters, and the cosy, quilted bedrooms, all whitewashed beams and terracotta floors, have a serene Provençal feel. Views fly over beautiful terracotta rooftops from the balconied suite, and handsome breakfasts are served on the terrace, complete with exceptional views to the Roman bridge.

Rooms	1 double: €110.
Meals	Restaurants 2-minute walk.
Closed	1 November to 1 April.

Rooms	3 twin/doubles: €87–€95.
	2 suites for 2-3: €125–€150.
	Singles €85–€125.
Meals	Restaurants nearby.
Closed	Christmas & New Year.

Martine & Julian Hollick
Annapurna,
38 rue des Fours,
84110 Vaison la Romaine,
Vaucluse
Tel   +33 (0)4 90 41 97 69
Email   annapurna.vaison@gmail.com
Web   vaison-cite-medievale.dudaone.com/fr

Aude & Jean-Loup Verdier
L'Évêché,
14 rue de l'Evêché, Cité Médiévale,
84110 Vaison la Romaine,
Vaucluse
Tel   +33 (0)4 90 36 13 46
Mobile   +33 (0)6 03 03 21 42
Email   eveche@aol.com
Web   www.eveche.com

Entry 648   Map 16

Entry 649   Map 16

Atelier du Renard Argenté

Delightfully wiggly lanes through the Forêt d'Uchaux lead you to the old 'mas' with pretty green shutters and a gorgeous garden with pool. You enter into the conservatory and dining area to be greeted by charming Gail and Christian, who ask only that you feel at home among the soft pastel colours, exposed stone walls, tinkling music and candlelight; it's all very plush but with quirky touches. Sleep peacefully on thick mattresses with clouds of goose down; breakfast on local yogurts, homemade cakes; proper lunches (or picnics) can be rustled up effortlessly, and dinner is sublime. A right royal pampering to be had here.

Aux Augustins

In the centre of Avignon, behind an unassuming shop front, a 14th-century convent lovingly renovated by owners Sabine and Patrick. No expense has been spared, from French linen to locally made wrought iron bedheads and sparkling new shower rooms. Exposed stone walls and archways lend character and all rooms have views into the peaceful inner courtyard, the perfect spot for a breakfast of croissants, fruit and hot chocolate. Park nearby for a price or further out for less, or leave the car at home: it's just five minutes' walk to shops and restaurants. Go boating on the Rhône, sample the local wines, walk the mountains.

Minimum stay: 2 nights; 7 nights during July festival.

Rooms	5 doubles: €130–€235.
Meals	Dinner gastronomique €45–€150.
	Lunches & picnics available.
Closed	Rarely.

Rooms	2 doubles: €105–€130.
	1 suite for 2: €135–€160.
	2 studios for 2: €115–€145.
Meals	Restaurants 5-minute walk.
Closed	Rarely.

	Gail Bodiguel
	Atelier du Renard Argenté,
	90 chemin des Chevres,
	84550 Mornas,
	Vaucluse
Mobile	+33 (0)6 09 39 33 14
Email	contact@atelier-renard-argente.com
Web	www.renarda.com

	Sabine & Patrick Eouagnignon
	Aux Augustins,
	16 rue Carreterie,
	84000 Avignon,
	Vaucluse
Tel	+33 (0)4 90 81 00 42
Email	contact@autourdupetitparadis.com
Web	www.autourdupetitparadis.com/fr

L'Observance

You couldn't be better placed for ambling round historic Avignon than at this B&B within the city's old walls. The latest incarnation of a building that has in its lifetime been part of a monastery, a barracks and a factory, there are now two light, spacious en-suite rooms in the main house and an annexe converted into a cosy apartment for four. Dutch hosts welcome you with a glass of wine and you start the day in the newly-glazed breakfast room with pastries, ham, cheese and eggs. Though the Palais des Papes and Pont d'Avignon are only a short stroll, it's blissfully calm. Cool off in the sparkling pool after a busy day sightseeing.

Minimum stay: 3 nights in high season.

Mas d'Arvieux

Caroline is a fabulous host, and her elegant manor house in Provence is full of colour. Big bedrooms, one in the tower wing, one with a carved mezzanine, have beams, stone walls, fine old armoires, luxurious bathrooms and long views. Arvieux's orchards drip with olives and luscious jam-worthy fruit; have afternoon tea or a delicious breakfast by the pool. Peaceful out of season, it's a great set-up for families in summer and the whole house can be booked; perfect for a wedding venue too. Cookery and art classes can be arranged, there are toys and games outside for little ones, and a boutique selling local pieces and estate produce.

Rooms	1 double, 1 twin/double: €95-€155. 1 apartment for 4: €140-€175. Extra bed/sofabed available €20 per person per night.
Meals	Restaurants 5-minute walk.
Closed	Rarely.

Rooms	2 doubles: €130-€160. 2 triples: €170-€190. Extra bed/sofabed available €10-€30 per person per night.
Meals	Lunch €15. Dinner €25. Restaurant 3km.
Closed	Rarely.

	Jacqueline & Jeroen Tutein Nolthenius L'Observance, Rue de l'Observance, 84000 Avignon, Vaucluse
Tel	+33 (0)4 13 66 05 85
Email	info@lobservance.com
Web	www.lobservance.com

	Caroline Villon Mas d'Arvieux, Route d'Avignon, 13150 Tarascon, Bouches-du-Rhône
Tel	+33 (0)4 90 90 78 77
Mobile	+33 (0)6 11 71 91 40
Email	mas@arvieux-provence.com
Web	www.arvieux-provence.com

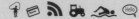

Entry 652   Map 16

Entry 653   Map 16

Mas du Vigueirat

High plane trees flank the drive to the dusky pink, grey-shuttered Provençal farmhouse and inside all is light, simplicity and gentle elegance. Bedrooms are uncluttered spaces of bleached colours, limed walls and terracotta floors. Views are over the beautiful garden with its small pool cascading into a larger one, or meadows, and ground-floor 'Maillane' has a private terrace. The high-beamed dining room/salon is a calm white space with a corner for sofas and books. If the weather's warm you'll take breakfast outside; after a dip in the pool or a jaunt on the bike, enjoy one of Catherine's lunches, fresh from the vegetable garden.

Mas de la Croix d'Arles

St Rémy is Provence on a plate: the ancient streets, artists, restaurants, the colourful weekly market, lush valleys and clear light which inspired Van Gogh. A short walk down the canal, a properly Provençal farmhouse distils this peace in a bubble of olives, vines and fruit trees. Tucked away in a pale stone bungalow are two light-filled B&B rooms, whose slate tiles, painted beams and fiery red splashes give a chic twist to Provençal style. You share a plunge pool with gîte guests, and breakfast on the terrace with lovely Jordane, who'll spill the area's best-kept secrets from hilltop Les Baux to the ochre-tinged Lubéron.

Rooms	3 doubles: €145–€165.
Meals	Picnic available. Poolside meals in summer €15–€20. Restaurants 3km.
Closed	Christmas.

Rooms	1 double, 1 twin: €75–€90.
Meals	Restaurants within 1km
Closed	Rarely.

Catherine Jeanniard
Mas du Vigueirat,
1977 chemin du Grand Bourbourel,
Route de Maillane,
13210 St Rémy de Provence,
Bouches-du-Rhône
Tel   +33 (0)4 90 92 56 07
Email   contact@mas-du-vigueirat.com
Web   www.mas-du-vigueirat.com

Jordane Marsot
Mas de la Croix d'Arles,
Chemin des Servières,
13210 St Rémy de Provence,
Bouches-du-Rhône
Tel   +33 (0)4 90 90 04 82
Mobile +33 (0)6 28 98 30 56
Email   masdelacroixdarles@sfr.fr
Web   www.masdelacroixdarles.com

Entry 654   Map 16

Entry 655   Map 16

La Taulière

These exceptional people – an Argentine artist, an eccentric English photographer and their four excellent children – will open their unconventional arms and carry you into their wide-ranging interests: art and history, travel and underwater photography at this old Provençal olive mill. Sleep cocooned in your great stone-vaulted room among natural materials and spots of colour; revel in the rain shower; enjoy Celina's delicious fruit salad among her generous paintings, Hugh's luscious photographs, and carefully chosen brocante. There's an easel should you find their inspiration infectious, or wander the woods, or worship Provence.

Minimum stay: 2 nights. Parking on-site.

Galerie Huit Arles

In the ancient heart of Arles, a fascinating 17th-century mansion. Warm vibrant Julia is curator of aesthetics, cultured conversation and a gallery that combines art with hospitality. Flagstones, fireplaces and original panelling abound, homemade jams at breakfast accompany a stylish tea selection and occasional dinners are paired with wine from friends' vineyards. And staircases wind past Chinese scrolls to your suite: exquisite tomette tiles, dreamy 'ciel de lit,' restored frescoes, marble touches and a small mosaic shower room with a gilded mirror. Explore Arles, a town ripe for discovery, enjoy the Camargue wilds!

Minimum stay: 2 nights.

Rooms	1 double: €115–€120.
Meals	Restaurants 2km.
Closed	Rarely.

Rooms	1 suite for 2: €95–€130.
	Extra bed €30.
Meals	Occasional dinner with wine, €35.
	Restaurants nearby.
Closed	Rarely.

Hugh & Celina Arnold
La Taulière,
Chemin de L'Ilon,
13310 St Martin de Crau,
Bouches-du-Rhône
Mobile   +33 (0)6 73 87 40 35
Email   hugh.arnold@wanadoo.fr
Web   www.latauliere.com

Julia de Bierre
Galerie Huit Arles,
8 rue de la Calade,
13200 Arles,
Bouches-du-Rhône
Mobile   +33 (0)6 82 04 39 60
Email   contact@galeriehuit.com
Web   www.galeriehuit.com

Entry 656   Map 16

Entry 657   Map 16

Mas de la Rabassière

Amazing views to the coast, fanfares of lilies at the door, Haydn inside and 'mine host' smiling in his 'Cordon Bleu' chef's apron. Vintage wines and a sculpted dancer grace the terrace table. Cookery classes with house olive oil and easy airport pick-up are all part of the elegant hospitality, aided by Thévi, Michael's serene assistant from Singapore. Big bedrooms and a drawing room with a roaring fire are comfortable in English country-house style: generous beds, erudite bookshelves, a tuned piano, Provençal antiques… and tennis, croquet, a pool. A little fading around some edges but stacks of character.

If you have to cancel/change your booking please contact owner as soon as possible.

Le petit Figuier

In a Provençal village known for its international piano festival, is a grand eighteenth-century house with two elegant B&B rooms. Bubbly Lis welcomes you into a chequerboard-tiled hall where musical guests can try out the old family piano. On the second floor, a cosy twin room has iron beds and garden views, while a chic country-style double has cream furniture, a sunny balcony and a smart en-suite. Breakfast on delicious croissants in a tranquil garden shaded with fig and olive trees. Take a dip in the pool or hop in the car to find beautiful villages and the Silvacane Abbey. In the evening you can stroll to good restaurants nearby.

Minimum stay: 2 nights.

Rooms	2 doubles: €85–€160. Singles €90. Dinner, B&B €140 per person. Extra bed/sofabed available at no charge.
Meals	Dinner with wine, €55. Vegetarian and vegan meals available on request.
Closed	Rarely.

Rooms	1 double, 1 twin: €110–€125. Extra bed/sofabed available €35 per person per night.
Meals	Summer kitchen. Restaurants 5-minute walk.
Closed	Rarely.

	Michael Frost
	Mas de la Rabassière,
	2137 chemin de la Rabassière,
	13250 Saint Chamas,
	Bouches-du-Rhône
Tel	+33 (0)4 90 50 70 40
Email	michaelfrost@rabassiere.com
Web	www.rabassiere.com

	Lis & Graham Steeden
	Le petit Figuier
	23 rue du Poilu,
	13640 La Roque d'Anthéron,
	Bouches-du-Rhône
Mobile	+33 (0)7 82 20 19 38 /
	+44 (0)7941 172388
Email	lis.steeden@hotmail.com
Web	www.lepetitfiguier.com

Entry 658   Map 16

Entry 659   Map 16

Les Arnauds

Come for a lovely old laid-back stone house, with pretty views of fields and hills. Here lives Sheila, with cats and ducks! You can share the family's living space or retreat to the guest sitting room, but summer evenings are usually spent outside, drinking in the scents and peace. Breakfasts with delicious fig, cherry and apricot jams set you up for the festivals and flower markets of Aix (6km). Return to comfortable beds on carpeted floors and ceiling fans to keep you cool. Time it right (July/October) and you can join in with the lavender and olive harvests: great fun.

Minimum stay: 2 nights.

La Bruissanne

Terraces of lavender, wisteria-covered pergolas, breakfasts beneath mulberry trees... Provençal living at its finest. Views from the 20th-century villa – from pool or private patio – over lawns and cypresses are uninterrupted. Rooms, with separate entrances, are furnished in country style; fresh, uncluttered, with tiled floors, white quilts and splashes of colour. Choose 'Marius' for space, 'Cesar' for intimacy, 'Fanny' for romance; 'Manon' has its own terrace. Find quiet corners for evening apéros, a summer kitchen for simple suppers. Stroll to Aix's museums, markets and restaurants; warmly efficient Sophie will advise.

Minimum stay: 2 nights.

Rooms	2 doubles: €80–€120.
	1 suite for 2: €115–€125.
Meals	Restaurant 3km.
Closed	Rarely.

Rooms	1 double, 3 twin/double: €120–€150.
	Extra bed/sofabed available €35 per person per night.
Meals	Summer kitchen.
	Restaurants 20-minute walk.
Closed	Rarely.

Sheila Spencer
Les Arnauds,
1902 chemin du Pont Rout,
13090 Aix en Provence,
Bouches-du-Rhône
Tel   +33 (0)4 42 20 17 96
Mobile +33 (0)6 78 90 38 85
Email   shspencer@gmail.com
Web   www.lesarnauds.com

Sophie Huet Legrand
La Bruissanne,
283 chemin du Vallon des Gardes
bas, Le Tholonet,
13100 Aix en Provence,
Bouches-du-Rhône
Tel   +33 (0)4 42 21 16 76
Email   labruissanneaix@gmail.com
Web   www.labruissanne.com

Le Clos des Frères Gris

In through the gates of Hubert's exquisitely tended park and well-tree'd gardens; you'd never guess the centre of Aix en Provence was a seven minute drive. Polyglot Caroline is a people person whose hospitality goes beyond her warm welcome. A passion for antiques is evident throughout her house, as is a talent with fabrics and colours; bedrooms combine comfort and cool elegance, fine linens, thick towels, special touches. Admire the rose and herb gardens on the way to boules or pool, then set off to discover the music and markets of Aix. A jewel of a bastide, a home from home and worth every sou.

Minimum stay: 2 nights.

Mas Sainte Anne

On its hilltop on the edge of pretty Peynier, the old *mas* stands in glory before Cézanne's Montagne Sainte Victoire: pull the cowbell, pass the wooden doors and the red-shuttered farmhouse rises from beds of roses. Beautifully restored, it once belonged to the painter Vincent Roux and memories of his life live on, thanks to your gracious and very helpful hostess. The Roux room is the nicest, all beams, terracotta tiles, fantastic ochre/green bathroom down the hall and delicious garden view. The house has a wonderful old-fashioned patina and the gardens are perfectly kept.

Minimum stay: 2 nights. Children accepted from 1 month old.

Rooms	4 doubles: €130–€190.
Meals	Restaurant 1km.
Closed	31 October to 1 April.

Rooms	1 double; 1 double with separate bathroom: €95–€115.
Meals	Summer kitchen. Restaurants in village.
Closed	3 weeks in August.

Caroline & Hubert Lecomte
Le Clos des Frères Gris,
2240 av Fortune Ferrini,
13080 Luynes,
Bouches-du-Rhône

Tel   +33 (0)4 42 24 13 37
Mobile   +33 (0)6 70 26 24 80
Email   freres.gris@free.fr
Web   freres.gris.free.fr

Jacqueline Lambert
Mas Sainte Anne,
3 rue d'Auriol,
13790 Peynier,
Bouches-du-Rhône

Tel   +33 (0)4 42 53 05 32
Email   stanpeynier@yahoo.fr
Web   www.massainteanne.com

Entry 662   Map 16

Entry 663   Map 16

La Bartavelle

French Myriam and English Alastair, kind helpful hosts, live with exceptional views across the valley and sunrises framed by oak woods in their traditionally styled modern farmhouse, a testament to deft planning. Ground-floor bedrooms spread themselves round a lovely central pool and a walled terrace loaded with pot plants while an airy sitting room provides music, mod cons and reading space. Alastair knows the history of the region off by heart and every path and trail; trek up through the woods to the ridge-perched village of Mimet, with charming restaurants and views to Marseille and the sea.

Maison°9

A beautifully restored, elegant 19th-century winemaker's farmhouse on a vineyard-braided hill. Plush bedrooms, all different, are on the 'outskirts' of the main house; one is down a bamboo-screened path. Expect big beds, excellent linen, cool terracotta floors and Italianate monsoon-head showers. The delicious little garden bursts with pots of herbs, kentia palms and olive trees; the raised limestone pool is lined with canvas loungers, and views are over wooded hills to the grandiose 'Charlemagne's Crown' cliff face. Enjoy a spectacular breakfast in the main house, then stroll to the beach. Simple, chic perfection.

Rooms	2 doubles, 2 twins: €85–€90. 1 suite for 3: €100–€110. Singles €65–€70.	Rooms	3 doubles, 1 double with sofabed: €215–€265.
Meals	Guest kitchen. Restaurants 3km.	Meals	Restaurant 2km.
Closed	Rarely.	Closed	November to March.

Myriam & Alastair Boyd
La Bartavelle,
348 chemin des Amandiers,
13105 Mimet,
Bouches-du-Rhône
Tel   +33 (0)4 42 58 85 90
Email   info@labartavelle.com
Web   www.labartavelle.com

Cynthia Kayser-Maus
Maison°9,
9 av du Docteur Yves Bourde,
13260 Cassis,
Bouches-du-Rhône
Tel   +33 (0)4 42 08 35 86
Email   contact@maison9.net
Web   www.maison9.net

Provence – Alps – Riviera

Bastide Ste Trinide

You'll love the simple lines and bright, airy décor of this renovated 18th-century farmhouse that once belonged to Pascale's grandparents. Prepare to be seduced by reds, whites and chocolate touches, fine linens, exposed beams, a choice of terraces for cooling breezes. One delight is the captivating chapel across the courtyard, another is the vibrant art: walls throughout are splashed with the canvasses of a family friend. You'll also love the blissful quiet up here in the hills, though the beaches are minutes away. Walks, riding, golf, exotic gardens, zoo; let your charming young hosts help you explore.

Mas des Avelines – Olives & Vines

Set among vineyards in beautiful countryside… a peaceful, homely B&B. Once a run-down farmhouse, it's now had new life breathed into it by owners Andy and Su. Come down from your light and airy bedroom, with its gorgeous views and sparkling en suite, and start your day with a convivial breakfast of pastries, bread, homemade jam, ham and cheese – either out on the terrace or at the large country-style table. Fully energised, you could explore hilltop medieval villages or take a spin around the nearby race track, but there's plenty here to entertain: a saltwater pool, beach volleyball court and gardens to roam.

Parking on-site.

Rooms	1 double, 1 twin/double: €70–€90.
Meals	Restaurants nearby.
Closed	Rarely.

Rooms	1 double,
	1 twin/doubles: €125–€225.
Meals	Restaurants 4km.
Closed	Rarely.

Pascale Couture & Grégoire Debord
Bastide Ste Trinide,
1671 chemin Chapelle Ste Trinide,
83110 Sanary sur Mer,
Var
Tel   +33 (0)4 94 34 57 75
Email   contact@bastidesaintetrinide.com
Web   www.bastidesaintetrinide.com

Su Stephens
Mas des Avelines – Olives & Vines,
183 chemin de Valdaray Le Brulat,
83330 Le Castellet,
Var
Mobile +33 (0)6 33 31 12 46
Email   info@olivesandvines.eu
Web   www.olivesandvines.eu

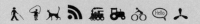

Entry 666   Map 16

Entry 667   Map 16

La Villa Mercedes

Beyond the holiday village, through the red gates, you enter a landscaped haven guarded by tabby Kiwi. The big villa has space for Frédéric, Karine and their children downstairs and the guest rooms upstairs, where a delightful Indochinese salon – Chinese lamps, fly whisk, ancient trunk (family mementoes) – leads to a terrace. Bedrooms, themed in quiet good taste, are supremely comfortable with excellent bathrooms. Your hosts left fast jobs in Paris to bring their family up in this small Mediterranean paradise, a hop-skip from the beach, and spend proper time with their guests. They will make you feel deeply welcome.

Parking on-site.

45 boulevard des Pêcheurs

From your private terrace gaze out to the sky-blue bay views – hillsides, islands, beaches, Corsica on a clear spring day – stunning. The many-windowed parquet-floored bedroom, restfully done in soft colours, feels like a lookout tower. Good bathroom, too. Breakfast is served in the family dining room or on the main terrace; the luxuriant garden and superb pool area lie beyond while the wide, welcoming, uncluttered salon has nice old French furniture and ship's binoculars for those views. Your host – charming, active and attentive Claudine – has lived in the area for over 30 years and knows it well. The centre of Le Levandou is a 15-minute walk.

Minimum stay: 2 nights.

Rooms	4 doubles: €110–€160.
	1 family room for 2: €110–€240.
	Cot & extra beds available.
	Under 12s, €25 per night.
Meals	Breakfast €10.
	Restaurants 15-minute walk.
Closed	Rarely.

Rooms	1 double: €80–€105.
Meals	Restaurants 15-minute walk
Closed	Rarely.

Frédéric & Karine Marie	
La Villa Mercedes,	
185 chemin de la Garenne,	
83250 La Londe les Maures,	
Var	
Tel	+33 (0)4 94 71 19 12
Email	villamercedes83@yahoo.fr
Web	www.villa-mercedes.com

Claudine Draganja	
45 boulevard des Pêcheurs,	
Super-Lavandou,	
83980 Le Lavandou,	
Var	
Tel	+33 (0)4 94 71 46 02
Mobile	+33 (0)6 84 07 38 67
Email	draganja83@gmail.com
Web	www.chambrehotes-draganja.com

Entry 668   Map 16

Entry 669   Map 16

Bastide Château Montagne

The rugged exterior of this 18th-century stone bastide belies the charm and comfort of its five elegant rooms – cool terracotta underfoot, venerable beams overhead, pale colours and clean lines throughout. Friendly owner Candy, who lives here with her young family, takes care of everything: a breakfast of local and home grown produce on the terrace, gourmet cooking and lashings of the family wine if you opt for dinner. Relaxation is key, whether it's in the big swimming pool or jacuzzi, wandering the tranquil gardens, playing pétanque or enjoying yoga classes in the attic. Peace and quiet just half an hour from the Med.

Minimum stay: 2 nights. Parking on-site.

La Maison de Rocbaron

Who would not love this beautifully restored stone bergerie in a riot of greenery and flowers, with terraces dotted about gardens and pool? Jeanne and Guy's welcome is warm and easy; he keeps guests happy over an apéritif as she delivers a dinner not to be missed. The glorious black fig of Solliès is one of her specialities; both Jeanne and Guy are passionate about Slow Food. Various staircases lead to elegant rooms – symphonies in pink, white and floral – and modern bathrooms. An early dip, a feast of a breakfast, and you're ready for the day's adventures. A happy place in harmony with the world – in a peaceful Provençal village.

Rooms	3 doubles: €75-€129. 1 suite for 2: €130-€154. Sofabed €8 per person per night.
Meals	Dinner €25. Restaurants 5km.
Closed	2 weeks in winter.

Rooms	3 doubles: €105-€120. 2 suites for 4 (for 2-4): €120-€130. Extra bed/sofabed available €30 per person per night.
Meals	Dinner with wine, €40. Guest fridge & microwave. Restaurants in village.
Closed	Rarely.

Candy Escriva
Bastide Château Montagne,
Château Montagne,
83390 Pierrefeu du Var,
Var
Mobile   +33 (0)6 64 76 89 56
Email   bastidechateaumontagne@outlook.fr
Web   www.bastidechateaumontagne.com

Jeanne Fischbach & Guy Laguilhemie
La Maison de Rocbaron,
3 rue St Sauveur,
83136 Rocbaron, Var
Tel   +33 (0)4 94 04 24 03
Email   contact@maisonderocbaron.com
Web   www.maisonderocbaron.com

Provence – Alps – Riviera

Une Campagne en Provence

In spring, water gushes through myriad irrigation channels dug by the Knights Templar! Martina and Claude, proud possessors of the European Ecolabel, have planted 3,750 trees on their vast estate. The bastide keeps its fortress-like proportions and, like its owners, has bags of charm. Simple furnishings are lit by huge windows, floors are terracotta, and breakfasts and dinners put the accent on Provençal produce and their own wine. A pool with a view, a sauna, a Turkish bath, a well-stocked library, a mini cinema in the cellar... an isolated paradise for all ages, overseen by a charming young family, two geese and one dog.

Pets by arrangement.

Rooms	3 doubles: €100-€134.
	1 suite for 2: €127-€150.
	1 studio for 2 with kitchenette: €140-€190.
Meals	Hosted dinner with wine, €39-€41; Thursday, Friday & Saturday only. Restaurant 3km.
Closed	January to mid-March.

Martina & Claude Fussler
Une Campagne en Provence,
Domaine le Peyrourier,
83149 Bras,
Var
Tel   +33 (0)4 98 05 10 20
Email   info@provence4u.com
Web   www.provence4u.com

Entry 672   Map 16

Provence – Alps – Riviera

Château Nestuby

Bravo, Nathalie! – in calm, friendly control of this gorgeous, well-restored 18th-century bastide. One whole wing is for guests: the light, airy, vineyard-view bedrooms, pastel-painted and Provençal-furnished with a happy mix of antique and modern (including WiFi), the big bourgeois sitting room (little used: it's too lovely outside), the spa on the roof terrace and the great spring-fed tank for swims. Stroll the lovely garden in the shade of 100-year-old plane trees; Jean-François runs the vineyard, the tastings and the wine talk at dinner with sweet-natured ease. Utterly relaxing and very close to perfection.

Minimum stay: 3 nights July/August.

Rooms	4 twin/doubles: €95.
	1 family room for 4: €85.
	1 triple: €95. Extra bed/sofabed available €20 per person per night. Jacuzzi available in twin/double; extra charge €85.
Meals	Dinner with wine, €27.
Closed	Mid-December to February.

Nathalie & Jean-François Roubaud
Château Nestuby,
4540 route de Montfort,
83570 Cotignac,
Var
Tel   +33 (0)4 94 04 60 02
Mobile +33 (0)6 86 16 27 93
Email   nestuby@wanadoo.fr
Web   www.nestuby-provence.com

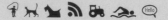

Entry 673   Map 16

La Bastide du Pin

It's a glamorous drive up from Nice to this gorgeous hideaway, set among gardens of lavender with views as far as the eye can see. Bedrooms are spacious and elegant with an understated feel, there's a beautiful shaded patio with only a fountain to disturb you, and billiards and books for evenings in. But best of all is Pierre, your interesting and attentive host, who gives you gorgeous breakfasts in a big dining room and holds court at dinner once a week in summer. A great spot from which to stroll into Lorgues, with its abbey, buzzing market, shops and bars; it's particularly alluring in spring.

Villa de Lorgues

Expect the unexpected in this stately 18th-century townhouse. From the basement spa to the traditional living rooms – level with the delicious garden and terrace – to the bedrooms at the top, all is pure enchantment. A red lantern here, a ceiling mirror there, four posters, fireplaces and candles just where you least expect them. Bedrooms combine superb comfort with an elegant minimalist décor and smart bathrooms. Come evening, fairy lights wink along the wrought-iron balustrades from top to bottom. Claudie juggles a busy freelance career with talent, taste, a warm welcome and a fabulous sense of humour.

Minimum stay: 2 nights July / August.

Rooms	4 doubles, 1 twin/double: €100–€165. 1 family room for 3: €125–€160.
Meals	Restaurants in Lorgues, 2km.
Closed	Rarely.

Rooms	2 doubles: €150–€200.
Meals	Restaurants within walking distance.
Closed	Rarely.

	Pierre Gissinger La Bastide du Pin, 1017 route de Salernes, 83510 Lorgues, Var
Tel	+33 (0)4 94 73 90 38
Email	contact@bastidedupin.com
Web	www.bastidedupin.com

	Claudie Cais Villa de Lorgues, 7 rue de la Bourgade, 83510 Lorgues, Var
Mobile	+33 (0)6 61 47 67 02
Email	villadelorgues@gmail.com
Web	www.villadelorgues.com

Entry 674   Map 16

Entry 675   Map 16

Mas la Jaïna

A large new house with villa-like arches surrounded by quiet farmland. Your eco-friendly hosts Ingrid and Johan – and their golden retrievers – usher you enthusiastically into a large room with a dining table and sofas. Bedrooms are themed and vary wildly – each sponsor a different cause – but all have very comfortable mattresses and can be reached from the outside. Breakfasts of fresh fruit salad, local cheese and eggs from their hens set you up for a lazy day by the natural swimming pool, in sauna and hot tub, or wandering through the herb garden and rows of lavender. Plenty of activities and space for children too.

Minimum stay: 7 nights in high season.

Rooms	2 doubles: €80–€150.
	2 suites for 2: €140–€235.
	2 family rooms for 3: €80–€180.
Meals	Restaurants next door.
Closed	Rarely.

Ingrid & Johan Hombergen
Mas la Jaïna,
Les Espourounes,
83830 Bargemon,
Var

Mobile	+33 (0)6 88 99 79 93
Email	maslajaina@me.com
Web	www.maslajaina.com

Entry 676   Map 16

La Ferrage

History and art buffs couldn't hope for a more gracious or cultured host or a better converted barn – formerly housing cows and farm tools, its swimming pool has been adapted from a basin once used to water the cows and field. Your warm and delicately decorated bedroom looks over the garden to distant hills from a house full of antiques, original paintings and signs of world travels. Denise and her late husband lived in many places and she talks perceptively about them and their treasures over breakfast of fresh fruit, local pâtisseries and jams – and cheeses if you like. But tear yourselves away, there's so much to do and see: climb, hike, glide, visit medieval marvels… Remarkable value.

Rooms	1 twin/double with separate bathroom: €85.
Meals	Restaurants 500m.
Closed	Rarely.

Denise Goss
La Ferrage,
Le Terme St Eloi,
83440 Fayence,
Var

| Tel | +33 (0)4 94 39 16 75 |
| Email | g.osco@wanadoo.fr |

Entry 677   Map 16

La Guillandonne

A very long drive, anticipation, then the house, the river, the cool forest. These lovely, civilised people, a former teacher of English and an architect, have treated their old house with delicacy and taste. Standing so Italianately red-ochre in its superb *parc* of great old trees and stream, it could have stepped out of a 19th-century novel. The interior speaks for your hosts' caring, imaginative approach (polished cement floors, rustic Salernes tiles). Bedrooms are full of personality, elegant and colourful; the living room is exquisite with vintage Italian hanging lamps and Le Corbusier chairs.

Rooms	2 doubles, 1 twin: €90.
Meals	Restaurants 1.5km.
Closed	Rarely.

Marie-Joëlle Salaün
La Guillandonne,
731a route des Tourettes,
83440 Tourrettes,
Var

Tel	+33 (0)4 94 76 04 71
Mobile	+33 (0)6 24 20 73 09
Email	guillandonne@wanadoo.fr

Entry 678   Map 16

Maison du Bonheur

In the hilltop village of Montauroux is this whitewashed townhouse with orange shutters, both elegant and understated. Behind, a big surprise: palm trees, lawns, lavenders, and a veranda with a heaven-sent view. Austrian Elisabeth, warm and delightful, gives you two small elegant bedrooms upstairs, and a smart bathroom in contemporary style. Explore the caves of St Cézaire and the vineyards of Provence Verte, enjoy a pizza and a *pastis* on the village square. Then home to an open-plan dining room full of light, and a sitting room cosy and enticing: white walls, chunky beams, sofas, books and beautiful art, some of it Elisabeth's.

Rooms	1 double, 1 twin/double sharing bathroom: €70-€95. Rooms let to same party only. Both rooms, €120.
Meals	Restaurants 2-minute walk.
Closed	30 September to 15 March.

Elisabeth Chuffart
Maison du Bonheur,
24 rue de l'Église,
83440 Montauroux,
Var

Tel	+33 (0)4 94 47 68 64
Email	ecmtx@orange.fr

Entry 679   Map 16

La Rivolte

Apricot-coloured villa, lavender-scented terraces, views to the shimmering Bay of Cannes; this is pure Provence. Rooms in the Belle Époque house, set above a spectacular garden, are light-filled and sorbet-coloured with rugs on tiled floors, wrought-iron bedsteads and charming brocante furnishings. One has a fireplace, another a private terrace, all have elegant bathrooms. Breakfast – home-made preserves – on the terrace or in the fire-warmed kitchen. Perfumed Grasse is strolling distance, the coast 25 minutes, or relax by the pool with views and the heady scents of flowers and fruit trees. Housekeeper Suzie is charmingly capable.

Minimum stay: 2 nights. Pool towels available.

Rooms	3 doubles, 2 twins: €105–€140.
Meals	Restaurants within walking distance
Closed	Mid-May to mid-September

Suzie Turner
La Rivolte,
1 chemin des Lierres,
06130 Grasse,
Alpes-Maritimes
Mobile +33 (0)6 50 97 33 31
Email suzie@larivolte.com
Web www.larivolte.com

Entry 680 Map 16

Mas Lou Peyloubet

Climb up to a gated estate and a terracotta farmhouse, perched high with views over valley to mountains. Lively Nick and Lise will greet you with a glass of well-chilled rosé and ask only that you make yourselves at home in their easy-going, spacious home; the dining room with Caribbean art work, the living room with plenty of sofas – all yours. Bedrooms are light and airy, one with an antique four-poster; bathrooms filled with Fragonard soaps, and most rooms gaze at far-reaching views. The garden is terraced – pool one side, olive groves the other. And breakfast is a feast (do try the marmalade from estate oranges). Super!

Parking on-site.

Rooms	3 doubles, 1 twin: €140–€220. 1 family room for 3 with separate bathroom: €140–€185. Extra bed €20–€45. Cot available. Whole property self-catering only in Jul/Aug.
Meals	Outdoor guest kitchen. Dinner €30, by arrangement. Wine list €12–€40. Restaurants 5km.
Closed	November to 5 March. Whole property self-catering Jul/Aug & Christmas.

Nick & Lise Davies
Mas Lou Peyloubet,
Chemin de Peyloubet,
06130 Grasse,
Alpes-Maritimes
Tel +33 (0)4 93 77 35 03
Mobile +33 (0)6 70 30 65 00
Email peyloubet@hotmail.com
Web www.peyloubet.com

Entry 681 Map 16

Le Relais du Peyloubet

A hint of Tuscany seeps through this ancient farmhouse, its shutters and terracotta tiles, standing on a hillside wrapped in olive groves. Once growing flowers for Grasse perfumers, its delicious terraces and orchards are now tended by Roby while Xavier, a pâtissier, whisks up the fabulous breakfasts. Dinners are do-it-yourself in the summer kitchen overlooking the peaceful hills. Beamed and parquet-floored bedrooms, all with private terraces, are furnished in country Provençal style. There are shady seats in the woods, glorious views, boules, pool, and the coast 20 minutes. Blissfully calm, easy and welcoming.

Villa du Roc Fleuri

You'll feel on top of the world in this square villa overlooking rooftops all the way to town – a labour of love for Fanny. Breakfast on homemade jams and crêpes, local pastries and plenty of teas in the great glass veranda, or out on the terrace. Do order dinner – your host's an inventive cook, or head into town for restaurants. Bedrooms are simple, light and airy with French doors and tall windows, the two at the front overlook a tropical garden across the road – all have modern bathrooms with waterfall showers. The suite is in a separate building and has its own terrace. Plenty to do from island hopping to beaches and culture.

Rooms	1 double, 2 twin/doubles: €80–€120. 2 suites for 4: €90–€130. Discounts available for longer stays. Extra bed/sofabed available €10–€20 per person per night.
Meals	Summer kitchen. Restaurant 3km.
Closed	Mid-November to mid-March.

Rooms	4 doubles: €90–€140. 1 suite for 4: €140–€200.
Meals	Dinner with wine, €35. Restaurants 1km.
Closed	Rarely.

	Xavier & Roby Stoeckel
	Le Relais du Peyloubet,
	65 chemin de la Plâtrière,
	06130 Grasse,
	Alpes-Maritimes
Tel	+33 (0)4 93 70 69 90
Mobile	+33 (0)6 16 90 67 39
Email	relais-peyloubet@wanadoo.fr
Web	www.relais-peyloubet.com.fr

	Fanny Larroze
	Villa du Roc Fleuri,
	11 rue du Rocher,
	06400 Cannes,
	Alpes-Maritimes
Mobile	+33 (0)6 30 20 82 41
Email	contact@villadurocfleuri.fr
Web	www.villadurocfleuri.fr

La Locandiera

Built for holidays and for early 20th-century entertaining, this Côte d'Azur villa is a literal stone's throw from the fishing port and beach, and charming Madame Rizzardo has forsaken Venice to restore it. Her villa exudes warmth, charm and peace – like stepping into the Riviera life of a more glamourous age – with gorgeous furnishings and, no doubt, witty conversation. Three of the cool, fresh, traditionally furnished bedrooms look straight out to sea over a walled garden whose jasmine-sweet corners are furnished for shaded retreat. Heaps of restaurants and smart places are reachable on foot.

Le Clos de Saint Paul

A young Provençal house on a lushly planted and screened piece of land where boundary hedging is high. In a guest wing, each pretty bedroom has its own patio, each bathroom is small and there's a summer kitchen for guests to share. Friendly energetic Madame has furnished in contemporary style – greys, yellows, painted chairs, the odd antique. She genuinely cares that you have the best, offers a welcome glass of rosé on her stunning shaded terrace and serves a very fresh breakfast in the garden. The large mosaic'd pool is a pleasure on a summer's day, and legendary St Paul de Vence is worth a trip.

Minimum stay: 2 nights.

Rooms	2 doubles, 1 twin: €120–€160. 2 suites for 2: €160–€190. Extra bed/sofabed available €35 per person per night.
Meals	Restaurants 100m.
Closed	Last 2 weeks in November.

Rooms	1 double, 1 twin/double, 1 twin/double with kitchenette: €75–€120. Singles €70–€85. Extra bed/sofabed available €20 per person per night. Pets on request, €10 per night.
Meals	Summer kitchen. Restaurant 1km.
Closed	Rarely.

	Daniela Rizzardo La Locandiera, 9 av Capitaine de Frégate Vial, 06800 Cagnes sur Mer, Alpes-Maritimes
Tel	+33 (0)4 97 22 25 86
Mobile	+33 (0)6 27 88 17 40
Email	daniela@lalocandieracagnes.com
Web	www.lalocandieracagnes.com

	Béatrice Ronin Pillet Le Clos de Saint Paul, 71 chemin de la Rouguière, 06480 La Colle sur Loup, Alpes-Maritimes
Tel	+33 (0)4 93 32 56 81
Email	leclossaintpaul@hotmail.com
Web	www.leclossaintpaul.com

Entry 684 Map 16

Entry 685 Map 16

Le Mas du Chanoine

Wake up and smell the roses from the patio (15 varieties share the garden, along with lavender bushes, bougainvillaea, fig and citrus trees), where you breakfast on Mariage Frères tea and Pascale's homemade jams and cakes in front of a striking stained-glass window. Inside, a treasure trove: Louis XVI Provençal cabinetry and marvellous stone fireplaces; oak parquet floors and marble bedside tables; a natural stone basin and a sunken bath. Explore the cobbled streets of St Paul de Vence, then soak tired limbs in the security pool with Opiocolor mosaic tiling. After dusk... pastis and boules on the floodlit court.

La Forge d'Hauterives

Discover a truly beautiful 18th-century 'bastide' basking between mountains and sea in the sunny Côte d'Azur close to stunning St Paul de Vence and Nice. Anne, a talented designer, has converted the south-west facing village mansion impeccably. Find ornamental gates, a courtyard paved with pebbles, gorgeous bedrooms with antiques – some with private terraces – and a lounge with a warming fireplace. Stroll through the fecund garden cooled by an ancient fountain that pours into a swimming pool. Meet like-minded folk around a big, convivial table for sublime regional meals or wander into the village for craft shops by the castle.

Minimum stay: 2 nights.

Rooms	3 suites for 2: €180–€220. Singles €170–€210. Extra bed/sofabed available €15–€50 per person per night.
Meals	Restaurants 2km.
Closed	Rarely.

Rooms	4 doubles: €100–€180. 1 family room for 4: €230–€260. Extra bed €35.
Meals	Dinner with wine, €40. Restaurants 150m.
Closed	Rarely.

Pascale Barissat
Le Mas du Chanoine,
831 chemin de la Bastide Rouge,
06570 St Paul de Vence,
Alpes-Maritimes

Tel	+33 (0)4 93 08 81 03
Email	contact@masduchanoine.com
Web	www.masduchanoine.com

Anne d'Hauterives
La Forge d'Hauterives,
44 rue Yves Klein,
06480 St Paul de Vence,
Alpes-Maritimes

Tel	+33 (0)4 93 89 73 34
Mobile	+33 (0)6 82 82 84 45
Email	annedhauterives@gmail.com
Web	www.laforgedhauterives.com

Entry 686   Map 16

Entry 687   Map 16

Les Orangers

Within walking distance of artistic St Paul de Vence, a tranquil hideaway with an enchanting garden shaded by palms and fruit trees. A slender pool is an oasis amid the abundant greenery. This was one of the village's original mas hotels, now Thomas and Marquesa have converted it into a delightful B&B. Five comfortable en suite rooms are furnished with antiques and painted in rose, blue and ochre. Garden-level rooms have little terraces ideal for sipping rosé as the sun drops beneath the horizon. Breakfast is a delicious spread of ham, cheese, home-made jams and marmalades, and fruit, along with freshly-squeezed oranges from the garden.

Minimum stay: 2 nights. Parking available.

Bleu Azur

Breakfast, ferried to the friendly communal table (or the elegant terrace) is a feast of croissants, fruits, jams and Jean-Yves' speciality: Breton crêpes. Nothing is too much trouble for these humorous hosts who have followed a long-held dream, to create an exceptional B&B. Their chosen patch, on the edge of a cobbled village between mountains and sea, has sumptuous gardens and shimmering views that reach to the Bay of Antibes. All six bedrooms (including those for families) are sophisticated, spacious and on the ground floor. After a glamorous day on the Riviera, come home to a dive in the pool.

Rooms	5 doubles: €140-€195.
Meals	Restaurants within walking distance
Closed	Rarely.

Rooms	3 twin/doubles: €145-€185. 3 apartments for 2: €185-€230. Extra bed/sofabed available €32 per person per night.
Meals	Dinner, 3 courses with wine, €28-€35. Restaurants 800m. Kitchen available.
Closed	Rarely.

Marquesa Portela
Les Orangers,
Quartier Les Fumerates,
06570 St Paul de Vence,
Alpes-Maritimes
Tel +33 (0)4 93 32 80 95
Email contact@lesorangers.fr
Web www.lesorangers.fr

Nadine Barrandon
Bleu Azur,
674 route des Queinières,
06140 Tourrettes-sur-loup,
Alpes-Maritimes
Tel +33 (0)4 93 32 58 55
Email contact@maisondhotes-bleuazur.com
Web www.maisondhotes-bleuazur.com

Entry 688   Map 16   Entry 689   Map 16

La Tour Manda

Such engaging hosts – nothing is too much trouble. Set well back from the busy dual carriageway, the house is convenient for airport, the new Allianz Riviera stadium and Nice (a 15-minute drive). And, inside, what a classic Côte d'Azur setting: generous bedrooms overlook a charming garden with palms (and pool). Jean-Claude was born in this house; it is colourful, like its owners. Expect light, space and heaps of southern style – family antiques, sofas with throws, posters and paintings. Breakfast, on the pretty terrace in summer, is delicious – be sure to try Jean-Claude's fruit salad! And you can stay all day.

Villa Kilauea

A grand Mediterranean villa that looks so settled in Nice's lush western hills you'd never know it was a 21st-century creation. There are balustrade-edged terraces, panoramic views and a blissful pool. Bedrooms above the pool house have a zen-like calm: wrought-iron four-posters draped in muslin, teak floors, white walls; orchids and silks hint at the exotic. The Lavender Room in the main house opens to the garden and is as feminine as the rest. Nathalie, the perfect host, kind, gentle and generous to a tee, delights in juggling family life with her B&B. Nice is a ten-minute drive down the hill.

Rooms	2 doubles: €100–€120.
	1 suite for 4: €100–€190.
	Extra bed €30.
Meals	Restaurants 10-minute walk.
Closed	Rarely.

Rooms	3 doubles: €130–€180.
	1 suite for 2: €180–€220.
Meals	Restaurants in Nice.
Closed	Rarely.

Jean-Claude & Brigitte Janer
La Tour Manda,
682 Boulevard du Mercantour,
06200 Nice,
Alpes-Maritimes
Tel +33 (0)4 93 29 81 32
Email latourmanda@wanadoo.fr
Web www.latourmanda.fr

Nathalie Graffagnino
Villa Kilauea,
6 chemin du Candeu,
06200 Nice,
Alpes-Maritimes
Mobile +33 (0)6 25 37 21 44
Email nathalie@villakilauea.com
Web www.villakilauea.com

Villa L'Aimée

In the northern part of Nice, a short tram ride from the city's rich culture (buses also stop virtually at the gate), Villa L'Aimée was built in 1929 and is typical of its period. Toni's decoration has restored the villa to a modern opulence. Much-travelled – one of her lives was in the art world – Toni, who is English, has created delightful bedrooms in subtle colours with damasks and silks, fine linen, tulle canopies and elegant furnishings, exuding an air of luxury. The original parquet is breathtaking, the breakfasts excellent. A peaceful corner of Nice from which to invade the bubblier downtown.

Over 12s welcome.

Rooms	2 twin/doubles, 1 twin: €110–€145.
Meals	Restaurants within walking distance.
Closed	December – March.

Toni Redding
Villa L'Aimée,
5 av Piatti, 06100 Nice,
Alpes-Maritimes
Tel   +33 (0)4 93 52 34 13
Mobile   +33 (0)6 71 82 67 72
Email   bookings@villa-aimee.co.uk
Web   www.villa-aimee.co.uk

Entry 692   Map 16

La Parare

Cradled in summer by cicada chant and the gentle wind, cocooned in winter in a romantic log-warmed bedroom, you will be bewitched by the subtle mix of clean-cut modernity and fine oriental detail that your much-travelled polyglot hosts have achieved in this craggy old house. Breakfast in bed? Bathtub for two? Elegant gourmet dinner? All of these and more: Karin from Sweden and French/Dutch Sydney love pampering people. The rough hills outside highlight the delicacy inside, the natural walled pool, the stunning bathrooms, the civilised conversation at dinner. Worth every centime.

Minimum stay: 2 nights at weekends; 4 nights in high season.

Rooms	4 doubles: €140–€170.
Meals	Dinner with wine, €35–€50.
Closed	Rarely.

Karin & Sydney van Volen
La Parare,
67 calade du Pastre,
06390 Châteauneuf Villevieille,
Alpes-Maritimes
Tel   +33 (0)4 93 79 22 62
Email   karin@laparare.com
Web   www.laparare.com

Entry 693   Map 16

Les Cyprès

Glorious views stretch over countryside and town from Frances's apricot-coloured villa. Its beautiful big garden bears olives, flowers and fruit in profusion – fig, cherry, strawberry... discover secret areas for dining or hiding away with a book. Bedrooms are traditional and minimalist with pretty bedspreads and smart bathrooms, and breakfast is scrumptious: bread, brioche, homemade jams galore. Explore the fascinating old town, tootle over to Nice, and get back in time truly delicious four-course dinners. Whet your whistle with an apéritif in the cosy-rustic sitting room... prepare to be spoiled.

Minimum stay: 2 nights July/August.

Rooms	3 doubles: €85–€90. Extra bed €25.
Meals	Dinner, 4 courses, €25.
	Light dinner with wine, €18.
	Restaurant 1km.
Closed	Christmas.

Frances Thompson
Les Cyprès,
289 route de Châteauneuf,
06390 Contes,
Alpes-Maritimes

Mobile	+33 (0)6 46 27 54 95
Email	contact@lescypres.fr
Web	www.lescypres.fr

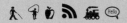

Entry 694   Map 16

Corsica

Corsica

Chambres d'Hôtes à Vallecalle

Welcome to the master house in Vallecalle, on the village edge, an eagle's nest with exquisite valley views. Here live Paul Henri and Myriam, warm, witty, welcoming, living the dream, raising a family, happy to advise you on their beloved adopted land — the food, the culture — or leave you in peace to explore their home, beautiful in its simplicity. Bedrooms, two with 18th-century floorboards, are spacious and gracious. The terraced gardens have oranges, olives, a hammock, corners for shade and sun, and, below, a river to bathe in. Myriam's dishes, always delicious, can be delicate, intriguing or hearty. Stay in!

Rooms	1 double: €66. 1 suite for 2-5: €71-€135. 1 family room for 4: €71-€100.
Meals	Dinner with wine, €25. Restaurant 7km.
Closed	Rarely.

Myriam & Paul Henri Gaucher
Chambres d'Hôtes à Vallecalle,
Village de Vallecalle,
20232 Vallecalle,
Haute-Corse
Tel   +33 (0)4 20 20 04 19
Email   phgaucher@sfr.fr
Web   www.chambresencorse.com

Entry 695   Map 16

Wheelchair-accessible

At least one bedroom and bathroom accessible for wheelchair users. Phone for details.

The North 1 • 17 • 20 • 24
Picardy 30
Champagne – Ardenne 47 • 55 • 56 • 57 • 59
Burgundy 95 • 96 • 97 • 102 •
Région Parisienne 117 • 124 • 134 • 140
Normandy 146 • 151 • 155 • 157 • 159 • 161 • 165 • 166
Brittany 241 • 245 • 248 • 249 • 253
Western Loire 255 • 278 • 280 • 285 • 288
Loire Valley 323 • 327 • 348
Poitou – Charentes 360 • 363 • 368 • 373 • 376 • 377
Aquitaine 388 • 394 • 403 • 404 • 410 • 411 • 418 • 423 • 437 • 440
Limousin 453
Auvergne 466
Midi   Pyrénées 489 • 513 •
Languedoc – Roussillon 544 • 546 • 552 • 571
Rhône Valley – Alps 602
Provence – Alps – Riviera 635 • 644 • 646 • 651 • 658 • 664 • 665 • 684 • 685 • 689

Pets

Pets welcome; please let the owner know if you want to bring pets.

The North 1 • 2 • 9 • 19 • 20 • 24
Picardy 26 • 33 • 37 • 40 • 44
Champagne – Ardenne 51 • 59 • 60 • 62

Burgundy 77 • 79 • 80 • 87 • 94 • 95 • 99 • 100 • 104 • 105 • 106 • 107 • 110
Région Parisienne 130 • 135 • 137 • 138
Normandy 145 • 146 • 150 • 155 • 164 • 165 • 168 • 171 • 179 • 184 • 186 • 190 • 191 • 192 • 197 • 200 • 204 • 206
Brittany 218 • 219 • 223 • 224 • 232 • 242 • 246 • 252 • 253
Western Loire 255 • 257 • 269 • 271 • 272 • 279 • 280 • 284 • 285 • 286 • 288 • 291
Loire Valley 299 • 304 • 306 • 311 • 314 • 318 • 319 • 320 • 323 • 325 • 338 • 341 • 348
Poitou – Charentes 351 • 361 • 365 • 366 • 367 • 370 • 374 • 378 • 380
Aquitaine 392 • 394 • 398 • 410 • 420 • 421 • 423 • 426 • 441 • 445 • 448
Limousin 450 • 452 • 453 • 459 • 461
Auvergne 470 • 477
Midi – Pyrénées 499 • 504 • 505 • 509 • 512 • 513 • 514 • 515 • 518 • 519 • 530 • 532
Languedoc – Roussillon 537 • 542 • 544 • 545 • 552 • 565 • 569 • 570 • 571 • 573 • 574 • 575 • 576 • 582 • 583
Rhône Valley – Alps 588 • 596 • 597 • 598 • 602 • 603 • 608 • 609 • 610 • 613
Provence – Alps – Riviera 622 • 623 • 625 • 627 • 628 • 630 • 632 • 634 • 635 • 637 • 640 • 646 • 673 • 676 • 680 • 683 • 684 • 685 • 687

Quick reference indices

Bikes

Bikes on the premises to hire or borrow.

The North 1 • 4 • 5 • 8 • 10 • 11 • 14 • 15 • 16 • 17 • 22 • 23 • 24

Picardy 26 • 27 • 28 • 29 • 30 • 31 • 32 • 34 • 35 • 38 • 39 • 40 • 43 • 45

Champagne – Ardenne 48 • 50 • 55 • 59 • 62

Lorraine 63

Alsace 65

Franche Comté 71 • 72 • 73

Burgundy 74 • 79 • 87 • 88 • 89 • 91 • 93 • 95 • 97 • 98 • 99 • 100 • 104 • 106 • 107 • 108 • 110 • 114 • 115

Région Parisienne 117 • 119 • 120 • 127 • 133 • 135 • 136 • 137 • 138 • 142

Normandy 145 • 147 • 151 • 152 • 153 • 157 • 158 • 164 • 166 • 167 • 170 • 174 • 176 • 178 • 180 • 185 • 188 • 189 • 190 • 191 • 196 • 197 • 199 • 203 • 207 • 208 • 211 • 213 • 214

Brittany 217 • 218 • 221 • 224 • 226 • 227 • 228 • 230 • 233 • 235 • 237 • 239 • 245 • 246 • 249 • 252

Western Loire 254 • 260 • 261 • 262 • 263 • 264 • 267 • 268 • 269 • 270 • 276 • 277 • 278 • 279 • 280 • 283 • 284 • 285 • 291 • 292 • 294

Loire Valley 296 • 298 • 300 • 301 • 302 • 304 • 306 • 307 • 309 • 311 • 314 • 315 • 316 • 317 • 318 • 320 • 321 • 323 • 325 • 328 • 329 • 333 • 334 • 337 • 338 • 341 • 343 • 344 • 346 • 348 • 349 • 350

Poitou – Charentes 351 • 354 • 356 • 357 • 358 • 360 • 361 • 362 • 363 • 365 • 366 • 367 • 368 • 370 • 372 • 377 • 380 • 382 • 384

Aquitaine 388 • 389 • 391 • 394 • 395 • 396 • 397 • 402 • 404 • 406 • 409 • 410 • 412 • 415 • 420 • 421 • 425 • 429 • 430 • 431 • 432 • 433 • 436 • 437 • 442 • 445 • 447 • 449

Limousin 451 • 456 • 459

Auvergne 463 • 469 • 477 • 479

Midi – Pyrénées 482 • 484 • 486 • 487 • 489 • 492 • 494 • 495 • 503 • 505 • 507 • 510 • 513 • 515 • 516 • 517 • 519 • 521 • 524 • 525 • 527 • 530 • 531

Languedoc – Roussillon 538 • 539 • 540 • 542 • 543 • 546 • 547 • 550 • 551 • 554 • 556 • 558 • 559 • 561 • 562 • 564 • 565 • 566 • 570 • 571 • 573 • 574 • 575 • 576 • 582

Rhône Valley – Alps 586 • 589 • 591 • 602 • 609 • 614

Provence – Alps – Riviera 626 • 628 • 630 • 631 • 635 • 636 • 640 • 644 • 645 • 650 • 652 • 655 • 658 • 661 • 666 • 672 • 676 • 683 • 684

Public transport

Places within 10 miles of a bus/coach/train station and the owner can arrange collection.

The North 1 • 2 • 3 • 4 • 5 • 7 • 9 • 10 • 11 • 12 • 13 • 14 • 17 • 19 • 23

Picardy 26 • 29 • 31 • 32 • 34 • 35 • 38 • 39 • 41 • 44 • 45

Quick reference indices

Swimming pool

Poon on the premises; use
may be by arrangement

Alastair Sawday has been publishing books for over 20 years, finding Special Places to Stay in Britain and abroad. All our properties are inspected by us and are chosen for their charm and individuality. And there are many more to explore on our perennially popular website: www.sawdays.co.uk. You can buy any of our books at a reader discount of 25%* on the RRP.

List of titles:	RRP	Discount price
British Bed & Breakfast	£15.99	£11.99
British Hotels and Inns	£15.99	£11.99
Pubs & Inns of England & Wales	£15.99	£11.99
Dog-friendly Breaks in Britain	£14.99	£11.24
French Bed & Breakfast	£15.99	£11.99
French Châteaux & Hotels	£15.99	£11.99
Italy	£15.99	£11.99

*postage and packaging is added to each order

How to order:
You can order online at: www.sawdays.co.uk/bookshop/
or call: **+44 (0)117 204 7810**

Sawday's

GO SNOW

COLLECTION

It's time to hit the slopes! From the cosy to the grand, find a chalet with a heated pool, an underground spa or a Michelin- starred restaurant. With handy tips about distances to lifts, the best places to hire equipment, and some great après-ski pampering, this is a superb place to start planning your close encounter of the snowy kind.

www.sawdays.co.uk/gosnow

Photo: Chaumarty, entry 509

Join us

TIME AWAY IS FAR TOO PRECIOUS TO
SPEND IN THE WRONG PLACE. THAT'S WHY,
BACK IN 1994, WE STARTED SAWDAY'S.

Twenty years on, we're still a family concern – and still
on a crusade to stamp out the bland and predictable,
and help our guests find truly special places to stay.

If you have one, we do hope you'll decide
to take the plunge and join us.

————

Alastair *Toby*

ALASTAIR & TOBY SAWDAY

"Trustworthy, friendly and helpful – with a reputation
for offering wonderful places and discerning visitors."

JULIA NAISMITH, HOLLYTREE COTTAGE

"Sawday's. Is there any other?"

SONIA HODGSON, HORRY MILL